Chemical Principles in the Laboratory

With Qualitative Analysis

REVISED EDITION

SAUNDERS GOLDEN SUNBURST SERIES

Emil J. Slowinski
Professor of Chemistry
Macalester College,
St. Paul, Minnesota

Wayne C. Wolsey
Associate Professor of Chemistry
Macalester College,
St. Paul, Minnesota

William L. Masterton
Professor of Chemistry
University of Connecticut,
Storrs, Connecticut

SAUNDERS COLLEGE PUBLISHING PHILADELPHIA

Saunders College Publishing
West Washington Square
Philadelphia, PA 19105

Chemical Principles in the Laboratory with Qualitative Analysis (Revised Edition)
ISBN 0-7216-8389-4

8901 147 9876543

PREFACE

In spite of its many successful theories, chemistry remains, and probably always will remain, an experimental science. Most of the research in chemistry, both in the universities and in industry, is done in the laboratory rather than in the office or computing room, and it behooves the young student of chemistry to devote a substantial portion of his time to the experimental aspects of the subject. It is not easy to become a good experimentalist, and it must be admitted that some famous chemists are not especially effective in the laboratory. Yet even those chemists who leave the actual work in the laboratory to a graduate student or an assistant must be completely familiar with the available experimental methods, the proper design of experiments, and the interpretation of experimental results. As beginning chemists, students will find that their efforts in the laboratory will be rewarded by a better understanding of the concepts of chemistry as well as an appreciation of what is required in the way of technique and interpretation if one is to be able to find or demonstrate any chemically significant relations.

In writing this manual the authors have attempted to illustrate many of the established principles of chemistry with experiments that are as interesting and challenging as possible. For the most part the experimental procedures and methods for calculation of data are described in great detail, so that students of widely varying backgrounds and abilities will be able to see how to perform the experiments properly and how to interpret them. Several of the experiments in this manual were not published previously and were developed and tested in the general chemistry laboratories at the University of Connecticut and at Macalester College. We have included more experiments than can be conveniently done in the usual laboratory program, so that instructors may select experiments in a flexible way to meet the needs of their particular courses. In many of the experiments unknowns are to be assigned to students to ensure their working independently and to introduce a measure of realism to the application of the chemical principle being investigated.

It is always difficult to get students in chemistry to prepare in advance for the laboratory sessions. If this is not done, a substantial amount of the laboratory period will be spent in trying to find out what the experiment is about and how to do it. It may result in the student not finishing the problem or having to take the report with him to complete it. In order to encourage preparation for the laboratory, we have included with each experiment an advance study assignment, which includes a few questions that require the student to read the experiment and understand it to the point where he can make calculations if given appropriate data. Students who complete the advance study assignments will be better able both to do the experiment properly and to complete it in the allotted time.

This manual is a revised edition of our manual by the same name that was first published in 1974. The choice and order of experiments were made to be as compatible as possible with our general chemistry text, *Chemical Principles with Qualitative Analysis.* In that text there is a full section on qualitative analysis, including considerable descriptive chemistry and a complete scheme for the analysis of the common cations and anions. That scheme is the one used in this manual, and differs from the one in the first version mainly in the procedure for analysis of the Group II cations, which we feel is much improved.

We believe that descriptive chemistry is best learned in the laboratory, and that, all things considered, qualitative analysis gives students the most interesting introduction to that area of chemistry. The combination of this manual and the text mentioned above offers the instructor the option to include varying amounts of descriptive chemistry in the general course. We hope that these books will be particularly useful in those schools in which general chemistry is a three-quarter course, with the third quarter devoted to qualitative analysis.

The authors would like to acknowledge the assistance of Miss Patricia Thiel of Macalester College, who tested the experiments for clarity and feasibility and checked and criticized the procedures used in the qualitative analysis experiments. We appreciate the very willing assistance of Mr. John Santee, also of Macalester College, who compiled the list of chemical and equipment requirements for each experiment as given in the instructor's manual. We are also grateful for the comments and criticisms we received from users, both students and teachers, of the first edition of the manual, and assure our readers that we will acknowledge and carefully consider any suggestions that they would like to make.

E. J. SLOWINSKI
W. L. MASTERTON
W. C. WOLSEY

SAFETY IN THE LABORATORY

A chemistry laboratory can be, and should be, a safe place in which to work. Yet each year in academic and industrial laboratories accidents occur which in some cases injure seriously, or kill, chemists. Most of these accidents could have been foreseen and prevented, had the chemists involved used the proper judgment and taken proper precautions.

The experiments you will be performing have been selected at least in part because they can be done safely. Instructions in the procedures should be followed carefully and in the order given. Where it seemed likely that a very simple error could produce a dangerous set of conditions, we have noted that error specifically. Sometimes even a change of concentration of one reagent is sufficient to change the conditions of a chemical reaction so as to make it occur in a different way, perhaps at a highly accelerated rate. Do not deviate from the procedure in the manual when performing experiments unless specifically told to do so by your instructor.

One of the simplest, and most important, things you can do to avoid injury in the laboratory is to protect your eyes by routinely wearing safety glasses. If you wear prescription glasses, they will serve the purpose; otherwise, use the plastic goggles that are available or buy a pair for your personal use.

The most common accident in the general chemistry laboratory occurs when a student tries to insert glass tubing, a thermometer, or a glass rod into a hole in a rubber stopper. The glass breaks because the student subjects it to excess force in the wrong direction, and sharp glass cuts the student's finger or hand, sometimes severely. Such accidents are completely unnecessary. When you are trying to put a piece of tubing into a rubber stopper, use common sense; we offer the following procedure for your consideration:

1. Make sure the hole in the stopper is only a little bit smaller than the tubing you are working with.
2. Keep both hands close to the stopper when working the tubing into the stopper. Don't hold a foot long piece of tubing by the end away from the stopper, but rather at a point an inch or two from the stopper.
3. Use a lubricant. A drop or two of glycerine, or even water, will make it much easier to work the tubing into the stopper.

Your laboratory assistant should show you the procedure to be used when you work with tubing and stoppers for the first time. If you do cut yourself go to the instructor, and he will decide on the proper treatment.

Although other kinds of accidents are less frequent, they do occasionally occur, and should be considered as possibilities. Your volatile organic liquid may ignite if you bring an open flame too close. You may spill a caustic reagent on yourself or your neighbor, or you may somehow get some chemical into your eye or mouth. A common response in such a situation is panic. All too frequently a student will, in the excitement of the incident, do something utterly irrational, such as running screaming from the room when the remedy for the accident was very close at hand. If you see an accident happen to another student, watch for signs of panic and tell the student what he should do; if it seems necessary, help him to do it. Call your instructor for assistance. Chemical spills are best handled by washing the area quickly with water from the nearest sink. More severe spills can be treated by using the showers or eye washes that may be available in your laboratory. In case of a fire, in a beaker, on the bench, on your clothing or that of another student, do not panic and run. Smother the fire with an extinguisher, a blanket, or with water, as seems most appropriate at the time. If the fire is in a piece of equipment or on the lab bench, and does not appear to require instant action, have your instructor put the fire out. In any event, learn where shower, eye wash, and the fire extinguishers are, so that you will not have to look all over if you ever need them in a hurry.

In this laboratory manual we have attempted to describe safe procedures and to employ chemicals that are safe when used properly. Many thousands of students have performed the experiments without having accidents, so you can too. However, we authors cannot be in the laboratory when you carry out the experiments to be sure that you observe the necessary precautions. You and your laboratory supervisor must, therefore, see to it that the experiments are done properly and assume responsibility for any accidents or injuries that may occur.

CONTENTS

Density = mass / VOLUME g/ml
Volume = d^3 mL or cm^3

SECTION 1

Properties of Matter. Chemical Separations

EXPERIMENT 1

The Densities of Liquids and Solids

One of the fundamental properties of any sample of matter is its density, which is its mass per unit of volume. Since one liter is defined as the volume occupied by exactly one kilogram of water at 4° C, the density of water at 4° C is 1.00000 kg/lit or, in the more usually employed dimensions, 1.00000 g/ml. Densities of liquids and solids range from values less than that of water to values considerably greater than that of water. Osmium metal has a density of 22.5 g/ml and is probably the densest material known at ordinary pressures. The densities of liquids and solids change with changes in temperature, in general decreasing slowly with increasing temperature, and slightly increasing with increasing pressure under ordinary conditions. Any change in the density of a given sample results from a change in volume, since the mass of a sample is not a function of temperature or pressure. The densities of gases can vary considerably with either pressure or temperature changes. Gas densities will be the subject of a later experiment.

In any density determination, two quantities must be determined—the mass and the volume of a given quantity of matter. The mass can easily be determined by finding the "weight" of the substance on a balance. The quantity we usually think of as "weight" is really the mass of a substance. In the process of "weighing," we find the mass, taken from a standard set of masses, that experiences the same gravitational force as that experienced by the given quantity of matter we are "weighing." The mass of a sample of liquid in a container can be found by taking the difference between the mass of the container plus the liquid and the mass of the empty container.

The volume of a liquid can easily be determined by means of a calibrated container. In the laboratory a graduated cylinder is often used for routine measurements of volume. Accurate measurement of liquid volume is made by using a pycnometer, which is simply a container having a precisely definable volume. The volume of a solid can be determined by direct measurement if the solid has a regular geometrical shape. Such is not usually the case, however, with ordinary solid samples. A convenient way to determine the volume of a solid is to measure accurately the volume of liquid displaced when an amount of the solid is immersed in the liquid. The liquid used in such an experiment should not react with or dissolve the solid and, as you may readily surmise, should have a lower density than the solid.

EXPERIMENTAL PROCEDURE

A. Mass of a Slug. After you are shown how to operate the analytical balance in your laboratory, obtain a numbered metal slug from your instructor. Weigh it on the balance to the nearest 0.001 g. Record the mass and the number of the slug and report it to your instructor. When he has approved your weighing, go to the stockroom and obtain a glass-stoppered flask, which will serve as a pycnometer, and samples of an unknown liquid and an unknown metal.

B. Density of a Liquid. If your flask is not clean and dry, clean it with soap and water, rinse it with a few ml of acetone, and dry it by letting it stand for a few minutes in the air or by gently blowing compressed air into it for a few moments.

Weigh the dry flask with its stopper on the analytical balance, or the toploading balance if so directed, to the nearest mg. Fill the flask with distilled water until the liquid level is nearly to the top of the ground surface in the neck. Put the stopper in the flask in order to drive out *all* the air and any excess water. Work the stopper gently into the flask, so that it is firmly seated in position. Wipe any water from the outside of the flask with a towel and soak up all excess water from around the top of the stopper.

Again weigh the flask, which should be completely dry on the outside and full of water, to the nearest mg. Given the density of water at the temperature of the laboratory and the mass of water in the flask, you should be able to determine the volume of the flask very precisely. Empty the flask, dry it, and fill it with your unknown liquid. Stopper and dry the flask as you did when working with the water and then weigh the stoppered flask full of the unknown liquid, making sure its surface is dry. This measurement, used in conjunction with those you made previously, will allow you to find accurately the density of your unknown liquid.

C. Density of a Solid. Pour your sample of liquid from the flask into its container. Rinse the flask with a small amount of acetone and dry it thoroughly. Add small chunks of the metal sample to the flask until the flask is about half full. Weigh the flask, with its stopper and the metal, to the nearest mg.

Leaving the metal in the flask, fill the flask with water and then replace the stopper. Roll the metal around in the flask to make sure that no air remains between the metal pieces. Refill the flask if necessary, and then weigh the dry, stoppered flask full of water plus the metal sample. Properly done, the measurements you have made in this experiment will allow a calculation of the density of your metal sample that will be accurate to about 0.1 per cent.

Pour the water from the flask. Put the metal in its container. Dry the flask and return it with its stopper and your metal sample to the stockroom.

Density = $\frac{\text{mass}}{\text{volume}}$ g/mL   V = $\frac{\text{mass}}{D}$

Volume = d^3 mL or cm^3 Name Stephanie Bortell Section ______

DATA AND CALCULATIONS: Densities of Liquids and Solids

Metal slug no. 48 Mass of slug 9.068 g

Unknown liquid no. 4 Unknown solid no. 1

Density of unknown liquid

Mass of empty flask plus stopper	30.614 g
Mass of stoppered flask plus water	59.648 g
Mass of stoppered flask plus liquid	76.806 g
Mass of water	29.034 g ÷ .9970
Volume of flask (density of H_2O at 25°C, 0.9970 g/ml; at 20°C, 0.9982 g/ml)	29.12 ml
Mass of liquid	46.192 g
Density of liquid	1.586 g/ml
To how many significant figures can the liquid density be properly reported?	4

Density of unknown metal

Mass of stoppered flask plus metal	49.248 g
Mass of stoppered flask plus metal plus water	75.633 g
Mass of metal	18.634 g
Mass of water	26.385 g
Volume of water	26.46 ml
Volume of metal	2.66 ml
Density of metal	7.01 g/ml

Would you expect the per cent error in the metal density to be higher or lower than the per cent error in the liquid density as obtained in this experiment? ______

Why?

EXP. 1 Name ______________________ Section ______________

ADVANCE STUDY ASSIGNMENT: Densities of Solids and Liquids

1. In an experiment a student was asked to measure the densities of liquid methanol and metallic cadmium. He was given a small flask with a ground-glass stopper, which he found weighed 34.334 g when empty. He filled the flask with water and weighed the full, stoppered flask, recording a mass of 68.321 g in a room at about 25° C. He dried the flask, filled it with methanol, and found that the flask then weighed 61.313 g. Then he dried the flask again and added some chunks of cadmium to it; the flask plus the cadmium weighed 76.720 g. He filled the flask with water, leaving the cadmium in the flask, and found that after he had removed all the air bubbles the flask with the metal and the water weighed 105.822 g. From the data the student obtained, calculate the density of methanol and the density of cadmium.

Density of methanol .79 g/ml

Density of cadmium 9.72 g/ml

2. Give the effects of the following errors on the value of the density of cadmium as obtained in Problem 1. Explain your reasoning in each case.

a. Air bubbles were present when the flask filled with water was weighed.

air bubbles present are going to give you an incorrect mass of water therefore the total volume of the flask will appear less than it really is. therefore the density of cadmium will go up.

b. The value recorded for the mass of the flask plus water was 69.321 g rather than 68.321 g.

Lower density as total capacity of the flask will be 34.98 1 mL more

EXPERIMENT 2

Resolution of Matter into Pure Substances, I. Fractional Crystallization

One of the important problems faced by chemists is that of determining the nature and state of purity of the substances with which they work. In order to perform meaningful experiments, chemists must ordinarily use essentially pure substances, which are often prepared by separation from complex mixtures.

In principle the separation of a mixture into its component substances can be accomplished by carrying the mixture through one or more physical changes, experimental operations in which the nature of the components remains unchanged. Because the physical properties of various pure substances are different, physical changes frequently allow an enrichment of one or more substances in one of the fractions that is obtained during the change. Many physical changes can be used to accomplish the resolution of a mixture, but in this experiment we will restrict our attention to one of the simpler ones in common use.

The solubilities of solid substances in different kinds of liquid solvents vary widely. Some substances are essentially insoluble in all known solvents; the materials we classify as macromolecular are typical examples. Most materials are noticeably soluble in one or more solvents. Those substances that we call salts often have very appreciable solubility in water but relatively little solubility in any other liquids. Organic compounds, whose molecules contain carbon and hydrogen atoms as their main constituents, are often soluble in organic liquids such as benzene or carbon tetrachloride.

We also often find that the solubility of a given substance in a liquid is sharply dependent on temperature. Most substances are more soluble in a given solvent at high temperatures than at low temperatures, although there are some materials whose solubility is practically temperature-independent and a few others that become less soluble as temperature increases.

By taking advantage of the differences in solubility of different substances we often find it possible to separate the components of a mixture in essentially pure form.

In this experiment you will be given a sample containing silicon carbide, potassium dichromate, and sodium chloride. Your problem will be to separate this mixture into its component parts, using water as a solvent. Silicon carbide SiC is a macromolecular substance and is insoluble in water. Potassium dichromate $K_2Cr_2O_7$ and sodium chloride NaCl are water soluble ionic substances, with different solubilities at different temperatures, as indicated in Figure 2.1. Sodium chloride exhibits little change in solubility between 0°C and 100°C, whereas the solubility of potassium dichromate increases about 16-fold over that temperature range. Given a water solution containing equal weights of NaCl and $K_2Cr_2O_7$ it should be clear that $K_2Cr_2O_7$ would most easily crystallize in pure form from the solution at low temperatures, and that at high temperatures the crystals that would first appear in the boiling solution would be essentially pure NaCl. The method by which we recover pure substances by making use of solubility properties such as those cited for NaCl and $K_2Cr_2O_7$ is called fractional crystallization, and this is one of the fundamental procedures used by chemists for isolating pure materials.

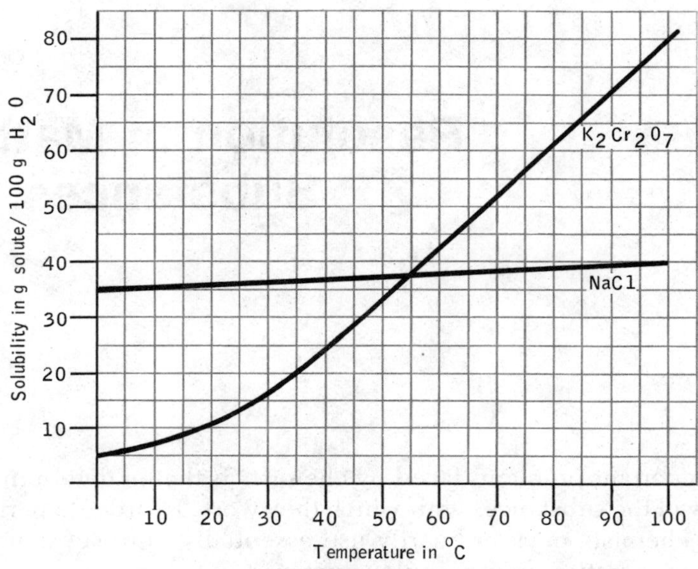

Figure 2.1

EXPERIMENTAL PROCEDURE { *WEAR YOUR SAFETY GLASSES WHILE PERFORMING THIS EXPERIMENT.*

Obtain from the stockroom a Buchner funnel, a suction flask and a sample (about 25 g) of your unknown solid.

Weigh the sample into a 250 ml beaker (±0.1 g). Add about 100 ml of distilled water, which will be enough to dissolve the soluble solids.

Support the beaker with its solution on a piece of wire gauze over an iron ring, and warm gently to about 40° C. Stir the solution to make sure that all soluble material is dissolved. Remove the insoluble silicon carbide by filtering the solution through a Buchner funnel with gentle suction. Transfer as much as you can of the solid carbide to the funnel with your rubber policeman. Transfer the orange filtrate to a clean 250 ml beaker. Reassemble the Buchner funnel, apply suction, and wash the SiC on the filter paper with distilled water. Continue suction for several minutes to dry the SiC. With the help of your spatula, lift the filter paper and the SiC crystals from the funnel and put the paper on the lab bench so that the crystals may dry in the air.

Heat the orange filtrate in the beaker to the boiling point and boil gently until white crystals of NaCl are visible in the liquid. The solution will have a tendency to bump, so do not heat it too strongly. Hot dichromate solution can give you a bad burn. When NaCl crystals are clearly apparent (the solution will usually appear cloudy at that point), stop heating and add 10 ml of distilled water to the solution. (This will be enough to dissolve the NaCl and prevent its crystallizing with the $K_2Cr_2O_7$.) Wash the crystallized solids from the walls of the beaker with your medicine dropper, using the solution in the beaker. Stir the solution with a glass rod to dissolve the solids; if necessary, you may heat the solution, but do not boil it.

Cool the solution to room temperature in a water bath, and then to about 0°C in an ice bath. Bright orange crystals of $K_2Cr_2O_7$ will precipitate. Stir the cold slurry of crystals for several minutes. Assemble the Buchner funnel; chill it by adding 100 ml ice-cold distilled water and, after a minute, drawing the water through with suction. *Discard* the water in the suction flask. Filter the $K_2Cr_2O_7$ slurry through the cold Buchner funnel into the empty flask. Your rubber policeman may be helpful when transferring the last of the crystals. Press the crystals dry with a clean piece of filter paper, and continue to apply suction for a minute or so. Turn off the suction and pour the filtrate, which contains most of the NaCl in the sample, into a clean 150 ml beaker. Heat the filtrate to boiling and boil gently.

Reassemble the Buchner funnel while you are waiting for the filtrate to boil, and, *without applying suction,* add a few ml of ice-cold distilled water from your wash bottle to the funnel; use just enough water to cover the crystals. Let the cold liquid remain in contact with the crystals for about ten seconds, and then apply suction; the liquid removed will contain most of the NaCl impurity. Continue to apply suction for about a minute to dry the purified $K_2Cr_2O_7$ crystals. Lift the filter paper and the crystals from the funnel and put the paper on the lab bench to let the crystals dry further in the air.

Continue to boil the solution containing the NaCl until the volume of NaCl crystals (which appear as the boiling proceeds) is about equal to half the volume of liquid above the crystals. Again, wash the crystallized solids from the walls of the beaker into the solution with your medicine dropper filled with solution from the beaker. Stir to dissolve any solid $K_2Cr_2O_7$ that may be present. Reheat the solution to the boiling point.

Assemble the Buchner funnel, turn on the suction, and, using your tongs to hold the beaker, filter the hot solution through the funnel. Transfer as much of the solid NaCl crystals as possible, first by swirling the slurry as you pour it, and then by using your rubber policeman. Press the crystals flat with a piece of dry filter paper. At this point the NaCl will appear yellow because of the presence of residual dichromate solution.

Turn off the suction by disconnecting the hose from the suction flask. Add about 15 drops 6 *M* HCl (dilute HCl) to the crystals. Wait about half a minute, and then reapply suction for a minute or so to remove the liquid, which will contain most of the yellow contaminant. Wash the crystals, with suction on, using a few ml of acetone, which will remove the residual HCl and will readily evaporate. If this operation has been done properly your purified NaCl crystals will be nearly colorless. Remove the filter paper with the crystals from the funnel and put it aside to let the NaCl dry further.

Weigh your dry SiC and $K_2Cr_2O_7$ crystals on separate preweighed sheets of paper, using the top loading or triple beam balance. Show your samples of SiC, $K_2Cr_2O_7$, and NaCl to your laboratory supervisor for his evaluation.

Name ______________________________ Section __________________

DATA AND CALCULATIONS: Resolution of Pure Substances, I. Fractional Crystallization

Unknown no. ______________

Weight of sample and container ______________g

Weight of container ______________g

Weight of sample ______________g

Weight of paper plus SiC ______________g

Weight of paper ______________g

Weight of SiC ______________g

Weight of paper plus $K_2Cr_2O_7$ ______________g

Weight of $K_2Cr_2O_7$ ______________g

Weight of $K_2Cr_2O_7$ in original sample if you recovered 80 per cent of it in this experiment. ______________g

Per cent SiC in sample ______________%

Per cent $K_2Cr_2O_7$ in sample (assuming 80 per cent recovery) ______________%

Per cent NaCl in sample (by difference) ______________%

 Name ____________________ **Section** ______________

ADVANCE STUDY ASSIGNMENT: Resolution of Matter into Pure Substances, I. Fractional Crystallization

1. From a mixture of SiC, $K_2Cr_2O_7$, and NaCl weighing 15.8 g, 3.5 g SiC and 7.8 g $K_2Cr_2O_7$ were recovered. Assuming that all of the SiC but only 80 per cent of the $K_2Cr_2O_7$ originally present were recovered and that the remainder of the sample was NaCl, what are the weight percentages of each component in the original mixture?

______________per cent SiC, ______________per cent $K_2Cr_2O_7$

______________per cent NaCl

2. What solid would crystallize first from a solution containing equal amounts of $K_2Cr_2O_7$ and NaCl if the solution was evaporated at:

(a) 100°C

(b) 60°C

(c) 20°C

3. A solution containing 30 g $K_2Cr_2O_7$ and 30 g NaCl in 100 g H_2O is cooled to 0°C. How much $K_2Cr_2O_7$ will crystallize out? How much NaCl? What per cent of the $K_2Cr_2O_7$ could be recovered by this crystallization?

EXPERIMENT 3

Resolution of Matter into Pure Substances, II. Paper Chromatography

The fact that different substances have different solubilities in a given solvent can be used in several ways to effect a separation of substances from mixtures in which they are present. We have seen in a previous experiment how fractional crystallization allows us to obtain pure substances by relatively simple procedures based on solubility properties. Another widely used resolution technique, which also depends on solubility differences, is chromatography.

In the chromatographic experiment a mixture is deposited on some solid adsorbing substance, which might consist of a strip of filter paper, a thin layer of silica gel on a piece of glass, some finely divided charcoal packed loosely in a glass tube, or even some microscopic glass beads coated very thinly with a suitable adsorbing substance and contained in a piece of copper tubing.

The components of a mixture are adsorbed on the solid to varying degrees, depending on the nature of the component, the nature of the adsorbent, and the temperature. A solvent is then caused to flow through the adsorbent solid under applied or gravitational pressure or by the capillary effect. As the solvent passes the deposited sample, the various components tend, to varying extents, to be dissolved and swept along the solid. The rate at which a component will move along the solid depends on its relative tendency to be dissolved in the solvent and adsorbed on the solid. The net effect is that, as the solvent passes slowly through the solid, the components separate from each other and move along as rather diffuse zones. With the proper choice of solvent and adsorbent, it is possible to resolve many complex mixtures by this procedure. If necessary, we can usually recover a given component by identifying the position of the zone containing the component, removing that part of the solid from the system, and eluting the desired component with a suitable good solvent.

The name given to a particular kind of chromatography depends upon the manner in which the experiment is conducted. Thus, we have column, thin-layer, paper, and vapor chromatography, all in very common use. Chromatography in its many possible variations offers the chemist one of the best methods, if not the best method, for resolving a mixture into pure substances, regardless of whether that mixture consists of a gas, a volatile liquid, or a group of nonvolatile, relatively unstable, complex organic compounds.

In this experiment we shall use paper chromatography to resolve a mixture of substances known as acid-base indicators. These materials are typically brilliant in color, with the colors depending on the acidity of the system in which they are present. A sample containing a few micrograms of the indicator is placed near one end of a strip of filter paper. That end of the paper is then immersed vertically in a solvent. As the solvent rises up the paper by capillary action it tends to carry the sample along with it, to a degree that depends on the solubility of the sample in the solvent and its tendency to adsorb on the paper. When the solvent has risen a distance of L centimeters, the solute, now spread into a somewhat diffuse zone or band, will have risen a smaller distance, say D centimeters. It is found that D/L is, for a given substance under specified conditions, a constant independent of the relative amount of that substance or other substances present. D/L is called the R_f value for that substance under the experimental conditions:

$$R_f = \frac{D}{L} = \frac{\text{distance solute moves}}{\text{distance solvent moves}}$$

The R_f value is a characteristic of the substance in a given chromatography experiment, and can be used to test for the presence of a particular substance in a mixture of substances with different R_f values.

The first part of the experiment will involve the determination of the R_f values for five common acid-base indicators. These substances have colors that will allow you to establish the positions of their bands at the conclusion of the experiment. When you have found the R_f value for each substance by studying it by itself, you will use these R_f values to analyze an unknown mixture.

EXPERIMENTAL PROCEDURE

Take a clean dry beaker and a clean dry test tube to the stockroom and obtain six paper strips and a sample of your unknown. Handle the strips carefully; whenever you need to work with them, handle them by their edges, because their surfaces can very easily be contaminated by your fingers.

Place the strips on a clean dry sheet of paper and make a pencil mark about 3/4 of an inch from one end of each strip (Figure 3.1).

Put two or three drops of the following indicators into separate, clean, dry, micro test tubes:

Bromthymol blue
Alizarin yellow
Bromcresol purple
Phenolphthalein
Phenol red

For an applicator use a fine capillary tube, which will be furnished to you by your instructor. Test the application procedure by dipping the applicator into one of the colored solutions and touching it momentarily to a round test piece of filter paper. The liquid from the applicator should form a spot no larger than 1/4 inch in diameter. Test this procedure several times.

Clean the applicator by dipping it in a few ml of acetone and blowing air through it to dry it. Dip it in one of the indicator solutions and put a 1/4 inch spot on the pencil line on one of the strips. Label the strip at point X (Figure 3.1) with the name of the indicator you applied. Clean the applicator and repeat the procedure on the other strips for each of the other indicators and the unknown. Apply the unknown three times for greater color intensity, *making sure* each time that the spot has *dried* before making the next application.

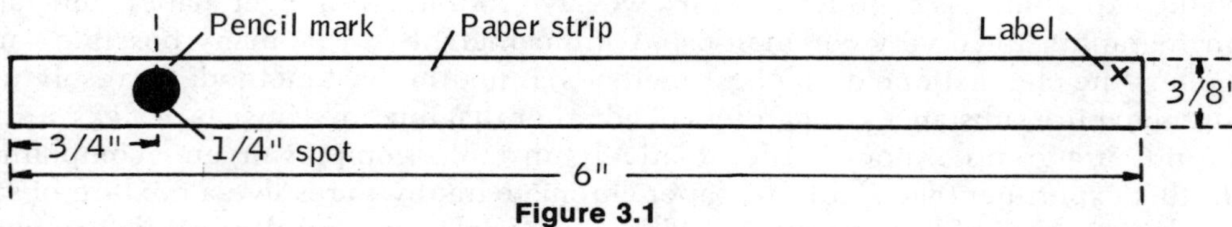

Figure 3.1

Draw 50 ml of eluting solvent from the supply on the reagent shelf. This solution is made by saturating normal butanol, an organic alcohol, with 1.5 M NH_3 solution. Pour this solution into three dry 250 ml Erlenmeyer flasks. These will serve as developing chambers in the experiment.

When you are sure the sample spots are dry, place two of the strips opposite each other on the side of a cork, and place the cork and the strips in the flask so that the ends of the strips, but not the sample spots, are in the solvent (see Figure 3.2). In the same way, place two strips in the second flask and two in the third.

Let solvent rise on the strips for 45 to 60 minutes, or until the solvent front has moved at least 3½ inches above the pencil lines. Remove the strips from the beakers and put them on the sheet of paper used earlier. Draw a pencil line along the solvent front on each of the strips and let the strips dry for several minutes.

When the strips have dried (you may need to hold them in the warm air over a piece of asbestos screen held over a small Bunsen flame), hold each strip over the open mouth of a bottle of 15 *M* NH_3,* and note the color of the band associated with each indicator when it is in this alkaline vapor. You will find that moistening the phenolphthalein strip with a damp paper towel prior to exposure to NH_3 produces a much more intense color. When you are sure that you know the position of the band to be associated with each indicator, measure the distance from the center of the band to the point where the indicator was applied. For each indicator, also measure the distance from the solvent front to the point of application. Calculate R_f values for each indicator.

On the strip containing the unknown, measure the R_f values and the colors for each band in the presence of NH_3 vapor, and identify those indicators which are in the unknown. The detection of phenolphthalein is again facilitated if the strip is moistened prior to exposure to NH_3 vapor.

*Labeled as "conc. NH_4OH."

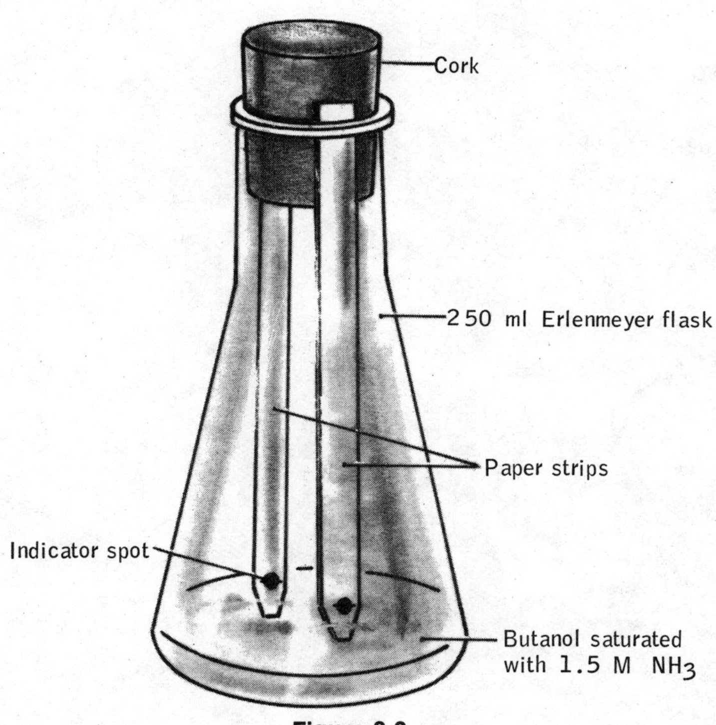

Figure 3.2

Name ______________________ Section ______________

DATA AND CALCULATIONS: Resolution of Matter into Pure Substances, III. Paper Chromatography

	Distance solvent moved (cm)	Distance sample moved (cm)	R_f	Color in NH_3 vapor
Bromthymol blue	________	________	________	________
Alizarin yellow	________	________	________	________
Bromcresol purple	________	________	________	________
Phenol red	________	________	________	________
Phenolphthalein	________	________	________	________
Unknown	________	________	________	________
		________	________	________
		________	________	________
		________	________	________
		________	________	________

Composition of unknown ____

Unknown no. ____________

EXP. 3 Name ______________________ Section ______________

ADVANCE STUDY ASSIGNMENT: **Resolution of Matter into Pure Substances, II. Paper Chromatography.**

1. A student chromatographs a mixture, and after developing the spots with a suitable reagent he observes the following:

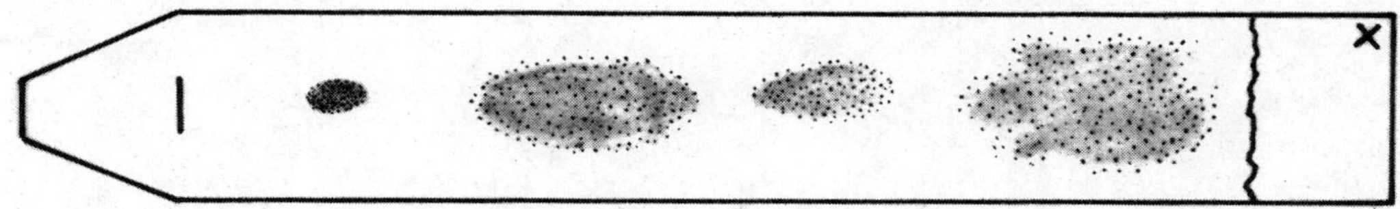

What are the R_f values measured to the centers of the spots?

2. Why should a pencil line be drawn to mark the spot to apply the samples in this experiment, rather than ink from a ball point or fountain pen?

3. The solvent moves the first inch in about 10 minutes. Why shouldn't the experiment be stopped at that time instead of waiting 45 to 60 minutes for the solvent to move 3 to 4 inches?

4. Chromatography gets its name from the fact that, as in this experiment, the positions of the bands obtained were first identified by the colors of the resolved substances. Modern chromatographic methods are ordinarily applied to substances that are colorless in the mixtures to be resolved. Can you suggest three methods that might be used to render apparent the positions of bands containing colorless substances?

SECTION 2

Formulas and Stoichiometry

EXPERIMENT 4

Law of Multiple Proportions

An early development in chemistry that brought some ordering to the study of composition of compounds was the recognition that there is a definite ratio between the amounts of any two elements in a compound. That is, in any pure substance the relative amount of each of the elements present is fixed. This relationship is known as the Law of Definite Proportions.

With binary compounds of any element and oxygen it was possible, given the composition, to calculate the amount of that element that was combined with 8.0000 grams of oxygen in the oxide. This quantity is called the gram equivalent weight (GEW) of the element. It was found that, once a group of gram equivalent weights of elements had been determined, they could often be used to calculate not only the composition of oxides but also that of other binary compounds. Knowing, for example, that the gram equivalent weight of magnesium is 12.16 g and that of sulfur is 16.03 g, one can correctly predict that these two elements will form a compound in which the weight ratio of magnesium to sulfur is 12.16:16.03, the general rule being that one GEW of an element combines with one GEW of another. The drawback of this approach was that many elements had more than one GEW since they formed more than one oxide, so that prediction of weight ratios of elements in compounds produced several possible values rather than one. The establishment of reliable atomic weights and chemical formulas eliminated the need for gram equivalent weights, but in the early days of chemistry they were extensively used, since they did systematize to some extent weight relationships among elements.

As we have noted, many elements form more than one compound with oxygen, and indeed with other nonmetals. These elements clearly must have more than one gram equivalent weight. The Law of Multiple Proportions, another very old chemical relation, states that in such cases the different gram equivalent weights of an element are related to each other by ratios of small whole numbers (2:1, 3:2, and so on). According to this law, if one value of the GEW of nitrogen was found to be 7.00 g, nitrogen might have other GEW's equal to 14.00 g, or 10.50 g, or 3.50 g; however, it would not be expected to have any gram equivalent weight equal to, say, 4.12. In this experiment* we will measure some gram equivalent weights by carrying out a few rather simple chemical reactions and will use the GEW's we find to illustrate the Law of Multiple Proportions.

---

*Similar to an experiment described by J. C. Bailar, J. Chem. Educ. 6, 1759 (1929).

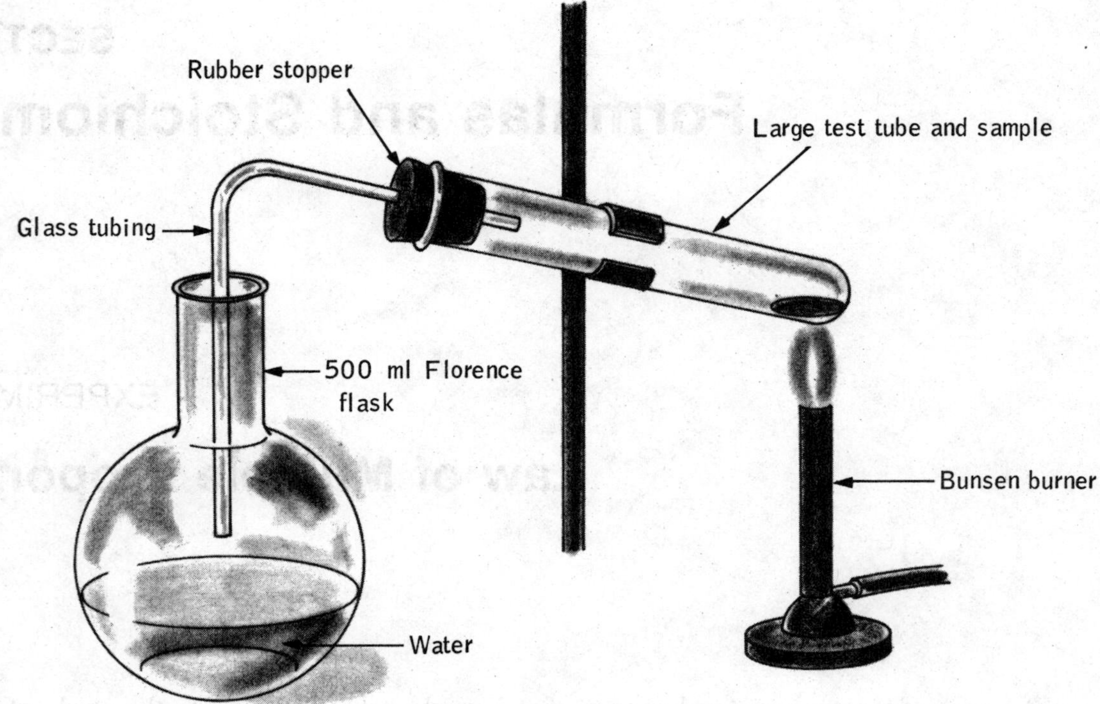

Figure 4.1

Copper and bromine form more than one compound with each other. A copper bromide (compound A) dissociates when heated, liberating bromine and forming another copper bromide (compound B). This second bromide is readily converted to an oxide (compound C) by treatment with nitric acid and subsequent heating. This oxide of copper can be easily reduced to copper metal with hydrogen. In this experiment you will carry a known mass of compound A through these reactions, measuring the related masses of compounds B and C. From these data, you will be able to calculate gram equivalent weights for copper and bromine. Knowing the atomic weights of copper and bromine, you can then establish the formulas of compounds A, B, and C.

EXPERIMENTAL PROCEDURE { *WEAR YOUR SAFETY GLASSES WHILE PERFORMING THIS EXPERIMENT.*

Place about one gram of the copper bromide (A) in a large, accurately weighed test tube. Weigh the test tube and its contents to the nearest 0.001 g. Clamp the test tube so that it is slightly inclined, and incorporate it into an apparatus like that shown in Figure 4.1. The bent glass tube should extend about an inch past the end of the rubber stopper and should dip to within about an inch of the surface of the water in the 500 ml Florence flask. Do not let the tube dip into the water; you do not want water to back up into the test tube during the experiment.

Heat the bromide sample, first gently and then rather strongly with the burner flame, until bromine, Br_2, is no longer evolved. (If the tube is heated to redness, the initial decomposition product may be further decomposed to copper, so use discretion when heating.) Carefully heat the upper end of the test tube, if necessary, to drive any condensed bromine out of the test tube. Bromine is very reactive and very poisonous. Do not inhale the bromine vapor or touch the liquid. Allow the test tube to cool and weigh it to find the amount of the second copper bromide (B) formed.

Add 2 ml of 15 M HNO_3 (carefully!) to the test tube and reassemble the apparatus as before. Heat the tube gently until the black substance formed, copper oxide (C), is completely dry. Weigh the test tube and its contents again to find the amount of copper oxide formed from the decomposition of the copper nitrate produced by the reaction of nitric acid with copper bromide.

In the next part of the experiment you will reduce the copper oxide (C) to copper with hydrogen gas. Set up the hydrogen generator described in Experiment 5, Figure 5.1, as directed in that experiment. Have your instructor check your apparatus before proceeding further.

Follow the procedure given in Experiment 5 for the generation of hydrogen gas and its use in the reduction of metal oxides. Be very careful when igniting the hydrogen jet, and follow the instructions exactly. Try to keep the jet burning throughout the reduction and to keep the flame at a constant size by the judicious addition of acid.

When the copper oxide has been completely reduced, let the test tube cool while hydrogen is still passing through it. Weigh the test tube and its contents.

This experiment ordinarily requires two laboratory sessions. You may conveniently stop after preparing and weighing the copper oxide, or you may proceed to construct the hydrogen generator if there is time. During the second session you can complete the reduction of the oxide and make the calculations. Be sure to save your sample of copper oxide; stopper it before putting it in your locker.

Name ______________________________ Section ________________

DATA: Law of Multiple Proportions

Weight of empty test tube ____________g

Weight of test tube plus copper bromide (A) ____________g

Weight of test tube plus copper bromide (B) ____________g

Weight of test tube plus copper oxide (C) ____________g

Weight of test tube plus copper ____________g

Weight of copper bromide (A) ____________g

Weight of copper bromide (B) ____________g

Weight of copper oxide (C) ____________g

Weight of copper ____________g

CALCULATIONS

A. Using the data you obtained and the definition of gram equivalent weight, calculate the GEW of copper in the oxide (C).

GEW Cu ____________g

B. Assuming that one GEW Cu combines with one GEW Br in any copper bromide compound, calculate the GEW Br in copper bromide (A) and copper bromide (B).

GEW Br in (A) ____________g

GEW Br in (B) ____________g

C. How do these results illustrate the Law of Multiple Proportions?

Continued on following page

D. Given the atomic weights for copper, bromine, and oxygen, find the chemical formulas for compounds A, B, and C.

Copper bromide (A) ____________

Copper bromide (B) ____________

Copper oxide (C) ____________

E. Write balanced chemical equations for the reactions that occurred when

1. Compound A was heated.

2. Compound C was heated in a stream of hydrogen.

Note: The calculations in this experiment are based on a constant gram equivalent weight for copper in its compounds. This leads to a set of GEW's for other elements which differ to some extent from those obtained using the usual assumption that the gram equivalent weight of oxygen is constant. The laws of chemistry are valid on either basis, and in this experiment it is certainly most convenient to assume, as we do, that the GEW of copper remains fixed.

 Name ______________________ **Section** ______________

ADVANCE STUDY ASSIGNMENT: Law of Multiple Proportions

1. Antimony forms two chlorides having widely different properties. One of the chlorides is a solid that melts at 73°C and contains 46.8 per cent chlorine by weight. The other chloride is a liquid that boils at 140°C and contains 59.3 per cent chlorine by weight. Antimony also forms an oxide which contains 16.5 per cent oxygen. On the basis of these data,

(a) Find the gram equivalent weight of antimony in its oxide.

______________g

(b) Based on the GEW of antimony calculated in (a), find two possible gram equivalent weights of chlorine.

______________g

______________g

(c) Show how the results of (a) and (b) illustrate the Law of Multiple Proportions.

2. In the experiment to be performed, a student did not completely reduce the copper oxide (C) to copper. How would this effect the values he obtained for the gram equivalent weights of bromine? Would the data still support the Law of Multiple Proportions?

EXPERIMENT 5

Weight Analysis of Metal Oxides

The gram equivalent weight of an element is most simply defined as the weight of that element which will combine with 8.000 g of oxygen. Gram equivalent weights of metals can in principle be determined by starting with a known weight of metal and determining the amount of oxide produced by reaction of the metal with oxygen. In this experiment you will find the gram equivalent weight of the metal by decomposing its oxide to the free metal. The gram equivalent weight of the metal can then be calculated from the weight of the oxide sample and the amount of metal produced.*

A few metal oxides, such as those of silver and mercury, can be decomposed to the free metal by heat alone. All others must react with some substance, called a reducing agent, that has a stronger affinity for oxygen than the metal in the metal oxide. In preparing metals from their oxide ores, carbon in the form of coke is used whenever possible, since it is relatively inexpensive. When reduction with carbon is not feasible, either because the reaction simply will not proceed or because undesirable carbides are formed, a more active metal such as aluminum is sometimes used. The metals with the most stable oxides, such as sodium and aluminum, are typically won from their ores by electrolysis.

In the laboratory, hydrogen gas is a very convenient reducing agent. It can be easily generated by the reaction of zinc metal with sulfuric acid:

$$Zn(s) + 2\ H^+(aq) \rightarrow H_2(g) + Zn^{2+}(aq)$$

At high temperatures hydrogen will reduce many metal oxides according to the following equation:

$$M_xO_y(s) + y\ H_2(g) \rightarrow x\ M(s) + y\ H_2O(g)$$

The experiment you will perform today involves this reaction. You will carry out the experiment by heating an unknown metal oxide in a stream of hydrogen gas until the oxide is completely reduced to the metal and the water vapor produced has been removed in the gas stream.

EXPERIMENTAL PROCEDURE {*WEAR YOUR SAFETY GLASSES WHILE PERFORMING THIS EXPERIMENT.*

Obtain from the stockroom a dropping funnel or thistle tube, a drying tube, and a sample of an unknown metal oxide.

Assemble the apparatus (Fig. 5.1) consisting of a hydrogen generator and a sample tube. Support the generator and sample tube on separate ringstands. The dropping funnel should nearly touch the bottom of the 250 ml Erlenmeyer flask. The jet issuing from the sample tube can be made from a piece of glass tubing by drawing out to a capillary and cutting back to a diameter of about 1/8 inch. The gas delivery tube from the drying tube should reach to about 2 inches from the bottom of the large test tube. Use proper caution and procedures when inserting glass tubing into the rubber stoppers. The drying tube should be filled with fresh $CaCl_2$.

*See W. L. Masterton and J. J. Demo, J. Chem. Educ. 35, 242–244, (1958).

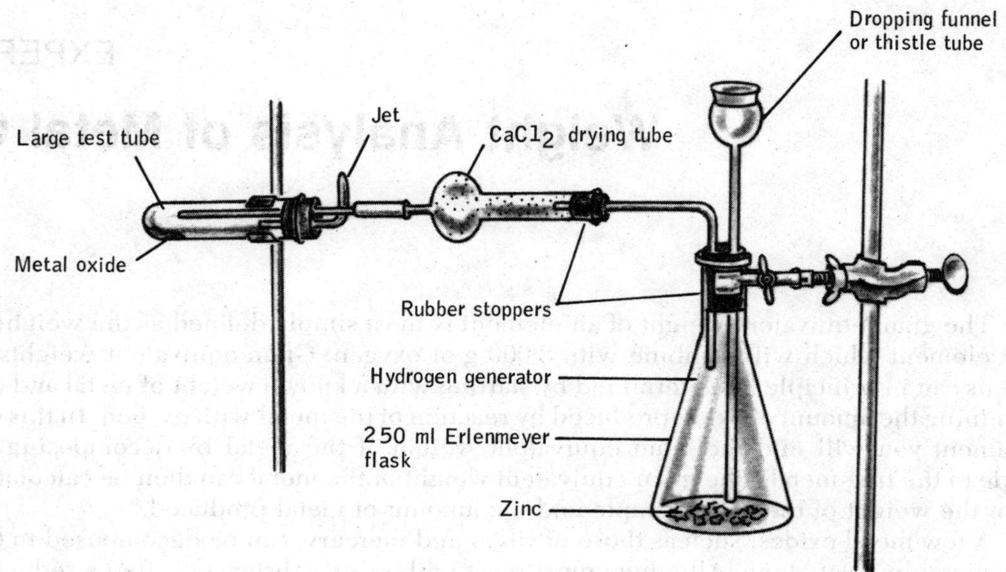

Figure 5.1

Weigh the empty test tube to 0.001 g on the analytical balance. If you use a two-pan balance, suspend the tube from the hook holding the balance pan. Place about one gram of your unknown metal oxide in the test tube and weigh it accurately.

Connect the test tube containing the sample to the generator, being careful not to let the gas delivery tube touch the sample. Add about 20 g of mossy zinc to the flask. Add a few drops of $CuSO_4$ solution and enough water to barely cover the zinc. The end of the dropping funnel or thistle tube should be under the water. Check with your instructor for approval of your apparatus before proceeding any further.

Add about 30 ml of 6 M H_2SO_4 through the dropping funnel. Hydrogen gas should begin to evolve and will soon flush the air from the whole apparatus. Although a hydrogen-air explosion is very unlikely, you should wrap the hydrogen generator in a towel as a safety precaution. Let the generator run for a few minutes, and then collect a sample of the gas escaping from the jet with a small inverted test tube. Ignite the hydrogen in the test tube by holding it close to the flame from your Bunsen burner. Then try to light the jet with the burning hydrogen in the small test tube. If the hydrogen coming from the jet is pure, the flame will last long enough for you to do this. *Never* light the jet of hydrogen with a match or burner flame, since this can result in an explosion.

Once the jet is burning, heat the sample of the metal oxide with your burner flame. As the heating proceeds and the oxide is reduced, the hydrogen flame may decrease in size. Add sulfuric acid as necessary to keep the size of the flame as constant as possible. If drops of water condensing in the glass tube in the generator or in the jet reduce the flow of hydrogen, the flame may sputter or even go out. If this happens, call your instructor and ask him for advice.

Continue to heat the sample with as hot a flame as possible for about 15 minutes. After you stop heating, let hydrogen pass through the apparatus until the sample is at room temperature. Warm samples may reoxidize if exposed to air. Weigh the tube and contents.

If time permits (at least 45 minutes will be required), check for completeness of reduction of the metal oxide by heating the sample again in a stream of hydrogen, following all of the precautions taken previously. The weights of metal as calculated after the first and second heatings should agree within 0.002 g.

Name ______________________ Section ______________

DATA: Weight Analysis of Metal Oxides

Weight of empty test tube ______________ g

Weight of test tube and metal oxide ______________ g

Weight of test tube and metal (first heating) ______________ g

Weight of test tube and metal (second heating) ______________ g

CALCULATIONS AND RESULTS

Weight of metal oxide ______________ g

Weight of metal contained in sample ______________ g

Weight of oxygen contained in sample ______________ g

______________ g metal ≏ ______________ g oxygen

______________ g metal ≏ 8.000 g oxygen

GEW metal = ______________ g

Per cent metal in oxide ______________

Unknown no. ______________

 Name ____________________ Section ______________

ADVANCE STUDY ASSIGNMENT: Weight Analysis of Metal Oxides

1. A sample of a certain metal oxide weighing 1.996 g yields 1.396 g of metal on reaction with hydrogen. Calculate the gram equivalent weight of the metal. Can you suggest what this metal might be? The formula of the oxide?

2. What effect would the following errors have on the value obtained for the GEW of the metal? Explain your reasoning.

   (a) The sample did not react completely with hydrogen.

   (b) The sample was cooled in air instead of in hydrogen.

   (c) Some water condensed on the upper end of the test tube and was weighed along with the metal.

3. Can you suggest a reason for using $CaCl_2$ to dry the hydrogen produced in this experiment?

EXPERIMENT 6

Water of Hydration

Most solid chemical compounds will contain some water if they have been exposed to the atmosphere for any length of time. In most cases the water is present in quite small amounts and is merely adsorbed on the surface of the crystals. This adsorbed water can usually be removed by gentle heating. Other solid compounds will contain larger amounts of water that are bound to the compound more strongly. These compounds are usually ionic salts. The water present in these salts, called water of hydration, is generally bound to the cations in the compound.

A few hydrated compounds lose water spontaneously to the atmosphere upon standing. Such compounds are called efflorescent. More generally, hydrated compounds may be dehydrated by heating. As the temperature is increased, the vapor pressure of water above the solid hydrate will increase until it exceeds the partial pressure of water in the atmosphere above it. At that temperature, dehydration occurs. As the water of hydration is lost from a hydrated compound, the compound may go through several color changes, which will correspond to the colors of the various hydrates formed by the salt. Thus $CoCl_2 \cdot 6H_2O$ is red, $CoCl_2 \cdot 2H_2O$ is violet, and $CoCl_2$ is blue.

Some anhydrous ionic compounds will absorb water from the atmosphere so strongly that they can be used to dry liquids or gases. These substances, called desiccants, are referred to as hygroscopic substances. A few ionic compounds will take up so much water from the atmosphere that they may eventually dissolve in their water of hydration; such substances are deliquescent.

In this experiment you will study the kinds of compounds that form hydrates. You will also determine the percentage of hydrate water lost by an unknown compound upon heating. You may be able to calculate the number of moles of water of hydration per mole of hydrated compound from the amount of water lost and the formula weight of the anhydrous compound.

EXPERIMENTAL PROCEDURE { *WEAR YOUR SAFETY GLASSES WHILE PERFORMING THIS EXPERIMENT.*

A. Identification of Hydrates. Place about 0.5 g of each of the compounds listed below in small dry test tubes. Observe carefully the behavior of each compound when you heat it gently with a burner flame. If droplets of water condense on the cool upper walls of the test tube, this is evidence that the compound may be a hydrate. Note the color and nature of the residue. See if the residue dissolves in water. If the residue is water soluble, then the original compound was probably a true hydrate. If the residue is not water soluble, then the compound is one that forms water as one of its products upon decomposition.

Sodium sulfate
Potassium chloride
Sodium tetraborate (borax)
Sugar
Potassium dichromate
Barium chloride

B. Reversibility of Hydration. Gently heat a few fine crystals of hydrated copper (II) sulfate $CuSO_4 \cdot 5H_2O$ in an evaporating dish until the color changes appear to be complete. Let a portion of the residue stand on a watch glass until the end of the laboratory period. Note any changes in color upon standing. Dissolve the rest of the residue in the evaporating dish in a few drops of water. Heat the resulting solution to boiling (CAUTION!) and allow to cool. Observe any color changes.

C. Deliquescence and Efflorescence. Place a few crystals of each of the compounds listed here on a watch glass and allow them to stand until the end of the laboratory period. Observe them occasionally and note any changes that occur.

$Na_2CO_3 \cdot 10H_2O$ (washing soda)	$MgSO_4 \cdot 7H_2O$ (Epsom salt)
$Na_2SO_4 \cdot 10H_2O$	$KAl(SO_4)_2 \cdot 12H_2O$ (alum)
$CaCl_2$	

D. Decomposition of $AlCl_3 \cdot 6H_2O$. Place a few crystals of $AlCl_3 \cdot 6H_2O$ in an evaporating dish. Heat gently and observe the color and odor of any vapor given off. Test the vapor with moist litmus paper to check for its acidity or basicity. If the vapor is acidic, the litmus will turn from blue to red; if it is basic, the litmus will turn from red to blue.

E. Percent Water in a Hydrate. Clean a porcelain crucible and its cover with 6 *M* HNO_3. Any stain that is not removed with this treatment will not interfere in this experiment. Rinse and dry the crucible and support it on a clay triangle. Heat the crucible with a flame, gently at first, then to redness. Allow it to cool to room temperature and weigh it on the analytical balance. Handle the crucible only with your crucible tongs.

Place about one gram of your unknown solid hydrate in the crucible and again weigh the crucible on the analytical balance. Place the crucible on the triangle and put the cover on it in an off-centered position so that the water vapor can escape. Heat the crucible gently at first and then to redness for about 10 minutes. Cover the crucible and allow it to cool to room temperature. Weigh the cooled crucible and its contents.

If there is time, repeat the heating and weighing procedure to be sure that all of the salt is completely dehydrated. You may assume that all of the water has been removed when two successive heatings and weighings give no significant (~2 or 3 mg) change in weight.

Examine the solid residue and see if it is water soluble. Calculate the percent of water in the hydrate.

Name ______________________ Section ______________

DATA AND OBSERVATIONS: Water of Hydration

A. Identification of Hydrates

	H_2O appears	Color of residue	Water soluble	Hydrate
Sodium sulfate				
Potassium chloride				
Sodium tetraborate				
Sugar				
Potassium dichromate				
Barium chloride				

B. Reversibility of Hydration

Summarize your observations on $CuSO_4 \cdot 5H_2O$:

Is the dehydration and hydration of $CuSO_4$ reversible?

C. Deliquescence and Efflorescence

	Observation	Conclusion
$Na_2CO_3 \cdot 10H_2O$		
$Na_2SO_4 \cdot 10H_2O$		
$CaCl_2$		
$MgSO_4 \cdot 7H_2O$		
$KAl(SO_4)_2 \cdot 12H_2O$		

Continued on following page

D. Decomposition of $AlCl_3 \cdot 6H_2O$

Observations:

What substance, in addition to H_2O, would you suggest is evolved when $AlCl_3 \cdot 6H_2O$ is heated?

E. Percent Water in a Hydrate

Weight of crucible and cover ____________ g

Weight of crucible, cover, and solid hydrate ____________ g

Weight of crucible, cover, and residue (first heating) ____________ g

Weight of crucible, cover, and residue (second heating) ____________ g

CALCULATIONS AND RESULTS

Weight of solid hydrate ____________ g

Weight of residue ____________ g

Weight of H_2O lost ____________ g

Percentage H_2O in the unknown hydrate ____________ %

Formula weight of anhydrous salt (if furnished) ____________

Number of moles of water per mole of unknown hydrate ____________

Unknown no. ____________

EXP. 6 **Name** ______________________ **Section** ______________

ADVANCE STUDY ASSIGNMENT: Water of Hydration

1. A solid hydrate weighing 2.125 g was heated to drive off the water. A solid anhydrous residue remained, which weighed 1.044 g. Calculate the per cent water in the hydrate. If the anhydrous residue has a formula weight of 104, how many moles of water are present in one mole of the hydrate?

______________% H_2O

______________moles H_2O

2. How can you tell if a compound that gives off water when heated is a true hydrate?

3. A very inexpensive hygrometer that is sold in novelty stores is based upon the color changes of cobalt(II) chloride as the relative humidity of the atmosphere changes. When the air is dry the color is blue; when the air is moist the color is pink. Suggest an explanation of these color changes.

SECTION 3
Calorimetry

EXPERIMENT 7
Heat Effects and Calorimetry

Heat is a form of energy, sometimes called thermal energy, which can pass spontaneously from an object at a high temperature to an object at a lower temperature. If the two objects are in contact they will, given sufficient time, both reach the same temperature.

Heat flow is ordinarily measured in a device called a calorimeter. A calorimeter is simply a container with insulating walls, made so that essentially no heat is exchanged between the contents of the calorimeter and the surroundings. Within the calorimeter chemical reactions may occur or heat may pass from one part of the contents to another, but no heat flows into or out of the calorimeter from or to the surroundings.

A. Specific Heat. When heat flows into a substance the temperature of that substance will increase. The quantity of heat Q required to cause a temperature rise Δt of any substance is proportional to the weight w of the substance and the temperature change, as shown in Equation (1). The proportionality constant C is called the specific heat of that substance.

$$Q = Cw\Delta t \qquad (1)$$

The specific heat can be considered to be the amount of heat required to raise the temperature of one gram of the substance by one degree centigrade. Amounts of heat are usually measured in calories. One calorie is defined as the amount of heat required to raise the temperature of one gram of water by one degree centigrade. Specific heat will therefore have the dimensions cal/g°C. The specific heat of a substance will change slightly with temperature, but for most purposes, it can be assumed to be a constant that is independent of temperature. Water has the highest specific heat (1.00 cal/g°C) of any ordinary substance.

The specific heat of a metal can readily be measured in a calorimeter. A weighed amount of metal is heated to some known temperature and is then quickly poured into a calorimeter that contains a measured amount of water at a known temperature. Heat flows from the metal to the water and the two equilibrate at some temperature between the initial temperatures of the metal and the water.

Assuming that no heat is lost from the calorimeter to the surroundings and that a negligible amount of heat is absorbed by the calorimeter walls, the amount of heat that flows from the metal as it cools is equal to the amount of heat absorbed by the water:

$$\begin{array}{c}\text{heat given off}\\ \text{by the metal}\end{array} = Q = C_m w_m \mid \Delta t_m \mid = \begin{array}{c}\text{heat absorbed}\\ \text{by the water}\end{array} = C_{H_2O} w_{H_2O} \mid \Delta t_{H_2O} \mid \quad (2)$$

If we measure the initial and final temperatures of the water and the metal and the weights of the water and metal used, we can use Equation (2) to find the specific heat C_m of the metal. In the first part of this experiment, you will measure the specific heat of an unknown metal by the method we have outlined.

The specific heat of a metal is related in a simple way to its atomic weight. Dulong and Petit discovered many years ago that about six calories were required to raise the temperature of one gram atomic weight of many metals by one degree centigrade. This relation, shown in Equation (3), is known as the Law of Dulong and Petit:

$$6 \text{ cal/deg} \cong C_m \times GAW_m \quad (3)$$

Once the specific heat of a metal is known, its approximate atomic weight can be calculated from Equation (3). The Law of Dulong and Petit was one of the few rules available to guide the early chemists in their studies of atomic weights.

B. Heat of Solution. When a solid substance and a liquid, both at the same initial temperature, are mixed and the solid dissolves in the liquid, the temperature of the solution formed is typically different from that of the initial system. The amount of heat which must flow into the solution to return it to the initial temperature of the system is called the heat of solution, $\Delta H_{solution}$, for the process. If, for example, the solution is colder than the initial system and 250 calories must be furnished to the solution to return it to the original temperature, then $\Delta H_{solution}$ equals 250 calories. Since heat must flow *into* the solution, the reaction is said to be *endo*thermic, and $\Delta H_{solution}$ is *positive.* If, on the other hand, the solution is warmer than the system was originally, and 320 calories have to be removed from the solution to bring it to the initial temperature, then $\Delta H_{solution}$ equals −320 calories. Since heat flows *from* the solution, the reaction is *exo*thermic, and $\Delta H_{solution}$ is *negative.* The heat flow for the solution of a mole of solute is called the molar heat of solution; this is the quantity that would be found in the literature for the solution reaction.

The heat of solution of a solid compound can be easily measured in a calorimetric experiment. The temperature change of the solvent water is measured and the quantity of heat that must be evolved or absorbed in returning the solution to its initial temperature is calculated from the known specific heats and the masses of the water and the solute. One can then calculate the molar heat of solution by multiplying the number of calories of heat absorbed or evolved per gram of solute by the formula weight of the solute.

EXPERIMENTAL PROCEDURE

A. Specific Heat. From the stockroom obtain a calorimeter, a sensitive thermometer, a sample of metal in a large test tube, and a sample of unknown solid. The thermometer is very expensive, so be careful when handling it.

The calorimeter consists of two nested expanded polystyrene coffee cups fitted with a styrofoam cover. There are two holes in the cover for a thermometer and a glass stirring rod that has a loop bent on one end. Assemble the experimental setup as shown in Figure 7.1.

Weigh your sample of unknown metal in the large test tube to the nearest 0.1 g on the top loading or triple beam balance. Pour the metal into a dry container and weigh the empty test tube. Replace the metal in the test tube and put the test tube in a beaker of water. The beaker should contain enough water so that the top of the metal is below the

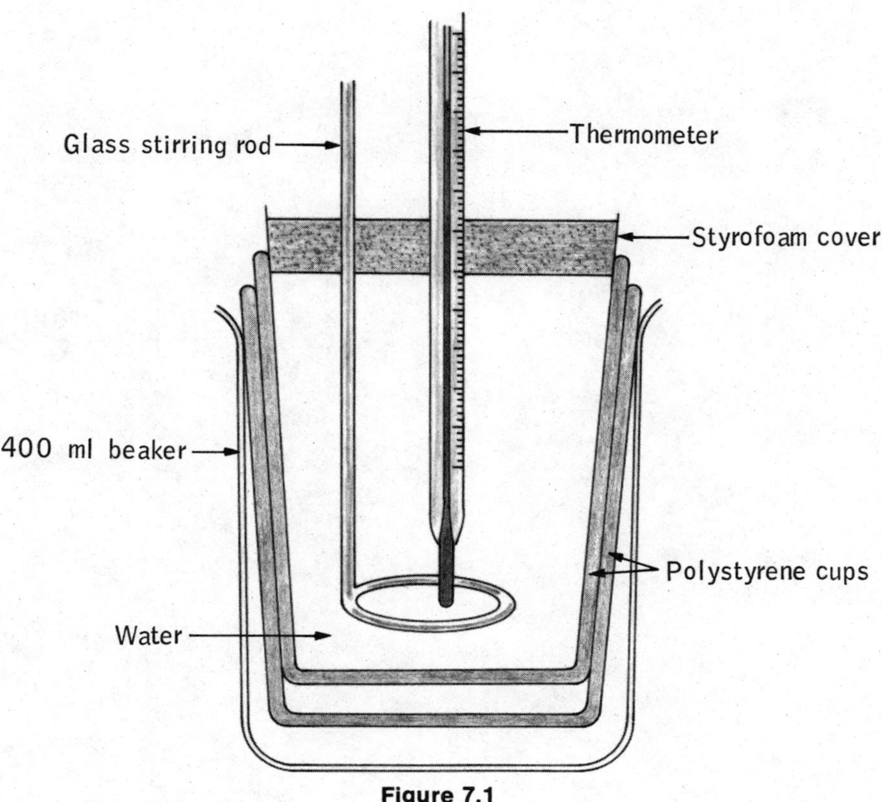

Figure 7.1

surface of the water. Heat the water to boiling and allow it to boil for a few minutes to ensure that the metal attains the temperature of the boiling water.

While the water is boiling, weigh the calorimeter to 0.1 g. Place about 40 ml of water in the calorimeter and weigh again. Insert the stirrer and thermometer into the cover and put it on the calorimeter. The thermometer bulb should be completely under the water.

Measure the temperature of the water in the calorimeter to 0.1°C. Take the test tube out of the beaker of boiling water and quickly pour the metal into the water in the calorimeter. Be careful that no water adhering to the outside of the test tube runs into the calorimeter when you are pouring the metal. Replace the calorimeter cover and agitate the water as best you can with the glass stirrer. Record to 0.1°C the maximum temperature reached by the water. Repeat the experiment, using about 50 ml of water in the calorimeter. Be sure to dry your metal before reusing it; this can be done by heating the metal briefly in the test tube in boiling water and then pouring the metal onto a paper towel to drain. You can dry the hot test tube with a little compressed air.

The metal used in this part of the experiment is to be returned to the stockroom in the test tube in which you obtained it.

B. Heat of Solution. Place about 50 ml of distilled water in the calorimeter and weigh as in the previous procedure. Measure the temperature of the water to 0.1°C. The temperature should be within a degree or two of room temperature. In a small beaker weigh out about 5 g of the solid compound assigned to you. Make the weighing of the beaker and of the beaker plus solid to 0.1 g. Add the compound to the calorimeter. Stirring continuously and occasionally swirling the calorimeter, determine to 0.1°C the maximum or minimum temperature reached as the solid dissolves. Check to make sure that all the solid dissolved. A temperature change of at least five degrees should be obtained in this experiment. If necessary, repeat the experiment, increasing the amount of solid used.

Name ______________________ Section ______________

DATA AND CALCULATIONS: Calorimetry

A. Specific Heat

	Trial 1		Trial 2
Weight of test tube plus metal	________g	→	________g
Weight of test tube	________g	→	________g
Weight of calorimeter	________g	→	________g
Weight of calorimeter and water	________g		________g
Weight of water	________g		________g
Weight of metal	________g	→	________g
Initial temperature of water in calorimeter	________°C		________°C
Initial temperature of metal (assume 100°C unless directed to do otherwise)	________°C	→	________°C
Equilibrium temperature of metal and water in calorimeter	________°C		________°C
Amount of heat gained by the water	________cal		________cal
Amount of heat lost by the metal	________cal		________cal
Specific heat of the metal	________cal/g°C		________cal/g°C
Approximate atomic weight of metal	________		________

Unknown no. ________

B. Heat of Solution

Weight of calorimeter plus water ________g

Weight of beaker ________g

Weight of beaker plus solid ________g

Continued on following page

Weight of water (w_w) ______________ g

Weight of solid (w_s) ______________ g

Original temperature (T_1) ______________ °C

Final temperature (T_2) ______________ °C

$Q_w = w_w(T_1 - T_2)$ (1.00 cal/g°C) ______________ cal

$Q_s = w_s(T_1 - T_2)$ (0.2 cal/g°C)* ______________ cal

$Q = Q_w + Q_s$ = heat flow into solution ______________ cal

The quantity you have just calculated is approximately equal to the heat of solution of your sample. Note that if $T_1 > T_2$, the reaction is endothermic, heat has to be absorbed to return the system to its original temperature, and Q has a positive sign. If $T_1 < T_2$, the reaction is exothermic and Q is a negative quantity.

Calculate the heat of solution per gram of solid.

ΔH per gram = ______________ cal

Solid Unknown No. ______________

(Optional)

Formula of substance used (if furnished by instructor) ______________

Formula weight of compound ______________ g

Heat of solution per mole of compound, ΔH_{molar} ______________ cal

---

*The specific heat will differ somewhat depending upon the nature of the solid, but the value used here, 0.2 cal/g°C, is close enough for our purposes in this experiment.

 Name ______________________ **Section** ______________

ADVANCE STUDY ASSIGNMENT: Heat Effects and Calorimetry

1. A metal sample weighing 45.2 g and at a temperature of 100°C was placed in 38.6 g of water contained in a calorimeter at 25.2°C. At equilibrium the temperature of the water and metal was 33.0°C. What is the specific heat of the metal? What is its approximate atomic weight?

Specific heat ____________ cal/g°C

Atomic weight ______________

2. When 3.6 g of KOH were dissolved in 54 ml of water in a calorimeter at 24.3°C, the temperature of the solution rose to 39.8°C. Following the procedure described on p. 48, calculate the heat of solution per gram of KOH and its molar heat of solution.

ΔH per gram ______________ cal

ΔH per mole ______________ cal

3. In the experiment we assume that the calorimeter is not only a good heat insulator but also that it absorbs only a very small amount of heat from its contents. Although these are good approximations for a calorimeter made of expanded polystyrene, some heat will actually be lost to the surroundings, and some will be absorbed by the calorimeter walls and the thermometer if the contents of the calorimeter are above room temperature. Would you expect that these effects would result in specific heat values that are larger or smaller than the true values? Why?

SECTION 4

Properties of Gases

EXPERIMENT 8

Analysis of an Aluminum-Zinc Alloy*

Some of the more active metals will react readily with solutions of strong acids, producing hydrogen gas and a solution of a salt of the metal. In a previous experiment you generated hydrogen by the action of sulfuric acid on metallic zinc:

$$Zn(s) + 2H^+(aq) \rightarrow H_2(g) + Zn^{2+}(aq) \quad (1)$$

From this equation it is clear that one mole of zinc produces one mole of hydrogen gas in this reaction. If the hydrogen were collected under known conditions, it would be possible to calculate the mass of zinc in a pure sample by measuring the amount of hydrogen it produced on reaction with acid.

Since aluminum reacts spontaneously with strong acids in a manner similar to that shown by zinc,

$$2\ Al(s) + 6\ H^+(aq) \rightarrow 2\ Al^{3+}(aq) + 3\ H_2(g) \quad (2)$$

we could find the amount of aluminum in a pure sample by measuring the amount of hydrogen produced by its reaction with an acid solution. In this case two moles of aluminum would produce three moles of hydrogen.

Since the amount of hydrogen produced by a gram of zinc is not the same as the amount produced by a gram of aluminum,

$$1 \text{ mole Zn} \rightarrow 1 \text{ mole } H_2,\ 65.4 \text{ g Zn} \rightarrow 1 \text{ mole } H_2\text{: } 1.00 \text{ g Zn} \rightarrow 0.0153 \text{ moles } H_2 \quad (3)$$

$$2 \text{ moles Al} \rightarrow 3 \text{ moles } H_2,\ 54.0 \text{ g Al} \rightarrow 3 \text{ moles } H_2\text{: } 1.00 \text{ g Al} \rightarrow 0.0556 \text{ moles } H_2 \quad (4)$$

it is possible to react an alloy of zinc and aluminum of known mass with acid, determine the amount of hydrogen gas evolved, and calculate the percentages of zinc and aluminum in the alloy, using relations (3) and (4). The object of this experiment is to make such an analysis.

In this experiment you will react a weighed sample of an aluminum-zinc alloy with an excess of acid and collect the hydrogen gas evolved over water (Fig. 8.1). If you meas-

*W. L. Masterton, J. Chem. Educ. *38*, 558 (1961).

ure the volume, temperature, and total pressure of the gas and use the Ideal Gas Law, taking proper account of the pressure of water vapor in the system, you can calculate the number of moles of hydrogen produced by the sample:

$$P_{H_2}V = n_{H_2}RT, \qquad n_{H_2} = \frac{P_{H_2}V}{RT} \tag{5}$$

The volume V and the temperature T of the hydrogen are easily obtained from the data. The pressure exerted by the dry hydrogen P_{H_2} requires more attention. The total pressure P of gas in the bottle is, by Dalton's Law, equal to the partial pressure of the hydrogen P_{H_2} plus the partial pressure of the water vapor P_{H_2O}:

$$P = P_{H_2} + P_{H_2O} \tag{6}$$

The water vapor in the bottle is present with liquid water, so the gas is saturated with water vapor; the pressure P_{H_2O} under these conditions is equal to the vapor pressure VP_{H_2O} of water at the temperature of the experiment. This value is constant at a given temperature, and will be found in Appendix I at the end of this manual. The total gas pressure P in the flask is very nearly equal to the barometric pressure P_{bar}.*

Substituting these values into (6) and solving for P_{H_2}, we obtain

$$P_{H_2} = P_{bar} - VP_{H_2O} \tag{7}$$

Using (5), you can now calculate n_{H_2}, the number of moles of hydrogen produced by your weighed sample. You can then calculate the percentages of Al and Zn in the sample by properly applying (3) and (4) to your results. For a sample containing g_{Al} grams Al and g_{Zn} grams Zn, it follows that

$$n_{H_2} = g_{Al} \times 0.0556 + g_{Zn} \times 0.0153 \tag{8}$$

For a one gram sample, g_{Al} and g_{Zn} represent the weight fractions of Al and Zn, that is, % Al/100 and % Zn/100. Therefore

$$N_{H_2} = \frac{\%\ \text{Al}}{100} \times 0.0556 + \frac{\%\ \text{Zn}}{100} \times 0.0153 \tag{9}$$

where N_{H_2} = number of moles of H_2 produced *per gram* of sample.

Since it is also true that

$$\%\ \text{Zn} = 100 - \%\ \text{Al} \tag{10}$$

(9) can be written in the form

$$N_{H_2} = \frac{\%\ \text{Al}}{100} \times 0.0556 + \frac{100 - \%\ \text{Al}}{100} \times 0.0153 \tag{11}$$

We can solve equation (11) directly for % Al if we know the number of moles of H_2 evolved per gram of sample. To save time in the laboratory and to avoid arithmetic errors, it is highly desirable to prepare in advance a graph giving N_{H_2} as a function of % Al. Then when N_{H_2} has been determined in the experiment, % Al in the sample can be read directly from the graph. Directions for preparing such a graph are given in Problem 1 in the Advance Study Assignment.

---

*In principle a small correction should be made for the difference in heights of the water levels inside and outside the sample bottle. In practice the error made by neglecting this effect is much smaller than other experimental errors.

EXPERIMENTAL PROCEDURE { WEAR YOUR SAFETY GLASSES WHILE PERFORMING THIS EXPERIMENT

Obtain a drying tube and sample of Al-Zn alloy from the stockroom. Assemble the apparatus as shown in Figure 8.1. The top of the funnel should be at least one inch higher than the top of the tube leading from the drying tube to the pneumatic trough.

Weigh the vial containing your unknown on the analytical balance. Transfer about half the alloy to a piece of paper and weigh the vial again. The sample transferred should weigh between 0.100 and 0.180 grams. When you have a sample of the proper weight, wrap it in some copper wool and place it in the drying tube.

Fill the apparatus by pouring water through the funnel. Close the clamp when all of the air is out of the apparatus. If bubbles of air appear in the tubing after the clamp is closed, check the rubber connections for leaks.

Fill a gas-collecting bottle with water and slide a glass plate across the mouth of the bottle in such a way that no air bubbles are trapped in the bottle. Invert the covered bottle in the trough and remove the glass plate. Insert the glass tube into the mouth of the bottle.

Pour 10 ml of 12 *M* HCl into the funnel. Open the clamp slowly to allow the acid to come into contact with the metal sample. Close the clamp when the metal starts to give off bubbles vigorously. When the reaction slows down, admit more acid. Be careful not to allow any air bubbles to get into the tube leading from the funnel. The second sample of metal can be weighed while the first sample is being allowed to react completely (approximately 15 minutes). When gas bubbles are no longer evolved from the metal, fill the funnel with water and open the clamp slowly to flush all the gas out of the tubing and into the collection bottle.

Measure the temperature of the water in the trough. Read the atmospheric pressure from the barometer. To measure the volume of gas inside the collection vessel, first cover the mouth of the bottle under the water and invert the bottle. Remove the glass plate and dry the outside of the bottle. Weigh it on a platform balance to ± 0.1 g. Fill the bottle completely with water and weigh again. The difference in the weights is the weight of water equivalent to the volume occupied by the gas produced in the reaction. Assuming that the density of water is 1.00 g/ml, we find that this is numerically equal to the volume of gas in ml.

Repeat the experiment using the second weighed sample of metal.

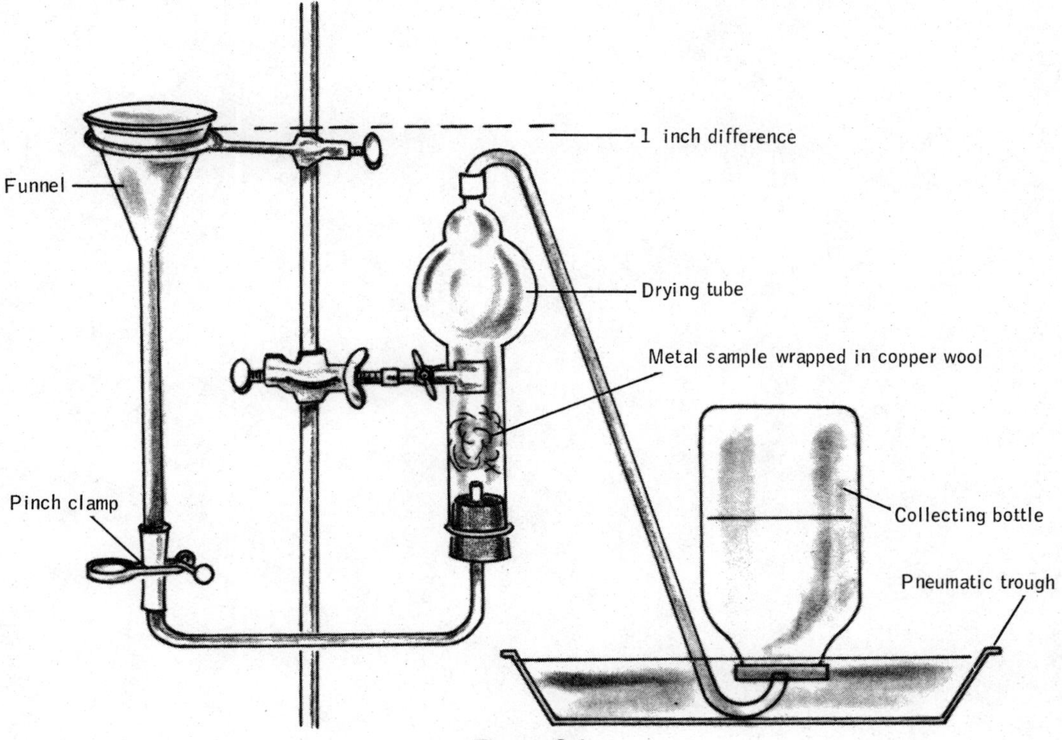

Figure 8.1

Name ______________________ Section ______________

DATA: Analysis of an Aluminum-Zinc Alloy

	Trial 1	Trial 2
Weight of sample plus vial	________ g	
Weight of about one-half the sample plus vial	________ g	________ g
Weight of vial plus any remaining sample		________ g
Temperature of water = temperature of H_2	________ °C	________ °C
Barometric pressure	________ mm Hg	________ mm Hg
Weight of bottle partially filled with water	________ g	________ g
Weight of bottle filled with water	________ g	________ g

CALCULATIONS

Weight of sample (0.10 to 0.18 g)	________ g	________ g
Volume of H_2, V	________ ml	________ ml
Temperature of H_2, T	________ °K	________ °K
Vapor pressure of H_2O at T, VP_{H_2O}, from Appendix I	________ mm Hg	________ mm Hg
Pressure of dry H_2, P_{H_2} (Eq. 7)	________ mm Hg	________ mm Hg
Moles H_2 from sample, n_{H_2} (Eq. 5)	________ moles	________ moles
Moles H_2 per gram of sample, N_{H_2}	________ moles/g	________ moles/g
% Al (read from graph)	________ %	________ %

Unknown no. ________

ADVANCE STUDY ASSIGNMENT: Analysis of an Aluminum-Zinc Alloy

1. On the following page, construct a graph of N_{H_2} vs. % Al. To do this, refer to Equation (11) and the discussion preceding it. Note that a plot of N_{H_2} vs. % Al should be a straight line (why?). To fix the position of a straight line, it is necessary to locate only two points. The most obvious way to do this is to calculate N_{H_2} when % Al = 0 and when % Al = 100. If you wish, you may also locate intermediate points (for example, N_{H_2} when % Al = 50, and so forth); all these points should be on the same straight line.

2. A student finds that a sample of an Al-Zn alloy weighing 0.220 g reacts with excess acid to generate 205 ml of hydrogen, measured over water at a temperature of 24°C and a total pressure of 738 mm Hg. Calculate:

(a) the partial pressure of dry H_2 (P_{H_2}) ______________

(b) the number of moles of H_2 evolved (n_{H_2}) ______________

(c) the number of moles H_2 per gram of sample ______________

(d) % Al, from graph ______________

(e) % Al, from Equation (11) ______________

3. The nature of the reaction of various metals with excess acid is as follows:

Mg 24.4 g Mg → 1 mole H_2 Cu no reaction

Ni 58.6 g Ni → 1 mole H_2 Ag no reaction

Co 59.0 g Co → 1 mole H_2

On this basis, indicate whether alloys of the following metals could be analyzed satisfactorily by the procedure of this experiment. Indicate your reasoning.

(a) Cu-Mg

(b) Mg-Ni

(c) Cu-Ag

(d) Co-Ni

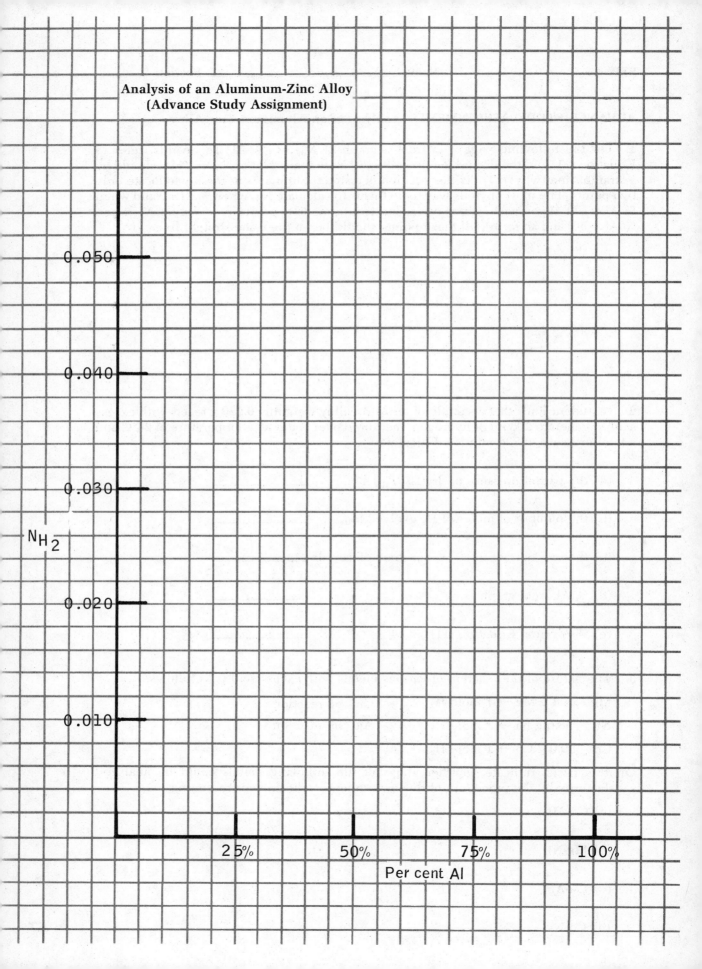

Analysis of an Aluminum-Zinc Alloy
(Advance Study Assignment)

EXPERIMENT 9

Molecular Weight of a Volatile Liquid

One of the important applications of the Ideal Gas Law is found in the experimental determination of the molecular weights of gases and vapors. In order to measure the molecular weight of a gas or vapor we need simply to determine the weight of a given sample of the gas under known conditions of temperature and pressure. If the gas obeys the Ideal Gas Law, we know that

$$PV = nRT \qquad (1)$$

If the pressure P is in atmospheres, the volume V in liters, the temperature T in °K, and the amount n in moles, then the gas constant R is equal to 0.0821 lit-atm/mole °K.

The number of moles n is equal to the weight g of the gas divided by its gram molecular weight *(M)*. Substituting into (1), we have:

$$PV = \frac{gRT}{M} \qquad M = \frac{gRT}{PV} \qquad (2)$$

This experiment involves measuring the gram molecular weight of a volatile liquid by using Equation (2). A small amount of the liquid is introduced into a weighed flask. The flask is then placed in boiling water, where the liquid will vaporize completely, driving out the air and filling the flask with vapor at barometric pressure and the temperature of the boiling water. If we cool the flask so that the vapor condenses, we can measure the weight of the vapor and calculate a value for M.

EXPERIMENTAL PROCEDURE* {WEAR YOUR SAFETY GLASSES WHILE PERFORMING THIS EXPERIMENT.

Obtain a special round bottom flask, a stopper and cap, and an unknown liquid from the storeroom. Support the flask on an evaporating dish or in a beaker at all times. If you should break or crack the flask, report it to your instructor immediately so that it can be repaired. With the stopper loosely inserted in the neck of the flask, weigh the empty dry flask on the analytical balance. Use a copper loop, if necessary, to suspend the flask from the hook of a two-pan balance.

Pour about half your unknown liquid, about 5 ml, into the flask. Assemble the apparatus as shown in Figure 9.1. Place the cap on the neck of the flask. Add a few boiling chips to the water in the 600 ml beaker and heat the water to the boiling point. Watch the liquid level in your flask; the level should gradually drop as vapor escapes through the cap. After all the liquid has disappeared and no more vapor comes out of the cap, continue to boil the water gently for 5 to 8 minutes. Measure the temperature of the boiling water. Shut off the burner and wait until the water has stopped boiling (about ½ minute) and then loosen the clamp holding the flask in place. Slide out the flask, remove the cap, and *immediately* insert the stopper used previously.

Remove the flask from the beaker of water, holding it by the neck, which will be cooler. Immerse the flask in a beaker of cool water to a depth of about 2 inches. After

*See W. L. Masterton and T. R. Williams, J. Chem. Educ. *36*, 528, (1959).

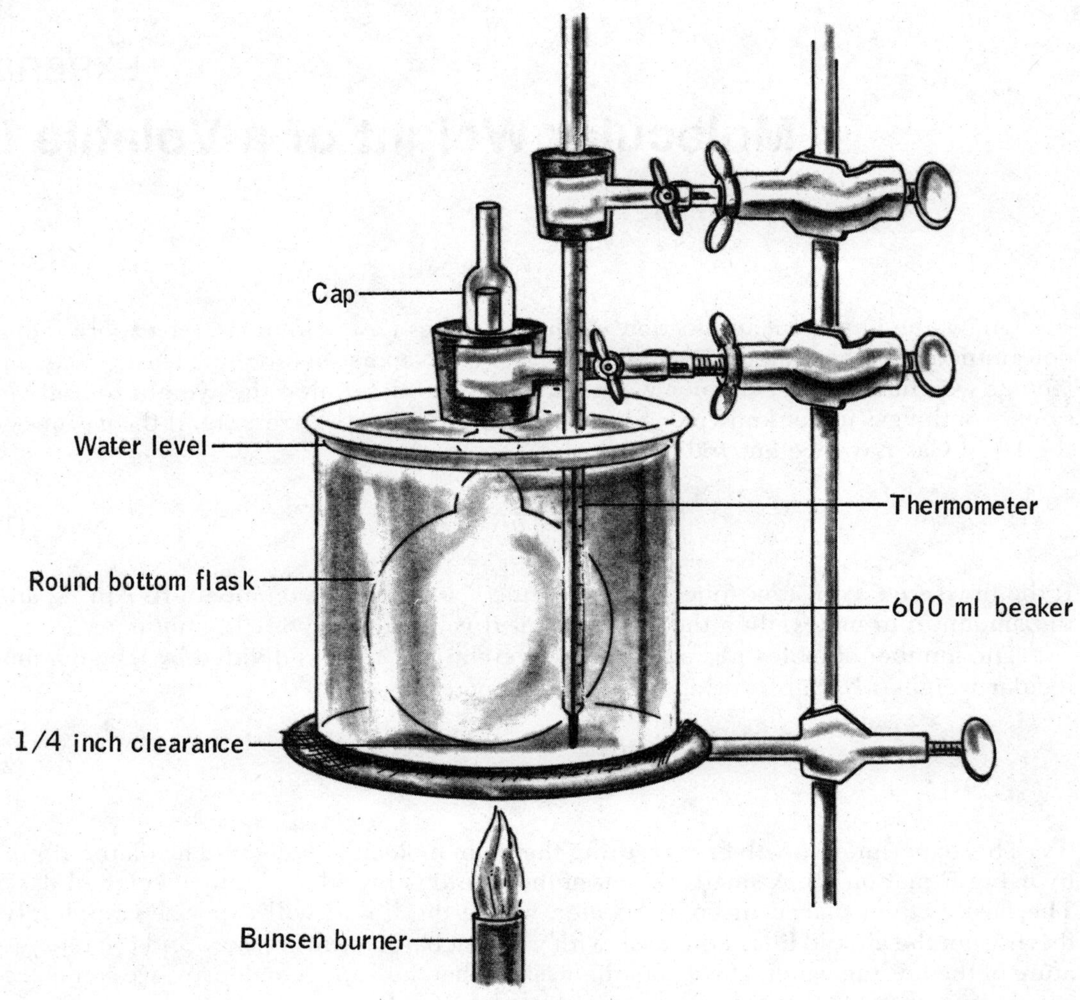

Figure 9.1

holding the flask in the water for about two minutes to allow it to cool, carefully remove the stopper *for not more than a second or two* to allow air to enter, and again insert the stopper. (As the flask cools the vapor inside condenses and the pressure drops, which explains why air rushes in when the stopper is removed.)

Dry the flask with a towel to remove the surface water. Loosen the stopper momentarily to equalize any pressure differences, and reweigh the flask. Read the atmospheric pressure from the barometer.

Repeat the procedure using the other half of your liquid sample.

You may obtain the volume of the flask from your instructor. Alternatively, he may direct you to measure its volume by weighing the flask stoppered and full of water on a rough balance. *Do not* fill the flask with water unless specifically told to do so.

When you have completed the experiment, return the flask to the storeroom; do not attempt to wash or clean it in any way.

Name ______________________ Section ______________

DATA: Molecular Weight of a Volatile Liquid

	Trial 1		Trial 2
Unknown no.	__________		
Weight of flask and stopper	__________ g	→	__________ g
Weight of flask, stopper, and condensed vapor	__________ g		__________ g
Weight of flask, stopper, and water (see directions)	__________ g	→	__________ g
Temperature of boiling water bath	__________ °C	→	__________ °C
Barometric pressure	__________ mm Hg	→	__________ mm Hg

CALCULATIONS AND RESULTS

	Trial 1	Trial 2
Pressure of vapor, P	__________ atm	__________ atm
Volume of flask (volume of vapor), V	__________ lit	__________ lit
Temperature of vapor, T	__________ °K	__________ °K
Weight of vapor, g	__________ g	__________ g
Gram molecular weight of unknown, M, as found by substitution into Equation (2)	__________ g	__________ g

 Name ________________ Section ________________

ADVANCE STUDY ASSIGNMENT: Molecular Weight of a Volatile Liquid

1. A sample of an unknown liquid is vaporized in a flask having a volume of 235 ml. At 100°C., 0.628 g of the vapor exert a pressure of 738 mm Hg. Calculate the gram molecular weight of the unknown liquid.

________________ g

2. How would each of the following procedural errors affect the results to be expected in this experiment? Give your reasoning in each case.

(a) All of the liquid was not vaporized before the flask was removed from the water bath.

(b) The flask was not allowed to remain in the boiling water long enough to reach thermal equilibrium.

(c) The flask was not dried before the final weighing with the condensed vapor inside.

(d) The flask was left open to the atmosphere while it was being cooled and the stopper was inserted just before the final weighing.

3. The liquids used in this experiment will all have appreciable vapor pressures at room temperature. What effect will this have upon the values of molecular weight obtained?

SECTION 5

Atomic Structure: Chemical Bonding

EXPERIMENT 10

The Atomic Spectrum of Hydrogen

According to the quantum theory, atoms and molecules can exist only in certain states, each of which has an associated fixed amount of energy. When an atom or molecule changes its state, it must absorb or emit an amount of energy equal to the difference between the energy of the initial and final states. This energy may be absorbed or emitted in the form of light, in which case the relationship between the change in energy and the wavelength of the light which is associated with the transition is given by the equation:

$$|\Delta E| = \frac{hc}{\lambda} \qquad (1)$$

where $|\Delta E|$ is the absolute value of the change in energy in ergs, h is Planck's constant, 6.6251×10^{-27} erg sec, c is the speed of light, 3.00×10^{10} cm/sec, and λ is the wavelength in cm. The change in energy, ΔE, of the atom or molecule is positive if light is absorbed and negative if it is emitted.

Atomic and molecular spectra are the result of changes in energy which occur in atoms and molecules when they are excited by various means. The emission spectrum of an atom gives us information about the spacings between the allowed energy levels of that atom. The different wavelengths present in the light can be used to establish the actual energy levels available to the atom. Conversely, given the set of energy levels for an atom, one can predict its atomic spectrum and determine which levels were involved in any observed line in the spectrum.

Since you are probably not familiar with the way in which Equation 1 is used, let us consider a specific example. On the left side of Figure 10.1, we have shown two of the lowest energy levels in which the sodium atom can exist. These occur at 8.25×10^{-12} ergs and 4.87×10^{-12} ergs, respectively, *below* the energy the atom has when it ionizes, which is arbitrarily assigned the value of zero. The actual energies on this basis are both negative, with the lower energy having the more negative value.

Ordinarily a sodium atom will exist in its lowest possible energy state, which is called its ground state. If the atom is excited, say in a flame, to its next higher state, it will be unstable and will very quickly make a transition back down to its ground state, as indicated by the arrow in Figure 10.1. In making the transition, the energy of the atom will decrease by about 3.38×10^{-12} ergs. This amount of energy may be radiated as light, which will have a wavelength given by Equation 1. Below the left side of the figure, we have calculated that wavelength, which turns out to be 5.88×10^{-5} cm. Wavelengths of light are ordinarily given in Å; since 1 Å equals 1×10^{-8} cm, the wavelength is 5880 Å. Atomic spectra arise from transitions of this sort, and the wavelengths associated with those transitions can all be calculated by the method we have used here.

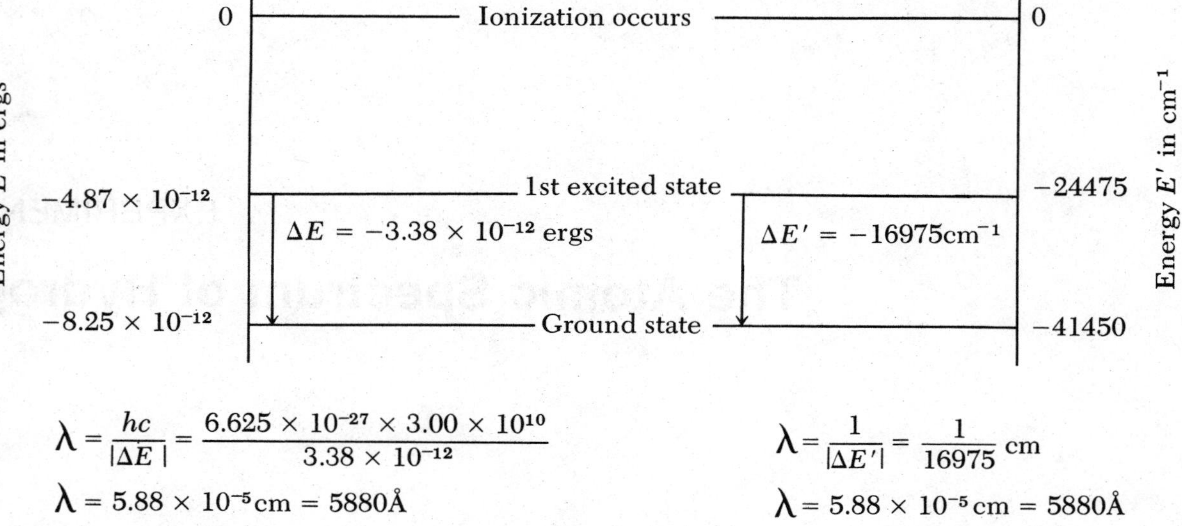

$$\lambda = \frac{hc}{|\Delta E|} = \frac{6.625 \times 10^{-27} \times 3.00 \times 10^{10}}{3.38 \times 10^{-12}}$$

$$\lambda = 5.88 \times 10^{-5}\,\text{cm} = 5880\text{Å}$$

$$\lambda = \frac{1}{|\Delta E'|} = \frac{1}{16975}\,\text{cm}$$

$$\lambda = 5.88 \times 10^{-5}\,\text{cm} = 5880\text{Å}$$

Figure 10.1. Calculations of a Wavelength in the Atomic Spectrum of Sodium

Many years ago spectroscopists recognized that wavelength calculations would be simplified if the energy in Equation 1 were expressed not in ergs, but in units of ergs/hc, which turn out to have the dimensions of cm^{-1} and are called wavenumbers, or reciprocal centimeters. Such energies we will call E', and on the right side of Figure 10.1, we have shown the same energy levels of the Na atom on that basis, with energies E' in cm^{-1}. The advantage of expressing E' in cm^{-1} is that Equation 1, written in terms of E', becomes simply

$$\frac{|\Delta E|}{hc} = |\Delta E'| = \frac{1}{\lambda} \quad \text{and} \quad \lambda = \frac{1}{|\Delta E'|} \tag{2}$$

To find the wavelength in cm for a transition, one need only take the reciprocal of $\Delta E'$. The calculation of λ by this approach is shown on the right side of Figure 10.1. You can see that it gives the same result as that obtained previously, but the mathematics required is somewhat easier.

The simplest atomic spectrum is that of the hydrogen atom. In 1886 Balmer showed that the lines in the spectrum of the hydrogen atom had wavelengths that could be expressed by a rather simple equation. Bohr, in 1913, explained the spectrum on a theoretical basis with his famous model of the hydrogen atom. According to Bohr's theory, the energies E'_n allowed to an H atom are all given by the following equation:

$$E'_n = -\frac{R}{n^2} \tag{3}$$

where R is a constant predicted by the theory and n is an integer, 1, 2, 3,. . ., called a quantum number. It has been found that all the lines in the atomic spectrum of hydrogen can be associated with energy levels in the atom which are predicted with great accuracy by Bohr's equation.

In this experiment we will furnish you with the wavelengths of some of the observed lines in the hydrogen atomic spectrum and ask you to explain the origin of each line in terms of the energy levels of the atom. The wavelengths to be considered are given in Table 10.1.

TABLE 10.1 SOME WAVELENGTHS (IN Å) IN THE SPECTRUM OF THE HYDROGEN ATOM AS MEASURED IN A VACUUM

Wavelength	Assignment $n_{hi} \longrightarrow n_{lo}$	Wavelength	Assignment $n_{hi} \longrightarrow n_{lo}$	Wavelength	Assignment $n_{hi} \longrightarrow n_{lo}$
972.5	________	4102.9	________	10053.	________
1025.7	________	4341.7	________	10941.	________
1215.7	________	4862.7	________	12822.	________
3890.2	________	6564.7	________	18756.	________
3971.4	________	9548.6	________	40,500	________

EXPERIMENTAL PROCEDURE

There are several ways in which one might analyze an atomic spectrum, given the energy levels of the atom, but a simple and powerful one is to calculate the wavelengths of some of the lines that are allowed and to see if they match those which are observed. We shall use this method in our experiment.

The value of R in Equation 3 can be measured very accurately and is found to be 109,677.58 cm^{-1}, perhaps the most accurately known of all physical constants. Since we will be working with electronic calculators, we can use most, or all, of the available precision. On this basis, Equation 3 takes the form

$$E'_n = -\frac{109{,}677.58}{n^2}\ \text{cm}^{-1} \qquad (4)$$

A. Calculations of the Energy Levels of the Hydrogen Atom. Given the expression for E'_n in Equation 4, it is possible to calculate the energy for each of the allowed levels of the H atom starting with $n = 1$. Using your calculator, calculate the energy in cm^{-1} of each of the ten lowest levels of the H atom. Note that the energies are all negative, so that the *lowest* energy will have the *largest* allowed negative value. Enter these values in the table of energy levels, Table 10.2. On the graph paper provided, plot along the y axis each of the six lowest energies, drawing a horizontal line at the allowed level and writing the value of the energy alongside the line near the y axis. Write the quantum number associated with the level to the right of the line.

B. Calculation of the Wavelength of the Lines in the Hydrogen Spectrum. The lines in the hydrogen spectrum all arise from jumps made by the atom from one energy level to another. The wavelengths in cm of these lines can be calculated by Equation 2, where $\Delta E'$ is the difference in energy between any two allowed levels. For example, to find the wavelength of the spectral line associated with a transition from the $n = 2$ level to the $n = 1$ level, calculate the difference, $\Delta E'$, between the energies of those two levels.

The reciprocal of $\Delta E'$ will, by Equation 2, be the wavelength in cm of the spectral line. To convert that wavelength to Å, use the conversion factor, $1 \text{ Å} = 1 \times 10^{-8}$ cm.

Using the procedure we have outlined, calculate the wavelengths in Å of all the lines we have indicated in Table 10.3. That is, calculate the wavelengths of all the lines that can arise from transitions between any two of the six lowest levels of the H atom. Enter these values in Table 10.3.

C. Assignment of Observed Lines in the Hydrogen Spectrum. Compare the wave lengths you have calculated with those which are listed in Table 10.1. If you have made your calculations properly, your wavelengths should match, within the error of your calculation, several of those which are observed. On the line opposite each wavelength in Table 10.1, write the quantum numbers of the upper and lower states for each line whose origin you can recognize by comparison of your calculated values with the observed values. On the energy level diagram, draw a vertical arrow pointing down (light is emitted, $\Delta E' < 0$) between those pairs of levels which you associate with any of the observed wavelengths. By each arrow write the wavelength of the line originating from that transition.

There are a few wavelengths in Table 10.1 which have not yet been calculated. By assignments already made and by an examination of the transitions you have marked on the graph, deduce the quantum states that are likely to be associated with one of the as yet unassigned lines. Calculate the wavelength for the transition between those states. When you have matched a calculated with an observed wavelength, write the associated quantum numbers as before in Table 10.1; continue until all the lines in the table have been assigned.

D. The Balmer Series. This is the most famous series in the atomic spectrum of hydrogen. Carry out calculations in connection with this series as directed in the Data and Calculations section.

Name ____________________ Section ____________________

DATA AND CALCULATIONS: The Atomic Spectrum of Hydrogen

A. The Energy Levels of the Hydrogen Atom

Energies are to be calculated from Equation 4 for the ten lowest energy states.

TABLE 10.2

Quantum Number	Energy, E'_n, in cm^{-1}	Quantum Number	Energy, E'_n, in cm^{-1}
______	______________	______	______________
______	______________	______	______________
______	______________	______	______________
______	______________	______	______________
______	______________	______	______________

B. Calculation of Wavelengths in the Spectrum of the H Atom

TABLE 10.3

n_{higher} / n_{lower}	6	5	4	3	2	1
1	— — —	— — —	— — —	— — —	— — —	
2	— — —	— — —	— — —	— — —		
3	— — —	— — —	— — —			
4	— — —	— — —				
5	— — —					

$$\Delta E' = E'_{n_{hi}} - E'_{n_{lo}} = \frac{1}{\lambda}\ cm^{-1}$$

$$\lambda(cm) = \frac{1}{\Delta E'}$$

$$\lambda(Å) = \lambda(cm) \times 1 \times 10^8$$

In the upper half of each box write $\Delta E'$, the difference in energy in cm^{-1} between $E'_{n_{hi}}$ and $E'_{n_{lo}}$. In the lower half of the box, write λ in Å associated with that value of $\Delta E'$.

Continued on following page

C. Assignment of Wavelengths

A. As directed in the procedure, assign n_{hi} and n_{lo} for each wavelength in Table 10.1 which corresponds to a wavelength calculated in Table 10.3.

B. List below any wavelengths you cannot yet assign and find their origin.

Wavelength, λ observed	Probable transition $n_{hi} \longrightarrow n_{lo}$	$\Delta E'$ transition	λ calculated in Å
________	________	________	________
________	________	________	________
________	________	________	________
________	________	________	________

D. 1. THE BALMER SERIES. When Balmer found his famous series for hydrogen in 1886, he was limited experimentally to wavelengths in the visible and near ultraviolet regions from 2500 Å to 7000 Å. All the lines in his series lie in this wavelength range. From the entries in Table 10.3, what other common characteristic do the lines in the Balmer Series have?

What would be the longest possible wavelength for a line in the Balmer series?

λ = ____________ Å

What would be the shortest possible wavelength that a line in the Balmer series could have?

λ = ____________ Å

Fundamentally, why must all the lines in the hydrogen spectrum between 2500 Å and 7000 Å belong to the Balmer series?

Continued on following page

2. THE IONIZATION ENERGY OF HYDROGEN. In a normal hydrogen atom, the electron is in the lowest energy state. The maximum energy that a hydrogen atom can have is 0 cm^{-1}, at which point the electron is essentially removed from the atom, and ionization occurs. How much energy in cm^{-1} does it take to ionize an H atom?

______________ cm^{-1}

Given the following conversion factors, find the ionization energy of the H atom in ergs, electron volts, and kcal/mole:

$$1 \text{ erg} \mathrel{\hat{=}} 5.0 \times 10^{15} \text{cm}^{-1}; \; 1 \text{ eV} \mathrel{\hat{=}} 1.6 \times 10^{-12} \text{erg} \mathrel{\hat{=}} 23 \text{ kcal/mole}$$

______________ ergs ______________ eV ______________ kcal/mole

Name ______________________ **Section** ________

The Spectrum of Hydrogen

(Data and Calculations)

ADVANCE STUDY ASSIGNMENT: The Atomic Spectrum of Hydrogen

1. The lowest energy level of the potassium atom lies 35,010 cm^{-1} below the energy required to ionize the atom. The first excited state of the K atom is at 22,025 cm^{-1} below ionization energy. What wavelength of light is emitted when a K atom makes a transition from the first excited state to the ground state? What is the ionization energy of the K atom in cm^{-1}? in ergs? in eV? See page 71 for conversion factors.

______________ Å

______________ cm^{-1}

______________ ergs

______________ eV

2. In the HCl molecule, the energy levels associated with rotation are given by the equation, $E_J^r = 10.4\ J(J + 1)\ cm^{-1}$, where J is a quantum number which may have the values 0, 1, 2, . . . Find the wavelength of the light which would be absorbed by the molecule in making a transition from the $J = 6$ to the $J = 7$ state. Would light of this wavelength be visible?

______________ Å

EXPERIMENT 11

The Alkaline Earths and the Halogens— Two Families in the Periodic Table

The periodic table arranges the elements in order of increasing atomic number in horizontal rows of such length that elements with similar properties recur periodically, i.e., they fall directly beneath each other in the table. The elements in a given vertical column are referred to as a family. By noting the gradual trends in properties of the members of a family, it is possible to arrange them in the order in which they fall in the periodic table. This is what you will be asked to do in this experiment for two particular families.

The families to be studied are the alkaline earths, Group II A, and the halogens, Group VII A. The alkaline earths are all active metals and include barium, beryllium, calcium, magnesium, radium, and strontium. Beryllium compounds, rarely encountered, are often very poisonous, and radium is highly radioactive, so we shall not include these two elements in the experiment. The elements in the halogen family are astatine, bromine, chlorine, fluorine, and iodine. Of these we will omit astatine, which is radioactive, and fluorine, which is the most chemically reactive of all the elements and somewhat dangerous to work with.

The experiments with the alkaline earths involve determining the relative solubilities of the salts formed by the alkaline earth cations with sulfate, carbonate, oxalate, and chromate ions. When solutions containing these M^{2+} cations are mixed with the above X^{2-} anions, the following reaction will occur if the salt MX is not very soluble:

$$M^{2+}(aq) + X^{2-}(aq) \longrightarrow MX(s) \qquad \textbf{(1)}$$

$$M^{2+} = Ba^{2+}, Ca^{2+}, Mg^{2+}, \text{ or } Sr^{2+}\ ; \quad X^{2-} = SO_4{}^{2-}, CO_3{}^{2-}, C_2O_4{}^{2-}, \text{ or } CrO_4{}^{2-}$$

The trends in solubilities of these salts are consistent with the order of the II A elements in the periodic table and can be used to establish that order.

The elementary halogens are all oxidizing agents, which means that they tend to react with other substances in such a way as to gain electrons; the reaction is called an oxidation-reduction reaction and results in the halogen (X_2) being reduced to a halide anion (X^-). Since the oxidizing powers of the elementary halogens are not the same, if we mix a solution of the halogen X_2 with a solution containing a halide ion Y^-, the following reaction may occur:

$$X_2(aq) + 2Y^-(aq) \longrightarrow Y_2(aq) + 2X^-(aq) \qquad \textbf{(2)}$$

The reaction will occur if X_2 is a better oxidizing agent than Y_2, since then X_2 can produce Y_2 by removing electrons from the Y^- ion. Conversely, if Y_2 is a stronger oxidizing agent than X_2, reaction 2 will not proceed as written, but will be spontaneous in the opposite direction.

We will test the oxidizing powers of the halogens using this approach. You will be able to tell whether a reaction proceeds by observing the colors of the solutions. The halogens have characteristic colors in water and, particularly, in 1,1,1-trichloroethane,

CCl_3CH_3 (TCE), and these will facilitate your tests. For example, Br_2 in solution in TCE has a reddish brown color, quite different from that of either Cl_2 or I_2 in TCE solution. (Bromide ion, Br^-, like all the halide ions, is colorless.) If we shake a solution of bromine water with TCE, most of the Br_2 will go into the TCE phase and impart its color to it. Then, if we add a solution of a salt containing an excess of another halide ion, say Cl^-, the following oxidation-reduction reaction may or may not occur:

$$Br_2(aq) + 2\,Cl^-(aq) \rightarrow Cl_2(aq) + 2\,Br^-(aq) \tag{3}$$

If the reaction occurs, the Br_2 color in the TCE will be replaced by that of Cl_2, whereas if it does not occur, there will be no appreciable color change. If, indeed, you observe a color change, indicating a reaction occurs, then you can say that Br_2 is a stronger oxidizing agent than Cl_2, since it can produce Cl_2 by oxidizing Cl^- ion. In the event no reaction occurs, as implied by the fact that the color of the TCE remains substantially unchanged, then Cl_2 is a stronger oxidizing agent than Br_2. Using this approach with the various possible mixtures of halogens and halide ions, it is quite easy to arrange the halogens in order of increasing oxidizing power.

We will also investigate the relative solubilities of the salts formed between the silver ion and the various halide ions. If a solution of silver nitrate, $AgNO_3$, is added to a solution of a halide salt, MX, the following reaction will occur:

$$Ag^+(aq) + X^-(aq) \longrightarrow AgX(s) \tag{4}$$

An insoluble precipitate of AgX forms immediately. This precipitate, although it is very insoluble in water, may dissolve in NH_3 solutions, since there the following reaction tends to occur:

$$AgX(s) + 2\,NH_3(aq) \longrightarrow Ag(NH_3)_2^+(aq) + X^-(aq) \tag{5}$$

The tendency for reaction 5 to proceed increases with increasing NH_3 concentration and with the increasing solubility of the silver halide.

The oxidizing powers of the halogens and the solubilities of their silver salts in NH_3 solutions will allow you to arrange the halogens in the order in which they should appear in the periodic table.

Given the properties of the alkaline earths and the halogens as observed in this experiment, it is possible to develop a systematic procedure for determining the presence of any Group II A cation and any given halide ion in a solution. In the last part of the experiment you will be asked to set up such a procedure and use it to establish the identity of an unknown solution containing a single alkaline earth halide.

EXPERIMENTAL PROCEDURE

I. Relative Solubilities of Some Salts of the Alkaline Earths. Add about 1 ml (approximately 12 drops) of 0.1 *M* solutions of the nitrate salts of barium, calcium, magnesium, and strontium to separate small test tubes. To each tube add 1 ml of 1 *M* H_2SO_4 and stir with your glass stirring rod. (Rinse your stirring rod in a beaker of water between tests.) Record your results in the table, noting whether a precipitate forms, as well as any characteristics that might distinguish it.

Repeat the experiment using 1 *M* Na_2CO_3 as the precipitating reagent and record your observations. Then test for the solubilities of the oxalate salts with 0.25 *M* $(NH_4)_2C_2O_4$. Finally, determine the relative solubilities of the chromate salts, using 1 ml of 1 *M* K_2CrO_4 plus 1 ml of 1 *M* acetic acid as the testing reagent.

II. Relative Oxidizing Powers of the Halogens. In a small test tube place a few ml of bromine-saturated water and add 1 ml of 1,1,1-trichloroethane. Stopper the test tube and shake until the bromine color is mostly in the TCE layer. *Caution:* Don't use your finger to stopper the tube, since halogen solutions can give you a bad chemical burn. Repeat the experiment using chlorine water and iodine water, noting any color changes as the bromine, chlorine, and iodine are extracted from the water into the TCE.

Shake 1 ml of bromine water with 1 ml of TCE in a small test tube. Add 1 ml 0.1 *M* NaCl solution, stopper, and shake. Using another sample of Br_2 solution with TCE, repeat the experiment using 0.1 *M* NaI solution. In each case observe the color of the TCE phase before and after addition of the halide to determine whether an oxidation-reduction reaction has occurred. Repeat the tests on 1 ml samples of the three halide solutions using chlorine water and then iodine water in TCE. Since mixtures of Cl^- with Cl_2 and I^- with I_2 will not aid in deciding on relative oxidizing powers, you will not need to test them. Record your observations for each test.

III. Solubilities of Silver Halide Salts. Add 1 ml of 0.1 *M* solutions of the three sodium halides to separate test tubes. Add a few drops of 0.1 *M* $AgNO_3$ to each test tube and stir. Note the color of each precipitate. Let the precipitates settle, centrifuge if necessary, and pour off the liquid. To the precipitate add 6 *M* NH_3 dropwise with stirring, noting the solubility in each case. With any precipitates which do not dissolve after addition of about 2 ml of ammonia, pour off the 6 *M* NH_3 and test for solubility of the solid in 15 *M* NH_3. Record your results.

IV. Identification of Unknown Salt. On the basis of your observations, devise a scheme by which you can establish which alkaline earth cation and which halide ion is present in a solution containing a single alkaline earth halide. Use your procedure to identify the salt in your unknown solution.

Name ______________________ Section ______________

DATA AND OBSERVATIONS: Periodicity of Chemical Properties

I. Solubilities of Salts of the Alkaline Earths

	1 *M* H_2SO_4	1 *M* Na_2CO_3	0.25 *M* $(NH_4)_2C_2O_4$	1 *M* K_2CrO_4 1 *M* Acetic Acid
$Ba(NO_3)_2$				
$Ca(NO_3)_2$				
$Mg(NO_3)_2$				
$Sr(NO_3)_2$				

P = precipitate forms; S = no precipitate.

Note any distinguishing characteristics of ppt.

Consider the relative solubilities of the Group II A cations in the various precipitating reagents. On the basis of the trends you observed, list the four alkaline earths in the order in which they should appear in the periodic table. *Start with the one which forms the most soluble oxalate.*

__________ __________ __________ __________

Why did you arrange the elements as you did? Is the order consistent with the properties of the cations in all of the precipitating reagents?

II. Relative Oxidizing Powers of the Halogens

A. Color of the halogen in solution:

	Br_2	Cl_2	I_2
Water	________	________	________
TCE	________	________	________

Continued on following page

B. Reactions between halogens and halides:

	Br^-	Cl^-	I^-
Br_2	X		
Cl_2		X	
I_2			X

State initial and final colors of TCE layer. R = reaction occurs; NR = no reaction occurs.

III. Properties of Silver Halide Salts

	AgBr	AgCl	AgI
1. Color	______	______	______
2. Solubility in NH_3 solution	______	______	______

S = soluble in 6 *M* NH_3; SS = soluble in 15 *M* NH_3; IS = insoluble in NH_3.

On the basis of trends in oxidizing power and in solubility of the silver halide salts in NH_3 solutions, arrange the halogens in the order in which they should be listed in the periodic table. Start with the strongest oxidizing agent.

________ ________ ________

IV. Given a solution known to contain one Group II A cation and one Group VII A anion, devise a scheme, based on the properties of these ions as you observed them in this experiment, which would allow you to determine which cation and which anion are present.

Continued on following page

Use your scheme to analyze your unknown solution.
Observations:

Cation present ______________ Anion present ______________

Unknown No. ______________

ADVANCE STUDY ASSIGNMENT: Periodic Properties of Substances

1. Calcium sulfate is slightly soluble (2 g/liter) in water, whereas barium sulfate is essentially insoluble (2 mg/liter). Would you expect magnesium sulfate to be more soluble or less soluble than strontium sulfate? Why?

2. Substances A, B, and C can all behave as oxidizing agents. When a solution of substance A is mixed with a solution containing B^- ions, substance B is formed. When a solution of A is mixed with a solution containing C^- ions, no C is produced. Arrange A, B, and C in order of increasing strength as oxidizing agents.

3. Hydrogen peroxide, H_2O_2, is a good oxidizing agent in acid solution, as is elementary iodine, I_2. In aqueous solution, H_2O_2 is colorless, while I_2 is brown. When H_2O_2 is added to an acidic solution of KI, the solution turns brown. Which is the stronger oxidizing agent under these conditions, H_2O_2 or I_2? Why?

EXPERIMENT 12

The Geometrical Structure of Molecules: An Experiment Using Molecular Models

Many years ago it was observed that in many of its compounds the carbon atom formed four chemical linkages to other atoms. As early as 1870, graphic formulas of carbon compounds were drawn as shown:

```
     H          H  H
     |          |  |
  H—C—H         C=C
     |          |  |
     H          H  H
  methane     ethylene
```

Although such drawings as these would imply that the atom-atom linkages, indicated by valence strokes, lie in a plane, chemical evidence, particularly the existence of only one substance with the graphic formula

```
     Cl
     |
  H—C—Cl
     |
     H
```

requires that the linkages be directed toward the corners of a tetrahedron, at the center of which is the carbon atom.

The concept of a tetrahedral carbon atom was developed and used extensively by organic chemists during the latter part of the nineteenth century. If carbon atoms are considered to be represented by tetrahedra in the manner indicated, single carbon-carbon bonds arise when two such tetrahedra share a common corner, double bonds arise when the tetrahedra share an edge, and triple bonds arise when the tetrahedra share a face. Long before physical methods for confirmation were available, the model correctly predicted that ethylene, $H_2C{=}CH_2$, would be a planar molecule and that acetylene, $HC{\equiv}CH$, would be linear.

The physical significance of the chemical linkages between atoms, expressed by the lines or valence strokes in molecular structure diagrams, became evident soon after the discovery of the electron. In 1916 in a classic paper, G. N. Lewis suggested, on the basis of chemical evidence, that the single bonds in graphic formulas involve two electrons and that an atom tends to hold eight electrons in its outermost or valence shell.

Lewis' proposal that atoms generally have eight electrons in their outer shell proved to be extremely useful and has come to be known as the octet rule. It can be applied to many atoms, but is particularly important in the treatment of covalent compounds of atoms in the second row of the periodic table. For atoms such as carbon, oxygen, nitrogen, and fluorine, the eight valence electrons occur in pairs that occupy tetrahedral positions around the central atom core. Some of the electron pairs do not participate directly in chemical bonding and are called unshared or nonbonding pairs; however, the structures of compounds containing such unshared pairs reflect the tetrahedral arrangement of the four pairs of valence shell electrons. In the H_2O molecule, which obeys the octet rule, the four pairs of electrons around the central oxygen atom occupy essentially tetrahedral positions; there are two unshared nonbonding pairs and two bonding pairs which are shared by the O atom and the two H atoms. The H —O— H bond angle is nearly but not exactly tetrahedral since the properties of shared and unshared pairs of electrons are not exactly alike.

```
  :Ö:
  /  \
 H    H
```

For some molecules with a given molecular formula, it is possible to satisfy the octet rule with different atomic arrangements. A simple example would be

```
   H  H                  H     H
   |  |                  |     |
H—C—C—Ö—H     and     H—C—Ö—C—H
   |  |   ..             |  .. |
   H  H                  H     H
```

The two molecules are called isomers of each other, and the phenomenon is called isomerism. Although the molecular formulas of both substances are the same, C_2H_6O, their properties differ markedly because of their different atomic arrangements.

Isomerism is very common, particularly in organic chemistry, and when double bonds are present, isomerism can occur in very small molecules:

```
 H       H           :Cl:      H           :Cl:      H
  \     /               \     /               \     /
   C=C        and        C=C        and        C=C
  /     \               /     \               /     \
:Cl:    :Cl:           H      :Cl:          :Cl:     H
```

The first two isomers result from the fact that there is no rotation around a double bond, although such rotation can occur around single bonds. The third isomeric structure cannot be converted to either of the first two without breaking bonds.

With certain molecules, given a fixed atomic geometry, it is possible to satisfy the octet rule with more than one bonding arrangement. The classic example is benzene, whose molecular formula is C_6H_6:

```
        H                       H
        |                       |
  H     C     H           H     C     H
   \  //  \  /             \  /  \\  /
    C       C               C       C
    |       ||     and      ||      |
    C       C               C       C
   /  \\  /  \             /  \  //  \
  H     C     H           H     C     H
        |                       |
        H                       H
```

These two structures are called resonance structures, and molecules such as benzene, which have two or more resonance structures, are said to exhibit resonance. The actual bonding in such molecules is thought to be an average of the bonding present in the resonance structures. The stability of molecules exhibiting resonance is found to be higher than that anticipated for any single resonance structure.

Once the symmetry of a species has been determined, it is possible to predict its polarity, that is, whether the molecule will contain a region of positive charge and a region of negative charge, and so have a dipole moment. Covalent bonds between different kinds of atoms in molecules are typically polar; all heteronuclear diatomic molecules are polar. In some molecules the polarity from one bond may be cancelled by that arising from others, so that the overall molecular polarity may vanish. Carbon dioxide CO_2, which is linear, is a nonpolar molecule; methane CH_4, which is tetrahedral, is also nonpolar. On the other hand, the related molecules of lower symmetry, COS and CH_3Cl, do not have complete cancellation of bond polarities and are therefore polar.

In this experiment, assuming that all atoms present in the species studied obey the octet rule, you will assemble models of some simple molecules and ions. On the basis of the models you will be able to draw electron dot diagrams and predict the geometrical structure of each species, the existence of isomers, the polarity of the species, and whether resonance structures would be likely to occur.

EXPERIMENTAL PROCEDURE

In this experiment you may work in pairs during the first portion of the laboratory period.

The models you will use consist of drilled wooden balls, short sticks, and springs. The balls represent atomic nuclei surrounded by the inner electron shells. The sticks and springs represent electron pairs and fit in the holes in the wooden balls. The model (molecule or ion) consists of wooden balls (atoms) connected by sticks or springs (chemical bonds). Some sticks may be connected to only one atom (non-bonding pairs).

In this experiment we will deal with atoms that obey the octet rule; such atoms have four electron pairs around the central core and will be represented by black or blue balls with four tetrahedral holes in which there are four sticks or springs. The only exception will be hydrogen atoms, which share two electrons in covalent compounds, and which will be represented by yellow balls with a single hole in which there is a single stick.

In assembling a molecular model of the kind we are considering, it is possible, indeed desirable, to proceed in a systematic manner. We will illustrate the recommended procedure by developing a model for a molecule with the formula CH_2O.

1. Draw electron dot diagrams for each atom in the molecule, letting dots represent valence electrons and the element symbols represent the atomic cores.

For carbon atoms: electron configuration $1s^22s^22p^2$

$$\text{four valence electrons} \quad \cdot\dot{\underset{\cdot}{\mathrm{C}}}\cdot$$

For hydrogen atoms: electron configuration 1s

$$\text{one valence electron} \quad \mathrm{H}\cdot$$

For oxygen atoms: electron configuration $1s^22s^22p^4$

$$\text{six valence electrons} \quad \cdot\ddot{\underset{\cdot}{\mathrm{O}}}:$$

Add up the valence electrons for all the atoms in the molecule. In this case there are 12 (four from the C atom, two from the two H atoms, and six from the O atom). If the particle is an ion, add one electron for each negative charge or subtract one for each positive charge on the ion.

2. Select wooden balls and sticks to represent the atoms and electron pairs in the molecule. You might use a black ball for the carbon atom core, a blue ball for the oxygen atom core, and yellow balls to represent the hydrogen atoms. Since there are 12 valence electrons in the molecule and electrons occur in pairs, you will need six sticks to represent the six electron pairs. The sticks will serve both as bonds between atoms and as nonbonding electron pairs.

3. Connect the balls with some of the sticks. (Assemble a skeleton structure for the molecule, joining atoms by single bonds.) In some cases this can only be done in one way. Usually, however, there are various possibilities, some of which are more reasonable than others. In CH_2O the model can be assembled by connecting the two yellow balls (H atoms) to the black ball (C atom) with two of the available sticks, and then using a third stick to connect the black ball to the blue one (O atom).

4. The next step is to use the sticks that are left over in such a way as to fill all the remaining holes in the balls. (Distribute the electron pairs so as to give each atom eight electrons and so satisfy the octet rule.) In the model we have assembled, there is one unfilled hole in the black ball, three unfilled holes in the blue ball, and three available sticks. An obvious way to meet the required condition is to use two sticks to fill two of the holes in the blue ball, and then use two springs instead of two sticks to connect the blue and black balls. The model as completed is shown in Figure 12.1.

5. Interpret the model in terms of the atoms and bonds represented. The sticks and spatial arrangement of the balls will closely correspond to the electronic and atomic arrangement in the molecule. Given our model, we would describe the CH_2O molecule as being planar with single bonds between carbon and hydrogen atoms and a double bond between the C and O atoms. The H—C—H angle is approximately tetrahedral. There are two nonbonding electron pairs on the O atom. Since all bonds are polar and the molecular symmetry does not cancel the polarity in CH_2O, the molecule is polar. The bonding sketch showing electronic structure is given below:

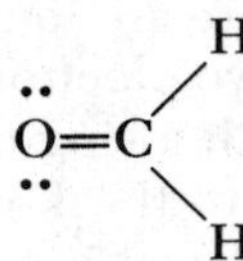

The drawing is really an electron dot structure, with each bond representing two electrons.

(The compound having molecules with the formula CH_2O is well-known and is called formaldehyde. The bonding and structure in CH_2O are as given by the model.)

6. Investigate the possibility of the existence of isomers or resonance structures in the model. It turns out that in the case of CH_2O one can easily construct an isomeric form which obeys the octet rule, in which the central atom is oxygen rather than carbon. It is found that this isomeric form of CH_2O does not exist in nature. Indeed, as a general rule, carbon atoms are almost never found at the end of a chain of atoms; put another way, nonbonding electron pairs on carbon atoms are very rare. Another useful rule of a similar nature is that if there are several oxygen atoms in a simple species containing one other atom, each oxygen atom is attached to that other atom. In the SO_4^{2-} ion, for example, the oxygen atoms are all chemically bound to the sulfur atom. Only rarely do oxygen atoms bond to one another, forming compounds known as peroxides.

Resonance structures are reasonably common. For resonance to occur, however, the atomic arrangement must remain fixed for two or more possible electronic structures. For CH_2O there are no resonance structures.

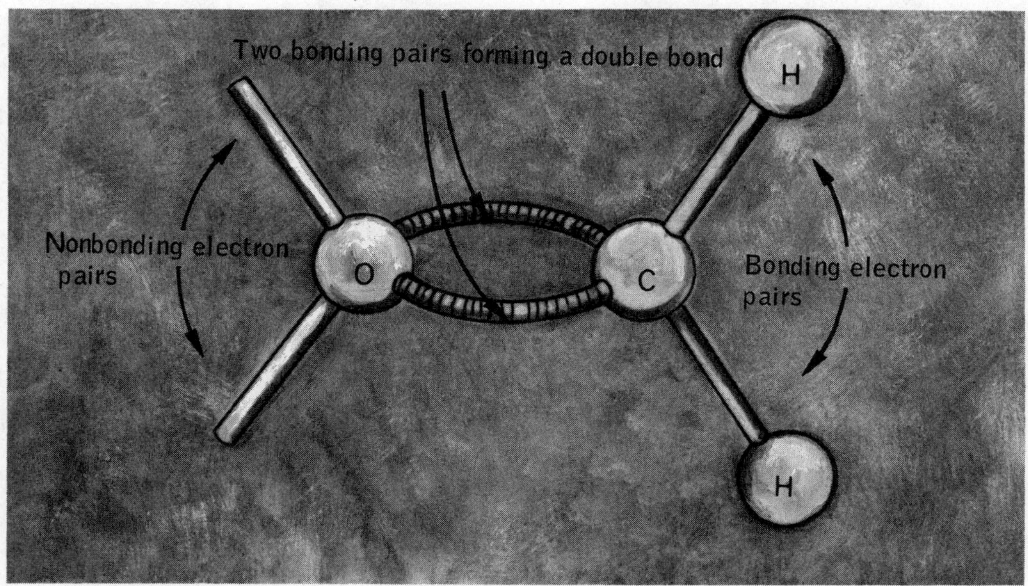

Figure 12.1

A. Using the procedure we have outlined, construct and report on models of the molecules and ions listed here and/or other species assigned by your instructor.

CH_4	H_3O^+	N_2	C_2H_2
CH_2Cl_2	HF	P_4	SO_2
CH_4O	NH_3	C_2H_4	SO_4^{2-}
H_2O	H_2O_2	$C_2H_2Br_2$	CO_2

B. Assuming that stability requires that each atom obey the octet rule, predict the stability of the following species:

PCl_3 CH_3 OH^- CO

C. When you have completed parts A and B, see your laboratory instructor, who will check your results and assign you a set of unknown species. Working now by yourself, assemble models for each species as in the previous section, and report on the geometry and bonding in each of the unknown species on the basis of the model you construct. Also consider and report on the polarity and the likelihood of existence of isomers and resonance structures for each species.

Name ____________________ Section ____________

REPORT: Geometrical Structures of Molecules Using Molecular Models

A. Species	Bonding Sketch	Geometry	Isomers or Resonance	Polarity	Species	Bonding Sketch	Geometry	Isomers or Resonance	Polarity
CH_4					HF				
CH_2Cl_2					NH_3				
CH_4O					H_2O_2				
H_2O					N_2				
H_3O^+					P_4				

Continued on following page

Continued

Species	Bonding Sketch	Geometry	Isomers or Resonance	Polarity	Species	Bonding Sketch	Geometry	Isomers or Resonance	Polarity
C_2H_4					SO_2				
$C_2H_2Br_2$					SO_4^{2-}				
C_2H_2					CO_2				

B. Stability predicted for PCl_3 __________ CH_3 __________ OH^- __________ CO __________

C. Unknowns

______ ______

______ ______

______ ______

EXPERIMENT 13

Classification of Chemical Substances

Depending on the kind of bonding present in a chemical substance, the substance may be called ionic, molecular, or metallic.

In a solid ionic compound there are ions; the large electrostatic forces between the positively and negatively charged ions are responsible for the bonding which holds these particles together.

In a molecular substance the bonding is caused by the sharing of electrons by atoms. When the stable aggregates resulting from covalent bonding contain relatively small numbers of atoms, they are called molecules. If the aggregates are very large and include essentially all the atoms in a macroscopic particle, the substance is called macromolecular.

Metals are characterized by a kind of bonding in which the electrons are much freer to move than in other kinds of substances. The metallic bond is stable but is probably less localized than other bonds.

The terms ionic, molecular, macromolecular, and metallic are somewhat arbitrary, and some substances have properties that would place them in a borderline category, somewhere intermediate between one group and another. It is useful, however, to consider some of the general characteristics of typical ionic, molecular, macromolecular, and metallic substances, since many very common substances can be readily assigned to one category or another.

IONIC SUBSTANCES

Ionic substances are all solids at room temperature. They are typically crystalline, but may exist as fine powders as well as clearly defined crystals. While many ionic substances are stable up to their melting points, some decompose on heating. It is very common for an ionic crystal to release loosely bound water of hydration at temperatures below 200°C. Anhydrous (dehydrated) ionic compounds have high melting points, usually above 300°C but below 1000°C. They are not readily volatilized and boil at only very high temperatures (Table 13.1).

When molten, ionic compounds conduct an electric current. In the solid state they do not conduct electricity. The conductivity in the molten liquid is attributed to the freedom of motion of the ions, which arises when the crystal lattice is no longer present.

Ionic substances are frequently but not always appreciably soluble in water. The solutions produced conduct the electric current rather well. The conductivity of a solution of a slightly soluble ionic substance is often several times that of the solvent water. Ionic substances are usually not nearly so soluble in other liquids as they are in water. For a liquid to be a good solvent for ionic compounds it must be highly polar, containing molecules with well-defined positive and negative regions with which the ions can interact.

TABLE 13.1 PHYSICAL PROPERTIES OF SOME REPRESENTATIVE CHEMICAL SUBSTANCES

Substance	M.P., °C	B.P., °C	Solubility *Water*	Solubility *Toluene*	Electrical Conductance	Classification
NaCl	801	1413	Sol	Insol	High in melt and in soln	Ionic
MgO	2800	–	Sl sol	Insol	Low in sat'd soln	Ionic
$CoCl_2$	Sublimes	1049	Sol	Insol	High in soln	Ionic
$CoCl_2 \cdot 6H_2O$	86	Dec	Sol	Insol	High in soln	Ionic hydrate, $-H_2O$ at 110°C
$C_{10}H_8$	70	255	Insol	Sol	Zero in melt	Molecular
C_6H_5COOH	122	249	Sl sol	Sol	Low in sat'd soln	Molecular-ionic
$FeCl_3$	282	315	Sol	Insol	High in soln	Molecular-ionic
SnI_4	144	341	Dec	Sol	Zero in melt	Molecular
SiO_2	1600	2590	Insol	Insol	Zero in solid	Macromolecular
Fe	1535	3000	Insol	Insol	High in solid	Metallic

Key: Sol = at least 0.1 mole/lit; Sl sol = appreciable solubility but <0.1 mole/lit; Insol = essentially insoluble; Dec = decomposes.

MOLECULAR SUBSTANCES

All gases and essentially all liquids at room temperature are molecular in nature. If the molecular weight of a substance is over about a hundred, it may be a solid at that temperature. The melting points of molecular substances are usually below 300°C; these substances are relatively volatile, but a good many will decompose before they boil. Most molecular substances do not conduct the electric current either when solid or when molten.

Organic compounds, which contain primarily carbon and hydrogen, often in combination with other nonmetals, are essentially molecular in nature. Since there are a great many organic substances, it is true that most substances are molecular. If an organic compound decomposes on heating, the residue is frequently a black carbonaceous material. Reasonably large numbers of inorganic substances are also molecular; those which are solids at room temperature include some of the binary compounds of elements in Groups IV A, V A, VI A, and VII A.

Molecular substances are frequently soluble in at least a few organic solvents, with the solubility being enhanced if the substance and the solvent are similar in molecular structure.

Some molecular compounds are markedly polar, which tends to increase their solubility in water and other polar solvents. Such substances may ionize appreciably in water, or even in the melt, so that they become conductors of electricity. Often the conductivity is considerably lower than that of an ionic material. Most polar molecular compounds in this category are organic, but a few, including some of the salts of the transition metals, are inorganic.

MACROMOLECULAR SUBSTANCES

Macromolecular substances are all solids at room temperature. They have very high melting points, usually above 1000°C, and low volatility. They are typically very resistant to thermal decomposition. They do not conduct electric current and are often good insulators. They are not soluble in water or any organic solvents. They are frequently chemically inert and may be used as abrasives or refractories.

METALLIC SUBSTANCES

The properties of metals appear to derive mainly from the freedom of movement of their bonding electrons. Metals are good electrical conductors in the solid form, and have characteristic luster and malleability. Most metals are solid at room temperature and have melting points that range from below 0°C to over 2000°C. They are not soluble in water or organic solvents. Some metals are prepared as black powders, which may not appear to be electrical conductors; if such powders are heated, the particles will coalesce to give good electrical conductivity.

EXPERIMENTAL PROCEDURE { *WEAR YOUR SAFETY GLASSES WHILE PERFORMING THIS EXPERIMENT.*

In this experiment you will investigate the properties of several substances with the purpose of determining whether they are ionic, molecular, macromolecular, or metallic. In some cases the classification will be very straightforward. In others you may find that the substance behaves in a way that would not clearly place it in a given category but in some intermediate group.

You may use any tests you wish to on the substances, but use due caution when using materials with which you are not familiar. It is suggested that approximate melting point, solubility in water or organic solvents, electrical conductivity of the solid, liquid, or solution, and tendency to decompose may readily be determined and might aid in classification.

Approximate melting points of substances can be determined rather easily. Substances with low melting points, less than 100°C, for example, will melt readily when warmed gently in a test tube. A test tube heated to about 300°C will impart a yellow-orange color to the Bunsen flame. This color becomes more pronounced between 300° and 550°C, at which temperature the Pyrex tube will begin to soften. When heating samples you should *loosely* stopper the test tube with a cork. Do not breathe any vapors that are given off. Look for water condensing on the cooler portions of the tube and for indications that sublimation is occurring. For the highest temperature studies possible in the lab, heat the sample in a nickel crucible with a strong Bunsen flame; a noticeable red color will appear in the crucible at about 600°C. If this temperature cannot be achieved with a Bunsen burner, use a Meker burner or a gas-air torch. Do not heat samples to 600°C unless their solubility and conductivity properties have been studied at lower temperatures with indecisive results.

Electrical conductivities of your solutions or melts will be measured for you by your laboratory supervisor, who has a portable test meter for that purpose. Distinguish between completely nonconducting, slightly conducting, and highly conducting liquids.

The substances to be studied in the first part of the experiment are on the laboratory tables along with two organic solvents, one polar and one nonpolar. Carry out enough tests on each substance to establish its classification as best you can. Report your observations on each substance, how you would classify it, and your reason for the classification.

When you have completed your tests, report to your laboratory supervisor, who will check your results and issue you two unknowns for characterization.

Name ____________________ Section ______________

OBSERVATIONS AND CONCLUSIONS: Classification of Chemical Substances

Substance No.	Approximate Melting Point, °C	Solubility			Conductivity			Classification and Reason
	(< 100, 100–300, 300–600, > 600)	H_2O	Nonpolar Organic	Polar Organic	Solid	Melt	Solution in H_2O	
I								
II								
III								
IV								
V								
VI								
Unknown no.								
________								
________								

Name ______________________ Section ______________

ADVANCE STUDY ASSIGNMENT: Classification of Substances

1. List the properties of a substance which would definitely establish that the material is molecular.

2. If we classify substances as ionic, molecular, macromolecular, or metallic, in which if any categories are all the members

(a) soluble in water?

(b) electrical conductors in the melt?

(c) insoluble in all common solvents?

(d) solids at room temperature?

3. A given substance is a white solid at 25°C. It melts at 350°C without decomposing and the melt conducts an electric current. What would be the classification of the substance, based on this information?

4. A white solid melts at 1000°C. The melt does not conduct electricity. Classify the substance as best you can from these properties.

SECTION 6

Organic Chemistry

EXPERIMENT 14

Preparation of Aspirin

One of the simpler organic reactions that one can carry out is the formation of an ester from an acid and an alcohol:

$$\underset{\text{an acid}}{R{-}\overset{\overset{\large O}{\|}}{C}{-}OH} + \underset{\text{an alcohol}}{HO{-}R'} \rightarrow \underset{\text{an ester}}{R{-}\overset{\overset{\large O}{\|}}{C}{-}O{-}R'} + H_2O \qquad (1)$$

In the equation, R and R′ are H atoms or organic fragments like CH_3, C_2H_5, or more complex aromatic groups. There are many esters, since there are many organic acids and alcohols, but they all can be formed, in principle at least, by Reaction 1. The driving force for the reaction is in general not very great, so that one ends up with an equilibrium mixture of ester, water, acid, and alcohol.

There are some esters which are solids because of their high molecular weight or other properties. Most of these esters are not soluble in water, so they can be separated from the mixture by crystallization. This experiment deals with an ester of this sort, the substance commonly called aspirin. Aspirin is the active component in headache pills and is one of the most effective, relatively nontoxic, pain killers.

Aspirin can be made by the reaction of the —OH group in the salicylic acid molecule with the carboxyl (—COOH) group in acetic acid:

$$\underset{\text{acetic acid}}{CH_3\overset{\overset{\large O}{\|}}{C}{-}OH} + \underset{\text{salicylic acid}}{HO{-}C_6H_4{-}C(=O){-}OH} \rightleftharpoons \underset{\text{aspirin}}{CH_3{-}\overset{\overset{\large O}{\|}}{C}{-}O{-}C_6H_4{-}C(=O){-}OH} + H_2O \qquad (2)$$

A better preparative method, which we will use in this experiment, employs acetic anhydride in the reaction instead of acetic acid. The anhydride can be considered to be the product of a reaction in which two acetic acid molecules combine, with the elimination of a molecule of water. The anhydride will react with the water produced in the esterification reaction and will tend to drive the reaction to the right. A catalyst, normally sulfuric or phosphoric acid, is also used to speed up the reaction.

$$(CH_3-CO)_2O + HO-C_6H_4-C(=O)OH \xrightarrow{H_3PO_4} CH_3-C(=O)-O-C_6H_4-C(=O)OH + CH_3-C(=O)-OH \qquad (3)$$

acetic anhydride, salicylic acid, aspirin, acetic acid

The aspirin you will prepare in this experiment is relatively impure and should certainly not be taken internally, even if the experiment gives you a bad headache.

EXPERIMENTAL PROCEDURE {WEAR YOUR SAFETY GLASSES WHILE PERFORMING THIS EXPERIMENT.

Weigh a 50 ml Erlenmeyer flask on a triple beam or top loading balance and add 2.0 g of salicylic acid. Measure out 5.0 ml of acetic anhydride in your graduated cylinder, and pour it into the flask in such a way as to wash any crystals of salicylic acid on the walls down to the bottom. Add 5 drops of 85 per cent phosphoric acid to serve as a catalyst. *Both acetic anhydride and phosphoric acid are reactive chemicals which can give you a bad chemical burn, so use due caution in handling them.* If you get any of either on your hands or clothes, wash thoroughly with soap and water.

Clamp the flask in place in a beaker of water supported on a wire gauze on a ring stand. Heat the water with a Bunsen burner to about 75°C, stirring the liquid in the flask occasionally with a stirring rod. Maintain this temperature for about 15 minutes, by which time the reaction should be complete. *Cautiously,* add 2 ml of water to the flask to decompose any excess acetic anhydride. There will be some hot acetic acid vapor evolved as a result of the decomposition.

When the liquid has stopped giving off vapors, remove the flask from the water bath and add 20 ml of water. Let the flask cool for a few minutes in air, during which time crystals of aspirin should begin to form. Put the flask in an ice bath to hasten crystallization and increase the yield of product. If crystals are slow to appear, it may be helpful to scratch the inside of the flask with a stirring rod.

Collect the aspirin by filtering the cold liquid through a Buchner funnel using suction. Turn off the suction and pour about 5 ml of ice-cold distilled water over the crystals; after about 15 seconds turn on the suction to remove the wash liquid along with most of the impurities. Repeat the washing process with another 5 ml sample of ice-cold water. Draw air through the funnel for a few minutes to help dry the crystals and then transfer them to a piece of dry filter paper.

While the aspirin is drying, test its solubility properties by taking samples of the solid the size of a pea on your spatula and putting them in separate 1 ml samples of each of the following solvents and stirring:

1. Toluene, $CH_3C_6H_5$, nonpolar aromatic
2. Hexane, C_6H_{14}, nonpolar aliphatic
3. Ethyl acetate, $C_2H_5OCOCH_3$, aliphatic ester
4. Ethyl alcohol, C_2H_5OH, polar aliphatic, hydrogen bonding
5. Acetone, CH_3COCH_3, polar aliphatic, nonhydrogen bonding

When the aspirin is dry, weigh the crystals by putting them into a small weighed beaker on the balance and reweighing to 0.1 g. Add 0.5 g to the weight of aspirin obtained to compensate for the amount used in the solubility tests.

Determine the melting point of the aspirin, which is one of the best criteria for its purity. This can be readily done in a small melting point tube, made from 5 mm tubing, as directed by your instructor. Add the crystals to the tube to a depth of about 1/4 inch, shaking the solid down by tapping the tube on the bench top. Place the tube as shown in Figure 14.1; heat the oil bath *slowly*, especially after the temperature gets over 100°C. As the melting point is approached, the crystals will begin to soften. Report the melting point as the temperature at which the last crystals disappear.

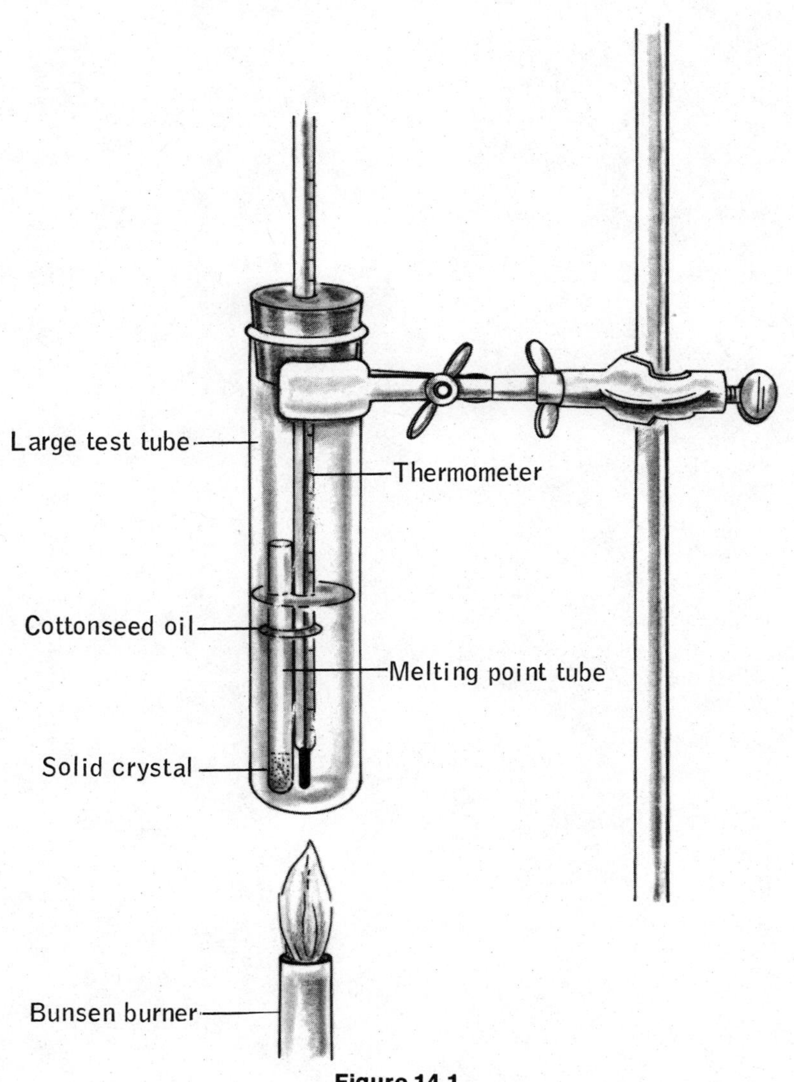

Figure 14.1

Name ______________________ Section ______________

DATA AND RESULTS: Preparation of Aspirin

Weight of salicylic acid used ____________ g

Volume of acetic anhydride used ____________ ml

Weight of acetic anhydride used (density = 1.08 g/ml) ____________ g

Weight of aspirin obtained ____________ g

Theoretical yield of aspirin ____________ g

Percentage yield of aspirin ____________ %

Melting point of aspirin ____________ °C

Solubility properties of aspirin

Water ____________ Ethyl acetate ____________

Toluene ____________ Ethyl alcohol ____________

Hexane ____________ Acetone ____________

S = soluble; I = insoluble; SS = slightly soluble

Comment on the likely ease in finding a good solvent for an organic solid with the general structural complexity of aspirin.

ADVANCE STUDY ASSIGNMENT: Preparation of Aspirin

1. Calculate the theoretical yield of aspirin to be obtained in this experiment, starting with 2.0 g of salicylic acid and 5.0 ml of acetic anhydride (density = 1.08 g/ml).

______________ g

2. If 2.2 g of aspirin were obtained in this experiment, what would be the percentage yield?

______________ %

3. The name acetic anhydride implies that that compound will react with water to form acetic acid. Write the equation for the reaction.

4. Identify R and R′ in Equation 1 when the ester, aspirin, is made from salicylic acid and acetic acid.

EXPERIMENT 15

Preparation of a Synthetic Resin

In this experiment we will prepare and examine the properties of one of the most common polymers, polystyrene, made from styrene, $C_6H_5—CH{=}CH_2$. Styrene is relatively easy to polymerize; the plastic made from it is typically quite hard and transparent. In pure polystyrene, the chain is unbranched:

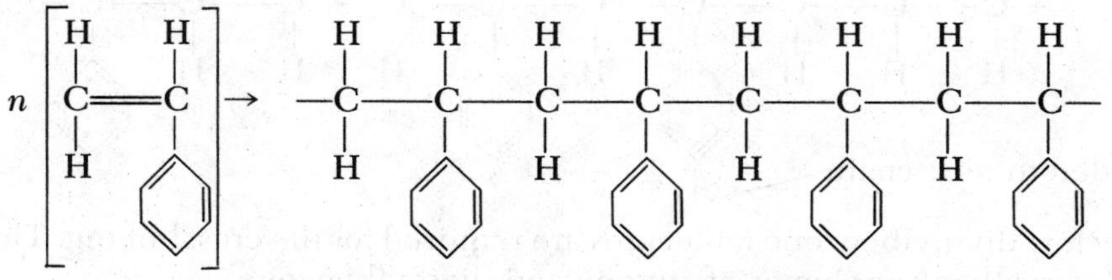

styrene   section of a polystyrene molecule

Polymers containing unbranched chains are thermoplastic, which means that they can be melted and then cast or extruded into various shapes. They also can usually be dissolved in some organic solvents, forming viscous liquids. If a polymer is cross-linked so that its chains are bonded together at regular or random positions, it will usually neither melt nor dissolve readily; such a material is called thermosetting and is usually polymerized in a mold in the shape of the article desired.

Styrene will polymerize to a crystalline solid if you simply heat it. The polymerization reaction itself evolves heat, however, and once the reaction gets started it tends to increase in rate and can get out of control; the simplest commercial process polymerizes styrene this way, and one of the important problems is to provide adequate cooling as the reaction proceeds.

We will polymerize styrene under somewhat different conditions, using an emulsion polymerization, in which the styrene is dispersed into droplets in water. In this process, temperature control is easy, and the polymer is produced in the form of easy-to-handle beads. By carrying out the reaction in the presence of divinylbenzene, which can react at two double-bonded positions, we will make a cross-linked polymer very similar in structure to that of an ion-exchange resin. Divinylbenzene is much like styrene except that there are two ethylene groups rather than one attached to each benzene ring. The compound has three isomers:

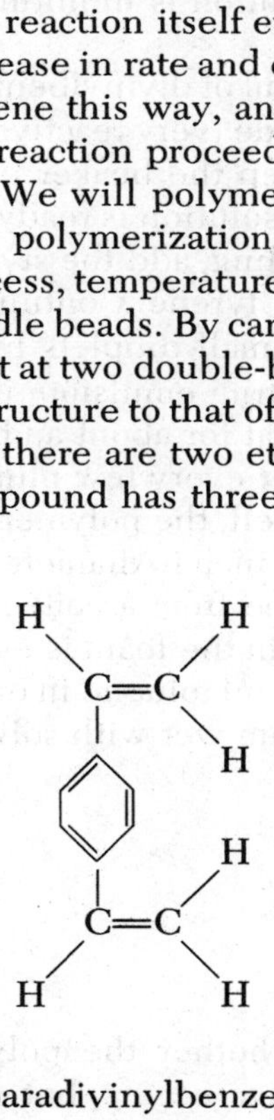

paradivinylbenzene 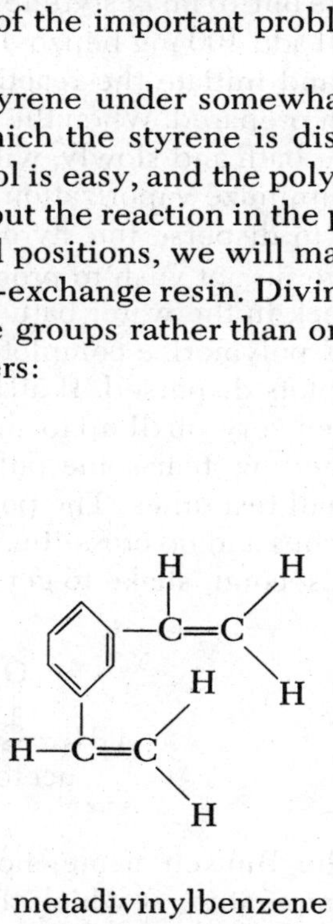   metadivinylbenzene 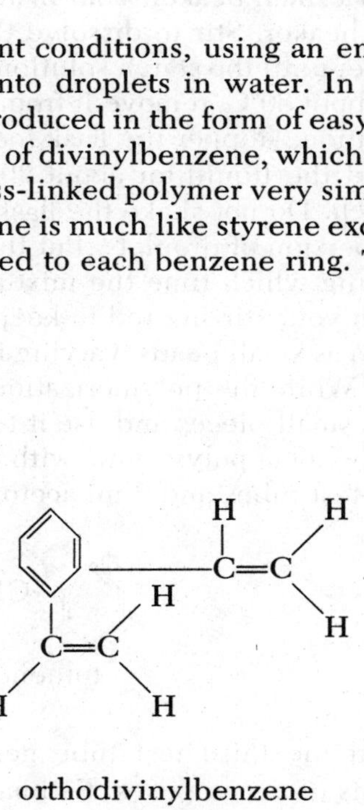   orthodivinylbenzene

The commercially available divinylbenzene which we use contains mainly the *para* and *meta* isomers, in about equal amounts.

The resin produced will have a structure similar to that indicated below:

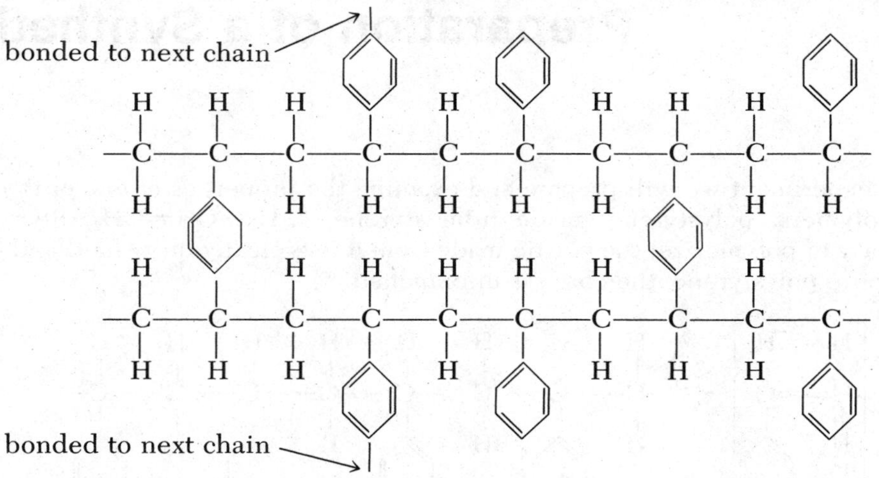

bonded to next chain

bonded to next chain

Relatively few divinylbenzene molecules are required for the crosslinking. The material produced is really a copolymer of styrene and divinylbenzene.

After preparing the polymer, we will compare its melting point and solubility properties with those of linear polystyrene.

EXPERIMENTAL PROCEDURE

Put 100 ml water in a 250 ml Erlenmeyer flask and heat the flask in a water bath set up as shown in Figure 15.1. When the water in the flask is at about 60°C, slowly add 1.0 g of starch, with stirring; continue stirring and heating until the solution is uniform and the starch completely dispersed.

While the water is heating, measure out 10 ml of styrene and 1 ml of divinylbenzene into a small beaker. Your instructor will add 100 mg benzoyl peroxide (very reactive!) to the beaker. Stir to dissolve the solid and initiate the reaction; keep the beaker in ice water until the starch solution has been prepared. When the starch solution is ready and at about 80°C, remove it from the water bath and slowly, with swirling, add the styrene solution; stopper the flask *loosely* to minimize vaporization of the styrene. Continue to swirl the liquid for about 20 seconds to disperse the styrene as small droplets in the starch. Do not shake the flask, since we do not wish to produce a true emulsion, just a dispersion of droplets. Put the flask back in the water bath and heat for about an hour, during which time the mixture should polymerize completely. Stir every few minutes with your stirring rod to keep the droplets dispersed. If all goes well, the polymer will form as small beads, varying in size from very small up to about 1/16 inch in diameter.

While the polymerization is proceeding, tear some polystyrene from a coffee cup into small pieces and use it to fill 3 small test tubes. The polymer in the foam is essentially linear polystyrene with few branches and no cross-links. Put 2 ml toluene in one of the test tubes and 2 ml acetone in the second; shake to get the foam wet with solvent.

C_6H_5—CH_3
toluene

CH_3—C(=O)—CH_3
acetone

Heat the third test tube gently in the Bunsen flame, noting whether the polymer melts or decomposes. Estimate the temperature at which the change occurs, but don't try to measure it. Poke the material with your stirring rod to aid in establishing its viscosity. Shake the tubes containing solvent and note whether the polymer has dissolved; if it hasn't, put the tubes in the boiling water in the bath to speed up the solution process. Do not boil the solvent, however. Note the properties of the final mixture, particularly viscosity and clarity of solution.

If you are able to obtain a solution with either solvent, pour a drop of the solution on to some water in a 600 ml beaker. Blow gently on the surface to evaporate the solvent completely. Pick up the film with a stirring rod and note its thickness and strength.

When the polymerization reaction is finished, remove the flask from the water bath and pour the slurry into a 600 ml beaker half full of distilled water. Stir and then let the beads settle. Decant the liquid and wash twice more to remove any residual starch. Pour the beads out on a paper towel and, when they are dry, weigh them.

Put a few of the beads in small test tubes and test them as before for solubility in toluene and acetone. Try to melt the beads; compare their behavior on heating with that of the polystyrene foam.

CAUTION: In this experiment we use several volatile organic liquids. Avoid breathing their vapors. If convenient, work in a hood or open the windows in the lab. Keep the polymerizing mixture loosely stoppered except when stirring it.

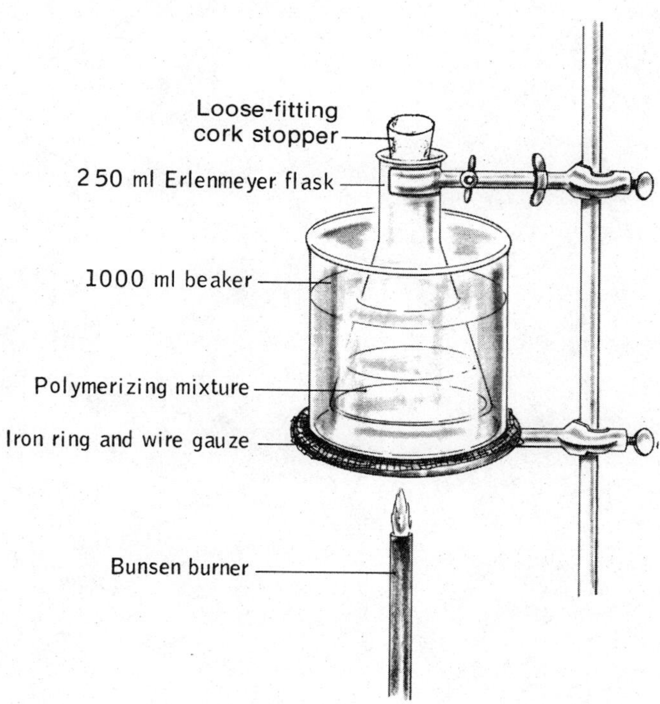

Figure 15.1

Name ____________________ Section ______________

DATA AND OBSERVATIONS: Preparation of a Synthetic Resin

Weight of styrene (density = 0.90 g/ml) ____________ g

Weight of divinylbenzene (density = 0.90 g/ml) ____________ g

Weight of resin ____________ g

Theoretical yield ____________ g

Percentage yield ____________ %

Properties of polystyrene and prepared resin

	Polystyrene (foam cup)	Prepared resin
Behavior on heating	____________	____________
	____________	____________
Solubility in toluene	____________	____________
Solubility in acetone	____________	____________

How do you explain the difference in solubility of polystyrene in the two solvents?

Comment on the effects of cross-linking on the properties of polystyrene.

 Name ______________________ Section ______________

ADVANCE STUDY ASSIGNMENT: Preparation of a Synthetic Resin

1. Polyvinyl chloride is made by addition polymerization of vinyl chloride, $CHCl{=}CH_2$. Sketch a section of the polyvinyl chloride molecule.

2. How much polyvinyl chloride could theoretically be made from 100 g of vinyl chloride?

______________ g

3. What per cent by weight of polyvinyl chloride is chlorine?

______________ %

4. Polystyrene foam such as that used in coffee cups is made by a procedure very analogous to that used in this experiment. Can you suggest how the foamable polymer might be made and how it would be converted to the form of a foam coffee cup?

SECTION 7

Properties of Liquids and Solutions

EXPERIMENT 16

Vapor Pressure and Heat of Vaporization of Liquids

The vapor pressure of a pure liquid is the total pressure at equilibrium in a container in which only the liquid and its vapor are present. In a container in which the liquid and another gas are both present, the vapor pressure of the liquid is equal to the partial pressure of its vapor in the container. In this experiment you will measure the vapor pressure of a liquid by determining the increase that occurs in the pressure in a closed container filled with air when the liquid is injected into it.

The vapor pressure of a liquid rises rapidly as the temperature is increased and reaches one atmosphere at the normal boiling point of the liquid. Thermodynamic arguments show that the vapor pressure of a liquid depends on temperature according to the equation:

$$\log_{10} VP = -\frac{\Delta H_{vap}}{2.3RT} + C \qquad (1)$$

where VP is the vapor pressure, ΔH_{vap} is the amount of heat in calories required to vaporize one mole of the liquid against a constant pressure, R is the gas constant, 1.99 cal/mole°K, in the units convenient to this expression, and T is the absolute temperature. You will note that this equation is of the form

$$Y = BX + C \qquad (2)$$

where $Y = \log_{10} VP$, $X = 1/T$ and $B = -\Delta H_{vap}/2.3R$. Consequently, if we measure the vapor pressure of a liquid at various temperatures and plot $\log_{10} VP$ vs. $1/T$, we should obtain a straight line. From the slope B of this line, we can calculate the heat of vaporization of the liquid, since $\Delta H_{vap} = -2.3RB$.

In the laboratory you will measure the vapor pressure of an unknown liquid at approximately 0°C, 20°C, and 40°C, as well as its boiling point at atmospheric pressure. Given the three vapor pressures, you will be able to calculate the heat of vaporization of the liquid by making a graph of $\log_{10} VP$ vs. $1/T$. The graph will then be used to predict the boiling point of the liquid, and the value obtained will be compared with that you found experimentally.

EXPERIMENTAL PROCEDURE

From the stockroom obtain a suction flask, a rubber stopper fitted with a small dropper, and a short length of rubber tubing. Also obtain a sample of an unknown liquid.

1. Assemble the apparatus, using the mercury manometer at your lab bench, as indicated in Figure 16.1. The flask should be dry on the inside. If it is not, rinse it with a few ml of acetone (*flammable*) and blow compressed air into it for a few moments until it is dry. Reassemble the apparatus. Pour some tap water into a beaker and bring it to about 20°C by adding some cold or warm water. Pour this water into the large beaker so that the level of water reaches as far as possible up the neck of the flask. Wait several minutes to ensure that the flask and air inside it are at the temperature of the water. Then remove the stopper from the flask. Pour a small amount of the unknown liquid into a small beaker, and draw about 2 ml of the liquid up into the dropper. Blot any excess liquid from the end of the dropper with a paper towel. Press the stopper *firmly* into the flask and connect the hose to the manometer. The mercury levels in the manometer should remain essentially equal.

Immediately squeeze the liquid from the dropper into the flask, where it will vaporize, diffuse, and exert its vapor pressure. This vapor pressure will be equal to the increase in gas pressure at equilibrium in the container. If you do not observe any appreciable ($\gtrsim$ 10 mm Hg) pressure increase within a minute or two after injecting the liquid, you probably have a leak in your apparatus and should consult your instructor. When the pressure in the flask becomes steady, in about 10 minutes, read and record the heights of the mercury levels in the manometer to ±1 mm. The difference in height is equal to the vapor pressure of the liquid in mm Hg at the temperature of the water bath. Record that temperature to ±0.2°C.

In this experiment it is essential that (1) the stopper is pressed firmly into the flask, so that the flask plus tubing plus manometer constitute a gas-tight system; (2) no liquid falls into the flask until the manometer is connected; (3) the operations of stoppering the flask, connecting the hose to the manometer, and squeezing the liquid into the flask are conducted promptly; (4) you take care when connecting the hose to the manometer, since mercury has a poisonous vapor and is not easily cleaned up when spilled.

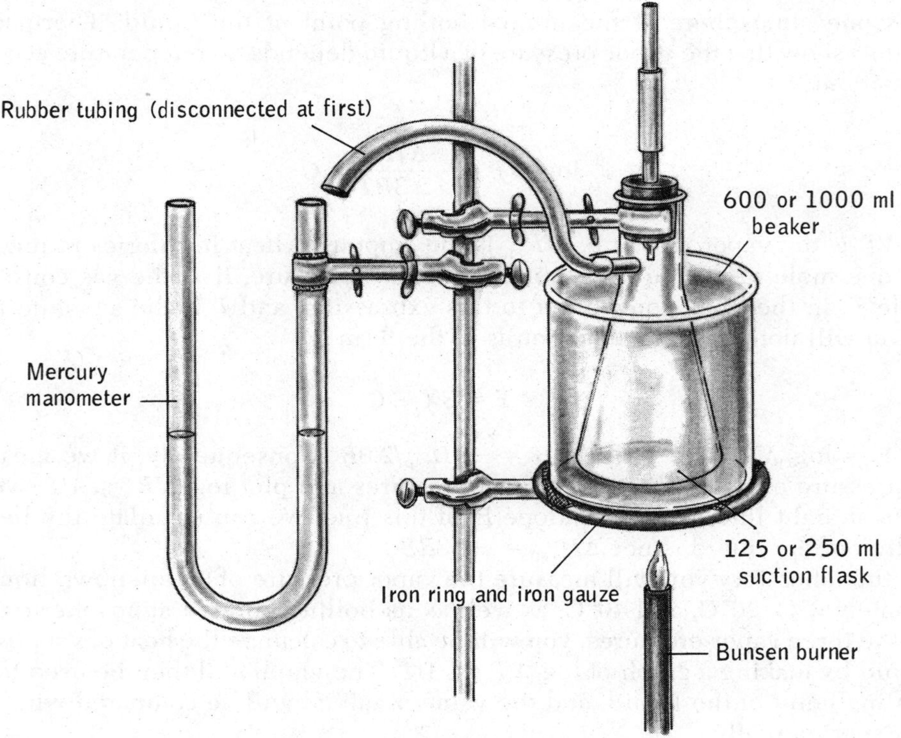

Figure 16.1

Remove the flask from the system. Dry it with compressed air, and dry the dropper by squeezing it several times in air.

2. Starting again at 1, carry out the same experiment at about 0°C. Use an ice-water bath for cooling the flask. Measure the latter temperature, rather than assuming it to be 0°C.

3. Repeat the experiment once again, this time holding the water bath at 40°C by judicious heating with a bunsen burner. Between each run, the flask and dropper must be thoroughly dried, and the precautions noted carefully observed.

4. In the last part of the experiment you will measure the boiling point of the liquid at the barometric pressure in the laboratory. This is done by pouring the remaining sample of unknown into a large test tube. Determine the boiling point of the liquid following the procedure which is indicated in Figure 16.2. The thermometer bulb should be just above the liquid surface. Heat the water bath until the liquid in the tube boils gently, with its vapor condensing *at least 2 inches below* the top of the test tube. Boiling chips may help in keeping the liquid boiling smoothly. The steady temperature obtained under these conditions is the boiling point of the liquid. The liquids used may be flammable, so *do not* heat the water bath so strongly that condensation of the vapors from the liquid occurs only at the top of the test tube.

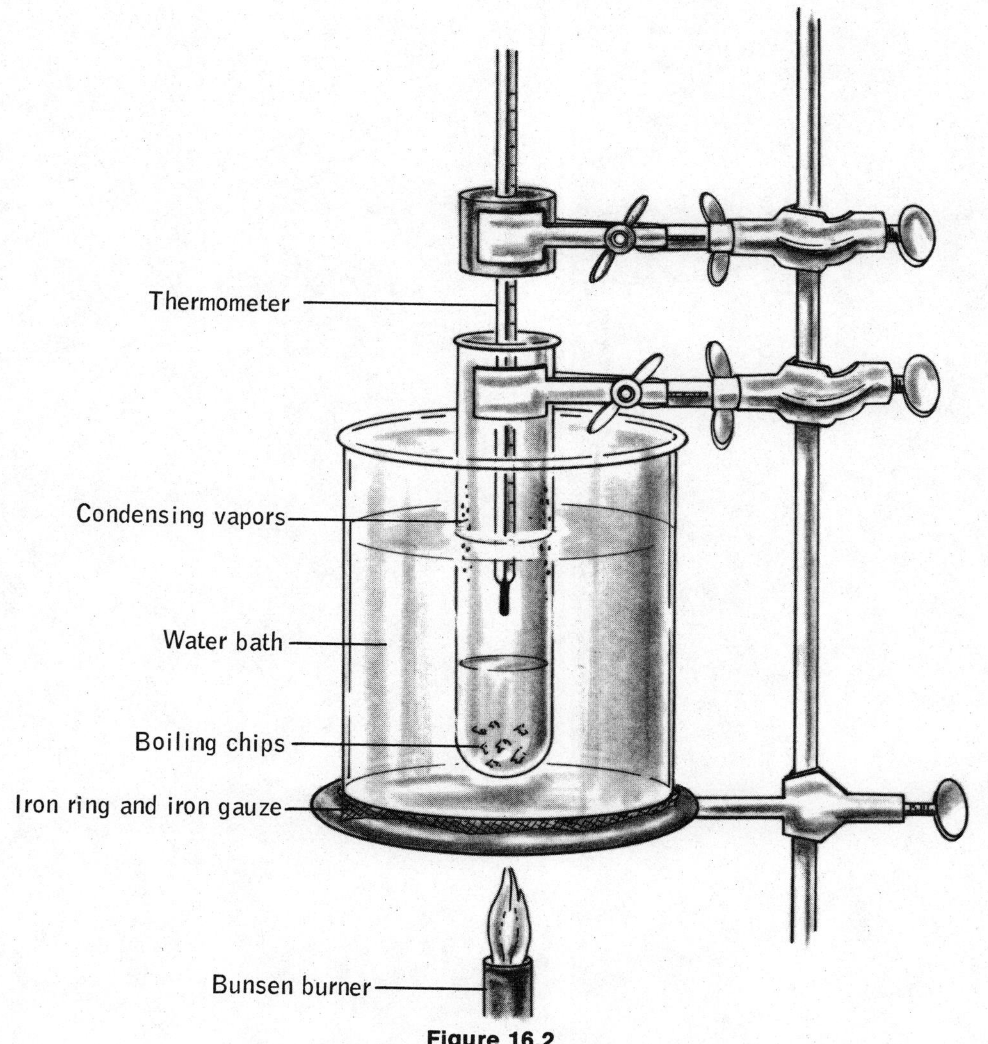

Figure 16.2

Name ______________________ Section ______________

DATA AND CALCULATIONS: Vapor Pressure and Heat of Vaporization of Liquids

	Temperature, t, in °C	Heights of manometer mercury levels in mm		Vapor pressure in mm Hg
1.	________	________	________	________
2.	________	________	________	________
3.	________	________	________	________

Boiling point ____________ °C

Barometric pressure ____________ mm Hg

Using the relation (1) between vapor pressure and temperature, we will calculate the molar heat of vaporization of the liquid and its boiling point from the vapor pressure data obtained. It would be useful to first make the calculations indicated in the following table:

Approximate temperature °C	t, actual temperature °C	T, temperature °K	$1/T$	Vapor pressure, VP, in mm Hg	$\log_{10} VP$
0	________	________	________	________	________
20	________	________	________	________	________
40	________	________	________	________	________

On the graph paper provided make a graph of $\log_{10}VP$ vs. $1/T$. Let $\log_{10}VP$ be the ordinate and plot $1/T$ on the abscissa. Since $\log_{10}VP$ is, by (1), a linear function of $1/T$, the line obtained should be nearly straight. Find the slope of the line, $\Delta\log_{10}VP/\Delta(1/T)$.

The slope of the line is equal to $-\Delta H_{vap}/2.3R$. Given that $R = 1.99$ cal/mole °K, calculate the molar heat of vaporization, ΔH_{vap}, of your liquid.

Slope $= \dfrac{\Delta \log_{10} VP}{\Delta\, 1/T} =$ ____________ $= \dfrac{-\Delta H_{vap}}{2.3R}$, $\Delta H_{vap} =$ ____________ cal/mole

Continued on following page

From the graph it is also possible to find the temperature at which your liquid will have any given vapor pressure. Recalling that a liquid will boil in an open container at the *temperature* at which its *vapor pressure* is equal to the *atmospheric pressure,* we can predict the boiling point of the liquid at the barometric pressure in the laboratory.

$P_{barometric}$ ______________ mm Hg

$\log_{10} P_{barometric}$ ______________

$1/T$ at this pressure ______________ $°K^{-1}$ (from graph)

T at this pressure ______________ °K

t at this pressure ______________ °C (boiling point predicted)

Boiling point observed experimentally ______________ °C

Unknown no. ______________

Comment on the validity of the equation:

$$\log_{10} VP = \frac{-\Delta H_{vap}}{2.3RT} + C$$

Name ____________________ Section ____________

VAPOR PRESSURE AND HEAT OF VAPORIZATION OF LIQUIDS
(Data and Calculations)

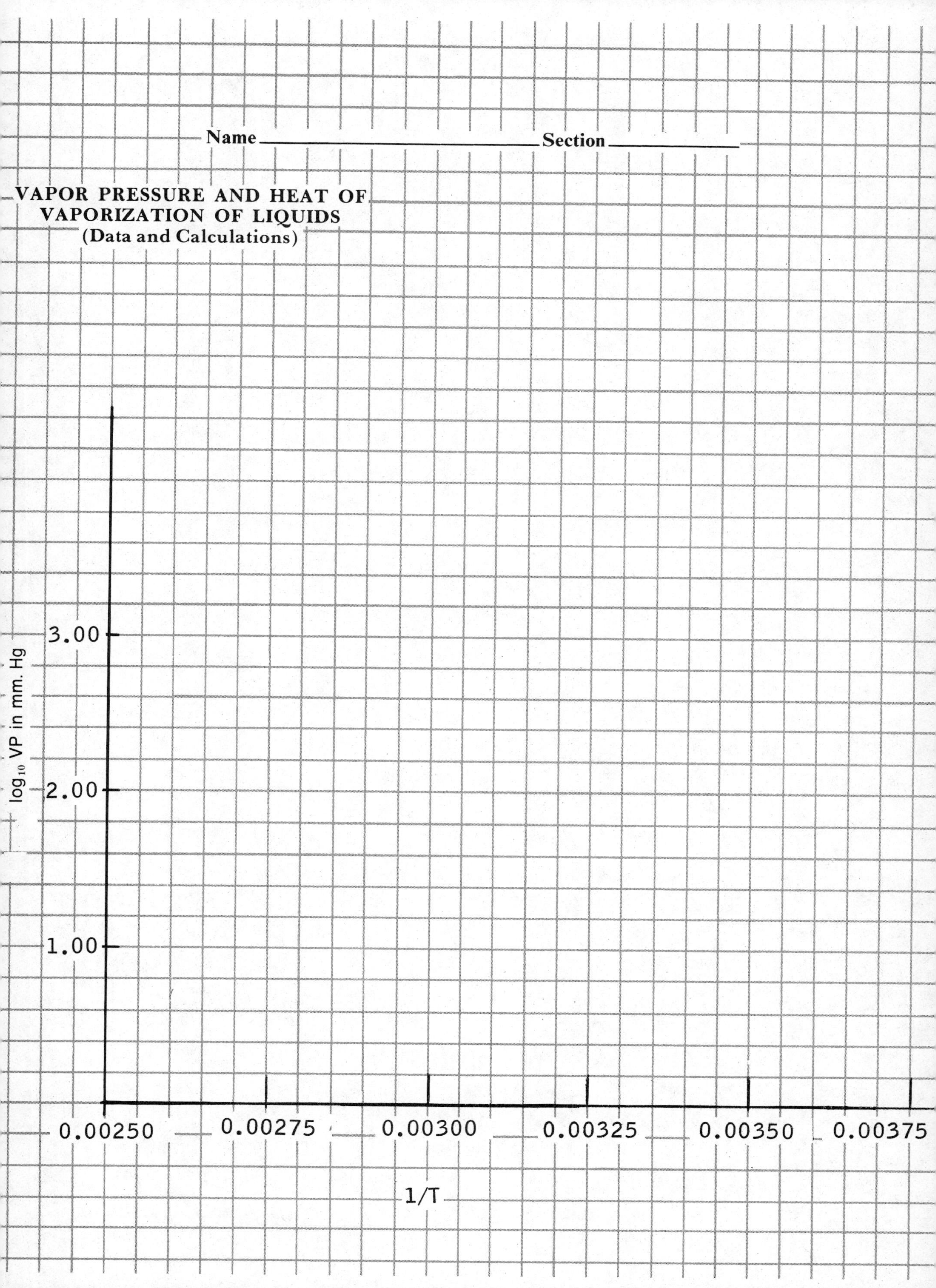

 Name ______________________ Section ______________

ADVANCE STUDY ASSIGNMENT: Vapor Pressure of Liquids

1. When a few ml of liquid carbon tetrachloride are introduced at 25°C into a closed container in which the gas pressure is 720 mm Hg, the pressure rises to 820 mm Hg, and the addition of more carbon tetrachloride does not increase the pressure. What is the vapor pressure of CCl_4 at 25°C?

______________ mm Hg

2. In a vapor pressure experiment on ethanol, C_2H_5OH, the following data were obtained:

t °C	0	30	60
$VP_{mm\ Hg}$	13	80	350

(a) Prepare a table of $\log_{10} VP$ vs. $1/T$ (T is in °K)

$\log_{10} VP$	$1/T$
____________	____________
____________	____________
____________	____________

(b) Using the graph paper, plot $\log_{10} VP$ vs. $1/T$.
(c) Draw a straight line through the three points.
(d) Determine the slope of the line.

Slope = ____________

(e) Using equations (1) and (2) from p. 117, calculate ΔH_{vap}, the molar heat of vaporization of ethanol.

ΔH_{vap} = ______________ cal/mole

3. Ethanol will boil in a beaker when its vapor pressure exceeds the barometric pressure at its surface. Using the graph made in Problem 2, find the temperature at which the vapor pressure of ethanol equals 760 mm Hg. This is the normal boiling point of ethanol.

BP = ______________ °C

BP observed = _____78_____ °C

Name____________________ Section__________

VAPOR PRESSURE OF LIQUIDS
(Advance Study Assignment)

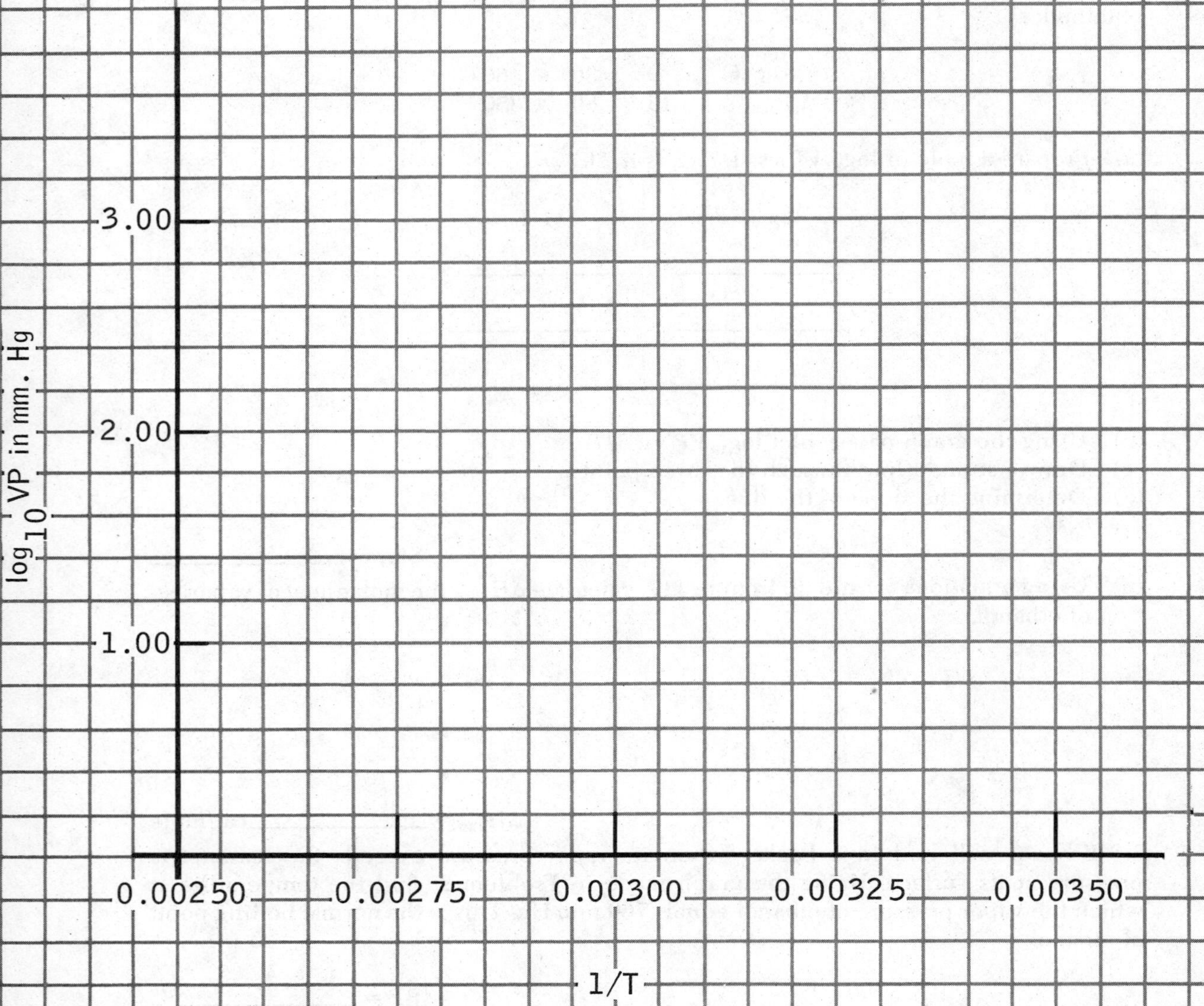

$\log_{10}$ VP in mm. Hg

3.00

2.00

1.00

0.00250 0.00275 0.00300 0.00325 0.00350

1/T

EXPERIMENT 17

Molecular Weight Determination by Depression of the Freezing Point

In the preceding experiment you observed the change of vapor pressure of a liquid as a function of temperature. If a nonvolatile solid compound (the solute) is dissolved in a liquid, the vapor pressure of the liquid solvent is lowered. This decrease in the vapor pressure of the solvent results in other easily observable physical changes; the boiling point of the solution is higher than that of the pure solvent and the freezing point is lower.

Many years ago chemists observed that at low solute concentrations the changes in the boiling point, the freezing point, and the vapor pressure of a solution are all proportional to the amount of solute that is dissolved in the solvent. These three properties are collectively known as colligative properties of solutions. The colligative properties of a solution depend only on the number of solute particles present in a given amount of solvent and not on the kind of particles dissolved.

When working with boiling point elevations or freezing point depressions of solutions, it is convenient to express the solute concentration in terms of its molality m defined by the relation:

$$\text{molality of A} = m_A = \frac{\text{no. of moles A dissolved}}{\text{no. of kg solvent in the solution}}$$

For this unit of concentration, the boiling point elevation, $T_b - T_b^\circ$ or ΔT_b, and the freezing point depression, $T_f^\circ - T_f$ or ΔT_f, in °C at low concentrations are given by the equations:

$$\Delta T_b = k_b m \qquad \Delta T_f = k_f m \tag{1}$$

where k_b and k_f are characteristic of the solvent used. For water, $k_b = 0.52$ and $k_f = 1.86$. For benzene, $k_b = 2.53$ and $k_f = 5.10$.

One of the main uses of the colligative properties of solutions is in connection with the determination of the molecular weights of unknown substances. If we dissolve a known amount of solute in a given amount of solvent and measure ΔT_b or ΔT_f of the solution produced, and if we know the appropriate k for the solvent, we can find the molality and hence the molecular weight of the solute. In the case of the freezing point depression, the relation would be:

$$\Delta T_f = k_f m = k_f \times \frac{\text{no. moles solute}}{\text{no. kg solvent}} = k_f \times \frac{\dfrac{\text{no. g solute}}{\text{GMW solute}}}{\text{no. kg solvent}} \tag{2}$$

In this experiment you will be asked to estimate the molecular weight of an unknown solute, using this equation. The solvent used will be paradichlorobenzene, which has a convenient melting point and a relatively large value for k_f, 7.10. The freezing points will be obtained by studying the rate at which liquid paradichlorobenzene and some of its solutions containing the unknown cool in air. Temperature-time graphs, called cooling curves, reveal the freezing points very well, since the rate at which a liquid cools is typically quite different from that of a liquid-solid equilibrium mixture.

EXPERIMENTAL PROCEDURE

A. Determination of the Freezing Point of Paradichlorobenzene. From the stockroom obtain a stopper fitted with a sensitive thermometer and a glass stirrer, a large test tube, and a sample of solid unknown. **Remember that the thermometer is both fragile and expensive, so handle it with due care.** Weigh the test tube on a top loading or triple beam balance to 0.01g. Add about 30 g of paradichlorobenzene, PDB, to the test tube and weigh again to the same precision.

Fill your 600 ml beaker almost full of hot water from the faucet. Support the beaker on an iron ring and wire gauze on a ring stand and heat the water with a Bunsen burner. Clamp the test tube to the ring stand and immerse the tube in the water as far as is convenient.

Heat the water to about 70 to 75°C (use your ordinary thermometer to follow the bath temperature), at which point most of the PDB will melt. Insert the stopper-thermometer-stirrer assembly in the test tube, adjusting the level of the thermometer so that the bulb is 1 cm above the bottom of the tube, well down into the melt. When the PDB is at about 65°C, stop heating. Stir, to dissolve any remaining solid PDB. Carefully lower the iron ring and water bath and put the beaker of hot water on the lab bench well away from the test tube. Dry the outside of the test tube with a towel.

Record the temperature of the paradichlorobenzene as it cools in the air. Stir the liquid slowly but continuously to avoid supercooling. Start readings at about 60°C and note the temperature every 30 seconds for eight minutes or until the solution has solidified to the point that you are no longer able to stir it. Near the melting point you will begin to observe crystals of PDB in the liquid, and these will increase in amount as cooling proceeds. Note the temperature at which the first solid PDB appears. In Figure 17.1 we have shown graphically how the temperature of pure PDB will typically vary with time in this experiment.

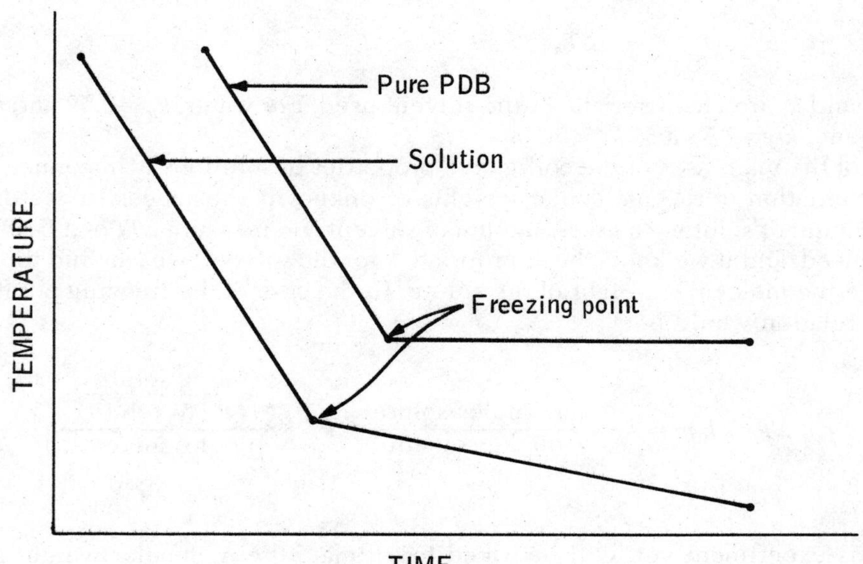

Figure 17.1

B. Determination of the Molecular Weight of an Unknown Compound. Weigh your unknown in its container to 0.01 g. Pour about half of the sample (about 2 g) into your test tube of PDB and reweigh the container.

Heat the test tube in the water bath until the PDB is again melted and the solid unknown is dissolved. When the melt has reached about 65° C, remove the bath, dry the test tube, and let it cool as before. Start readings at about 60° C and continue to take readings, with stirring, for eight minutes.

The dependence of temperature on time with the solution will be similar to that observed for pure PDB, except that the first crystals will appear at a lower temperature, and the temperature of the solid-solution system will gradually fall as cooling proceeds. There may be some supercooling, as evidenced by a rise in temperature shortly after the first appearance of PDB crystals. In this case the freezing point of the solution is best taken as the temperature at which the two lines on the temperature-time graph intersect (Figure 17.1).

Repeat the experiment with this same solution to check for reproducibility of your data.

Add the rest of your unknown (about 2 g) to the PDB solution and again weigh the container. Melt the PDB as before, heating it to about 65°C before removing the water bath. Repeat the entire procedure described above, again checking for reproducibility of data.

Name ______________________ Section ______________

DATA AND CALCULATIONS: Molecular Weight Determination by Freezing Point Depression

Weight of large test tube ______________ g

Weight of test tube plus about 30 g of paradichlorobenzene ______________ g

Weight of container plus unknown ______________ g

Weight of container less Sample I ______________ g

Weight of container less Sample II ______________ g

Time-Temperature Readings

Time (minutes)	Temperature				
	Paradichloro- benzene	Solution I 1st run	Solution I 2nd run	Solution II 1st run	Solution II 2nd run
0					
1/2					
1					
1 1/2					
2					
2 1/2					
3					
3 1/2					
4					
4 1/2					
5					
5 1/2					

Continued on following page

6	______	______	______	______	______
6½	______	______	______	______	______
7	______	______	______	______	______
7½	______	______	______	______	______
8	______	______	______	______	______

Approximate temperature at which first solid appeared

______ ______ ______ ______ ______

Estimation of Freezing Point

On the graph paper provided, plot your temperature vs. time readings for pure paradichlorobenzene and each run of the two solutions. To avoid overlapping graphs, add four minutes to all observed times in making the graph of the cooling curve for pure paradichlorobenzene. Add three minutes to all times for Solution I, run 1; two minutes for Solution I, run 2; one minute for Solution II, run 1; and use times as observed for Solution II, run 2. The freezing point of the liquid may, in each case, be taken to be the point of intersection of the approximately straight line portions of the cooling curve.

Freezing point (from graph)

______ ______ ______ ______ ______

Calculation of Molecular Weight

	Solution I	Solution II
Weight of unknown used (total amount in solution)	______ g	______ g
Weight of paradichlorobenzene used	______ g	______ g
Freezing point of pure paradichlorobenzene	______ °C	______ °C
Freezing point of solution (average values of runs 1 and 2)	______ °C	______ °C
Freezing point depression (total depression)	______ °C	______ °C

Continued on following page

Total molal concentration m of unknown solution (from Equation 2) ($k_f = 7.10$) ____________ ____________

Gram molecular weight of unknown, GMW (from Equation 2) ____________g ____________g

Average GMW ____________g

Unknown no. ____________

Name ______________ Section ______________

Molecular Weight Determination by Freezing Point Depression

(Data and Calculations)

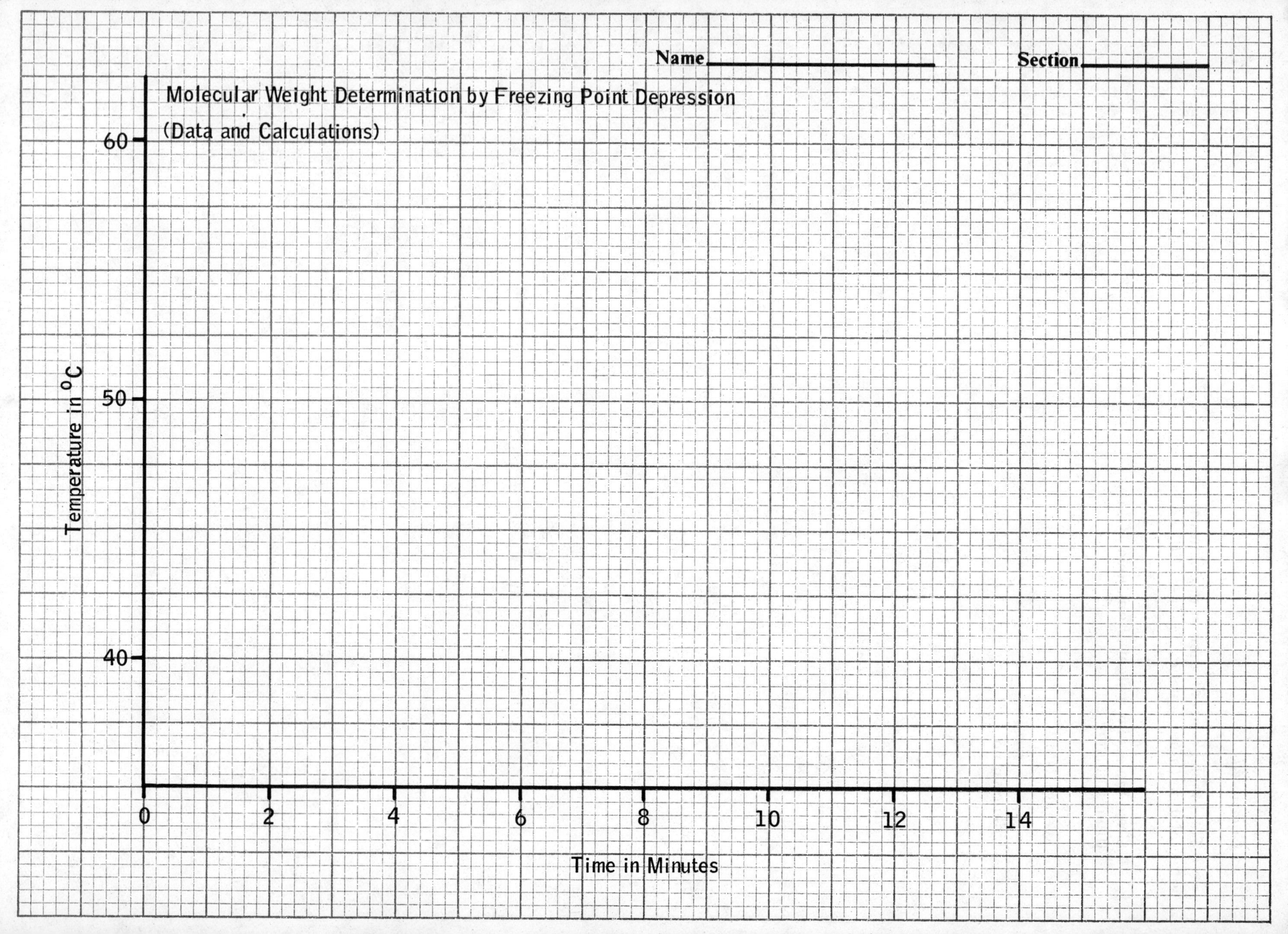

 Name ____________________ Section ____________

ADVANCE STUDY ASSIGNMENT: Determination of Molecular Weight by Freezing Point Depression

1. A student determines the freezing point of a solution of 1.96 g of naphthalene in 25.64 g of paradichlorobenzene. He obtains the following temperature-time readings.

Time (min)	0	1/2	1	1 1/2	2	2 1/2
Temperature (°C)	59.7	58.0	56.5	54.8	53.4	52.1

Time (min)	3	3 1/2	4	4 1/2	5	5 1/2
Temperature (°C)	50.9	49.5	48.4	48.6	48.7	48.6

Time (min)	6	6 1/2	7	7 1/2	8
Temperature (°C)	48.5	48.4	48.3	48.2	48.1

(a) Plot these data on the graph paper provided. Estimate the freezing point of the solution to ±0.1°C by determining the intersection of the straight line portions of the cooling curves.

____________°C

(b) Taking k_f for paradichlorobenzene to be 7.10, find the gram molecular weight of the solid. Assume 53.0°C to be the freezing point of pure paradichlorobenzene.

GMW = ____________ g

2. Precise freezing point determinations show that Equation 2 is really valid only for dilute solutions and that at high concentrations, the molecular weights obtained are appreciably in error. By calculating apparent molecular weights at various concentrations by Equation 2 and extrapolating those values to zero concentration, one can obtain the best value possible for the molecular weight of a given solute.

Continued on following page

Sucrose solutions in water, in very precise experiments, are found to have the following freezing points:

g sucrose/kg H_2O	T_f, °C	m(effective)	MW (apparent)
100	−0.56	__________	__________
200	−1.15	__________	__________
400	−2.42	__________	__________
600	−4.05	__________	__________

Given that k_f for water is 1.86, use Equation 2 to calculate the effective molality m and the apparent molecular weight of sucrose in each solution. Make a graph of MW (apparent) vs. g sucrose/kg H_2O present, and extrapolate the line to g sucrose/kg H_2O equals zero to find the best value of the molecular weight of sucrose. (We will not use this procedure in the experiment you perform, since experimental errors are too high. Under such conditions, averaged results are probably best.)

Best value for MW __________

Name ______________________ Section ______________

DETERMINATION OF MOLECULAR WEIGHT BY FREEZING POINT DEPRESSION

(Advance Study Assignment)

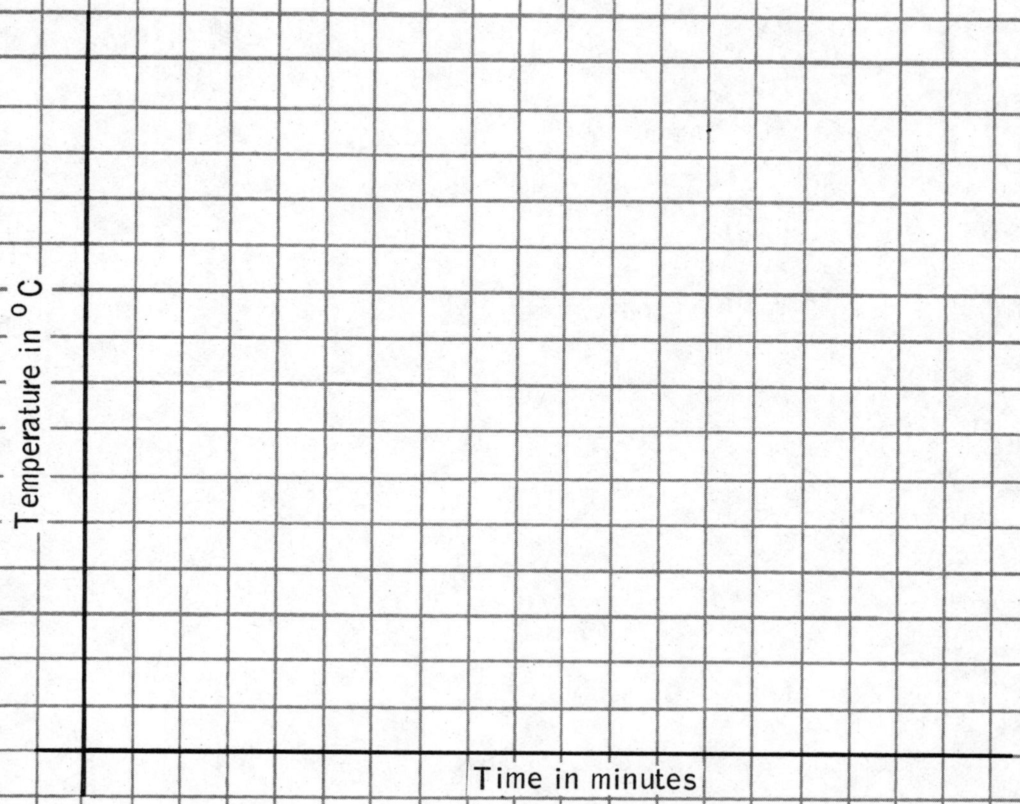

Temperature in °C

Time in minutes

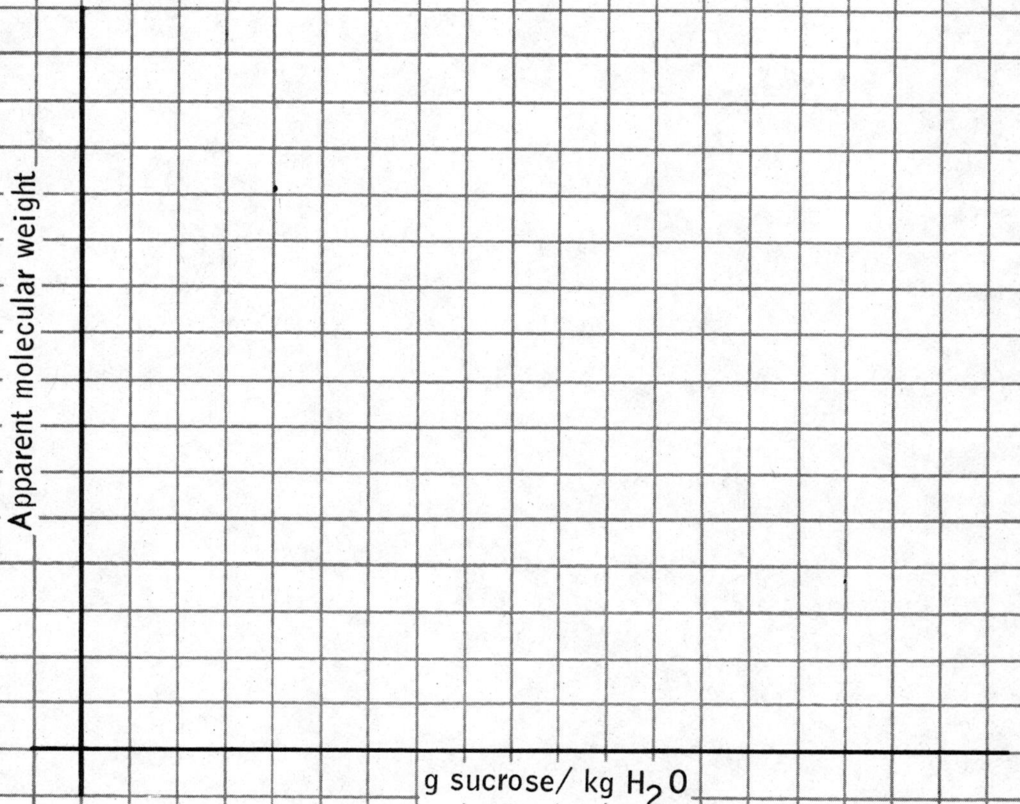

Apparent molecular weight

g sucrose/ kg H_2O

SECTION 8

Chemical Equilibrium

EXPERIMENT 18

Determination of the Equilibrium Constant for a Chemical Reaction

Every chemical reaction has a characteristic condition of equilibrium at a given temperature. If two reactants are mixed, they will tend to react to form products until a state is reached where the amounts of reactants and products no longer change. Under such conditions the reactants and products are in chemical equilibrium and will remain so until the system is altered in some way. Associated with the equilibrium state there is a number called the equilibrium constant, K_c, which expresses the necessary condition on the concentrations of reactants and products for the reaction. For the reaction

$$aA + bB \rightleftharpoons cC + dD \tag{1}$$

the equilibrium condition* is that

$$\frac{[C]^c[D]^d}{[A]^a[B]^b} = K_c \tag{2}$$

where A, B, C, and D are solutes in solution or are gases, and the bracketed expressions are their concentrations in moles per liter at equilibrium. The equilibrium constant K_c

---

*The expression for the equilibrium constant K_c is fundamental and will appear in several of its many possible forms in many of the experiments in the latter part of this manual.

Strictly speaking, the expression for K_c should be set up in terms of the activities of the species A, B, C, and D, rather than their concentrations. The activity of a species may be considered to be its effective concentration in a system, rather than its actual concentration. At low concentrations the activities of solute and gaseous species and their concentrations are nearly equal. In most applications of the equilibrium concept, whether they be in homogeneous systems (as in this experiment) or in heterogeneous systems, in which solubilities are of concern, concentrations of species are used rather than activities in the expression for K_c. This practice will be followed in all experiments involving chemical equilibria that appear in this manual.

In the experiments on equilibrium systems an attempt will be made to illustrate various aspects of equilibrium theory. In order to make the experiments tractable, it will be necessary in some cases to make simplifying assumptions about the system being studied. In addition to assuming that concentrations may be employed instead of activities, we will in general limit the number of equilibria to be considered in any given system. Since there are many equilibria that are simultaneously satisfied in some systems, this limitation may produce results that are not in complete accord with data in the literature. In some instances, we admit, we have sacrificed a complete treatment of a system in order to more clearly illustrate a valid principle.

will have a fixed value for the reaction at any given temperature. If A, B, C, and D are mixed in arbitrary amounts in a container they will tend to react until their concentrations satisfy Equation 2. Depending on the magnitude of K_c and the amounts of species used initially, Reaction 1 will proceed to the right or to the left until equilibrium is attained.

In this experiment we will study the equilibrium properties of the reaction between iron(III) ion and thiocyanic acid:

$$Fe^{3+}(aq) + HSCN(aq) \rightleftharpoons FeSCN^{2+}(aq) + H^{+}(aq) \tag{3}$$

When solutions containing Fe^{3+} ion and thiocyanic acid are mixed, Reaction 3 occurs to some extent, forming the $FeSCN^{2+}$ complex ion, which has a deep red color, and H^+ ion. As a result of the reaction, the equilibrium amounts of Fe^{3+} and HSCN will be less than they would have been if no reaction occurred; for every mole of $FeSCN^{2+}$ that is formed, one mole of Fe^{3+} and one mole of HSCN will react. According to the general law, K_c for Reaction 3 takes the form

$$\frac{[FeSCN^{2+}]\,[H^+]}{[Fe^{3+}]\,[HSCN]} = K_c \tag{4}$$

Our purpose in the experiment will be to evaluate K_c for the reaction by determining the equilibrium concentrations of the four species in Equation 4 in several solutions made up in different ways. The equilibrium constant K_c for the reaction has a convenient magnitude and the color of the $FeSCN^{2+}$ ion makes for an easy analysis of the equilibrium mixture.

The solutions will be prepared by mixing solutions containing known concentrations of iron(III) nitrate and thiocyanic acid. The color of the $FeSCN^{2+}$ ion formed will allow us to determine its equilibrium concentration. Knowing the initial composition of the solution and the equilibrium concentration of $FeSCN^{2+}$, we can calculate the equilibrium concentrations of the rest of the pertinent species and then calculate K_c.

Since the calculations that are necessary to find K_c may not be apparent, let us consider a specific example. Assume that we prepare our solution by mixing 10.0 ml 2.00×10^{-3} M $Fe(NO_3)_3$ with 10.0 ml 2.00×10^{-3} M HSCN under conditions which keep $[H^+]$ equal to 0.50. The Fe^{3+} in the iron(III) nitrate reacts with the HSCN to produce some red $FeSCN^{2+}$ complex ion. By a method of analysis described below it is found that $[FeSCN^{2+}]$ at equilibrium is about 1.50×10^{-4} M.

To find K_c for the reaction from these data it is convenient first to determine how many moles of reactant species were initially present, before the reaction occurred. By the definition of the molarity M of a species A,

$$M_A = \frac{\text{no. moles A}}{\text{no. liters solution}} \quad \text{or} \quad \text{no. moles A} = M_A V$$

where V is the volume of solution in liters.

$$\text{Initial no. moles } Fe^{3+} = M_{Fe^{3+}}\,V_{Fe(NO_3)_3} = 2.00 \times 10^{-3} \times \frac{10.0 \text{ ml}}{1000 \text{ ml/lit}} = 20.0 \times 10^{-6}$$

$$\text{Initial no. moles HSCN} = M_{HSCN}\,V_{HSCN} = 2.00 \times 10^{-3} \times \frac{10.0 \text{ ml}}{1000 \text{ ml/lit}} = 20.0 \times 10^{-6}$$

The number of moles $FeSCN^{2+}$ present at equilibrium is found from the analysis and the volume of the solution:

$$\text{Equilibrium no. moles } FeSCN^{2+} = M_{FeSCN^{2+}}\,V = 1.50 \times 10^{-4} \times \frac{20.0 \text{ ml}}{1000 \text{ ml/lit}} = 3.00 \times 10^{-6}$$

since the volume of the solution containing the complex ion is 20.0 ml. The $FeSCN^{2+}$ ion is produced by Reaction 3:

$$Fe^{3+}(aq) + HSCN(aq) \rightarrow FeSCN^{2+}(aq) + H^+(aq)$$

Therefore, for every mole of $FeSCN^{2+}$ present in the equilibrium mixture, one mole Fe^{3+} and one mole HSCN are reacted. We can see then that

Equilibrium no. moles Fe^{3+} = no. moles Fe^{3+} initially present − no. moles $FeSCN^{2+}$ at equilibrium

$$= 20.0 \times 10^{-6} - 3.00 \times 10^{-6} = 17.0 \times 10^{-6}$$

Similarly,

Equilibrium no. moles HSCN = no. moles HSCN initially present − no. moles $FeSCN^{2+}$ at equilibrium

$$= 20.0 \times 10^{-6} - 3.00 \times 10^{-6} = 17.0 \times 10^{-6}$$

Knowing the no. moles Fe^{3+} and HSCN present in the equilibrium mixture, and the volume of the mixture, we can easily find the concentrations of those two species:

$$[Fe^{3+}] = \frac{\text{no. moles } Fe^{3+}}{\text{no. lit solution}} = \frac{17.0 \times 10^{-6}}{20.0 \times 10^{-3}} = 8.5 \times 10^{-4}\ M$$

$$[HSCN] = \frac{\text{no. moles HSCN}}{\text{no. lit solution}} = \frac{17.0 \times 10^{-6}}{20.0 \times 10^{-3}} = 8.5 \times 10^{-4}\ M$$

We now can substitute into Equation 4 to find the equilibrium constant for this reaction:

$$K_c = \frac{[FeSCN^{2+}][H^+]}{[Fe^{3+}][HSCN]} = \frac{1.50 \times 10^{-4} \times 0.50}{8.5 \times 10^{-4} \times 8.5 \times 10^{-4}} = 104$$

(The data in this calculation correspond to a different temperature than the one at which you will be working, so the actual value of K_c you will obtain will not be the one found above.)

Two methods of analysis can be easily used to determine $[FeSCN^{2+}]$ in the equilibrium mixtures. The more precise method makes use of a spectrophotometer, which measures the amount of light absorbed by the red complex at 4470 Å, the wavelength at which the complex most strongly absorbs. The absorbance A of the complex is proportional to its concentration M and can be measured directly on the spectrophotometer:

$$A = kM \tag{5}$$

Your instructor will show you how to operate the spectrophotometer if these are available to your laboratory and will provide you with a calibration curve from which you can find $[FeSCN^{2+}]$ once you have determined the absorbance of your solutions.

In the other method for analysis a solution of known concentration of $FeSCN^{2+}$ is prepared. By determining the depth of this standard solution, which matches in color intensity the unknown solution of known depth, one can calculate $[FeSCN^{2+}]$.

In all the solutions to be mixed we will maintain $[H^+]$ at a value of 0.5 M. This large amount of H^+ ion will ensure that essentially all the HSCN present remains undissociated and that no Fe^{3+} reacts to form other brown colored species such as $FeOH^{2+}$. Since H^+ will be present in large excess as compared to the other reactants, its concentration will not be appreciably affected by the reaction which occurs and can be assumed to remain constant and equal to 0.5 M.

EXPERIMENTAL PROCEDURE

Label five test tubes 1 through 5. Pipet 5.0 ml of 2.00×10^{-3} *M* $Fe(NO_3)_3$ in 0.50 *M* HNO_3 into each test tube. Into each of the test tubes labeled 1 to 5, pipet the corresponding number of ml (1 to 5) of 2.00×10^{-3} *M* HSCN in 0.50 *M* HNO_3. Add enough 0.50 *M* HNO_3 to each test tube to make the total volume equal to 10.0 ml. Mix each solution thoroughly with a glass stirring rod. Be sure to dry the stirring rod after mixing each solution.

Method I. Analysis by Spectrophotometric Measurement. Place a portion of each solution in a spectrophotometer cell as shown by your instructor and measure the absorbance of the solution at 4470 Å. Determine the concentration of $FeSCN^{2+}$ from the calibration curve provided for each instrument. Record these values on the data page.

Method II. Analysis by Comparison with a Standard. Prepare a solution of known $[FeSCN^{2+}]$ by pipetting 5.0 ml 0.200 *M* $Fe(NO_3)_3$ in 0.50 *M* HNO_3 into a test tube and adding 1.0 ml 0.002 *M* HSCN in 0.50 *M* HNO_3. Dilute to 20 ml with 0.50 *M* HNO_3. Mix the solution thoroughly with a stirring rod.

Since in this solution $[Fe^{3+}] >> [HSCN]$, Reaction 3 is driven strongly to the right. You can assume without serious error that essentially all the HSCN added is converted to $FeSCN^{2+}$. Assuming that this is the case, calculate $[FeSCN^{2+}]$ in the standard solution and record the value on the data page.

The $[FeSCN^{2+}]$ in the unknown solutions in test tubes 1 to 5 can be found by comparing the intensity of the red color in those solutions with that in the standard solution. This can be done by placing the test tube containing Solution 1 side by side with the test tube containing the standard. Look down both test tubes toward a well-illuminated piece of white paper on the laboratory bench.

Pour out the standard solution into a dry clean beaker until the color intensity you see down the tube containing the standard matches that which you see when looking down the tube containing the unknown. When the colors match, the following relation is valid:

$$[FeSCN^{2+}]_{unknown} \times \text{depth of unknown solution} = [FeSCN^{2+}]_{standard} \times \text{depth of standard solution} \qquad (6)$$

Measure the depths of the matching solutions with a rule and record them. Repeat the measurement for solutions 2 through 5, recording the depth of each unknown and that of the standard solution which matches it in intensity.

Name ______________________ Section ______________

DATA: Determination of the Equilibrium Constant for a Chemical Reaction

SOLUTION	MILLILITERS 2.00×10^{-3} *M* $Fe(NO_3)_3$	MILLILITERS 2.00×10^{-3} *M* HSCN	MILLILITERS 0.5 *M* HNO_3	METHOD I absorbance	METHOD II depth (mm) standard	METHOD II depth (mm) unknown	$[FeSCN^{2+}]$
1	______	______	______	______	______	______	______ $\times 10^{-4}$
2	______	______	______	______	______	______	______ $\times 10^{-4}$
3	______	______	______	______	______	______	______ $\times 10^{-4}$
4	______	______	______	______	______	______	______ $\times 10^{-4}$
5	______	______	______	______	______	______	______ $\times 10^{-4}$

If Method II was used: $[FeSCN^{2+}]_{standard}$ ______________ $\times 10^{-4}$ *M*; $[FeSCN^{2+}]$ in solutions 1 to 5 calculated by Relation 6.

CALCULATIONS

A. Calculation of K_c assuming the reaction: $Fe^{3+}(aq) + HSCN(aq) \rightleftharpoons FeSCN^{2+}(aq) + H^+(aq)$

This calculation is most readily carried out by completing the table on p. 144 as follows:

1. Knowing the initial concentration and volume of Fe^{3+} and HSCN, calculate the initial no. of moles of these species (express as a number $\times 10^{-6}$).
2. Record $[FeSCN^{2+}]$ from above. Calculate the no. of moles of $FeSCN^{2+}$ in your 10 ml of solution. Again, express as a number $\times 10^{-6}$.
3. Realizing that 1 mole of $FeSCN^{2+}$ is formed at the expense of 1 mole of Fe^{3+} and 1 mole of HSCN, calculate the number of moles of Fe^{3+} and HSCN at equilibrium.
4. Knowing the no. of moles of Fe^{3+} and HSCN at equilibrium and the volume (10 ml), calculate $[Fe^{3+}]$ and [HSCN]. Express as a number $\times 10^{-4}$.
5. Use Equation 4 to calculate K_c.

Continued on following page

SOLUTION	INITIAL NO. MOLES Fe^{3+}	HSCN	EQUILIBRIUM NO. MOLES Fe^{3+}	HSCN	$FeSCN^{2+}$	EQUILIBRIUM CONCENTRATIONS $[Fe^{3+}]$	[HSCN]	$[FeSCN^{2+}]$	$[H^+]$	K_c
1	___ $\times 10^{-6}$	___ $\times 10^{-6}$	___ $\times 10^{-6}$	___ $\times 10^{-6}$	___ $\times 10^{-6}$	___ $\times 10^{-4}$	___ $\times 10^{-4}$	___ $\times 10^{-4}$	0.50	___
2	___	___	___	___	___	___	___	___	0.50	___
3	___	___	___	___	___	___	___	___	0.50	___
4	___	___	___	___	___	___	___	___	0.50	___
5	___	___	___	___	___	___	___	___	0.50	___

B. In calculating K_c in Part **A**, we assumed that the formula of the complex ion is $FeSCN^{2+}$. It is by no means obvious that this is the case, and one might have assumed, for instance, that $Fe(SCN)_2^+$ was the species formed. The reaction would then be:

$$Fe^{3+}(aq) + 2\ HSCN(aq) \rightleftharpoons Fe(SCN)_2^+(aq) + 2\ H^+(aq) \qquad (7)$$

If one analyzed the equilibrium system we have studied, assuming that Reaction 7 occurs rather than Reaction 3, we would presumably obtain nonconstant values of K_c. Using the same kind of procedure as in Part **A**, calculate K_c for solutions 1, 3, and 5 on the basis that $Fe(SCN)_2^+$ is the formula of the complex ion formed by reaction between Fe^{3+} and HSCN. Because of the procedure used for calibrating the system by Method I or Method II, $[Fe(SCN)_2^+]$ will equal *one-half* the $[FeSCN^{2+}]$ obtained for each solution in Part **A.** Note that *two* moles HSCN are needed to form *one* mole $Fe(SCN)_2^+$; this changes not only the relative numbers of moles from the previous case but also the expression for K_c.

SOLUTION	INITIAL NO. MOLES Fe^{3+}	HSCN	EQUILIBRIUM NO. MOLES $Fe(SCN)_2^+$	Fe^{3+}	HSCN	EQUILIBRIUM CONCENTRATIONS $[Fe(SCN)_2^+]$	$[Fe^{3+}]$	[HSCN]	$[H^+]$	K_c
1	___	___	___	___	___	___	___	___	___	___
3	___	___	___	___	___	___	___	___	___	___
5	___	___	___	___	___	___	___	___	___	___

On the basis of the results of Part **A**, what can you conclude about the validity of the equilibrium concept, as exemplified by Equation 4? What can you conclude about the formula of the iron(III) thiocyanate complex ion?

 Name ______________ Section ______________

ADVANCE STUDY ASSIGNMENT: Determination of the Equilibrium Constant for a Chemical Reaction

1. When Fe^{3+} and HSCN react to an equilibrium with $FeSCN^{2+}$ and H^+, what happens to the concentration of Fe^{3+}? How are the numbers of moles $FeSCN^{2+}$ produced and the number of moles Fe^{3+} used up related to each other?

2. In an experiment similar to the one you will be doing, the $FeSCN^{2+}$ *equilibrium* concentration was found to be $0.32 \times 10^{-4}\,M$ in a solution made by mixing 5 ml of 0.001 *M* $Fe(NO_3)_3$ with 5 ml 0.001 *M* HSCN. The H^+ concentration was maintained at 0.50 *M*.

a. How many moles $FeSCN^{2+}$ are present at equilibrium? ______ $\times 10^{-6}$

b. How many moles of Fe^{3+} and HSCN were initially present? ______ $\times 10^{-6}$

c. How many moles Fe^{3+} remain unreacted in the solution? ______ $\times 10^{-6}$

d. How many moles HSCN remain unreacted? ______ $\times 10^{-6}$

e. Find $[Fe^{3+}]$ and [HSCN] in the equilibrium solution. ______ $\times 10^{-4}M$

f. Calculate the value of K_c for the reaction.

____

3. In this experiment we assume that the complex ion formed is $FeSCN^{2+}$. It would be possible, however, to form $Fe(SCN)_2^+$ under certain conditions.

a. Write the equation for the reaction between Fe^{3+} and HSCN in which $Fe(SCN)_2^+$ is produced.

b. Formulate the expression for the equilibrium constant K_c associated with the reaction in part a.

SECTION 9
Chemical Kinetics

EXPERIMENT 19
Rates of Chemical Reactions, I. The Bromination of Acetone

The rate at which a chemical reaction occurs depends on several factors: the nature of the reaction, the concentrations of the reactants, the temperature, and the presence of possible catalysts. All of these factors can markedly influence the observed rate of reaction.

Some reactions at a given temperature are very slow indeed; the oxidation of gaseous hydrogen or wood at room temperature would not appreciably proceed in a century. Other reactions are essentially instantaneous; the precipitation of silver chloride when solutions containing silver ions and chloride ions are mixed and the formation of water when acidic and basic solutions are mixed are examples of extremely rapid reactions. In this experiment we will study a reaction which, in the vicinity of room temperature, proceeds at a moderate, relatively easily measured rate.

For a given reaction, the rate typically increases with an increase in the concentration of any reactant. The relation between rate and concentration is a remarkably simple one in many cases, and for the reaction

$$aA + bB \rightarrow cC$$

the rate can usually be expressed by the equation

$$\text{rate} = k\,(A)^m\,(B)^n \tag{1}$$

where m and n are generally, but not always, integers, 0, 1, 2, or possibly 3; (A) and (B) are the concentrations of A and B (ordinarily in moles per liter); and k is a constant, called the *rate constant* of the reaction, which makes the relation quantitatively correct. The numbers m and n are called the *orders of the reaction* with respect to A and to B. If m is 1 the reaction is said to be *first order* with respect to the reactant A. If n is 2 the reaction is second order with respect to reactant B.

The rate of a reaction is also significantly dependent on the temperature at which the reaction occurs. An increase in temperature increases the rate, an often cited rule being that a 10° C rise in temperature will double the rate. This rule is only approximately correct; nevertheless, it is clear that a rise of temperature of, say, 100° C could change the rate of a reaction appreciably.

As with the concentration, there is a quantitative relation between reaction rate and temperature, but here the relation is somewhat more complicated. This relation is based on the idea that in order to react, the reactant species must have a certain minimum amount of energy present at the time the reactants collide in the reaction step; this amount of energy, which is typically furnished by the kinetic energy of motion of the species present, is called the *activation energy* for the reaction. The equation relating the rate constant k to the absolute temperature T and the activation energy E_a is

$$\log_{10} k = \frac{-E_a}{2.30RT} + \text{constant} \qquad (2)$$

where R is the gas constant (1.99 cal/mole °K for E_a in calories per mole). This equation is identical in form to Equation 1 in Exp. 16. By measuring k at different temperatures we can determine graphically the activation energy for a reaction.

In this experiment we will study the kinetics of the reaction between bromine and acetone:

$$CH_3{-}\overset{\overset{\displaystyle O}{\|}}{C}{-}CH_3(aq) + Br_2(aq) \rightarrow CH_3{-}\overset{\overset{\displaystyle O}{\|}}{C}{-}CH_2Br(aq) + H^+(aq) + Br^-(aq)$$

The rate of this reaction is found to depend on the concentration of hydrogen ion in the solution as well as presumably on the concentrations of the two reactants. By Equation 1, the rate law for this reaction is

$$\text{rate} = k(\text{acetone})^m (Br_2)^n (H^+)^p \qquad (3)$$

where m, n, and p are the orders of the reaction with respect to acetone, bromine, and hydrogen ion respectively, and k is the rate constant for the reaction.

The rate of this reaction can be expressed as the (small) change in the concentration of Br_2, $\Delta(Br_2)$, which occurs, divided by the time interval Δt required for the change:

$$\text{rate} = \frac{\Delta(Br_2)}{\Delta t} \qquad (4)$$

Ordinarily, since rate varies as the concentrations of the reactants according to Equation 3, in a rate study it would be necessary to measure, directly or indirectly, the concentration of each reactant as a function of time; the rate would typically vary markedly with time, decreasing to very low values as the concentration of at least one reactant becomes very low. This makes reaction rate studies relatively difficult to carry out and introduces mathematical complexities that are difficult for beginning students to understand.

The bromination of acetone is a rather atypical reaction, in that it can be very easily investigated experimentally. First of all, bromine has color, so that one can readily follow changes in bromine concentration visually. A second and very important characteristic of this reaction is that it turns out to be zero order in Br_2 concentration. This means (see Equation 3) that the rate of the reaction does not depend on (Br_2) at all; $(Br_2)^0 = 1$, no matter what the value of (Br_2) is, as long as it is not itself zero.

Since the rate of the reaction does not depend on (Br_2), we can study the rate by simply making Br_2 the limiting reagent present in a large excess of acetone and H^+ ion. We then measure the time required for a known initial concentration of Br_2 to be completely used up. If both acetone and H^+ are present at much higher concentrations than that of Br_2, their concentrations will not change appreciably during the course of the reaction, and the rate will remain, by Equation 3, effectively constant until all the bromine is gone, at which time the reaction will stop. Under such circumstances, if it takes t seconds for the color of a solution having an initial concentration of Br_2 equal to $(Br_2)_0$ to disappear, the rate of the reaction, by Equation 4, would be

$$\text{rate} = \frac{\Delta(Br_2)}{\Delta t} = \frac{(Br_2)_0}{t} \tag{5}$$

Although the rate of the reaction is constant during its course under the conditions we have set up, we can vary it by changing the initial concentrations of acetone and H^+ ion. If, for example, we should *double* the initial concentration of *acetone* over that in Reaction 1, keeping (H^+) and (Br_2) at the *same* values they had previously, then the rate of Reaction 2 would, according to Equation 3, be different from that in Reaction 1:

$$\text{rate } 2 = k(2A)^m\,(Br_2)^0\,(H^+)^p$$
$$\text{rate } 1 = k(A)^m\,(Br_2)^0\,(H^+)^p$$

Dividing the first equation by the second, we see that the *k's* cancel, as do the terms in the bromine and hydrogen ion concentrations, since they have the same values in both reactions, and we obtain simply

$$\frac{\text{rate } 2}{\text{rate } 1} = \frac{(2A)^m}{(A)^m} = \left(\frac{2A}{A}\right)^m = 2^m \tag{6}$$

Having measured both rate 2 and rate 1 by Equation 5, we can find their ratio, which must be equal to 2^m. We can then solve for m either by inspection or using logarithms and so find the *order* of the reaction with respect to acetone.

By a similar procedure we can measure the order of the reaction with respect to H^+ ion concentration and also confirm the fact that the reaction is zero order with respect to Br_2. Having found the order with respect to each reactant, we can then evaluate k, the rate constant for the reaction.

The determination of the orders m and p, the confirmation of the fact that n, the order with respect to Br_2, equals zero, and the evaluation of the rate constant k for the reaction at room temperature comprise your assignment in this experiment. You will be furnished with standard solutions of acetone, bromine, and hydrogen ion, and with the composition of one solution that will give a reasonable rate. The rest of the planning and the execution of the experiment will be your responsibility.

An optional part of the experiment is to study the rate of this reaction at different temperatures in order to find its activation energy. The general procedure here would be to study the rate of reaction in one of the mixtures at room temperature and at two other temperatures, one above and one below room temperature. Knowing the rates, and hence the *k's*, at the three temperatures, you can then find E_a, the energy of activation for the reaction, by plotting log k vs. $1/T$. The slope of the resultant straight line, by Equation 2, must be $-E_a/2.30R$.

EXPERIMENTAL PROCEDURE

Select two six-inch test tubes; when filled with distilled water, they should appear to have identical color when you view them down the tubes against a white background.

Draw 50 ml of each of the following solutions into clean dry 100 ml beakers, one solution to a beaker: 4 M acetone, 1 M HCl, and 0.02 M Br_2. Cover each beaker with a watch glass.

With your graduated cylinder, measure out 10.0 ml of the 4 M acetone solution and pour it into a clean 125 ml Erlenmeyer flask. Then measure out 10.0 ml 1 M HCl and add that to the acetone in the flask. Add 20.0 ml distilled H_2O to the flask. Drain the graduated cylinder, shaking out any excess water, and then use the cylinder to measure out 10.0 ml 0.02 *M* Br_2 solution. Be careful not to spill the bromine solution on your hands or clothes.

Noting the time on your wrist watch or the wall clock to one second, pour the bromine solution into the Erlenmeyer flask and quickly swirl the flask to thoroughly mix the reagents. The reaction mixture will appear yellow because of the presence of the bromine, and the color will fade slowly as the bromine reacts with the acetone. Fill one of the test tubes ¾ full with the reaction mixture, and fill the other test tube to the same depth with distilled water. Stopper the Erlenmeyer flask. Look down the test tubes toward a well-lit piece of white paper, and note the time when the color of the bromine just disappears. Measure the temperature of the mixture in the test tube.

Repeat the experiment, using as a reference the reacted solution instead of distilled water. The amount of time required in the two runs should agree within about 30 seconds.

The rate of the reaction equals the initial concentration of Br_2 *in the reaction mixture* divided by the elapsed time. Since the reaction is zero order in Br_2, and since both acetone and H^+ ion are present in great excess, the rate is constant throughout the reaction and the concentrations of both acetone and H^+ remain essentially at their initial values.

Having found the rate of the reaction for one composition of the system, change the composition of the reaction mixture by changing the volume, and hence the concentration, of acetone, keeping the total volume at 50 ml, so that by measuring the rate of reaction in the new mixture you can find the order of the reaction with respect to acetone. (Remember that the concentrations of H^+ and Br_2 must be the same as in the initial experiment!) Do the experiment twice with this mixture; the times needed for reaction should not differ by more than about 20 seconds. Keep the temperature within about a degree of that in the first experiment. Calculate the rate of the reaction. Compare the rate with that found in the first mixture, and then calculate m, the order of the reaction with respect to acetone, using an equation similar to (6).

Again change the composition of the reaction mixture so that this time a measurement of the reaction rate will give you information about the order of the reaction with respect to H^+. Do the experiment twice with this mixture to find the reaction time to within 20 seconds, again making sure that the temperature is within about a degree of that observed previously. From the rate you determine for this mixture find p, the order of the reaction with respect to H^+.

Finally, change the reaction mixture composition in such a way as to allow you to show that the order of the reaction with respect to Br_2 is zero. Measure the rate of the reaction twice, and calculate n, the order with respect to Br_2.

Having found the order of the reaction for each species on which the rate depends, evaluate k, the rate constant for the reaction, from the rate and concentration data in each of the mixtures you studied. If the temperatures at which the reactions were run are all equal to within a degree or two, k should be about the same for each mixture.

As a final reaction, make up a mixture using reactant volumes that you did not use in any previous experiments. Using Equation 3, the values of concentrations in the mixtures, the orders, and the rate constant you calculated from your experimental data, predict how long it will take for the Br_2 color to disappear from your mixture. Measure the time for the reaction and compare it with your prediction.

If time permits, select one of the reaction mixtures you have already used which gave a convenient time, and use that mixture to measure the rate of reaction at about 10° C and at about 40° C. From the two rates you find, plus the rate at room temperature, calculate the energy of activation for the reaction, using Equation 2.

CAUTION: The reagents used in this experiment are volatile. Avoid exposure to their vapors by keeping the reagents and reaction mixtures covered, and, if convenient, opening the windows in the lab.

Name ______________________ Section ______________

DATA AND CALCULATIONS: The Bromination of Acetone

I. Reaction Rate Data

Mixture	Vol (ml) 4 *M* acetone	Vol (ml) 1 *M* HCl	Vol (ml) 0.02 *M* Br_2	Volume in ml H_2O	Time for Reaction in sec 1st Run	2nd Run	Temp °C
I	10	10	10	20			
II							
III							
IV							
V							

II. Determination of Reaction Orders with Respect to Acetone, Br_2, and H^+ Ion

$$\text{rate} = k\,(\text{acetone})^m\,(Br_2)^n\,(H^+)^p$$

Mixture	(acetone)	(H^+)	$(Br_2)_0$	$\text{rate} = \dfrac{(Br_2)_0}{\text{ave. time}}$
I	0.8 *M*	0.2 *M*	0.004 *M*	
II				
III				
IV				

$$\frac{\text{rate II}}{\text{rate I}} = \_\_\_\_\_\_\_\_ = \left(\_\_\_\_\_\_\_\_\right)^m;\ m = \_\_\_\_\_\_\_\_$$

$$\frac{\text{rate III}}{\text{rate}\,\_\_\_} = \_\_\_\_\_\_\_\_ = \left(\_\_\_\_\_\_\_\_\right)^p;\ p = \_\_\_\_\_\_\_\_$$

Continued on following page

$$\frac{\text{rate IV}}{\text{rate}\_\_\_} = \_\_\_\_\_\_\_\_\_\_ = \left(\_\_\_\_\_\_\_\_\_\_\right)^n;\ n = \_\_\_\_\_\_\_\_\_\_$$

III. Determination of Rate Constant *k*

Mixture	I	II	III	IV	
k	________	________	________	________	________ average

IV. Prediction of Reaction Rate

Reaction mixture

Volume in ml 4 *M* acetone _____	Volume in ml 1 *M* HCl _____	Volume in ml 0.02 *M* Br_2 _____	Volume in ml H_2O _____

(acetone) ________*M* (H^+) ________*M* (Br_2) ________*M*

Predicted rate ____________

Predicted time for reaction ____________ sec

Observed time for reaction ____________ sec

V. Determination of Energy of Activation (Optional)

Reaction mixture used ____________ (same for all temperatures)

Time for reaction at about 10°C ____________ sec temperature ____________ °C

Time for reaction at about 40°C ____________ sec temperature ____________ °C

Time for reaction at room temp. ____________ sec temperature ____________ °C

Continued on following page

Calculate the rate constant at each temperature from your data, following the procedure in III.

	rate	k	$\log k$	$\frac{1}{T(°K)}$
~10°C	________	________	________	________
~40°C	________	________	________	________
room temp.	________	________	________	________

Plot $\log k$ vs. $1/T$. Find the slope of the best straight line through the points.

Slope = ____________

By Equation 2:

$$E_a = -(2.30)\,(1.99)\,(\text{slope})$$

E_a = ____________ cal

Name ______________________ Section __________

THE BROMINATION OF ACETONE
(Data and Calculations)

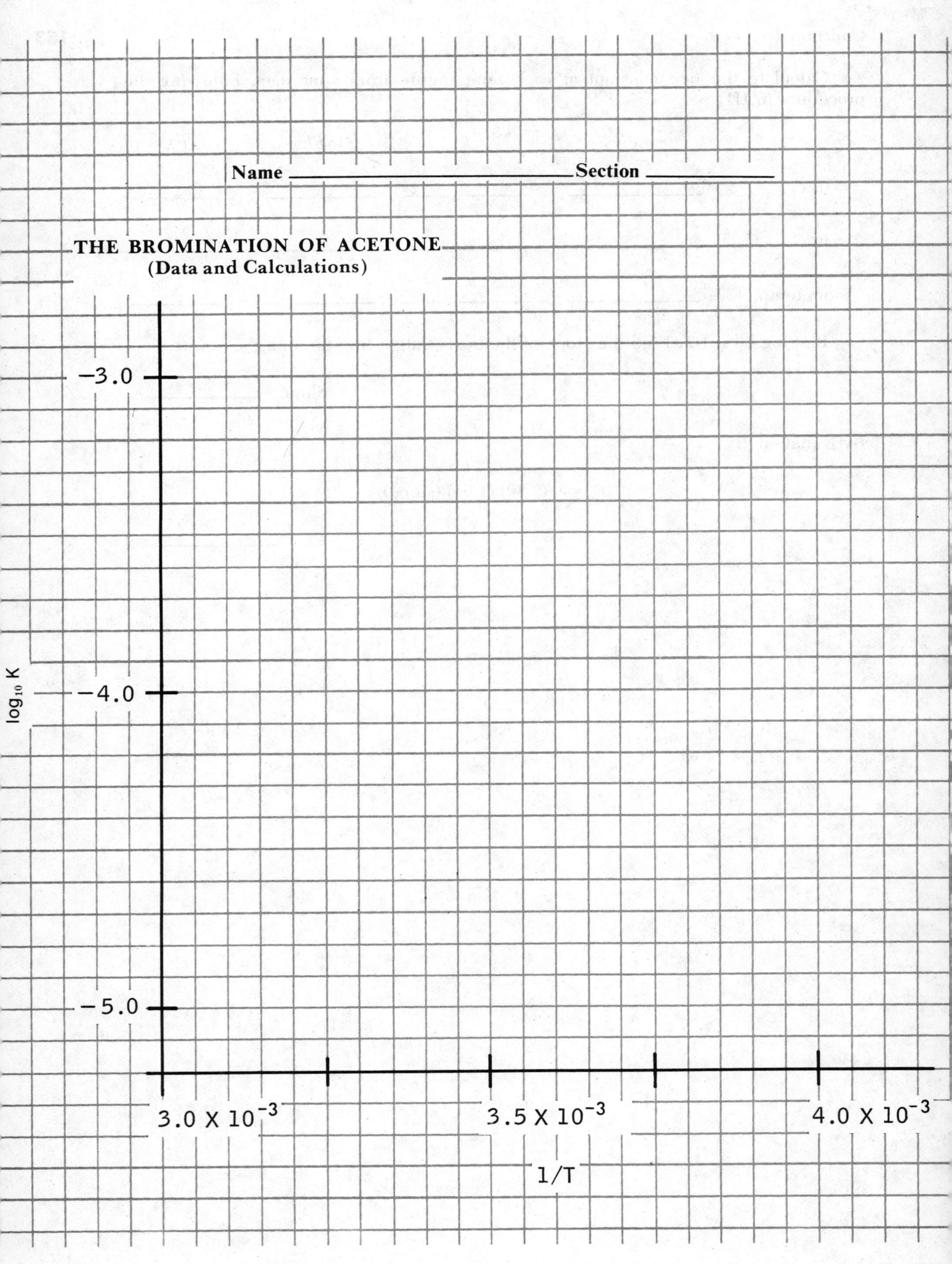

 Name ______________________ Section ______________

ADVANCE STUDY ASSIGNMENT: The Bromination of Acetone

1. In a reaction involving the bromination of acetone, the following initial concentrations were present in the reaction mixture:

$$(\text{acetone}) = 0.8\ M;\ (H^+) = 0.2\ M;\ (Br_2) = 0.004\ M$$

In the reaction at 25°C, it took 280 seconds before the Br_2 color had disappeared from the solution. If the reaction is zero order in Br_2, how long would it take before the color of Br_2 is discharged from a reaction mixture at 25°C exactly like the one above except that the concentration was initially 0.006 *M* in Br_2?

______________ sec

2. The following data were obtained at 27°C for the reaction:

$$aA + bB \longrightarrow cC$$

Reaction mixture	1	2	3	4
Initial (*A*) in moles/lit	0.100	0.200	0.200	0.300
Initial (*B*) in moles/lit	0.200	0.200	0.400	0.100
Initial rate in moles *A*/lit-sec × 10^3	0.50	1.00	4.00	0.38

What is the order of the reaction with respect to *A*? ______________

What is the order of the reaction with respect to *B*? ______________

3. (a) What volume of each of the solutions listed below would you use to prepare 50 ml of the reaction mixture referred to in Problem 1?

______________ ml 4 *M* acetone ______________ ml 1 *M* HCl

______________ ml 0.020 *M* Br_2 ______________ ml water

(b) How would you make up 50 ml of a mixture in which the concentrations of acetone, HCl, and Br_2 are 0.8 *M*, 0.4 *M*, and 0.004 *M* respectively?

______________ ml 4 *M* acetone ______________ ml 1 *M* HCl

______________ ml 0.020 *M* Br_2 ______________ ml water

EXPERIMENT 20

Rates of Chemical Reactions, II. A Clock Reaction

In the previous experiment we discussed the factors that influence the rate of a chemical reaction and presented the terminology used in quantitative relations in studies of the kinetics of chemical reactions. That material is also pertinent to this experiment and should be studied before you proceed further.

This experiment involves the study of the rate properties, or chemical kinetics, of the following reaction between iodide ion and peroxydisulfate ion:*

$$2I^-(aq) + S_2O_8^{2-}(aq) \rightarrow I_2(aq) + 2SO_4^{2-}(aq) \quad (1)$$

This reaction proceeds reasonably slowly at room temperature, its rate depending on the concentrations of the I^- and $S_2O_8^{2-}$ ions according to the rate law discussed in the previous experiment. For this reaction the rate law takes the form:

$$\text{rate} = k(I^-)^m\,(S_2O_8^{2-})^n \quad (2)$$

One of the main purposes of the experiment will be to evaluate the rate constant k and the reaction orders m and n for this reaction. We will also investigate the manner in which the reaction rate depends on temperature and will evaluate the activation energy E_a for the reaction. Finally we shall briefly examine the effect of a catalyst on the rate of the reaction.

Our method for measuring the rate of the reaction involves what is frequently called a "clock" reaction. In addition to Reaction 1, whose kinetics we will study, the following reaction will also be made to occur simultaneously in the reaction flask:

$$I_2(aq) + 2S_2O_3^{2-}(aq) \rightarrow 2I^-(aq) + S_4O_6^{2-}(aq) \quad (3)$$

As compared with (1) this reaction is essentially instantaneous. The I_2 produced in (1) reacts completely with the thiosulfate, $S_2O_3^{2-}$, ion present in the solution, so that until all the thiosulfate ion has reacted, the concentration of I_2 is effectively zero. As soon as the $S_2O_3^{2-}$ is gone from the system, the I_2 produced by (1) remains in the solution and its concentration begins to increase. The presence of I_2 is made strikingly apparent by a starch indicator which is added to the reaction mixture, since I_2 even in small concentrations reacts with starch solution to produce a deep blue color.

By carrying out Reaction 1 in the presence of $S_2O_3^{2-}$ ion and a starch indicator, we introduce a built-in "clock" into the the system. Our clock tells us when sufficient I_2 has been produced by Reaction 1 to use up all the $S_2O_3^{2-}$ ion originally added. Since, however, one mole of I_2 is produced for each mole of $S_2O_8^{2-}$ reacted, and each mole of I_2 reacts in (3) with two moles of $S_2O_3^{2-}$ ion, the color change also occurs at the time when a certain amount of $S_2O_8^{2-}$ ion has reacted, namely an amount in moles equal to one-half the number of moles $S_2O_3^{2-}$ initially present in the reaction flask. If we fix the amount of $S_2O_3^{2-}$ ion used at a value that is small compared to the amount of I^- and $S_2O_8^{2-}$ used, the color change will occur before any appreciable amounts of reactants are used up, and the concentrations of reactants and the rate in (2) will remain essentially constant during the time interval over which the rate is measured.

---

*Similar to Experiment 25 in Chemical Principles in the Laboratory, by H. W. Franz and L. E. Malm, Freeman, 1966.

The reaction between I^- and $S_2O_8^{2-}$ ions will be conducted under the conditions in the discussion above. Carefully measured amounts of I^- and $S_2O_8^{2-}$ ion in water solution will be mixed in the presence of a relatively small amount of $S_2O_3^{2-}$ ion and a starch indicator. The time it takes for the solution to turn blue will be measured for several different solutions in which the amounts and hence concentrations of I^- and $S_2O_8^{2-}$ ions are varied, but in which the amount of $S_2O_3^{2-}$ ion is held constant. Essentially, what we will measure in each case is the time required for the concentration of the $S_2O_8^{2-}$ ion to decrease by a constant predetermined amount. Since the rate of a reaction is equal to minus the change (small) in concentration of a reactant divided by the time required for the change to occur, the experimental data will furnish the information needed to find the rate of reaction in each solution. The calculation of the value of the rate constant k and the orders of the reaction with respect to I^- and $S_2O_8^{2-}$ follow from the dependence of reaction rate on reactant concentrations. The calculation of the activation energy E_a for the reaction is made from data obtained on the dependence of the reaction rate on temperature.

EXPERIMENTAL PROCEDURE

A. Dependence of Reaction Rate on Concentration

TABLE OF REACTION MIXTURES AT ROOM TEMPERATURE

Reaction	*Reaction Flask*	*50 ml Flask*
1	20.0 ml 0.200 M KI	20.0 ml 0.100 M $(NH_4)_2S_2O_8$
2	10.0 ml 0.200 M KI 10.0 ml 0.200 M KCl	20.0 ml 0.100 M $(NH_4)_2S_2O_8$
3	20.0 ml 0.200 M KI	10.0 ml 0.100 M $(NH_4)_2S_2O_8$ 10.0 ml 0.100 M $(NH_4)_2SO_4$
4	20.0 ml 0.200 M KI	5.0 ml 0.100 M $(NH_4)_2S_2O_8$ 15.0 ml 0.100 M $(NH_4)_2SO_4$
5	8.0 ml 0.200 M KI 12.0 ml 0.200 M KCl	20.0 ml 0.100 M $(NH_4)_2S_2O_8$
6	15.0 ml 0.200 M KI 5.0 ml 0.200 M KCl	15.0 ml 0.100 M $(NH_4)_2S_2O_8$ 5.0 ml 0.100 M $(NH_4)_2SO_4$

This table summarizes the volumes of reactants to be used in making up six different reaction mixtures. The actual procedure for carrying out each reaction will be much the same, and we will describe it now for Reaction 1.

Using a graduated cylinder, measure out 20.0 ml of 0.200 M KI into a 250 ml Erlenmeyer flask, which we will call the reaction flask and which will serve as a container for the reaction. Add 10.0 ml 0.005 M $Na_2S_2O_3$ to this flask along with 3 or 4 drops of starch solution. Rinse the graduated cylinder with distilled water, and let it drain for several seconds; then use it to measure out 20.0 ml 0.100 M $(NH_4)_2S_2O_8$ into a 50 ml Erlenmeyer flask.

Put a thermometer into the reaction flask. Have a watch with a second hand available, or use the second hand on the wall clock.

Pour the solution from the 50 ml flask into the reaction flask and swirl to mix the solutions thoroughly. Note the time at which the solutions were mixed. Continue swirling the solution; it should turn blue in less than a minute. Record the time at the instant the blue color appears. Also record the temperature of the solution to ±0.2°C.

Repeat the experiment with the other mixtures in the table. In each case use 10.0 ml 0.005 M $Na_2S_2O_3$ solution and a few drops of indicator in the reaction flask. The flasks should be rinsed with distilled water between experiments and drained before being used again. The graduated cylinder should be rinsed whenever you switch from one reagent to another. Use your wash bottle to rinse the cylinder, and let it drain thoroughly before measuring out the next solution. The solutions of KCl and $(NH_4)_2SO_4$ are used (rather than water) in diluting the reaction mixtures so that the ionic strength of the mixture, which has some effect on the reaction rate, can be kept substantially constant. The temperature should be maintained at the same value, within 0.2°C, for all the reactions. Repeat any experiments that for any reason do not appear to proceed properly.

B. Dependence of Reaction Rate on Temperature. In this part of the experiment the reaction will be carried out at several different temperatures, but with the same concentrations of all reactants. The Table indicates the reaction conditions.

TABLE OF REACTION MIXTURES AT DIFFERENT TEMPERATURES

Reaction	*Temperature*	*Reaction Mixture*
1	about 20°C	as in Reaction 1
7	about 40°C	as in Reaction 1
8	about 10°C	as in Reaction 1
9	about 0°C	as in Reaction 1

The rate of the reaction at about 20° C can be obtained from the data on Reaction 1.

Reaction 7 is carried out by first measuring out the same solutions in the same volumes as those used in Reaction 1: 20.0 ml of 0.200 *M* KI, 10.0 ml of 0.005 *M* $Na_2S_2O_3$, and a few drops of starch indicator into the reaction flask, and 20.0 ml of 0.100 *M* $(NH_4)_2S_2O_8$ into the smaller flask.

Instead of mixing the solutions at room temperature, put the two flasks in water at 40° C in one or more large beakers. Make sure that the water in the large beakers is all at about 40° C, and leave the flasks in the water for several minutes so that they will be at the proper temperature. Put the thermometer in the reaction flask, and when the temperature is about 40° C, mix the solutions together, noting the time of mixing. Swirl as before, keeping the reacting mixture in the warm water. Record the time at which the color change occurs and the temperature of the mixture at that point.

Repeat the experiment at about 10° C, cooling all reactants in a water bath to that temperature before starting the reaction. Record the time required for the reaction and the final temperature of the reaction mixture. Repeat once again at about 0° C, this time using an ice-water bath to cool the reactant solutions.

C. Dependence of Reaction Rate on the Presence of a Catalyst (Optional). Metallic cations have a pronounced catalytic effect on the rate of this reaction. Observe this effect by repeating Reaction 1 with a catalyst at room temperature. Before mixing the three solutions, add five drops of 0.1 *M* $CuSO_4$ to the flask containing the 0.1 *M* $(NH_4)_2S_2O_8$. Swirl the flask for a minute to mix the catalyst thoroughly. Then mix the solutions, and when the color change occurs record the time and temperature.

Name ______________________ Section ____________

DATA AND CALCULATIONS: Rates of Chemical Reactions, II. A Clock Reaction

A. Orders of the Reaction. Rate constant determination

$$\text{Reaction:}\quad 2I^-(aq) + S_2O_8^{2-}(aq) \rightarrow I_2(aq) + 2SO_4^{2-}(aq) \qquad (1)$$

$$\text{rate} = k(I^-)^m\,(S_2O_8^{2-})^n = \frac{-\Delta(S_2O_8^{2-})}{t} \qquad (4)$$

In all the reaction mixtures used in the experiment, the color change occurred when a constant predetermined number of moles of $S_2O_8^{2-}$ had been used up by the reaction. The color "clock" allows you to measure the *time required* for this *fixed number of moles of* $S_2O_8^{2-}$ *to react*. The rate of each reaction is determined by the time t required for the color to change; since in Equation 4 the change in concentration of $S_2O_8^{2-}$ ion, $\Delta(S_2O_8^{2-})$, is the same in each mixture, the relative rate of each reaction is inversely proportional to the time t. Since we are mainly concerned with relative rather than absolute rate, we will for convenience take all relative rates as being equal to $100/t$. Fill in the table below, calculating reactant concentrations and relative reaction rate for each mixture.

Reaction	Time t (sec) for Color to Change	Initial Concentrations in Reaction Flask I^-	$S_2O_8^{2-}$	Relative Rate of Reaction, $100/t$
1	________	________	________	________
2	________	________	________	________
3	________	________	________	________
4	________	________	________	________
5	________	________	________	________
6	________	________	________	________

Temperature of Reaction 1 ____________ °C

Consider the relative rates of Reactions 1 to 6. These rates differ because the concentrations of I^- and $S_2O_8^{2-}$ ions differ in the various reaction mixtures. We can relate the rates of each of these reactions to the concentrations by modifying Equation 2 to read

$$\text{Relative rate} = k'(I^-)^m\,(S_2O_8^{2-})^n \qquad (5)$$

where k' is a relative rate constant. The problem now is to find values for m, n, and k' such that the data in the above table are consistent with Equation 5.

The solution to this problem is not as difficult as it might first appear. Note that the concentrations of I^- and $S_2O_8^{2-}$ ions change in a simple manner, as one goes from one mixture to the next; one concentration remains constant while the other changes by a factor of 2 or a rational fraction. This means that Equation 5 for one reaction mixture can be related to Equation 5 for another in such a way as will permit easy evaluation of m and n.

Continued on following page

Write Equation 5 below for Reactions 1 and 2, substituting the known concentrations of I^- and $S_2O_8^{2-}$ ions:

Relative rate 1 = ______________ = $k'($ $)^m$ ($)^n$

Relative rate 2 = ______________ = $k'($ $)^m$ ($)^n$

Divide the first equation by the second:

=

If you have done this properly, you will have an equation involving only m as an unknown. Solve this equation for m, the order of the reaction with respect to I^- ion.

m = ______________ (ordinarily an integer)

Applying the same approach to Reactions 1 and 3, find the value of n, the order of the reaction with respect to $S_2O_8^{2-}$ ion.

Relative rate 1 = ______________ = $k'($ $)^m$ ($)^n$

Relative rate 3 = ______________ = $k'($ $)^m$ ($)^n$

Dividing one equation by the other:

=

n = ______________

Having found m and n, the relative rate constant, k', can be calculated by substitution of m, n, and the known rates and reactant concentrations into Equation 5. Evaluate k' for Reactions 1 to 5.

Reaction	1	2	3	4	5		
k'	________	________	________	________	________	k'_{ave}	________

Why should k' have nearly the same value for each of the above reactions?

Using k'_{ave}, predict the relative rate and time t for Reaction 6.

relative rate_{pred} ______________ t_{pred} ______________ t_{obs} ______________

Comment on the validity of the reaction rate law (5) and hence (2) for the mixtures studied.

Continued on following page

B. The Effect of Temperature on Reaction Rate: The Activation Energy. To find the activation energy for the reaction you will find it convenient to complete the table below.

The temperature dependence of the rate constant, k', for a reaction is given by Equation 2 in Experiment 19:

$$\log_{10} k' = \frac{-E_a}{2.3RT} + \text{constant} \qquad \textbf{(6)}$$

where the terms in the equation have the meanings given in the discussion in that experiment. To set up the terms in $1/T$, fill in (b), (e), and (f) in the table.

Since the reactions in mixtures 1, 7, 8, and 9 all involve the same reactant concentrations, the rate constants, k', for two different mixtures will have the same ratio as the reaction rates themselves for the two mixtures. This means that in the calculation of E_a, we can use the observed relative rates instead of rate constants. Proceeding as before, calculate the relative rates of reaction in each of the mixtures and enter these values in (c) below. Take the $\log_{10}$ rate for each mixture and enter these values in (d).

	Reaction			
	1	7	8	9
(a) Time t in seconds for color to appear	______	______	______	______
(b) Temperature of the reaction mixture in °C	______	______	______	______
(c) Relative rate = $100/t$	______	______	______	______
(d) Log_{10} of relative rate	______	______	______	______
(e) Temperature T in °K	______	______	______	______
(f) $1/T$, $°K^{-1}$	______	______	______	______

To evaluate E_a, make a graph of log (relative rate) vs. $1/T$ on the graph paper provided.

Find the slope of the line obtained by drawing the best straight line through the experimental points.

Slope = ______________

The slope of the line equals $-E_a/2.3R$, where $R = 1.98$ cal/mole°K if E_a is to be in calories per mole. Find the activation energy, E_a, for the reaction.

E_a = ____________ cal

Continued on following page

C. Effect of a Catalyst on Reaction Rate

	Reaction 1	Catalyzed Reaction 1
Time for color to appear (seconds)	______	______

Would you expect the activation energy, E_a, for the catalyzed reaction to be greater than, less than, or equal to the activation energy for the uncatalyzed reaction? Why?

Name ______________________ Section ____________

RATES OF CHEMICAL REACTIONS, II. A CLOCK REACTION
(Data and Calculations)

$\log_{10}$ relative rate

0.00300 0.00350 0.00400

1/T

 Name ____________________ Section ____________

ADVANCE STUDY ASSIGNMENT: Rate of Chemical Reactions, II. A Clock Reaction

1. In a clock reaction, 20 ml of 0.20 *M* KI, 20 ml of 0.10 *M* $(NH_4)_2S_2O_8$, and 10 ml of 0.005 *M* $Na_2S_2O_3$ were mixed in the presence of a starch indicator. The solution turned blue in 80 seconds.

   (a) What were the concentrations of I^-, $S_2O_8^{2-}$, and $S_2O_3^{2-}$ in the reaction mixture?

(I^-) = ____________ *M*;

$(S_2O_8^{2-})$ = ____________ *M*;

$(S_2O_3^{2-})$ = ____________ *M*

   (b) What fraction of the $S_2O_8^{2-}$ had reacted when the mixture turned blue?

____

2. If $(2.0/1.0)^m = 1.8$, what is the approximate value of *m*? The exact value? (Hint: take logarithms of both sides of the equation.)

____________ approx.; ____________ exact

3. In the reaction $A + B \rightarrow C$, it took 25 seconds for 1 per cent of B to react in a certain mixture of A and B. When the concentration of A in the mixture was decreased by a factor of 2, keeping the concentration of B constant, it took 95 seconds for 1 per cent of B to react at the same temperature. What is the order of the reaction with respect to A?

____

SECTION 10

Precipitation Reactions

EXPERIMENT 21

Determination of an Unknown Chloride

One of the important applications of precipitation reactions lies in the area of quantitative analysis. Many substances that can be precipitated from solution are so slightly soluble that the precipitation reaction by which they are formed can be considered to proceed to completion. Silver chloride is an example of such a substance.

$$AgCl(s) \rightleftharpoons Ag^+(aq) + Cl^-(aq) \qquad K_{sp} = [Ag^+][Cl^-] = 1.6 \times 10^{-10}$$

Although silver chloride is in chemical equilibrium with its ions in solution, the equilibrium constant K_{sp} for the reaction is so low that if AgCl is precipitated by the addition of a solution containing Ag^+ ion to one containing Cl^- ion, essentially all the Ag^+ added will precipitate as AgCl until essentially all the Cl^- is used up. When the amount of Ag^+ added to the solution is equal to the amount of Cl^- originally present, the precipitation of Cl^- ion will be, for all practical purposes, complete.

A convenient method for chloride analysis using AgCl has been devised. A solution of $AgNO_3$ is added to a chloride solution just to the point where the number of moles of Ag^+ added is equal to the number of moles of Cl^- initially present. We analyze for Cl^- by simply measuring how many moles of $AgNO_3$ are required. Surprisingly enough, this measurement is rather easily made by an experimental procedure called a *titration.*

In the titration a solution of $AgNO_3$ of known concentration (in moles $AgNO_3$ per liter of solution) is added from a calibrated buret to a solution containing a measured amount of unknown. The titration is stopped when a color change occurs in the solution, indicating that stoichiometrically equivalent amounts of Ag^+ and Cl^- are present. The color change is caused by a chemical reagent, called an indicator, which is added to the solution at the beginning of the titration.

The volume of $AgNO_3$ solution that has been added up to the time of the color change can be measured accurately with the buret, and the number of moles of Ag^+ added can be calculated from the known concentration of the solution.

In the Mohr method for the volumetric analysis of chloride, which we will employ in this experiment, the indicator used is K_2CrO_4. The chromate ion present in solutions of this substance will react with silver ion to form a red precipitate of Ag_2CrO_4. This precipitate will form as soon as $[Ag^+]^2 \times [CrO_4^{2-}]$ exceeds the solubility product of Ag_2CrO_4, which is about 1×10^{-12}. Under the conditions of the titration, the Ag^+ added to the solution reacts preferentially with Cl^- until that ion is essentially quantitatively removed from the system, at which point Ag_2CrO_4 begins to precipitate and the solution color changes from yellow to buff. The end point of the titration is that point at which the color change is first observed.

In this experiment, weighed samples containing an unknown percentage of chloride will be titrated with a standardized solution of $AgNO_3$, and the volumes of $AgNO_3$ solution required to reach the end point of each titration will be measured. Given the molarity of the $AgNO_3$, we can easily calculate the number of moles of Ag^+ used:

$$\text{no. of moles } Ag^+ = \text{no. of moles } AgNO_3 = M_{AgNO_3} \times V_{AgNO_3}$$

where the volume of $AgNO_3$ is expressed in liters and the molarity M_{AgNO_3} is in moles per liter of solution. At the end point of the titration,

$$\text{no. of moles } Ag^+ \text{ added} = \text{no. of moles } Cl^- \text{ present in unknown}$$

$$\text{no. of grams } Cl^- \text{ present} = \text{no. of moles } Cl^- \text{ present} \times GAW \text{ Cl}$$

$$\% \text{ Cl} = \frac{\text{no. of grams } Cl^-}{\text{no. of grams unknown}} \times 100$$

EXPERIMENTAL PROCEDURE

Obtain from the stockroom a buret and a vial containing a sample of an unknown solid chloride. Weigh out accurately on the analytical balance three samples of the chloride, each sample weighing about 0.2 grams. This weighing is best done by accurately weighing the vial and its contents and pouring out the sample a little at a time into a 250 ml Erlenmeyer flask until the vial has lost about 0.2 g of chloride sample. Again weigh the sample vial accurately to obtain the exact amount of chloride sample poured into the flask. Put two other samples of similar weight into clean, dry, small beakers, weighing the vial accurately after the size of each sample has been decided upon.

Add 50 ml of distilled water to the flask to dissolve the sample and add 3 drops of some 1 *M* K_2CrO_4 indicator solution. Using the graduated cylinder at the reagent shelf, measure out about 100 ml of the standardized $AgNO_3$ solution into a clean *dry* 125 ml Erlenmeyer flask. This will be your total supply for the entire experiment so do not waste it. Clean your buret thoroughly with soap solution and rinse it with distilled water. Pour three successive 2 or 3 ml portions of the $AgNO_3$ solution into the buret and tip it back and forth to rinse the inside walls. Allow the $AgNO_3$ solution to drain out the buret tip completely each time. Fill the buret with the $AgNO_3$ solution. Open the buret stopcock momentarily to flush any air bubbles out of the tip of the buret. Be sure your stopcock fits snugly and that the buret does not leak.

Read the initial buret level to 0.02 ml. Your may find it useful when making readings to put a white card marked with a thick, black stripe behind the meniscus. If the black line is held just below the level to be read, its reflection in the surface of the meniscus will help you obtain a very accurate reading. Begin to add the $AgNO_3$ solution to the chloride solution in the Erlenmeyer flask. A white precipitate of AgCl will form immediately, and the amount will increase during the course of the titration. At the beginning of the titration, you can add the $AgNO_3$ fairly rapidly, a few ml at a time, swirling the flask as best you can to mix the solution. You will find that at the point where the $AgNO_3$ hits the solution, there will be a red spot of Ag_2CrO_4, which disappears when you stop adding nitrate and swirl the flask. As you proceed with the titration, the red spot will persist more and more, since the amount of excess chloride ion, which reacts with the Ag_2CrO_4 to form AgCl, will slowly decrease. Gradually decrease the rate at which you add $AgNO_3$ as the red color becomes stronger. At some stage you may find it convenient to set your buret stopcock to deliver $AgNO_3$ slowly, drop by drop, while you swirl the flask. When you are near the end point, add the $AgNO_3$ drop by drop, swirling between drops. The end point of the titration is that point where the mixture first takes on a permanent reddish-yellow or buff color which does not revert to pure yellow on swirling. If you are careful, you can hit the end point within one drop of $AgNO_3$. When you have reached the end point, stop the titration and record the buret level.

Rinse out the 250 ml Erlenmeyer flask in which you carried out the titration. Take your second sample and carefully pour it from the beaker into the Erlenmeyer flask. Wash out the beaker a few times with distilled water from your wash bottle and pour the washings into the sample flask. *All the sample* must be transferred if the analysis is to be accurate. Add water to the sample flask to a volume of about 50 ml and swirl to dissolve the solid. Refill your buret, take a volume reading, add the indicator, and proceed to titrate to an end point as before. This titration should be more accurate than the first, since the volume of $AgNO_3$ used is proportional to the sample size and can therefore be estimated rather well on the basis of the relative weights of the two samples.

Titrate the third sample as you did the second.

Name ________________ Section ________________

DATA: Determination of an Unknown Chloride

Unknown sample no. ________

Molarity of standard $AgNO_3$ solution ________

	I	II	III
Weight of vial and chloride unknown	______ g	______ g	______ g
Weight of vial less sample	______ g	______ g	______ g
Initial buret reading	______ ml	______ ml	______ ml
Final buret reading	______ ml	______ ml	______ ml

Calculations and Results

Weight of sample	______ g	______ g	______ g
Volume of $AgNO_3$ used to titrate sample	______ ml	______ ml	______ ml
No. of moles of $AgNO_3$ used to titrate sample	______	______	______
No. of moles of Cl^- present in sample	______	______	______
Weight of Cl^- present in sample	______ g	______ g	______ g
% Cl^- in sample	______ %	______ %	______ %
Mean value of % Cl^- in unknown	______ %		

 Name ____________________ Section ____________

ADVANCE STUDY ASSIGNMENT: Determination of an Unknown Chloride

1. A sample containing 0.150 g Cl^- is dissolved in 75 ml of water. What is the concentration of Cl^- in moles/liter in the solution?

______________ M

2. The solution in Problem 1 is titrated with $AgNO_3$ to an end point. If at that point $[Ag^+]$ equals $[Cl^-]$, as it should, find $[Cl^-]$ in the solution. If the final volume of the solution is 100 ml, how many grams of Cl^- are present in solution? What per cent of the Cl^- originally present remains unprecipitated? $K_{sp}AgCl = 1.6 \times 10^{-10}$

______________ M, ______________ g, ______________ %

3. In the Mohr titration, the first formation of red Ag_2CrO_4 is taken to indicate the end point. In the solution being titrated, $[CrO_4^{2-}]$ is about 0.01 M. What is the $[Ag^+]$ when Ag_2CrO_4 first begins to precipitate? This concentration of Ag^+ is also in equilibrium with AgCl(s), which is present in the system. What is $[Cl^-]$ in the solution when Ag_2CrO_4 first starts to appear? If the solution was initially 0.05 M in Cl^-, what fraction of Cl^- remains in solution at the Mohr end point? $K_{sp}Ag_2CrO_4 = 1 \times 10^{-12}$

$[Ag^+] =$ ______________ M, $[Cl^-] =$ ______________ M

______________ % in solution

4. A solid chloride sample weighing 0.217 g required 42.63 ml of 0.113 M $AgNO_3$ to reach the Ag_2CrO_4 end point. What is the per cent chloride in the sample?

______________ %

EXPERIMENT 22

Determination of the Solubility Product of PbI_2

In this experiment you will determine the solubility product of lead iodide, PbI_2. Lead iodide is relatively insoluble, having a solubility of less than 0.002 moles per liter at 20°C. The equation for the solution reaction of PbI_2 is

$$PbI_2(s) \rightleftarrows Pb^{2+}(aq) + 2\,I^-(aq) \quad (1)$$

The solubility product expression associated with this reaction is

$$K_{sp} = [Pb^{2+}]\,[I^-]^2 \quad (2)$$

Equation 2 implies that in any system containing solid PbI_2 in equilibrium with its ions, the product of $[Pb^{2+}]$ times $[I^-]^2$ will at a given temperature have a fixed magnitude, independent of how the equilibrium system was initially made up.

In the first part of the experiment, known volumes of standard solutions of $Pb(NO_3)_2$ and KI will be mixed in several different proportions. The yellow precipitate of PbI_2 formed will be allowed to come to equilibrium with the solution. The value of $[I^-]$ in the solution will be measured experimentally. The $[Pb^{2+}]$ will be calculated from the initial composition of the system, the measured value of $[I^-]$, and the stoichiometric relation between Pb^{2+} and I^- in Equation 1.

In the second part of the experiment, a precipitate of PbI_2 will be prepared, washed clean of excess ions, and then dissolved in an inert salt solution. The $[I^-]$ in the saturated solution will be measured and the value of $[Pb^{2+}]$ found from the relation in Equation 1.

The concentration of I^- ion will be found spectrophotometrically, as in Experiment 18. Although the iodide ion is not colored, it is relatively easily oxidized to I_2, which is brown in water solution. Our procedure will be to separate the solid PbI_2 from the solution and then to oxidize the I^- in solution with potassium nitrite, KNO_2, under slightly acidic conditions, where the conversion to I_2 is quantitative. Although the concentration of I_2 will be rather low in the solutions you will prepare, the absorption of light by I_2 in the vicinity of 525 mμ is sufficiently intense to make accurate analyses possible.

In all of the solutions prepared, potassium nitrate KNO_3 (note this distinction between KNO_2 and KNO_3!) will be present as an inert salt. This salt serves to keep the ionic strength of the solution essentially constant at 0.2 *M*, which helps to maintain constant the observed values of K_{sp}.

EXPERIMENTAL PROCEDURE

Label five test tubes 1 to 5. Pipette 5.0 ml of 0.012 *M* $Pb(NO_3)_2$ in 0.20 *M* KNO_3 into each of the first four test tubes. Add 2.0 ml of 0.03 *M* KI in 0.20 *M* KNO_3 to test tube 1. Add 3.0, 4.0, and 5.0 ml of this solution to test tubes 2, 3, and 4, respectively. Add enough 0.20 *M* KNO_3 to the first three test tubes to make the total volume 10.0

ml. Stopper each test tube and shake *thoroughly* at intervals of several minutes while you are proceeding with the next part of the experiment.

In a fifth test tube mix about 10 ml of 0.012 *M* $Pb(NO_3)_2$ in KNO_3 with 10 ml of 0.03 *M* KI in KNO_3. Shake the mixture vigorously for a minute or so. Let the solid settle for a few minutes and then decant and discard three-fourths of the supernatant solution. Transfer the solid PbI_2 and the rest of the solution to a small test tube and centrifuge. Discard the liquid, retaining the solid precipitate. Add 3 ml 0.20 *M* KNO_3 and shake to wash the solid free of excess Pb^{2+} or I^-. Centrifuge again, and discard the liquid. By this procedure you should now have prepared a small sample of essentially pure PbI_2 in a little KNO_3 solution. Add 0.20 *M* KNO_3 to the solid until the tube is about three-fourths full. Shake well at several one minute intervals to saturate the solution with PbI_2.

In this experiment it is essential that the volumes of reagents used to make up the mixtures in test tubes 1 to 4 be measured accurately. It is also essential that all five mixtures be shaken thoroughly so that equilibrium can be established. Insufficient shaking of the first four test tubes will result in not enough PbI_2 precipitating to reach true equilibrium; if the small test tube is not shaken sufficiently, not enough PbI_2 will dissolve to attain equilibrium.

When each of the mixtures has been shaken for at least 15 minutes, let the tubes stand for three to four minutes to let the solid settle. Pour the supernatant liquid in test tube 1 into a small dry test tube and centrifuge for about three minutes to settle the solid PbI_2. Pour the liquid into another small dry test tube; if there are any solid particles or yellow color remaining in the liquid, centrifuge again. When you have a clear liquid, dip a small piece of clean, dry paper towel into the liquid to remove floating PbI_2 particles from the surface. Pipette 3.0 ml of 0.02 *M* KNO_2 into a clean, dry spectrophotometer tube and add 2 drops 6 *M* HCl. Then add enough of the clear centrifuged solution (about 3 ml) to fill the spectrophotometer tube just to the level indicated by your instructor. Shake gently to mix the reagents and then measure the absorbance of the solution as directed by your instructor. The calibration curve which is provided will allow you to determine directly the concentration of I^- ion that was in equilibrium with PbI_2. Use the same procedure to analyze the solutions in test tubes 2 through 5, completing each analysis before you proceed to the next.

Name ______________________ Section ______________

DATA AND CALCULATIONS: Determination of the Solubility Product of PbI_2

From the experimental data we obtain $[I^-]$ directly. To obtain K_{sp} for PbI_2 we must calculate $[Pb^{2+}]$ in each equilibrium system. This is most easily done by constructing an equilibrium table. We first find the initial amounts of I^- and Pb^{2+} ions in each system from the way the mixtures were made up. Knowing $[I^-]$ and the formula of lead iodide allows us to calculate $[Pb^{2+}]$. K_{sp} then follows directly. The calculations are similar to those in Experiment 18.

$$PbI_2(s) \rightleftharpoons Pb^{2+}(aq) + 2\,I^-(aq) \qquad K_{sp} = [Pb^{2+}][I^-]^2$$

DATA

Test tube no.	1	2	3	4	Saturated solution of PbI_2
ml 0.012 *M* $Pb(NO_3)_2$	______	______	______	______	
ml 0.03 *M* KI	______	______	______	______	
ml 0.20 *M* KNO_3	______	______	______	______	
Total volume in ml	______	______	______	______	
Absorbance of solution	______	______	______	______	______
$[I^-]$ in moles/lit at equilibrium	______	______	______	______	______

CALCULATIONS

Initial no. moles Pb^{2+}	____ $\times 10^{-5}$	____ $\times 10^{-5}$	____ $\times 10^{-5}$	____ $\times 10^{-5}$	
Initial no. moles I^-	____ $\times 10^{-5}$	____ $\times 10^{-5}$	____ $\times 10^{-5}$	____ $\times 10^{-5}$	
No. moles I^- at equilibrium	____ $\times 10^{-5}$	____ $\times 10^{-5}$	____ $\times 10^{-5}$	____ $\times 10^{-5}$	
No. moles I^- precipitated	____ $\times 10^{-5}$	____ $\times 10^{-5}$	____ $\times 10^{-5}$	____ $\times 10^{-5}$	
No. moles Pb^{2+} precipitated	____ $\times 10^{-5}$	____ $\times 10^{-5}$	____ $\times 10^{-5}$	____ $\times 10^{-5}$	
No. moles Pb^{2+} at equilibrium	____ $\times 10^{-5}$	____ $\times 10^{-5}$	____ $\times 10^{-5}$	____ $\times 10^{-5}$	
$[Pb^{2+}]$ at equilibrium	______	______	______	______	______
K_{sp} PbI_2	______	______	______	______	______

 Name ____________________ Section ____________

ADVANCE STUDY ASSIGNMENT: Determination of the Solubility Product of PbI_2

1. State in words the meaning of the solubility product equation for PbI_2:

$$K_{sp} = [Pb^{2+}]\,[I^-]^2$$

2. When 12.0 ml of 0.012 *M* $Pb(NO_3)_2$ are mixed with 8.0 ml of 0.030 *M* KI, a yellow precipitate of $PbI_2(s)$ forms.

(a) How many moles of Pb^{2+} are originally present?

____________ moles

(b) How many moles of I^- are originally present?

____________ moles

(c) In a colorimeter the equilibrium solution is analyzed for I^-, and its concentration is found to be 5×10^{-3} moles/liter. How many moles of I^- are present in the solution (20 ml)?

____________ moles

(d) How many moles of I^- precipitated?

____________ moles

(e) How many moles of Pb^{2+} precipitated?

____________ moles

(f) How many moles of Pb^{2+} are left in solution?

____________ moles

(g) What is the concentration of Pb^{2+} at equilibrium?

____________ *M*

(h) Find a value for K_{sp} of PbI_2 from these data.

____

SECTION 11

Acids and Bases

EXPERIMENT 23

pH, Its Measurement and Applications

One of the more important properties of an aqueous solution is its concentration of hydrogen ion. The H^+ or H_3O^+ ion has great effect on the solubility of many inorganic and organic species, on the nature of complex metallic cations found in solutions, and on the rates of many chemical reactions. It is important that we know how to measure the concentration of hydrogen ion and understand its effect on solution properties.

For convenience the concentration of H^+ ion is frequently expressed as the pH of the solution rather than as molarity or normality. The pH of a solution is defined by the following equation:

$$pH = -\log [H^+] \quad (1)^*$$

where the logarithm is taken to the base 10. If $[H^+]$ is 1×10^{-4} moles per liter, the pH of the solution is, by the equation, 4. If the $[H^+]$ is 5×10^{-2} M, the pH is 1.3.

Basic solutions can also be described in terms of pH. In water solutions the following equilibrium relation will always be obeyed:

$$[H^+] \times [OH^-] = K_w = 1 \times 10^{-14} \quad \text{at } 25°C \quad (2)$$

Since $[H^+]$ equals $[OH^-]$ in distilled water, by Equation 2, $[H^+]$ must be 1×10^{-7} M. Therefore, the pH of distilled water is 7. Solutions in which $[H^+] > [OH^-]$ are said to be acidic and will have a $pH<7$; if $[H^+] < [OH^-]$, the solution is basic and its $pH>7$. A solution with a pH of 10 will have a $[H^+]$ of 1×10^{-10} M and a $[OH^-]$ of 1×10^{-4} M.

We measure the pH of a solution experimentally in two ways. In the first of these we use a chemical called an indicator, which is sensitive to pH. These substances have colors that change over a relatively short pH range (about 2 pH units) and can, when properly chosen, be used to roughly determine the pH of a solution. Two very common indicators are litmus, usually used on paper, and phenolphthalein, the most common indicator in acid-base titrations. Litmus changes from red to blue as the pH of a solution goes from about 6 to about 8. Phenolphthalein changes from colorless to red as the pH goes from 8 to 10. A given indicator is useful for determining pH only in the region in which it changes color. Indicators are available for measurement of pH in all the important ranges of acidity and basicity. Universal indicators, which contain a mixture of several indicators and show color changes over a wide pH range, are also in common use.

The other method for finding pH involves the use of an instrument called a pH meter. With this device the pH is determined from a measurement of the potential which develops between two particular electrodes when they are in the solution being investigated. This potential varies with pH and is used to activate a meter, which is calibrated so as to read pH directly. A pH meter can furnish much more precise measurement of pH than is possible with indicators, and is almost always used when accurate knowledge or control of pH is necessary.

Most substances when dissolved in water will form solutions in which the pH is not 7. If the pH of the solution is less than 7, the dissolved substance behaves as an acid, while if the pH is greater than 7, it is a base. Some acids, like HCl and HNO_3, ionize completely in solution; in a 1 M HCl solution, $[H^+]$ is one mole per liter, and there are

*See Experiment 18 for a discussion of the approximation made in this equation and the other equations based on equilibrium theory that appear in this experiment.

essentially no HCl molecules in the system. A substance which behaves in this way is called a *strong* acid. Similarly, there are some bases, like NaOH, which ionize completely in solution; in 0.5 *M* NaOH, $[OH^-]$ is 0.5 *M*, and there are practically no NaOH molecules present. NaOH is one of the few examples of a *strong* base.

Many substances in addition to the strong acids will produce acidic solutions. These substances are called *weak* acids because they do not dissociate completely in solution. We can write the general formula of a weak acid as HA; in water this acid will ionize to some extent according to the equation:

$$HA(aq) \rightleftarrows H^+(aq) + A^-(aq) \tag{3}$$

The species in solution will obey the law of chemical equilibrium, so that

$$\frac{[H^+][A^-]}{[HA]} = K_a \tag{4}$$

The condition imposed by Equation 4 will be obeyed in any solution in which some HA molecules are present. K_a, the equilibrium constant for the reaction, is called the *dissociation constant* of HA, and will have a constant value at any given temperature.

The species HA may be an organic acid, like acetic acid, $HC_2H_3O_2$; a hydrated metallic cation, such as $Cu(H_2O)_4^{2+}$; ammonium ion, NH_4^+; or an inorganic molecule or anion, like H_2CO_3 or HSO_4^-. The reactions analogous to Equation 3 for these species are

$$HC_2H_3O_2(aq) \rightleftarrows H^+(aq) + C_2H_3O_2^-(aq) \tag{5}$$

$$Cu(H_2O)_4^{2+}(aq) \rightleftarrows H^+(aq) + Cu(H_2O)_3OH^+(aq) \tag{6}$$

$$NH_4^+(aq) \rightleftarrows H^+(aq) + NH_3(aq) \tag{7}$$

$$H_2CO_3(aq) \rightleftarrows H^+(aq) + HCO_3^-(aq) \tag{8}$$

$$HSO_4^-(aq) \rightleftarrows H^+(aq) + SO_4^{2-}(aq) \tag{9}$$

Clearly there are many substances, including many salts, in addition to those species which are called acids, which form acidic solutions. The extent of the dissociation reaction is usually small, with perhaps 1 per cent of the acid-forming species undergoing reactions. In 0.1 *M* $HC_2H_3O_2$, $[H^+]$ equals about 0.001 *M*, $[C_2H_3O_2^-]$ is also 0.001 *M*, $[HC_2H_3O_2]$ is just about 0.1 *M*, and the pH of the solution is 3. In solutions of $HC_2H_3O_2$, in contrast to those of HCl, there are many undissociated acid molecules.

There are also many substances in addition to NaOH which form basic solutions. These materials are all related in a simple way to the weak acids. Consider the properties of the A^- ion from the weak acid HA, say as they would be observed in a solution of the salt NaA. Since HA is a weak acid, A^- ions in solution will tend to combine with any H^+ ions present to form HA molecules. In a solution of NaA, the A^- ions will tend to extract protons from the solvent water molecules, according to the equation:

$$A^-(aq) + H_2O \rightleftarrows OH^-(aq) + HA(aq) \tag{10}$$

In the solution Reaction 10 usually will not go very far, since *K* is typically very small, but even if it proceeds to a small extent, excess OH^- ions will be produced and the solution will be *basic*. Because of Reaction 10, the A^- ion is a *weak* base. As a general rule, we can say that *the sodium salts of weak acids behave as weak bases.*

There is only one common weak base that is molecular, and that is ammonia, NH_3. (You can see that NH_3, in Equation 7, plays the same role as $C_2H_3O_2^-$ in Equation 5; both of these species are analogous to the A^- ion and both will behave as weak bases.) The reaction similar to 10 in which NH_3 participates is

$$NH_3(aq) + H_2O \rightleftarrows NH_4^+(aq) + OH^-(aq) \tag{11}$$

Ammonia is the weak base most commonly encountered in the laboratory. In 0.1 *M* NH_3 about 1 per cent of the NH_3 reacts according to Equation 11; therefore, in that solution,

$[OH^-]$ is about 0.001 M, $[NH_4^+]$ is also 0.001 M, and $[NH_3]$ is just about 0.1 M.

The dissociation constant K_a of an acid is one of its characteristic properties. In this experiment we will determine the value of K_a for acetic acid by measuring the pH of some solutions of known acetic acid molarity. From the pH we can find $[H^+]$. By Equation 5 we can find $[C_2H_3O_2^-]$. Since acetic acid is only slightly dissociated, $[HC_2H_3O_2]$ is very nearly equal to the original acid molarity. K_a for the acid is obtained on substitution of these values into Equation 4.

Another very simple way to find K_a for a weak acid will also be employed in this experiment. Consider again Equation 4. The acid HA will obey the condition imposed by that equation in all solutions in which HA is present. Suppose that by some means we prepare a solution in which $[A^-]$ equals [HA]; in such a solution $[A^-]/[HA]$ will equal one, and K_a for the acid, by Equation 4, will equal $[H^+]$.

It turns out that it is very easy to prepare a solution which meets the condition we have just described. Given a solution of the acid HA, we divide it into two parts of equal volume, so that each part contains the same number of moles of HA. We then titrate one of the parts with an NaOH solution, causing essentially all of the HA molecules to react according to the equation:

$$HA(aq) + OH^-(aq) \rightleftarrows A^-(aq) + H_2O \qquad K \text{ is large} \qquad (12)$$

Since K is very large for the reaction, we generate by the titration a number of moles of A^- ion equal to the number of moles of HA in the other portion of acid. We mix the two portions, and can be sure that in the resulting solution [HA] equals $[A^-]$ (as long as the HA is essentially undissociated in the solution, which will be the case for nearly all weak acids). Measurement of the pH of the resulting solution will furnish $[H^+]$ and, hence, the value of K_a. This approach has the distinct advantage that you don't have to know the original molarity of the acid. We will use this method to find K_a for an unknown acid.

The solution used to find K_a by the method just described has the property that it resists changes in pH relatively well. If a small amount of 1 M HCl were added to that solution, the added H^+ ion would react with the A^- present to form HA, keeping $[H^+]$ just about where it was before the acid was added. Similarly, addition of a little 1 M NaOH would cause Reaction 12 to occur, removing the added OH^- ion and leaving a solution whose pH is almost unchanged.

Solutions which resist changes in pH are called *buffers*, and, like the solution we have just discussed, typically contain both a weak acid HA and its anion A^-. The pH of a buffer solution is fixed by establishing the ratio $[A^-]/[HA]$ in the solution. If this ratio is one, as in the solution we use to find K_a for an unknown acid, $[H^+]$ is, by Equation 4, simply equal to K_a. By changing the ratio to other values, which can be easily accomplished, we can fix $[H^+]$, and so the pH, of the buffer at some preselected value. Since the ratio can't be much greater than about 10 or much less than 0.1, the range of concentration of H^+ is not very large for any given buffer, but in the useful range $[H^+]$ can be fixed quite accurately. In the last part of this experiment you will be asked to prepare a buffer having a pH selected by your instructor.

EXPERIMENTAL PROCEDURE

You may work in pairs on the first two parts of this experiment.

A. Measurement of the pH of Some Typical Acidic and Basic Solutions

Using the stock solution of 1.0 M HCl, prepare by appropriate dilutions with distilled water about 25 ml of each of two solutions, 0.1 M and 0.01 M. Using a 150 ml beaker as a container for the solutions, measure and record the pH of the 1.0 M, the 0.1 M, and the 0.01 M HCl with the pH meter. To each of the solutions add two drops of methyl violet indicator and record the indicator color.

Repeat these measurements with acetic acid, starting with the 1.0 M $HC_2H_3O_2$ solution. After measuring a pH, pour a few ml of the acid into a test tube and test the solution with a drop of methyl violet indicator. Test another portion of that solution in another test tube, using methyl yellow indicator.

Carry out the same measurements on ammonia, using 1.0 M NH_3 as your stock solution. As the indicator for these solutions, use alizarin yellow

B. Measurement of the pH of Some Typical Salt Solutions

Using the pH meter and 25 ml samples, determine and record the pH of the following stock solutions: 0.1 *M* NaCl, 0.1 *M* $NaC_2H_3O_2$, 0.1 *M* Na_2CO_3, 0.1 *M* NH_4NO_3, 0.1 *M* $ZnCl_2$, 0.1 *M* $Cu(NO_3)_2$.

C. Determination of the Dissociation Constant of a Weak Acid

In the rest of the experiment each student is to work independently.

Obtain from the stockroom a sample of an unknown acid and a buret. Measure out 100 ml of distilled water in a graduated cylinder and pour it into a clean 250 ml Erlenmeyer flask. Dissolve about half your acid sample in the water and stir thoroughly.

Pour half the solution into another 250 ml Erlenmeyer flask. Use the solution levels in the two flasks to decide when the volumes of solution in the two flasks are equal. Titrate the acid in one of the flasks to a phenolphthalein end point, using 0.2 *M* NaOH in the buret. (See Exp. 24; volume readings do not have to be taken here.) This should take less than 50 ml of the NaOH. Add the hydroxide solution slowly while rotating the flask. As the end point approaches, add the solution drop by drop until the solution has a permanent pink color.

Mix the neutralized solution with the acid solution in the other flask and determine the pH of the resulting half-neutralized solution. From the observed pH calculate K_a for the unknown acid.

D. The Preparation and Properties of a Buffer (optional)

Report the values of pH and K_a you obtained in C to your laboratory supervisor, who will then assign you the pH of a buffer to prepare from the rest of your solid acid.

Dissolve the remaining portion of your acid sample in 100 ml water, divide the solution into two equal parts, and titrate one portion with 0.2 *M* NaOH in a 250 ml flask as in C. Record the volume of NaOH solution required.

You now have a solution of the acid in one flask and a solution of its sodium salt in the other. To make the concentration of acid equal to the concentration of salt, add to the acid solution a volume of water equal to that of the 0.2 *M* NaOH solution used to titrate the acid portion.

Calculate on the report sheet the ratio of anion concentration to undissociated acid concentration required in the buffer. Since the anion and undissociated acid concentrations are equal in the two solutions you have prepared, in the buffer to be made by mixing these solutions,

$$\frac{\text{volume salt solution needed}}{\text{volume acid solution needed}} = \frac{[A^-]}{[HA]}$$

Using this ratio of volumes, make up at least 50 ml of your buffer and measure its pH. Compare the observed pH with the value you wished to obtain.

To 25 ml of your buffer solution add 5 drops 0.1 *M* NaOH and stir thoroughly. Measure the pH of the resulting solution.

To another 25 ml sample of your buffer add 5 drops 0.1 *M* HCl, mix thoroughly, and measure the pH of the mixed solution.

Measure the pH of the distilled water in the laboratory. To one 25 ml sample of water add 5 drops 0.1 *M* NaOH and to another add 5 drops 0.1 *M* HCl. After mixing, measure the pH of the two solutions.

Name ______________________ Section ______________

OBSERVATIONS, CALCULATIONS, AND EXPLANATIONS: pH, Its Measurement and Applications

A. Measurement of the pH of Some Typical Acidic and Basic Solutions

Record the pH of the solutions and the indicator colors.

		1.0 *M*	0.1 *M*	0.01 *M*
HCl	pH	________	________	________
	color—methyl violet	________	________	________
$HC_2H_3O_2$	pH	________	________	________
	color—methyl violet	________	________	________
	color—methyl yellow	________	________	________
NH_3	pH	________	________	________
	color—alizarin yellow	________	________	________

1. What is the per cent ionization of each of the $HC_2H_3O_2$ solutions? How does the per cent ionization of the acid vary with its concentration? Hint: First find $[H^+]$ in each solution; then compare it with $[H^+]$ if the acid completely dissociated.

2. Which indicator would you suggest would be useful in determining the pH of a 5.0×10^{-4} *M* HCl solution? Why?

3. From the pH measurements you obtained, calculate K_a for acetic acid. (Obtain a value for K_a for each solution, using (4) and the method outlined in the discussion.)

B. Measurement of the pH of Some Typical Salt Solutions

Record the pH of the solutions studied.

0.1 *M* NaCl ____________ 0.1 *M* NH_4NO_3 ____________

Continued on following page

0.1 *M* $NaC_2H_3O_2$ ____________ 0.1 *M* $ZnCl_2$ ____________

0.1 *M* Na_2CO_3 ____________ 0.1 *M* $Cu(NO_3)_2$ ____________

Explain the observation of any pH in these solutions that is not within 1 pH unit of 7 by writing the net ionic equation for the reaction responsible for the pH change:

C. Determination of the Dissociation Constant of a Weak Acid

pH of half-neutralized acid solution ____________

$[H^+]$ in half-neutralized solution ____________ *M*

K_a for unknown acid ____________ Unknown no. ____________

D. Preparation and Properties of a Buffer

pH of buffer to be prepared ____________

$[H^+]$ in buffer ____________ *M*

$\frac{[A^-]}{[HA]}$ in buffer solution $= \frac{\text{Volume salt solution}}{\text{Volume acid solution}}$ in buffer ____________

Buffer was made by mixing ____________ ml salt solution with ____________ ml acid solution.

pH of prepared buffer ____________

Properties of prepared buffer:

pH of buffer ____________ pH of H_2O ____________

pH of buffer + 5 drops 0.1 *M* NaOH ____________ pH of H_2O + 5 drops 0.1 *M* NaOH ____________

pH of buffer + 5 drops 0.1 *M* HCl ____________ pH of H_2O + 5 drops 0.1 *M* HCl ____________

Conclusions:

 Name ______________ Section ______________

ADVANCE STUDY ASSIGNMENT: pH, Its Measurement and Applications

1. The pH of a solution was found to be 4.0. Find $[H^+]$ in the solution.

______________ M

2. A solution of NaCN has a pH of 9.5. Find the $[H^+]$ and $[OH^-]$ in the solution. Is the solution acidic or basic?

$[H^+] =$ ______________ M; $[OH^-] =$ ______________ M; ______________

3. A 0.1 M solution of the weak acid HB has a pH of 3.0. What is the per cent dissociation of HB in the solution? What is K_a for HB?

______________ %; $K_a =$ ______________

4. A solid acid is dissolved in water. Half the solution is titrated to a phenolphthalein end point with NaOH solution. The neutralized and acid solutions are then mixed and the pH of the resulting solution is found to be 4.6. Find K_a of the solid acid.

$K_a =$ ______________

5. Acetic acid has a K_a of about 2×10^{-5}. A buffer is to be prepared with a pH of 4.0 from 0.1 M solutions of $HC_2H_3O_2$ and $NaC_2H_3O_2$. How many ml of 0.1 M $NaC_2H_3O_2$ would have to be added to 100 ml of 0.1 M $HC_2H_3O_2$ to make the proper buffer solution?

EXPERIMENT 24

The Standardization of a Basic Solution and the Determination of the Gram Equivalent Weight of a Solid Acid

When a solution of a strong acid is mixed with a solution of a strong base, a chemical reaction occurs that can be represented by the following net ionic equation:

$$H^+(aq) + OH^-(aq) \rightarrow H_2O$$

This is called a neutralization reaction, and chemists use it extensively to change the acidic or basic properties of solutions. The equilibrium constant for the reaction is about 10^{14} at room temperature, so that the reaction can be considered to proceed completely to the right, using up whichever of the ions is present in the lesser amount and leaving the solution either acidic or basic, depending on whether H^+ or OH^- ion was in excess.

Since the reaction is essentially quantitative, it can be used to determine the concentrations of acidic or basic solutions. A frequently used procedure involves the titration of an acid with a base. In the titration, a basic solution is added from a buret to a measured volume of acid solution until the number of moles of OH^- ion added is just equal to the number of moles of H^+ ion present in the acid. At that point the volume of basic solution that has been added is measured.

Recalling the definition of the concentration term called molarity,

$$\text{molarity } M \text{ of Species } S = \frac{\text{no. moles } S \text{ in the solution}}{\text{volume of the solution in liters}}$$

or, no. moles S in solution = molarity of $S \times$ volume of solution in liters. We can see that at the end point of a titration of an acid with a base,

$$\text{no. moles } H^+ \text{ originally present} = \text{no. moles } OH^- \text{ added}$$

$$M_{H^+} \times V_{acid} = M_{OH^-} \times V_{base}$$

Therefore, if the molarity of either the H^+ or the OH^- ion in its solution is known, the molarity of the other ion can be found from the titration.

The equivalence point or end point in the titration is determined by using a chemical, called an indicator, that changes color at the proper point. The indicators used in acid-base titrations are weak organic acids or bases which have colors that depend on the pH. One of the most common indicators is phenolphthalein, which is colorless in acid solutions but becomes red when the pH of the solution becomes 9 or higher.

When a solution of a strong acid is titrated with a solution of a strong base, the pH at the end point will be about 7. At the end point a drop of acid or base added to the solution will change its pH by several pH units, so that phenolphthalein can be used as an indicator in such titrations. If a weak acid is titrated with a strong base, the pH at the equivalence point is somewhat higher than 7, perhaps 8 or 9, and phenolphthalein is still a very satisfactory indicator. If, however, a solution of a weak base such as ammonia is titrated with a strong acid, the pH will be a unit or two less than 7 at the end point, and phenolphthalein will not be as good an indicator for that titration as, for example, methyl red, whose color changes from red to yellow as the pH changes from about 4 to 6. Ordinarily, indicators will be chosen so that their color change occurs at about the pH at the equivalence point of a given acid-base titration.

In this experiment you will determine the molarity of OH^- ion in an NaOH solution by titrating that solution against a standardized solution of HCl. Since in these solutions one mole of acid in solution furnishes one mole of H^+ ion and one mole of base produces one mole of OH^- ion, $M_{HCl} = M_{H^+}$ in the acid solution, and $M_{NaOH} = M_{OH^-}$ in the basic solution. Therefore the titration will allow you to find M_{NaOH} as well as M_{OH^-}. You will note, however, that in order to be able to calculate M_{NaOH} you must know the formula of the base.

To establish the accuracy with which you standardize your NaOH solution you will use it to titrate a sample of a pure solid organic acid. By titrating a weighed sample of unknown acid with your standardized NaOH solution you can easily determine the number of moles of H^+ ion available in the sample. From the number of moles of H^+ and the weight of the sample you can calculate the number of grams of acid that would contain one mole of H^+ ion. This is called the gram equivalent weight of the acid. If one mole of the acid can produce one mole of H^+, then the weight of a mole of the acid and its gram equivalent weight are equal. If, however, the acid has three moles of available H^+ ion per mole of acid, the *GMW* is $3 \times GEW$. Since you will not be given the formula of the acid, you will be able to determine only the gram equivalent weight of the acid by titration with NaOH.

EXPERIMENTAL PROCEDURE

Note: This experiment is relatively long unless you know precisely what you are to do. Study the experiment carefully before coming to class, so that you don't have to spend a lot of time finding out what the experiment is all about.

Obtain two burets and a sample of solid unknown acid from the stockroom.

A. Standardization of NaOH Solution. Into a small graduated cylinder draw about 7 ml of the stock 6 *M* NaOH solution provided in the laboratory and dilute to about 400 ml with distilled water in a 500 ml Florence flask. Stopper the flask tightly and mix the solution thoroughly at intervals over a period of at least 15 minutes before using the solution.

Draw into a clean *dry* 125 ml Erlenmeyer flask about 75 ml of standardized HCl solution (about 0.1 *M*) from the stock solution on the reagent shelf. This amount should provide all the standard acid you will need, so do not waste it.

Prepare for the titration using the procedure given in Experiment 21. Clean the two burets and rinse with distilled water. Then rinse the first buret three times with a few ml of the HCl solution. Fill the buret with HCl; open the stopcock momentarily to fill the tip. Proceed to clean and fill the other buret with your NaOH solution in a similar manner. Carefully label the two burets. Check to see that your burets do not leak and that there are no air bubbles in either buret tip. Read the levels in both burets to 0.02 ml.

Draw about 25 ml of the HCl solution from the buret into a clean 250 ml Erlenmeyer flask; add to the flask about 25 ml of distilled H_2O and 2 or 3 drops of phenolphthalein indicator solution. Place a white sheet of paper under the flask to aid in the detection of any color change. Add the NaOH solution intermittently from its buret to the solution in the flask, noting the pink phenolphthalein color that appears and disappears as the drops hit the liquid and are mixed with it. Swirl the liquid in the flask gently and continuously as you add the NaOH solution. When the pink color begins to persist, slow down the rate of addition of NaOH. In the final stages of the titration add the NaOH drop by drop until the entire solution just turns a pale pink color that will persist for about 30 seconds. If you go past the end point and obtain a red solution, add a few drops of the HCl solution to remove the color, and then add NaOH a drop at a time until the pink color persists. Carefully record the final readings on the HCl and NaOH burets.

To the 250 ml Erlenmeyer flask containing the titrated solution, add about 10 ml more of the standard HCl solution. Titrate this as before with the NaOH to an end point, and carefully record both buret readings once again. To this solution add about 10 ml more HCl and titrate a third time with NaOH.

You have now completed three titrations, with *total* HCl volumes of about 25, 35, and 45 ml. Find the ratio $V_{HCl}:V_{NaOH}$ at the end point of each of the titrations, using *total* volumes of each reagent reacted up to that end point. At least two of these volume ratios should agree to within one per cent. If they do, proceed to the next part of the experiment. If they do not, repeat these titrations until two volume ratios do agree.

B. Determination of the Gram Equivalent Weight of an Acid. Weigh the vial containing your solid acid on the analytical balance. Carefully pour out about half the sample into a clean but not necessarily dry 250 ml Erlenmeyer flask. Weigh the vial accurately. Add about 50 ml of distilled water and 2 or 3 drops of phenolphthalein to the flask. The acid may be relatively insoluble, so don't worry if it doesn't all dissolve.

Fill your NaOH buret with your (now standardized) NaOH solution and read the level accurately.

Titrate the acid solution to an end point as before. As the acid is neutralized by the NaOH, it will tend to dissolve in the solution. If your unknown is so insoluble that the phenolphthalein color persists before all the solid dissolves, add 25 ml of ethanol to the solution to increase the solubility. Record the NaOH buret reading at the end point.

Pour the rest of your acid sample into a 250 ml Erlenmeyer flask and weigh the vial accurately. Titrate the acid as before with NaOH solution. If you go past the end point in these titrations, it is possible, though more complicated in calculations, to back-titrate with a little of the standard HCl solution. Measure the volume of HCl used and subtract the number of moles HCl in that volume from the number of moles NaOH used in the titration. The difference will equal the number of moles NaOH used to neutralize the acid sample.

Name ______________________ Section ____________

DATA: Standardization of a Basic Solution.
Determination of the GEW of an Acid

A. Standardization of the NaOH Solution

	Trial 1	Trial 2	Trial 3
Final reading HCl buret	______ ml	______ ml	______ ml
Initial reading HCl buret	______ ml		
Final reading NaOH buret	______ ml	______ ml	______ ml
Initial reading NaOH buret	______ ml		

B. Gram Equivalent Weight of Unknown Acid

Weight of vial plus contents ______ g

Weight of vial plus contents less sample 1 ______ g

Weight less sample 2 ______ g

	Trial 1	Trial 2
Final reading NaOH buret	______ ml	______ ml
Initial reading NaOH buret	______ ml	______ ml

CALCULATIONS

A. Standardization of NaOH Solution

	Trial 1	Trial 2	Trial 3
Total volume HCl	______ ml	______ ml	______ ml
Total volume NaOH	______ ml	______ ml	______ ml

Continued on following page

Volume ratio: V_{HCl}/V_{NaOH} (should agree within 1 per cent) __________ __________ __________

Molarity M_A of standardized HCl __________ M

No. moles acid $= \frac{V_A M_A}{1000}$ = no. moles base $= \frac{V_B M_B}{1000}$ (where V_A, V_B are in ml)

Molarity M_B of NaOH solution __________ M __________ M __________ M

Average molarity of NaOH solution __________ M

B. Gram Equivalent Weight of an Unknown Acid

	Trial 1	Trial 2
Weight of sample of acid	__________ g	__________ g
Volume NaOH used	__________ ml	__________ ml
No. moles NaOH $= \frac{V_{NaOH} M_{NaOH}}{1000}$	__________	__________
No. moles OH^- = no. moles NaOH	__________	__________
No. moles H^+ in sample	__________	__________
GEW $= \frac{\text{weight acid in sample}}{\text{no. moles } H^+ \text{ in sample}}$	__________ g	__________ g
Unknown No.	__________	

 Name ______________________ Section ______________

ADVANCE STUDY ASSIGNMENT: Gram Equivalent Weight of an Unknown Acid

1. If 7.0 ml of 6.0 *M* NaOH are diluted with water to a volume of 400 ml, what is the molarity of the resulting solution?

______________ *M*

2. In an acid-base titration, 24.28 ml of an NaOH solution were required to neutralize 21.16 ml of a 0.1046 *M* HCl solution. What is the molarity of the NaOH solution?

______________ *M*

3. A gram equivalent weight, or an equivalent, of an acid contains one mole of acid hydrogen. How many equivalents of acid would there be in 0.2 moles of HNO_3? In 0.3 moles of H_2SO_4?

______________ ______________

4. A 0.2625 g sample of an unknown solid acid required 36.45 ml of 0.1185 *M* NaOH for neutralization to a phenolphthalein end point. What is the gram equivalent weight of the acid?

______________ g

5. Why is it not possible to find the molecular weight of an unknown acid by the method used in this experiment? How might the molecular weight of the acid be found?

SECTION 12

Complex Ions

EXPERIMENT 25

Relative Stabilities of Complex Ions and Precipitates Prepared from Solutions of Copper (II)

In aqueous solution, typical cations, particularly those produced from atoms of the transition metals, do not exist as free ions but rather consist of the metal ion in combination with some water molecules. Such cations are called complex ions. The water molecules, usually 2, 4, or 6 in number, are bound chemically to the metallic cation, but often rather loosely, with the electrons in the chemical bonds being furnished by one of the unshared electron pairs from the oxygen atoms in the H_2O molecules. Zinc ion in aqueous solution may exist as $Zn(H_2O)_4^{2+}$, with the water molecules arranged tetrahedrally around the central metal ion.

If a hydrated cation such as $Zn(H_2O)_4^{2+}$ is mixed with other species that can, like water, form coordinate covalent bonds with Zn^{2+}, those species, called ligands, may displace one or more H_2O molecules and form other complex ions containing the new ligands. For instance, NH_3, a reasonably good coordinating species, may replace H_2O from the hydrated zinc ion, $Zn(H_2O)_4^{2+}$, to form $Zn(H_2O)_3NH_3^{2+}$, $Zn(H_2O)_2(NH_3)_2^{2+}$, $Zn(H_2O)(NH_3)_3^{2+}$, or $Zn(NH_3)_4^{2+}$. At moderate concentrations of NH_3, essentially all the H_2O molecules around the zinc ion are replaced by NH_3 molecules, forming the zinc ammonia complex ion.

Coordinating ligands differ in their tendency to form bonds with metallic cations, so that in a solution containing a given cation and several possible ligands, an equilibrium will develop in which most of the cations are coordinated with those ligands with which they form the most stable bonds. There are many kinds of ligands, but they all share the common property that they possess an unshared pair of electrons which they can donate to form a coordinate covalent bond with a metal ion. In addition to H_2O and NH_3, other uncharged coordinating species include CO and ethylenediamine; some common anions that can form complexes include OH^-, Cl^-, CN^-, SCN^-, and $S_2O_3^{2-}$.

As you know, when solutions containing metallic cations are mixed with other solutions containing ions, precipitates are sometimes formed. When a solution of 0.1 *M* zinc nitrate is mixed with a little 1 *M* NH_3 solution, a precipitate forms and then dissolves in excess ammonia. The formation of the precipitate helps us to understand what is occurring as NH_3 is added. The precipitate is hydrous zinc hydroxide, formed by reaction of the hydrated zinc ion with the small amount of hydroxide ion present in the NH_3 solution. The fact that this reaction occurs means that even at very low OH^- ion concentration $Zn(OH)_2(H_2O)_2(s)$ is a more stable species than $Zn(H_2O)_4^{2+}$ ion.

Addition of more NH_3 causes the solid to redissolve. The zinc species then in solution cannot be the hydrated zinc ion. (Why?) It must be some other complex ion, and is, indeed, the $Zn(NH_3)_4^{2+}$ ion. The implication of this reaction is that the $Zn(NH_3)_4^{2+}$ ion is also more stable in NH_3 solution than is the hydrated zinc ion. To deduce in addition that the zinc ammonia complex ion is also more stable in general than $Zn(OH)_2(H_2O)_2(s)$ is not warranted, since under the conditions in the solution $[NH_3]$ is much larger than $[OH^-]$, and given a higher concentration of hydroxide ion, the solid hydrous zinc hydroxide might possibly precipitate even in the presence of substantial concentrations of NH_3.

To resolve this question, you might proceed to add a little 1 *M* NaOH solution to the solution containing the $Zn(NH_3)_4^{2+}$ ion. If you do this you find that $Zn(OH)_2(H_2O)_2(s)$ does indeed precipitate, but that on addition of more 1 *M* NaOH, it too redissolves.

We can conclude from these observations that $Zn(OH)_2(H_2O)_2(s)$ is more stable than $Zn(NH_3)_4^{2+}$ in solutions in which the ligand concentrations (OH^- and NH_3) are roughly equal, but also that there is yet another species formed in the presence of high OH^- ion concentrations that is even more stable than the solid zinc hydroxide. That species we can identify chemically as $Zn(OH)_4^{2-}$.

The zinc species that will be present in a system depends, as we have just seen, on the conditions in the system. We cannot say in general that one species will be more stable than another; the stability of a given species depends in large measure on the kinds and concentrations of other species that are also present with it.

Another way of looking at the matter of stability is through equilibrium theory. Each of the zinc species we have mentioned can be formed in a reaction between the hydrated zinc ion and a complexing or precipitating ligand; each reaction will have an associated equilibrium constant, which we might call a formation constant for that species. The pertinent formation reactions and their constants for the zinc species we have been considering are listed here:

$$Zn(H_2O)_4^{2+}(aq) + 4\,NH_3(aq) \rightleftharpoons Zn(NH_3)_4^{2+}(aq) + 4\,H_2O \qquad K_1 = 3 \times 10^9 \qquad (1)$$

$$Zn(H_2O)_4^{2+}(aq) + 2\,OH^-(aq) \rightleftharpoons Zn(OH)_2(H_2O)_2(s) + 2\,H_2O \qquad K_2 = 2 \times 10^{16} \qquad (2)$$

$$Zn(H_2O)_4^{2+}(aq) + 4\,OH^-(aq) \rightleftharpoons Zn(OH)_4^{2-}(aq) + 4\,H_2O \qquad K_3 = 3 \times 10^{15} \qquad (3)$$

The formation constants for these reactions do not involve $[H_2O]$ terms, which are essentially constant in aqueous systems and are included in the magnitude of K in each case. The large size of each formation constant indicates that the tendency for the hydrated zinc ion to react with the ligands listed is very high.

In terms of these data, let us compare the stability of the $Zn(NH_3)_4^{2+}$ complex ion with that of the $Zn(OH)_4^{2-}$ complex ion. This is most readily done by considering the reaction

$$Zn(NH_3)_4^{2+}(aq) + 4\,OH^-(aq) \rightleftharpoons Zn(OH)_4^{2-}(aq) + 4\,NH_3(aq)$$

$$K = \frac{[Zn(OH)_4^{2-}]\,[NH_3]^4}{[Zn(NH_3)_4^{2+}]\,[OH^-]^4} \qquad (4)$$

Since $K_1 = \dfrac{[Zn(NH_3)_4^{2+}]}{[Zn(H_2O)_4^{2+}]\,[NH_3]^4}$ and $K_3 = \dfrac{[Zn(OH)_4^{2-}]}{[Zn(H_2O)_4^{2+}]\,[OH^-]^4}$

and since all three equilibria must be satisfied in the solution, it is clear that

$$K = \frac{K_3}{K_1} = \frac{3 \times 10^{15}}{3 \times 10^9} = 10^6$$

From the expression for K in Equation 4, we can calculate that in a solution in which the NH_3 and OH^- ligand concentrations are about equal,

$$\frac{[Zn(OH)_4{}^{2-}]}{[Zn(NH_3)_4{}^{2+}]} = 10^6$$

which means that the zinc is primarily in the form of the hydroxide complex. But that is exactly what we discovered by treating the hydrated zinc ion first with ammonia and then with an equivalent amount of hydroxide ion.

Summarizing the experimental behavior of the zinc ion, we can conclude that since the hydroxide complex ion is the one that exists when zinc ion is exposed to equal concentrations of ammonia and hydroxide ion, the hydroxide complex is more stable under those conditions, *and* the equilibrium constant for the formation of the hydroxide complex is larger than the constant for the formation of the ammonia complex. By determining, then, which species is present when a cation is in the presence of equal ligand concentrations, we can speak meaningfully of stability under such conditions and can rank the formation constants for the possible complex ions, and indeed for precipitates, in order of their increasing magnitudes.

In this experiment you will carry out formation reactions for a group of complex ions and precipitates involving the Cu^{2+} ion. You can make these species by mixing a solution of $Cu(NO_3)_2$ with solutions containing NH_3 or anions, which may form either precipitates or complex ions by reaction with $Cu(H_2O)_4{}^{2+}$, the cation present in aqueous solutions of copper(II) nitrate. By examining whether the precipitates or complex ions formed by the reaction of hydrated copper(II) ion with a given species can, on addition of a second ligand, be dissolved or transformed to another species, you will be able to rank the relative stabilities of the precipitates and complex ions made from Cu^{2+} with respect to one another, and thus rank the equilibrium formation constants for each species in order of increasing magnitude. The species to be reacted with Cu^{2+} ion in aqueous solution are NH_3, Cl^-, OH^-, $CO_3{}^{2-}$, $C_2O_4{}^{2-}$, S^{2-}, $NO_2{}^-$, and $PO_4{}^{3-}$. In each case the test for relative stability will be made in the presence of essentially equal concentrations of the two ligands. When you have completed your ranking of the known species you will be given an unknown species to incorporate into your list.

EXPERIMENTAL PROCEDURE

Obtain from the stockroom an unknown and enough medium size test tubes so that you have a total of eight.

Add about two ml 0.1 M $Cu(NO_3)_2$ solution to each of the test tubes.

To each of the test tubes add about two ml 1 M NH_3 solution, drop by drop. Report your observation in the space corresponding to NH_3–NH_3 in the table on your data page. Report the color of any precipitate that forms, and if the precipitate redissolves in excess NH_3, report the color of the resulting solution. At the bottom of the space indicate the formula of the species present in excess NH_3. If a solution is present, the Cu^{2+} ion is present in a complex, with four ligand NH_3 molecules coordinated to it. If a precipitate is present, the species is neutral and in the case of NH_3 would be a hydrous copper hydroxide, $Cu(H_2O)_2(OH)_2(s)$.

To test the stability of the copper species present in excess NH_3 relative to those possibly present with other precipitating or coordinating species, add two ml of 1 M solutions of the anions in the horizontal row in the table to the test tubes you have just prepared, one solution to a test tube. Note in the appropriate spaces in the table any changes which occur. A change in color of the solution or the formation of a new precipitate implies that a reaction has occurred between the added ligand or precipitating anion and the species originally present. Recognizing that the formulas of precipitates are neutral and that copper(II) ion typically exhibits a coordination number of four, write the formula of the species present in a system containing both excess NH_3 and the added species. If a new species is formed on addition of the second reagent, is that species more or less stable than the one originally present?

Repeat the above series of experiments, using 1 *M* Cl^- as the species originally added to the $Cu(NO_3)_2$ solution. In each case record the color of any precipitates or solutions formed on addition of the reagents in the horizontal row, and the formulas of the species present when an excess of both Cl^- ion and the added species is present in the solution. Since these reactions are reversible, it is not necessary to retest Cl^- with NH_3, since the same results would be obtained as when the NH_3 solution was tested with Cl^- solution.

Repeat the series of experiments for each of the anions in the vertical row in the table, omitting those tests where decisions as to relative stabilities are already clear. Where both ligands produce precipitates it may be helpful to check the effect of the addition of the other ligand to those precipitates. When complete, your table should have at least 36 entries.

Examine your table and decide on the relative stabilities of all species you observed to be present in all the spaces of the table. There should be eight such species; rank them as best you can in order of increasing stability. There is only one correct ranking, and you should be prepared to defend your choices. Although we did not in general prepare the species by direct reaction of $Cu(H_2O)_4^{2+}$ with the added ligand or precipitating anion, the equilibrium formation constants for those species for the direct reactions will have magnitudes that increase in the same order as the relative stabilities of the species you have established.

When you are satisfied that your ranking order is correct, carry out the necessary tests on your unknown to determine its proper position in the list. Your unknown may be one of the species you have already observed, or it may be a different species, present in excess of its ligand or precipitating anion.

Name ______________________ Section ______________

DATA AND OBSERVATIONS: Relative Stabilities of Complex Ions and Precipitates Containing Cu(II)

Table of Observations

	NH_3	Cl^-	OH^-	CO_3^{2-}	$C_2O_4^{2-}$	S^{2-}	NO_2^-	PO_4^{3-}
NH_3								
Cl^-								
OH^-								
CO_3^{2-}								
$C_2O_4^{2-}$								
S^{2-}								
NO_2^-								
PO_4^{3-}								
Unknown								

Continued on following page

Determination of Relative Stabilities

In each row of the table you can compare the stabilities of species involving the reagent in the horizontal row with those of the species containing the reagent initially added. In the first row of the table, the copper(II)–NH_3 species can be seen to be more stable than some of the species obtained by addition of the other reagents, and less stable than others. Examining each row, make a list of all the complex ions and precipitates you have in the table in order of increasing stability and formation constant.

Reasons

Lowest ______________________ ______________________

______________________ ______________________

______________________ ______________________

______________________ ______________________

______________________ ______________________

______________________ ______________________

______________________ ______________________

Highest ______________________ ______________________

Stability of Unknown

Indicate the position your unknown would occupy in the above list.

Reasons:

Unknown no. __________

ADVANCE STUDY ASSIGNMENT: Stabilities of Complex Ions and Precipitates

1. For the formation of AgCl from ions in solution,

$$Ag^+(aq) + Cl^-(aq) \rightleftharpoons AgCl(s) \qquad K_1 = 1 \times 10^{10}$$

For the formation of AgBr from the ions in solution,

$$Ag^+(aq) + Br^-(aq) \rightleftharpoons AgBr(s) \qquad K_2 = 1 \times 10^{13}$$

Find the equilibrium constant for the reaction

$$AgCl(s) + Br^-(aq) \rightleftharpoons AgBr(s) + Cl^-(aq)$$

____

What would be the silver-containing species present at equilibrium when 2 ml 1 *M* NaCl and 2 ml 1 *M* NaBr are added in succession to 2 ml 0.1 *M* $AgNO_3$?

____

2. Copper(II) nitrate solution yields a precipitate when treated with a reagent containing A^-. The precipitate dissolves both in a reagent containing B^- and in a reagent containing C^-.

If the reagent containing C^- is added to a solution made by mixing copper(II) nitrate with a solution of B^-, the color of the solution does not change. However, if B^- is added to a solution made by mixing copper nitrate with a solution of C^-, a change in color is observed.

Write the formulas of the copper-containing species present when copper(II) nitrate is mixed with a solution containing A^-, B^-, or C^-. Rank these species in order of increasing equilibrium formation constants.

Increasing → ______________ ______________ ______________

3. One way of considering relative stabilities of species of the sort studied in this experiment is to note that the more stable of two possible species will be in equilibrium with the lower concentration of hydrated cation. Calculate $[Zn(H_2O)_4^{2+}]$ in equilibrium with $Zn(NH_3)_4^{2+}$ in a solution in which $[NH_3]$ is 1 *M* and $[Zn(NH_3)_4^{2+}]$ is 0.1 *M*.

______________ *M*

EXPERIMENT 26

Determination of the Hardness of Water

One of the factors that establishes the quality of a water supply is its degree of hardness. The hardness of water is defined in terms of its content of calcium and magnesium ions. Since the analysis does not distinguish between Ca^{2+} and Mg^{2+}, and since most hardness is caused by carbonate deposits in the earth, hardness is usually reported as total parts per million calcium carbonate by weight. A water supply with a hardness of 100 parts per million would contain the equivalent of 100 grams of $CaCO_3$ in 1 million grams of water or 0.1 gram in one liter of water. In the days when soap was more commonly used for washing clothes, and when people bathed in tubs instead of using showers, water hardness was more often directly observed than it is now, since Ca^{2+} and Mg^{2+} form insoluble salts with soaps and make a scum that sticks to clothes or to the bath tub. Detergents have the distinct advantage of being effective in hard water, and this is really what allowed them to displace soaps for laundry purposes.

Water hardness can be readily determined by titration with the chelating agent EDTA (ethylenediaminetetraacetic acid). This reagent is a weak acid that can lose four protons on complete neutralization; its structural formula is

$$\begin{array}{ccc} HOOC{-}CH_2 & & CH_2{-}COOH \\ & \diagdown \quad\quad\quad\quad\quad\quad\quad \diagup & \\ & N{-}CH_2{-}CH_2{-}N & \\ & \diagup \quad\quad\quad\quad\quad\quad\quad \diagdown & \\ HOOC{-}CH_2 & & CH_2{-}COOH \end{array}$$

The four acid sites and the two nitrogen atoms all contain unshared electron pairs, so that a single EDTA ion can form a complex with up to six sites on a given cation. The complex is typically quite stable, and the conditions of its formation can ordinarily be controlled so that it contains EDTA and the metal ion in a 1:1 mole ratio. In a titration to establish the concentration of a metal ion, the EDTA which is added combines quantitatively with the cation to form the complex. The end point occurs when essentially all of the cation has reacted.

In this experiment we will standardize a solution of EDTA by titration against a standard solution made from calcium carbonate, $CaCO_3$. We will then use the EDTA solution to determine the hardness of an unknown water sample. Since both EDTA and Ca^{2+} are colorless, it is necessary to use a rather special indicator to detect the end point of the titration. The indicator we will employ is called Eriochrome Black T, which forms a rather stable wine-red complex, $MgIn^-$, with the magnesium ion. A tiny amount of this complex will be present in the solution during the titration. As EDTA is added, it will complex free Ca^{2+} and Mg^{2+} ions, leaving the $MgIn^-$ complex alone until essentially all of the calcium and magnesium has been converted to chelates. At this point EDTA concentration will increase sufficiently to displace Mg^{2+} from the indicator complex; the indicator reverts to an acid form, which is sky blue, and this establishes the end point of the titration.

The titration is carried out at a pH of 10, in an $NH_3{-}NH_4^+$ buffer, which keeps the EDTA (H_4Y) mainly in the half-neutralized form, H_2Y^{2-}, where it complexes the Group IIA ions very well but does not tend to react as readily with other cations such as Fe^{3+} that might be present as impurities in the water. Taking H_4Y and H_3In as the formulas for EDTA and Eriochrome Black T respectively, the equations for the reactions which occur during the titration are:

(main reaction) $H_2Y^{2-}(aq) + Ca^{2+}(aq) \rightarrow CaY^{2-}(aq) + 2\,H^+(aq)$ (same for Mg^{2+})

(at end point) $H_2Y^{2-}(aq) + MgIn^-(aq) \rightarrow MgY^{2-}(aq) + HIn^{2-}(aq) + H^+(aq)$
wine red sky blue

Since the indicator requires a trace of Mg^{2+} to operate properly, we will add a little magnesium ion to each solution and titrate it as a blank.

EXPERIMENTAL PROCEDURE

Obtain a 50 ml buret, a 250 ml volumetric flask, and 25 and 50 ml pipets from the stockroom.

Put about a half gram of calcium carbonate in a small 50 ml beaker and weigh the beaker and contents on the analytical balance. Using a spatula, transfer about 0.4 g of the carbonate to a 250 ml beaker and weigh again, determining the mass of the $CaCO_3$ sample by difference.

Add 25 ml of distilled water to the large beaker and then, slowly, about 20 drops of 12 *M* HCl. Cover the beaker with a watch glass and allow the reaction to proceed until all of the solid carbonate has dissolved. Rinse the walls of the beaker down with distilled water from your wash bottle and heat the solution until it just begins to boil. (Be sure not to be confused by the evolution of CO_2 which occurs with the boiling.) Add 50 ml of distilled water to the beaker and carefully transfer the solution, using a stirring rod as a pathway, to the volumetric flask. Rinse the beaker several times with small portions of distilled water and transfer each portion to the flask. All of the Ca^{2+} originally in the beaker should then be in the volumetric flask; the solution is one of slightly acidic $CaCl_2$. Fill the volumetric flask with distilled water, adding the last few ml a drop at a time with your wash bottle or medicine dropper. When the bottom of the meniscus is just even with the horizontal mark on the flask, stopper the flask and mix the solution thoroughly by inverting the flask at least a dozen times and shaking at intervals over a period of five minutes.

Clean your buret thoroughly. Draw about 200 ml of the stock EDTA solution from the carboy into a dry 250 ml Erlenmeyer flask. Rinse the buret with a few ml of the solution at least three times. Drain through the stopcock and then fill the buret with the EDTA solution.

Determine a blank by adding 25 ml distilled water and 5 ml of the pH 10 buffer to a 250 ml Erlenmeyer flask. Add two drops of Eriochrome Black T indicator. The solution should turn blue. Add 15 drops 0.03 *M* $MgCl_2$, which should contain enough Mg^{2+} to turn the solution wine red. Read the buret to 0.02 ml and add EDTA to the solution until the last tinge of purple just disappears. Read the buret again to determine the volume required for the blank. This volume must be subtracted from the total EDTA volume used in each titration. Save the solution as a reference for the end point in all your titrations.

Pipet three 25 ml portions of the Ca^{2+} solution in the volumetric flask into clean 250 ml Erlenmeyer flasks. To each flask add 5 ml of the pH 10 buffer, 2 drops of indicator, and 15 drops of 0.03 *M* $MgCl_2$. Titrate the solution in one of the flasks until its color matches that of your reference solution; the end point is a reasonably good one, and you should be able to hit it within a few drops if you are careful. Read the buret. Refill the buret, read it, and titrate the second solution, then the third.

Your instructor will furnish you a sample of water for hardness analysis. Since the concentration of Ca^{2+} is probably lower than that in the standard calcium solution you prepared, pipet 50 ml of the water sample for each titration. As before, add 2 drops of indicator, 5 ml of pH 10 buffer, and 15 drops of 0.03 *M* $MgCl_2$ before titrating. Carry out as many titrations as necessary to obtain two volumes of EDTA that agree within about 3 per cent. If the volume of EDTA required in the first titration is low due to the fact that the water is not very hard, increase the volume of the water sample so that in succeeding titrations, it takes at least 20 ml of EDTA to reach the end point.

Name ____________________ Section ____________

DATA AND CALCULATIONS: Determination of the Hardness of Water

Weight of beaker plus $CaCO_3$ ____________ g

Volume Ca^{2+} solution prepared ____________ ml

Weight of beaker less sample ____________ g

Molarity of Ca^{2+} ____________ *M*

Weight of $CaCO_3$ sample ____________ g

Moles Ca^{2+} in each aliquot titrated ____________ moles

Number of moles $CaCO_3$ in sample (Formula weight = 100.1) ____________ moles

Standardization of EDTA Solution

Determination of blank:

Initial buret reading ____________ ml

Final buret reading ____________ ml

Volume of blank ____________ ml

Titration:	I	II	III
Initial buret reading	____________ ml	____________ ml	____________ ml
Final buret reading	____________ ml	____________ ml	____________ ml
Volume of EDTA	____________ ml	____________ ml	____________ ml
Volume EDTA used to titrate blank	____________ ml	____________ ml	____________ ml
Volume EDTA used to titrate Ca^{2+}	____________ ml	____________ ml	____________ ml

Average volume of EDTA required to titrate Ca^{2+} ____________ ml

$$\text{Molarity of EDTA} = \frac{\text{no. moles } Ca^{2+} \text{ in aliquot} \times 1000}{\text{average volume EDTA required (ml)}} = \underline{\hspace{3cm}}\ M$$

Continued on following page

Determination of Water Hardness

Titration:	I	II	III
Volume of water used	______ ml	______ ml	______ ml
Initial buret reading	______ ml	______ ml	______ ml
Final buret reading	______ ml	______ ml	______ ml
Volume of EDTA	______ ml	______ ml	______ ml
Volume of EDTA used to titrate blank	______ ml	______ ml	______ ml
Volume of EDTA required to titrate water	______ ml	______ ml	______ ml
Volume of EDTA required per liter of water	______ ml	______ ml	______ ml
Average volume EDTA per liter of water	______ ml		

No. moles EDTA per liter water ______ = No. moles $CaCO_3$ per liter water

No. grams $CaCO_3$ per liter water ______ g   Water hardness (1 ppm = 1 mg/liter) ______ ppm $CaCO_3$

Unknown No. ______

 Name ______________________ Section ______________

ADVANCE STUDY ASSIGNMENT: Determination of the Hardness of Water

1. A 0.4505 g sample of $CaCO_3$ was dissolved in HCl and the resulting solution diluted to 250.0 ml in a volumetric flask. A 25.00 ml sample of the solution required 24.25 ml of an EDTA solution for titration to the Eriochrome Black T end point.

(a) How many moles of $CaCO_3$ were used?

______________ moles

(b) What is the concentration of Ca^{2+} in the 250 ml of $CaCl_2$ solution?

______________ moles/lit

(c) How many moles of Ca^{2+} are contained in a 25.00 ml sample?

______________ moles

(d) How many moles of EDTA are contained in the 24.25 ml used for titration?

______________ moles

(e) What is the concentration of the EDTA solution?

______________ moles/lit

2. If 100 ml of a water sample required 23.24 ml of EDTA of the concentration found in Problem 1(e), what is the hardness of the water in terms of ppm $CaCO_3$? (1 ppm = 1 mg/lit)

______________ ppm $CaCO_3$

EXPERIMENT 27

Synthesis of Some Coordination Compounds

Some of the most interesting research in inorganic chemistry has involved the preparation and study of the properties of those substances known as coordination compounds. These compounds, sometimes called complexes, are typically salts that contain *complex ions.* A complex ion is an ion that contains a central metal ion to which are bonded small polar molecules or simple ions; the bonding in the complex ion is through coordinate covalent bonds, which ordinarily are relatively weak.

In this experiment we shall be concerned with the synthesis of four coordination compounds:

A. $[Cu(NH_3)_4]\ SO_4 \cdot H_2O$ B. $[Co(NH_3)_5H_2O]\ Cl_3$

C. $[Co(NH_3)_6]\ Cl_3$ D. $[Co(NH_3)_5Cl]\ Cl_2$

The complex ions in these substances are enclosed in brackets to indicate those species which are bonded to the central ion. In this experiment you will prepare the complex ions by making use of reactions in which substituting *ligands,* or coordinating species, replace other ligands on the central ion. The reactions will usually be carried out in water solution, in which the metallic cation will initially be present in the simple hydrated form; addition of a reagent containing a complexing ligand will result in an exchange reaction of the sort

$$Cu(H_2O)_4{}^{2+}(aq) + 4\ NH_3(aq) \rightleftharpoons Cu(NH_3)_4{}^{2+}(aq) + 4\ H_2O \quad (1)$$

In many reactions involving complex ion formation the rate of reaction is very rapid, so that the thermodynamically stable form of the ion is the one produced. Such reactions obey the law of chemical equilibrium and can thus be readily controlled as to direction by a change in the reaction conditions. Reaction 1 proceeds readily to the right in the presence of NH_3 in moderate concentrations. However, by decreasing the NH_3 concentration, for example by the addition of acid to the system, we can easily regenerate the hydrated copper cation. Complex ions that undergo very fast exchange reactions, such as those in Reaction 1, are called *labile.*

Most but by no means all complex ions are labile. Some complex ions, including some to be studied in this experiment, will exchange ligands only slowly. For such species, called *inert* or *nonlabile,* the complex ion produced in a substitution reaction may be the one which is kinetically rather than thermodynamically favored. Alteration of reaction conditions, perhaps by the addition of a catalyst, may change the relative rates of formation of possible complex products and so change the complex ion produced in the reaction. In your experiment, you will find that under one set of conditions the cobalt complex ion in substance B listed previously will be formed, whereas by addition of a catalyst the complex ion in substance C is produced in the presence of the same ligands.

Many complex ions are highly colored, both in solution and in the solid salt. An easy way to determine whether a complex ion is labile is to note whether a color change occurs in a solution containing the ion when a good complexing ligand is added. We will use this method to observe relative rates of substitution reactions for the complex ions we prepare.

The experiment as described here will ordinarily take two weeks. If only one week of laboratory time is available, your instructor will tell you which sections of the experiment you should perform and how he wishes to evaluate your product.

EXPERIMENTAL PROCEDURE

WEAR YOUR SAFETY GLASSES WHILE PERFORMING ANY OF THESE EXPERIMENTS.

A. Preparation of $[Cu(NH_3)_4]SO_4 \cdot H_2O$

$$Cu(H_2O)_4^{2+}(aq) + SO_4^{2-}(aq) + 4\,NH_3(aq) \rightarrow [Cu(NH_3)_4]SO_4 \cdot H_2O(s) + 3\,H_2O$$

Weigh out 7.0 g of $CuSO_4 \cdot 5H_2O$ on a triple-beam or other rough balance. Weigh the solid either on a piece of paper or in a small beaker and not directly on the balance pan. Transfer the solid copper sulfate to a 125 ml Erlenmeyer flask and add 15 ml of water. Heat the flask to dissolve the solid, then cool to room temperature.

Carry out the remaining steps under the hood. Add 15 *M* NH_3 solution, a few ml at a time, swirling the flask to mix the reagents, until the first precipitate has completely dissolved. All the copper should now be present in solution as the complex ion $Cu(NH_3)_4^{2+}$.

The sulfate salt of this complex cation can be precipitated by the addition of a liquid, such as methyl alcohol, in which $Cu(NH_3)_4SO_4 \cdot H_2O$ is insoluble. Add 10 ml of methyl alcohol* to the solution; this should result in the formation of a deep blue precipitate of $Cu(NH_3)_4SO_4 \cdot H_2O$. Filter the solution through a Buchner funnel, using suction. Wash the solid in the funnel by adding two 5 ml portions of methyl alcohol. Dry the solid by pressing it between two pieces of filter paper. Put the crystals on a piece of filter paper and let them dry further in the air. When they are thoroughly dry, weigh them on the paper.

B. Synthesis of Aquopentamminecobalt (III) Chloride, $[Co(NH_3)_5H_2O]Cl_3$

$$2\,Co(H_2O)_6^{2+}(aq) + 6\,Cl^-(aq) + 10\,NH_3(aq) + H_2O_2(aq) \rightarrow 2\,[Co(NH_3)_5H_2O]Cl_3(s) + 10\,H_2O + 2\,OH^-(aq)$$

Obtain a 5 ml sample of cobalt(II) chloride solution from your laboratory instructor. This sample contains 1.0 g of $CoCl_2$. Place the cobalt solution in a 150 ml beaker and add 0.2 g of ammonium chloride, NH_4Cl, and 11 ml of 15 *M* NH_3 solution. Pour 5 ml of 10 per cent hydrogen peroxide, H_2O_2, solution into a 10 ml graduated cylinder. Slowly add the H_2O_2 solution to the $CoCl_2$ solution, stirring constantly. When the bubbling has stopped, place the beaker containing the dark red cobalt solution under the hood and gently aerate for 1 hour using a glass eyedropper and rubber tubing connected to the air jet. Be careful not to turn on the compressed air so vigorously that the solution splatters out of the beaker.

After the compressed air has been stopped, add 15 ml of 12 *M* HCl to the cobalt solution. If a red precipitate does not form in a few minutes, add 5 ml more of the HCl solution. Isolate the red precipitate of $[Co(NH_3)_5H_2O]Cl_3$ by filtration through a Buchner funnel, using suction. Continue to draw air through the precipitate by suction for several minutes after the solvent has been removed to partially dry the solid. Press the solid dry between pieces of filter paper and then transfer it to a fresh piece of filter paper. Weigh the crystals after they are dry.

C. Synthesis of Hexamminecobalt(III) Chloride, $[Co(NH_3)_6]Cl_3$

$$2\,Co(H_2O)_6^{2+}(aq) + 6\,Cl^-(aq) + 12\,NH_3(aq) + H_2O_2(aq) \rightarrow 2\,[Co(NH_3)_6]Cl_3(s) + 12\,H_2O + 2\,OH^-(aq)$$

---

*Methyl alcohol (not to be confused with ethyl alcohol) is extremely poisonous. Avoid inhalation and contact with the skin.

Obtain a 5 ml sample of cobalt(II) chloride solution (containing 1.0 g $CoCl_2$). Place this solution in a 150 ml beaker and add 0.2 gram of ammonium chloride, NH_4Cl, 0.1 gram of activated charcoal (Norite) and 5 ml of 15 *M* NH_3. Into a 10 ml graduated cylinder draw 5 ml of 10 per cent hydrogen peroxide, H_2O_2, solution. Add the H_2O_2 solution very slowly to the $CoCl_2$ solution, stirring constantly. When the bubbling has stopped, gently heat the cobalt solution in the hood for 5 minutes with a small Bunsen flame. Allow the mixture to stand for 1/2 hour. Remove the activated charcoal by passing the solution through filter paper on a Buchner funnel, using suction. Pour the filtrate into a 150 ml beaker and add 20 ml of 12 *M* HCl. Stir the solution thoroughly and isolate the orange precipitate of $[Co(NH_3)_6]Cl_3$ by filtration through the Buchner funnel with suction. Continue to draw air through the funnel for several minutes to help dry the solid. Dry the product further by pressing the crystals between two pieces of filter paper. Let the crystals finish drying on a piece of filter paper and then weigh them.

D. Synthesis of Chloropentamminecobalt(III) Chloride, $[Co(NH_3)_5Cl]Cl_2$

$$[Co(NH_3)_5H_2O]Cl_3(s) \rightarrow [Co(NH_3)_5Cl]Cl_2(s) + H_2O(g)$$

Place the aquopentamminecobalt(III) chloride which was prepared in Part B on a small watch glass. Place the watch glass on a piece of asbestos-covered wire gauze supported on a ring stand. Adjust the height of the ring so that the gauze is about 2 inches above the top of a Bunsen burner tip. Spread the $[Co(NH_3)_5H_2O]Cl_3$ into a thin layer on the watch glass, using a spatula. Ignite the Bunsen burner and adjust the flame until the blue flame is about 3/4 inch high. Heat the wire gauze in the center (gently!) and observe the $[Co(NH_3)_5H_2O]Cl_3$. When the center of the red solid begins to darken, remove the flame. Move any remaining red solid to the center of the watch glass with a spatula, spreading the solid thin! Gently reheat the watch glass until only the purple product, $[Co(NH_3)_5Cl]Cl_2$, is left. Weigh the final product.

E. Relative Lability of Complex Ions

Put about 0.5 g of each of the complexes you prepared in separate small test tubes. Dissolve the solids in a few ml of water. Note the color and observe the effect of adding a few drops of 12 *M* HCl.

CAUTION: In these experiments you will be using 15 *M* NH_3, 12 *M* HCl, and a 10% solution of H_2O_2. Avoid getting these reagents on your skin or clothing and don't breathe the vapors of NH_3 or HCl. Wash off any spilled reagents thoroughly with water.

Name ______________________ Section ______________

DATA AND OBSERVATIONS: Synthesis of Some Coordination Compounds

	A	B	C	D
Yield of products	________ g	________ g	________ g	________ g
Theoretical yield of products	________ g	________ g	________ g	________ g
Percentage yield of products	________ %	________ %	________ %	________ %

Observations Regarding Lability of Complexes (Part E)

complex	color of solid	color in H_2O solution	color on addition of HCl
________	________	________	________
________	________	________	________
________	________	________	________

Conclusions

What evidence, if any, do you have that any of the formulas we have given for the compounds prepared in Parts A, B, C, and D are correct, either as to the nature of the atoms or groups present or as to the number of the groups present?

EXP. 27 Name ____________________ Section ____________

ADVANCE STUDY ASSIGNMENT: Synthesis of Some Coordination Compounds

1. a. Calculate the theoretical yields of all compounds to be prepared in the first four parts of this experiment. The metal ion in all cases is the limiting reagent.

A.

____________ g

B.

____________ g

C.

____________ g

D.

____________ g

b. Show that the cobalt ion is indeed the limiting reagent in Part B.

2. How would you name the compound $[Cu(NH_3)_4]\ SO_4 \cdot H_2O$ prepared in Part A?

3. What species would you expect to be present in aqueous solutions of each of the complexes to be prepared in these experiments?

A. C.

B. D.

SECTION 13

Oxidation-Reduction Reactions

EXPERIMENT 28

Determination of a Gram Equivalent Weight by Electrolysis

The gram equivalent weight of an element was defined in earlier experiments as that weight of the element which will combine with 8.000 grams of oxygen or with one gram equivalent weight of any other element. Experiments 4 and 5 dealt with the determination of gram equivalent weights by straightforward chemical means.

Experimentally we find that the gram equivalent weight of an element can also be related in a fundamental way to the chemical effects observed in that phenomenon known as *electrolysis*. As you know, some liquids, because they contain ions, will conduct an electric current. If the two terminals on a storage battery, or any other source of D.C. voltage, are connected through metal electrodes to a conducting liquid, an electric current will pass through the liquid and chemical reactions will occur at the two metal electrodes; in this experiment electrolysis is said to occur, and the liquid is said to be electrolyzed.

At the electrode connected to the *negative* pole of the battery, a *reduction* reaction will invariably be observed. In this reaction electrons will usually be accepted by one of the species present in the liquid, which, in the experiment we shall be doing, will be an aqueous solution. The species reduced will ordinarily be a metallic cation or the H^+ ion or possibly water itself; the reaction which is actually observed will be the one that occurs with the least expenditure of electrical energy, and will depend on the composition of the solution. In the electrolysis cell we shall study, the reduction reaction of interest will occur in an acid medium; hydrogen gas will be produced by the reduction of hydrogen ion:

$$2\,H^+(aq) + 2\,e^- \rightarrow H_2(g) \qquad (1)$$

In this reduction reaction, which will occur at the negative pole, or *cathode*, of the cell, for every H^+ ion reduced *one* electron will be required, and for every molecule of H_2 formed, *two* electrons will be needed.

Ordinarily in chemistry we deal not with individual ions or molecules but rather with moles of substances. In terms of moles, we can say that, by Equation 1,

The reduction of one mole of H^+ ion requires one mole of electrons
The production of one mole of $H_2(g)$ requires two moles of electrons

A mole of electrons is a fundamental amount of electricity in the same way that a mole of pure substance is a fundamental unit of matter, at least from a chemical point of view. A mole of electrons is called a *faraday*, after Michael Faraday, who discovered the basic laws of electrolysis. The amount of a species which will react with a *mole* of *electrons*, or *one faraday*, is equal to the *gram equivalent weight* of that species. Since one faraday will reduce one mole of H^+ ion, we say that the gram equivalent weight of hydrogen is 1.008 grams, the mass of one mole of H^+ ion (or one-half mole of $H_2(g)$). To form one mole of $H_2(g)$ one would have to pass two faradays through the electrolysis cell.

In the electrolysis experiment we will perform we will measure the volume of hydrogen gas produced under known conditions of temperature and pressure. By using the ideal gas law we will be able to calculate how many moles of H_2 were formed, and hence how many faradays of electricity passed through the cell.

At the positive pole of an electrolysis cell (the metal electrode that is connected to the + terminal of the battery), an *oxidation* reaction will occur, in which some species will give up electrons. This reaction, which takes place at the *anode* in the cell, may involve again an ionic or neutral species in the solution or the metallic electrode itself. In the cell that you will be studying, the pertinent oxidation reaction will be that in which a metal under study will participate:

$$M(s) \rightarrow M^{n+}(aq) + ne^- \tag{2}$$

During the course of the electrolysis the atoms in the metal electrode will be converted to metallic cations and will go into the solution. The mass of the metal electrode will decrease, depending on the amount of electricity passing through the cell and the nature of the metal. In order to oxidize one mole, or one gram atomic weight, of the metal, it would take n faradays, where n is the charge on the cation which is formed. By definition, one faraday of electricity would cause one gram equivalent weight, GEW, of metal to go into solution. The gram atomic weight, GAW, and the gram equivalent weight of the metal are clearly related by the equation:

$$\text{GAW} = \text{GEW} \times n \tag{3}$$

In an electrolysis experiment, since n is not determined independently, it is not possible to find the gram atomic weight of a substance. It is possible, however, to find gram equivalent weights of many metals, and that will be our purpose.

The general method we will use is implied by the discussion. We will oxidize a sample of an unknown metal at the positive pole of an electrolysis cell, weighing the metal before and after the electrolysis and so determining its loss in weight. We will use the same amount of electricity, the same number of electrons, to reduce hydrogen ion at the negative pole of an electrolysis cell. From the volume of H_2 gas which is produced under known conditions we can calculate the number of moles of H_2 formed, and hence the number of faradays which passed through the cell. (See Problem 2 in the advance study assignment for illustrative data.) The gram equivalent weight of the metal is then calculated as the amount of metal which would be oxidized if one faraday were used.

EXPERIMENTAL PROCEDURE

Obtain from the stockroom a buret and a sample of a metal unknown. Weigh the metal sample on the analytical balance.

Set up the electrolysis apparatus as indicated in Figure 28.1. There should be about 100 ml 1 *M* H_2SO_4 in the beaker with the gas buret. Immerse the end of the buret in the acid and attach a length of rubber tubing to its upper end. Open the stopcock on the buret and, with suction, carefully draw the acid up to the top of the graduations. Close the stopcock. Insert the bare coiled end of the heavy copper wire up into the end of the buret; all but the coil end of the wire should be covered with watertight insulation. Check the acid level after a few minutes to make sure the stopcock does not leak.

The hydrogen cell is connected to the other cell by a piece of heavy nichrome wire, which serves as an anode in one cell and a cathode in the other. The reactions that occur at the nichrome electrodes are not of concern in this experiment. The second 125 ml beaker should contain about 100 ml 0.5 *M* KNO_3. The anode in that beaker is made from your sample of unknown metal. Connect the metal to the + pole of the power source with an alligator clip and immerse the metal but not the clip in the KNO_3 solution. Read and record the liquid level in the buret.

Begin electrolysis by connecting the copper electrode to the negative pole of the power source. Hydrogen gas should immediately begin to bubble from the copper cathode. Collect the gas until about 50 ml have been produced. At that point, stop the electrolysis by disconnecting the cell from the power source. Record the liquid level in

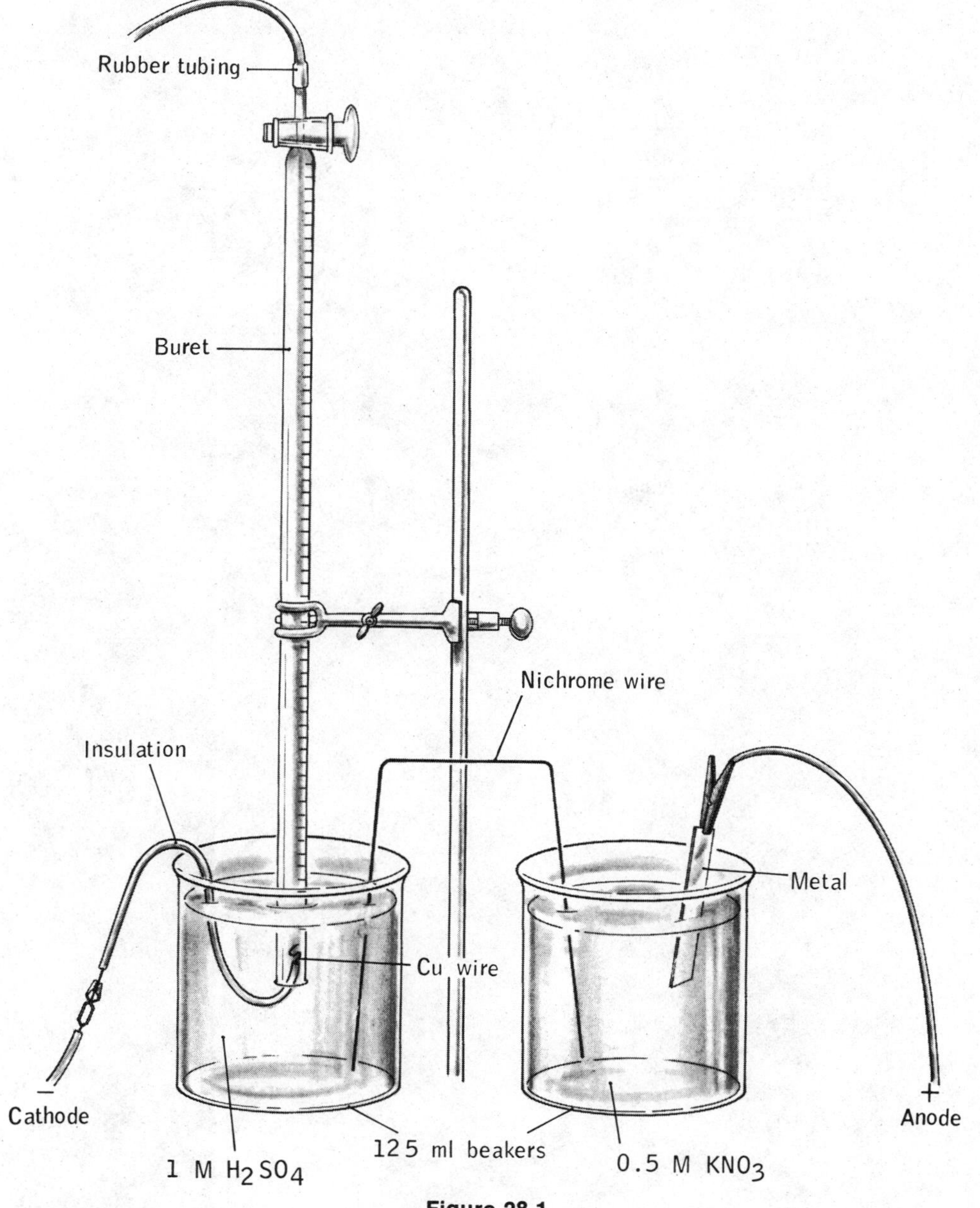

Figure 28.1

the buret. (In some cases a cloudiness will appear in the KNO_3 solution during the electrolysis; this is caused by formation of a metal hydroxide, and will have no adverse effect on the experiment.) Open the stopcock on the buret and again draw the acid up to the top of the graduations. Read the buret, reconnect the electrical wires, and generate another 50 ml of hydrogen as before.

Record the liquid level in the buret and the temperature and barometric pressure in the laboratory. Remove the metal anode from the electrolysis cell and rinse it with 0.1 *M* or, if necessary, 1 *M* acetic acid; if it has a flaky coating, scrape this off and rinse the electrode again; dry it by immersing it in acetone and letting the acetone evaporate in the air. Weigh the metal anode.

Name ______________________ Section ______________

DATA AND CALCULATIONS: Determination of a Gram Equivalent Weight by Electrolysis

Weight of metal anode ____________ g

Weight of anode after electrolysis ____________ g

Initial buret reading ____________ ml

Buret reading after first electrolysis ____________ ml

Buret reading after refilling ____________ ml

Buret reading after second electrolysis ____________ ml

Barometric pressure ____________ mm Hg

Temperature t ____________ °C

Vapor pressure of H_2O at t ____________ mm Hg

Total volume of H_2 produced, V ____________ ml

Temperature T ____________ °K

Pressure exerted by dry H_2: $P = P_{Bar} - VP_{H_2O}$
(ignore any pressure effect due to liquid levels in buret) ____________ mm Hg

No. moles H_2 produced, n
(use Ideal Gas Law, $PV = nRT$) ____________ moles

No. of faradays passed ____________

Loss in weight by anode ____________ g

Gram equivalent weight of metal ____________ g

Unknown metal number ____________

EXP. 28 **Name** ____________________ **Section** ____________

ADVANCE STUDY ASSIGNMENT: Determination of a Gram Equivalent Weight by Electrolysis

1. In the electrolysis experiment, two cells are used. Why is it possible to relate the effect at the cathode of one cell to the anode of the other?

2. A current passing through an electrolytic cell such as the one employed in this experiment liberates 27.2 ml of H_2 at the cathode and causes a weight loss of 0.232 g at the metal anode. If the barometric pressure is 752 mm Hg, and the temperature in the laboratory is 24°C, what is the gram equivalent weight of the metal? At 24°C the vapor pressure of water is 22.4 mm Hg.

P_{H_2} = ____________ mm Hg = ____________ atm

V_{H_2} = ____________ ml = ____________ lit

T = ____________ °K

n_{H_2} = ____________ moles

1 mole H_2 requires ____________ faradays

No. faradays passed = ____________ = No. GEW metal oxidized

No. g metal oxidized = ____________ g

$$\text{GEW metal} = \frac{\text{No. g oxidized}}{\text{No. faradays passed}} = \_\_\_\_\_\_\_\_ = \_\_\_\_\_\_\_\_ \text{g}$$

3. In this experiment we make the assumption that the reactions occurring at the cathode and anode are the only reactions which take place. That is, we assume that the electrode processes are 100% efficient. If other reactions also occur at the electrodes of interest, the results of the experiment will be incorrect. What effect would the evolution of O_2 occurring simultaneously with the oxidation of the metal anode have on the value of the GEW of the metal which would be obtained?

EXPERIMENT 29

Voltaic Cell Measurements

Many chemical reactions can be classified as oxidation-reduction reactions, since they involve the oxidation of one species and the reduction of another. Such reactions can conveniently be considered as the result of two half reactions, one of oxidation and the other reduction. In the case of the oxidation-reduction reaction

$$Zn(s) + Pb^{2+}(aq) \rightarrow Zn^{2+}(aq) + Pb(s)$$

which would occur if a piece of metallic zinc were put into a solution of lead nitrate, the two reactions would be

$$Zn(s) \rightarrow Zn^{2+}(aq) + 2e^- \qquad \text{oxidation}$$

$$2e^- + Pb^{2+}(aq) \rightarrow Pb(s) \qquad \text{reduction}$$

The tendency for an oxidation-reduction reaction to occur can be measured if the two reactions are made to occur in separate regions connected by a barrier that is porous to ion movement. An apparatus called a *voltaic cell* in which this reaction might be carried out under these conditions is shown in Figure 29.1.

If we connect a voltmeter between the two electrodes we will find that there is a voltage, or potential, between them. The magnitude of the potential is a direct measure

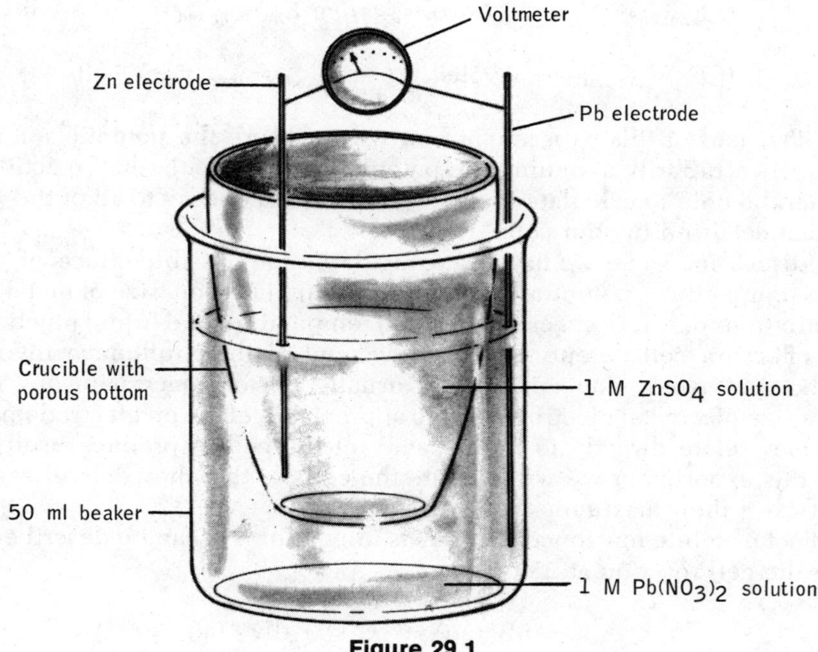

Figure 29.1

of the driving force or thermodynamic tendency of the oxidation-reduction reaction to occur.

If we study several oxidation-reduction reactions we find that the potential of each associated voltaic cell can be considered to be the sum of a potential for the oxidation reaction and a potential for the reduction reaction. In the Zn, Zn^{2+}||Pb^{2+}, Pb cell we have been discussing, for example,

$$E_{cell} = E_{Zn,\,Zn^{2+}\text{oxidation reaction}} + E_{Pb^{2+},\,Pb\text{ reduction reaction}} \tag{1}$$

By convention, the negative electrode in a voltaic cell is taken to be the one from which electrons are emitted (i.e., where oxidation occurs), so here Zn is negative.

Since any cell potential is the sum of two electrode potentials, it is not possible, by measuring cell potentials, to determine individual absolute electrode potentials. However, if a value of potential is arbitrarily assigned to one electrode reaction, then other electrode potentials can be given definite values, based on the assigned value. The usual procedure is to assign a value of 0.0000 volts to the standard potential for the electrode reaction

$$2\,H^+(aq) + 2\,e^- \rightarrow H_2(g); \quad E_{H^+,H_2\text{ red}} = 0.0000\,v$$

For the Zn, Zn^{2+}||H^+, H_2 cell, the measured potential is 0.76 v, and the zinc electrode is negative. Zinc metal is therefore oxidized, and the cell reaction must be

$$Zn(s) + 2\,H^+(aq) \rightarrow Zn^{2+}(aq) + H_2(g); \quad E_{cell} = 0.76v$$

Given this information, one can readily find the potential for the oxidation of Zn to Zn^{2+}.

$$E_{cell} = E_{Zn,\,Zn^{2+}\text{ oxid}} + E_{H^+,\,H_2\text{ red}}$$

$$0.76\text{ v} = E_{Zn,\,Zn^{2+}\text{ oxid}} + 0.00\text{ v}; \quad E_{Zn,\,Zn^{2+}\text{ oxid}} = +0.76\text{ v}$$

If the potential for a half reaction is known, the potential for the reverse reaction can be obtained by changing the sign. For example:

$$\textit{if } E_{Zn,\,Zn^{2+}\text{ oxid}} = +0.76\text{ volts}, \quad \textit{then } E_{Zn^{2+},\,Zn\text{ red}} = -0.76\text{ volts}$$

$$\textit{if } E_{Pb^{2+},\,Pb\text{ red}} = +Y\text{ volts}, \quad \textit{then } E_{Pb,\,Pb^{2+}\text{ oxid}} = -Y\text{ volts}$$

In the first part of this experiment you will measure the potentials of several different cells. By arbitrarily assigning the potential of a particular half reaction as 0.00 v, you will then be able to calculate the potentials corresponding to all of the various half reactions that occurred in your cells.

In our discussion so far we have not considered the possible effects of such system variables as temperature, potential at the liquid-liquid junction, size of metal electrodes, and concentrations of solute species. Although temperature and liquid junctions do have a definite effect on cell potentials, taking account of their influence involves rather complex thermodynamic concepts and is usually not of concern in any elementary course. The size of a metal electrode has no appreciable effect on electrode potential, although it does relate directly to the capacity of the cell to produce useful electrical energy. In this experiment we will operate the cells so that they deliver essentially no energy but exert their maximum potentials.

The effect of solute ion concentrations is important and can be described relatively easily. For the cell reaction at 25°C:

$$aA(s) + bB^+(aq) \rightarrow cC(s) + dD^{2+}(aq)$$

$$E_{cell} = E^\circ_{cell} - \frac{0.06}{n}\log\frac{(D^{2+})^d}{(B^+)^b} \tag{2}$$

where E°_{cell} is a constant for a given reaction and is called the standard cell potential, and n is the number of electrons in either electrode reaction. (Strictly speaking, in Equation (2) the so-called activities of the ions should be used rather than their molarities. See footnote in Experiment 18.)

By Equation 2 you can see that the measured cell potential, E_{cell}, will equal the standard cell potential if the molarities of D^{2+} and B^+ are both unity, or, if d equals b, if they are simply equal to each other. We will carry out our experiments under such conditions that the cell potentials you observe will be very close to the standard potentials given in the tables in your chemistry text.

Considering the $Cu,Cu^{2+}\|Ag^+,Ag$ cell as a specific example, the observed cell reaction would be

$$Cu(s) + 2\,Ag^+(aq) \rightarrow Cu^{2+}(aq) + 2\,Ag(s)$$

For this cell, Equation 2 takes the form

$$E_{cell} = E^\circ_{cell} - \frac{0.06}{2} \log \frac{(Cu^{2+})}{(Ag^+)^2} \qquad (3)$$

In the equation n is 2 because in the cell reaction, two electrons are transferred in each of the two half reactions. E°_{cell} would be the cell potential when the copper and silver salt solutions are both 1 M, since then the logarithm term is equal to zero.

If we decrease the Cu^{2+} concentration, keeping that of Ag^+ at 1 M, the potential of the cell will go up by about 0.03 volts for every factor of ten by which we decrease conc. Cu^{2+}. Ordinarily it is not convenient to change concentrations of an ion by several orders of magnitude, so in general, concentration effects in cells are relatively small. However, if we should add a complexing or precipitating species to the copper salt solution, the value of (Cu^{2+}) would drop drastically, and the voltage change would be appreciable. In the experiment we will illustrate this effect by using NH_3 to complex the Cu^{2+}. Using Equation 3, we can actually calculate (Cu^{2+}) in the solution of its complex ion.

In an analogous experiment we will determine the solubility product of AgCl. In this case we will surround the Ag electrode in a $Cu,Cu^{2+}\|Ag^+,Ag$ cell with a solution of known Cl^- ion concentration which is saturated with AgCl. From the measured cell potential, we can use Equation 3 to calculate the very small value of (Ag^+) in the chloride-containing solution. Knowing the concentrations of Ag^+ and Cl^- in a solution in equilibrium with AgCl(s) allows us to find K_{sp} for AgCl.

EXPERIMENTAL PROCEDURE

You may work in pairs in this experiment.

A. Cell Potentials. In this part of the experiment you will be working with these seven electrode systems:

Ag^+, Ag(s)	Br_2(l), Br^-, Pt
Cu^{2+}, Cu(s)	Cl_2(g, 1 atm), Cl^-, Pt
Fe^{3+}, Fe^{2+}, Pt	I_2(s), I^-, Pt
Zn^{2+}, Zn(s)	

Your purpose will be to measure enough voltaic cell potentials to allow you to determine the electrode potentials of each electrode by comparing it with an arbitrarily chosen electrode potential.

Using the apparatus shown in Figure 29.1, set up a voltaic cell involving any two of the electrodes in the list. The solute ion concentrations may be assumed to be one molar and all other species may be assumed to be at unit activity, so that the potential of the cell you set up will be essentially the standard potential. Measure the cell potential and record it along with which electrode has negative polarity.

In a similar manner set up and measure the cell potentials and polarities of other cells, sufficient in number to include all of the electrode systems on the list at least once. Do not combine the silver electrode system with any of the halogen electrode systems, since a precipitate will form; any other combinations may be used. The data from this part of the experiment should be entered in the first three columns of the table in Part A.1 of your report.

B. Effect of Concentration on Cell Potentials

1. COMPLEX ION FORMATION. Set up the Cu,Cu^{2+}||Ag^+, Ag cell, using 10 ml of the $CuSO_4$ solution in the crucible and the solution of $AgNO_3$ in the beaker. Measure the potential of the cell. While the potential is being measured, add 10 ml of 6*M* NH_3 to the $CuSO_4$ solution, stirring carefully with your stirring rod. Measure the potential when it becomes steady.

2. DETERMINATION OF THE SOLUBILITY PRODUCT OF AgCl. Remove the crucible from the cell you have just studied and discard the solution of $Cu(NH_3)_4^{2+}$. Clean the crucible by drawing a little 6 *M* NH_3 through it, using the adapter and suction flask. Then draw some distilled water through it. Reassemble the Cu-Ag cell, this time using the beaker for the Cu-$CuSO_4$ electrode system. Immerse the Ag electrode in the crucible in 1 *M* KCl; add a drop of $AgNO_3$ solution to form a little AgCl, so that an equilibrium between Ag^+ and Cl^- can be established. Measure the potential of this cell, noting which electrode is negative. In this case (Ag^+) will be very low, which will decrease the potential of the cell to such an extent that its polarity may change from that observed previously.

Name ______________________ Section ______________

DATA AND CALCULATIONS: Voltaic Cell Measurements

A. 1. Cell Potentials

	Electrode systems used in cell	Cell potential, E°_{cell} (volts)	Negative electrode	Oxidation reaction	$E^\circ_{oxidation}$ in volts	Reduction reaction	$E^\circ_{reduction}$ in volts
1.							
2.							
3.							
4.							
5.							
6.							
7.							

CALCULATIONS

A. Noting that oxidation occurs at the negative pole in a cell, write the oxidation reaction in each of the cells. The other electrode system must undergo reduction; write the reduction reaction which occurs in each cell.

B. Assume that $E^\circ_{Ag^+,\ Ag} = 0.00$ volts (whether in reduction or oxidation). Enter that value in the table for all of the silver electrode systems you used in your cells. Since $E^\circ_{cell} = E^\circ_{oxidation} + E^\circ_{reduction}$, you can calculate E° values for all the electrode systems in which the Ag, Ag^+ system was involved. Enter those values in the table.

C. Using the values and relations in B and taking advantage of the fact that for any given electrode system, $E^\circ_{oxidation} = -E^\circ_{reduction}$, complete the table of E° values. The best way to do this is to use one of the E° values you found in B in another cell with that electrode system. That potential, along with E°_{cell}, will allow you to find the potential of the other electrode. Continue this process with other cells until all the electrode potentials have been determined.

Continued on following page

A.2. Table of Electrode Potentials

In Table A.1, you should have a value for $E°_{red}$ or $E°_{oxid}$ for each of the electrode systems you have studied. Remembering that for any electrode system, $E°_{red} = -E°_{oxid}$, you can find the value for $E°_{red}$ for each system. List those potentials in the left column of the table below in order of decreasing value.

$E°_{reduction}$ ($E°_{Ag^+, Ag} = 0.00$ volts)	Electrode reaction in reduction	$E°_{reduction}$ ($E°_{H^+, H_2} = 0.00$ volts)
____________	____________	____________
____________	____________	____________
____________	____________	____________
____________	____________	____________
____________	____________	____________
____________	____________	____________
____________	____________	____________

The electrode potentials you have determined are based on $E°_{Ag^+, Ag} = 0.00$ volts. The usual assumption is that $E°_{H^+, H_2} = 0.00$ volts, under which conditions $E°_{Ag^+, Ag\ red} = 0.80$ volts. Convert from one base to the other by adding 0.80 volts to each of the electrode potentials and enter these values in the third column of the table.

Why are the values of $E°_{red}$ on the two bases related to each other in such a simple way?

What is the most powerful reducing species you studied in this experiment? Give your reasoning.

Calculate the standard potential of the $Ag,Ag^+||I_2(s),I^-$ cell. Which electrode would be negative?

____________ volts

Continued on following page

B. Effect of Concentration on Cell Potentials

1. Complex ion formation:

Potential, E°_{cell}, before addition of 6 *M* NH_3 __________volts

Potential, E_{cell}, after $Cu(NH_3)_4^{2+}$ formed __________volts

Given Equation 3

$$E_{cell} = E^\circ_{cell} - \frac{0.06}{2} \log \frac{(Cu^{2+})}{(Ag^+)^2} \qquad (3)$$

calculate the residual concentration of free Cu^{2+} ion in equilibrium with $Cu(NH_3)_4^{2+}$ in the solution in the crucible.

$(Cu^{2+})=$ __________ *M*

2. Solubility product of AgCl:

Potential, E°_{cell}, of the Cu, $Cu^{2+}||Ag^+$, Ag cell (from B.1)

______v Negative electrode______

Potential, E_{cell}, with 1 *M* KCl present ______v Negative electrode ______

Using Equation 3, calculate (Ag^+) in the cell, where it is in equilibrium with 1 *M* Cl^- ion. (E_{cell} in Equation 3 is the *negative* of the measured value if the polarity is not the same as in the standard cell.)

$(Ag^+) =$ __________ *M*

Determine K_{sp} AgCl on the basis of your results.

$K_{sp} =$ __________

EXP. 29 **Name** ______________________ **Section** ______________

ADVANCE STUDY ASSIGNMENT: Voltaic Cell Measurements

1. Write the electrode reactions associated with the following oxidation-reduction reaction: $Ni(s) + Hg_2^{2+}(aq) \rightarrow 2\ Hg(l) + Ni^{2+}(aq)$

2. Describe how you would make a voltaic cell to study this reaction.

3. If the reaction in Problem 1 occurs spontaneously in the cell, which electrode will be negative?

4. How would the cell potential change if the reaction above were written for two moles of Ni(s)?

5. If the cell potential as measured is 1.04 volts and the reaction is that described in Problem 1, what would be the reduction potential associated with the Ni^{2+}, Ni electrode if

(a) the Hg, Hg_2^{2+} electrode is assigned a potential of 0.000 volts?
(b) the Hg, Hg_2^{2+} electrode is assigned a reduction potential of 0.80 volts?

(a) ____________ volts

(b) ____________ volts

6. Referring to Equation 3, what voltage would you expect to obtain for a Cu, Cu^{2+}|| Ag^+, Ag cell in which the solution surrounding the Ag electrode is 1 M in Br^- and saturated with AgBr (K_{sp}AgBr $= 1 \times 10^{-13}$)? Assume $E°_{cell} = 0.46$ v.

____________ volts

EXPERIMENT 30

Preparation of Copper(I) Chloride

Oxidation-reduction reactions, like the other kinds of reactions we have studied, are often used in the preparation of inorganic substances. In this experiment we will employ a series of chemical changes involving oxidation-reduction, precipitation, acid-base, and complex ion formation reactions to prepare one of the less commonly encountered compounds of copper, copper(I) chloride. Most copper compounds contain copper(II), but copper(I) is present in a few slightly soluble or complex copper salts.

We begin the synthesis of CuCl by dissolving copper metal in nitric acid:

$$Cu(s) + 4\,H^+(aq) + 2\,NO_3^-(aq) \rightarrow Cu^{2+}(aq) + 2\,NO_2(g) + 2\,H_2O \qquad (1)$$

The solution obtained is treated with sodium carbonate in excess, which neutralizes the remaining acid with evolution of CO_2 and precipitates Cu(II) as the carbonate:

$$2\,H^+(aq) + CO_3^{2-}(aq) \rightleftharpoons (H_2CO_3)\,(aq) \rightleftharpoons CO_2(g) + H_2O \qquad (2)$$

$$Cu^{2+}(aq) + CO_3^{2-}(aq) \rightleftharpoons CuCO_3(s) \qquad (3)$$

The $CuCO_3$ will be purified by filtration and washing and dissolved in hydrochloric acid. Copper metal added to the highly acidic solution then reduces the Cu(II) to Cu(I) and is itself oxidized to Cu(I). In the presence of excess chloride, the copper will be present as a $CuCl_4^{3-}$ complex ion. Addition of this solution to water destroys the complex, and white CuCl precipitates.

$$CuCO_3(s) + 2\,H^+(aq) + 4\,Cl^-(aq) \rightarrow CuCl_4^{2-}(aq) + CO_2(g) + H_2O \qquad (4)$$

$$CuCl_4^{2-}(aq) + Cu(s) + 4\,Cl^-(aq) \rightarrow 2\,CuCl_4^{3-}(aq) \qquad (5)$$

$$CuCl_4^{3-}(aq) \xrightarrow{H_2O} CuCl(s) + 3\,Cl^-(aq) \qquad (6)$$

Since CuCl is readily oxidized, due care must be taken to minimize its exposure to air during its preparation and while it is being dried.

EXPERIMENTAL PROCEDURE { *WEAR YOUR SAFETY GLASSES WHILE PERFORMING THIS EXPERIMENT.*

Obtain a 1 g sample of copper metal, a Buchner funnel, and a filter flask from the stockroom. Weigh the copper metal on the top loading or triple beam balance to 0.1 g.

Put the metal in a 150 ml beaker and *under a hood* add 5 ml 15 *M* HNO_3. Brown NO_2 gas will be evolved and an acidic blue solution of $Cu(NO_3)_2$ produced. If it is necessary, you may warm the beaker gently with a Bunsen burner to dissolve all of the copper. When all of the copper is in solution, add 50 ml of water to the solution and allow it to cool.

Weigh out about 5 grams of sodium carbonate in a small beaker on a rough balance. Add small amounts of the Na_2CO_3 to the solution with your spatula, adding the solid as necessary when the evolution of CO_2 subsides. Stir the solution to expose it to the solid.

When the acid is neutralized, a blue-green precipitate of $CuCO_3$ will begin to form. At that point, add the rest of the Na_2CO_3, stirring the mixture well to ensure complete precipitation of the copper carbonate.

Transfer the precipitate to the Buchner funnel and use suction to remove the excess liquid. Use your rubber policeman and a spray from your wash bottle to make a complete transfer of the solid. Wash the precipitate well with distilled water with suction on, then let it remain on the filter paper with suction on for a minute or two.

Remove the filter paper from the funnel and transfer the solid $CuCO_3$ to the 150 ml beaker. Add 25 ml water and then 10 ml 12 *M* HCl slowly to the solid, stirring continuously. When the $CuCO_3$ has all dissolved, add 1.5 g Cu foil cut in small pieces to the beaker and cover it with a watch glass.

Heat the mixture in the beaker to the boiling point and keep it at that temperature, just simmering, for 30 to 40 minutes. It may be that the dark-colored solution which forms will clear to a yellow color before that time is up, and if it does, you may stop heating and proceed with the next step.

While the mixture is heating, put 150 ml distilled water in a 400 ml beaker and put the beaker in an ice bath. Cover the beaker with a watch glass. After you have heated the acidic Cu-$CuCl_2$ mixture for 40 minutes or as soon as it turns light-colored, carefully decant the hot liquid into the beaker of water, taking care not to transfer any of the excess Cu metal to the beaker. White crystals of CuCl should form. Continue to cool the beaker in the ice bath to promote crystallization and to increase the yield of solid.

Pour 25 ml glacial acetic acid (*careful, it's a caustic reagent*) and 25 ml acetone into separate small beakers. Filter the crystals of CuCl in the Buchner funnel using suction. Swirl the beaker to aid in transferring the solid to the funnel. Just as the last of the liquid is being pulled through, wash the CuCl with one third of the glacial acetic acid. Rinse the last of the CuCl into the funnel with another portion of the acid and use the final third to rewash the solid. Turn off suction and add one half of the acetone to the funnel; wait about ten seconds and turn on the suction. Repeat this operation with the other half of the acetone. Draw air through the sample for a few minutes to dry it. If you have properly washed the solid, it will be pure white; if the moist compound is allowed to come into contact with air, it will tend to turn pale green, due to oxidation of Cu(I) to Cu(II). Weigh the CuCl in a previously weighed beaker to 0.1 g. Show your sample to your instructor for his evaluation.

(Optional) Analysis of CuCl. It will take one laboratory period to do this analysis.

It is reasonably easy to carry out a complete elemental analysis of the CuCl you prepared to prove that its formula is as given. We will only outline the procedure here, to the point where you should be able to design the experimental steps yourself.

ANALYSIS FOR CL. Dissolve a carefully weighed sample of CuCl (~0.25 g) in 5 ml 6 *M* HNO_3; add a few drops of 3% H_2O_2 if necessary to hasten the solution process. Add 25 ml distilled water and 30 ml 0.1 *M* $AgNO_3$. Mix well, and let the AgCl settle. Filter through a weighed porous crucible, using suction; transfer all of the AgCl to the crucible. Wash with acetone and dry the AgCl with suction and then in air. Reweigh the crucible. From the number of grams AgCl, calculate the number of grams Cl and number of moles Cl in the sample.

ANALYSIS FOR CU. Dissolve a carefully weighed sample of CuCl (~0.25 g) in 25 ml $NH_4Fe(SO_4)_2 \cdot 12H_2O$ (ferric alum) solution. (Make alum solution by dissolving about 100 g alum in 500 ml distilled water and diluting to one liter with 6 *M* H_2SO_4.) This solution will oxidize all of the Cu(I) to Cu(II), simultaneously reducing an equal number of moles of Fe(III) to Fe(II). Without delay, titrate the solution to a pink end point with standardized $KMnO_4$ solution (~0.02 *M*). In the titration reaction, 1 mole $KMnO_4$ oxidizes 5 moles Fe(II). Calculate the number of moles Fe(II) oxidized, which equals the number of moles Cu(I) in the sample.

Obtain the formula of the copper chloride from the relative number of moles of copper and chlorine in the sample.

Name ______________________ Section ______________

DATA AND RESULTS: Preparation of CuCl

Weight of Cu sample	________ g
Weight of watch glass	________ g
Weight of beaker plus CuCl	________ g
Weight of CuCl prepared	________ g
Theoretical yield	________ g
Percentage yield	________ %

EXP. 30 Name ______________________ Section ______________

ADVANCED STUDY ASSIGNMENT: Preparation of Copper(I) Chloride

1. The Cu^{2+} ions in this experiment are produced from the reaction of 1.0 g of copper foil with excess nitric acid. How many moles of Cu^{2+} are produced?

______________moles Cu^{2+}

2. Why isn't hydrochloric acid used in a direct reaction with copper wire to prepare the $CuCl_2$ solution?

3. How many grams of metallic copper are required to react with the number of moles of Cu^{2+} calculated in Problem 1 to form the CuCl?

______________g Cu

4. What is the maximum weight of CuCl that can be prepared from the reaction sequence of this experiment if 1.0 g of Cu foil is used to prepare the Cu^{2+} solution?

______________g CuCl

SECTION 14

Nuclear Chemistry

EXPERIMENT 31

Determination of the Half-life of a Radioactive Isotope

Some atomic nuclei are radioactive; that is to say, they can spontaneously undergo reactions in which they converted to different nuclei, which may or may not belong to different elements. For example $^{20}_{9}F$ nuclei may spontaneously emit electrons in a reaction in which $^{20}_{10}$ Ne nuclei are produced:

$$^{20}_{9}\mathrm{F} \rightarrow {}^{20}_{10}\mathrm{Ne} + {}^{0}_{-1}\mathrm{e}$$

Reactions such as this differ from ordinary chemical reactions in several ways. Typically they produce electrons, He^{2+} nuclei, γ-rays, or some combination of these, all having very high associated energies. The reactions ordinarily involve relatively few atoms, and we usually study them by measuring the high energy particles or radiations that are emitted. Neither the temperature nor the state of chemical combination of the substances containing the active nuclei affect appreciably either the rate at which the reaction occurs or the energies of the emitted species.

The rate at which given radioactive nuclei decay depends only on the kind and number of nuclei present. In any fixed time interval Δt a certain fraction of the active nuclei will undergo reaction according to the equation

$$\frac{\Delta n}{n} = -k\Delta t \qquad (1)$$

where n is the number of active nuclei in the sample and Δn is the change in the number of active nuclei (or minus the number undergoing decay) in the time interval Δt. Equation 1 can be rewritten to read

$$\frac{\Delta n}{\Delta t} = -kn \qquad (2)$$

which tells us that the rate of radioactive decay, $\Delta n/\Delta t$, is proportional to the number of active nuclei present. The proportionality constant k is called the rate constant for the decay, and the minus sign indicates that the number of active nuclei in the sample decreases with time.

By the methods of the calculus, Equation 2 can be integrated to produce an equation that allows us to calculate the number of active nuclei n in a sample at a given time, given the initial number of nuclei n_0 and the associated decay constant:

$$\log_{10} n = \log_{10} n_0 - \frac{kt}{2.3} \tag{3}$$

The time t required for half of the active nuclei in a sample to decay is called the half-life of the nuclei, $t_{1/2}$. If, in Equation 3, $t = t_{1/2}$, then n equals $n_0/2$, and it becomes clear that $t_{1/2}$ and k are related by the equation

$$\log_{10} 1/2 = \frac{-kt_{1/2}}{2.3} \quad \text{or} \quad t_{1/2} = \frac{-0.301 \times 2.303}{-k} = \frac{0.693}{k} \tag{4}$$

If by some means we can find k for a given active isotope, we can find its half-life by Equation 4.

Devices have been developed that are sensitive to the high-energy particles emitted in the nuclear reactions that occur during radioactive decay processes. Upon entering such a device, usually called a counter, a high-energy particle causes an electric discharge in the counter. This discharge is automatically recorded on a digital readout meter. In a typical experiment the active sample is placed near the counter, and the number of particles emitted in the direction of the detector is determined. If the number of particles entering the counter is measured as a function of time, we can measure in a relative way the number of active atoms in the whole sample; for example, if after 10 minutes the number of counts per minute is only 80 per cent of the number at the beginning of the experiment, there are only 80 per cent as many active nuclei in the sample as there were at the start. This means that if the counting rate is called A, the activity of the sample, Equation 3 can be written in terms of A as well as n, in a relative way, to give

$$\log_{10} \frac{n}{n_0} = \log_{10} \frac{A}{A_0} = -\frac{kt}{2.3} \quad \text{or} \log A = \log A_0 - \frac{kt}{2.3} \tag{5}$$

To determine the decay constant k for a given active nucleus, we need merely to measure the activity of a sample containing that kind of nucleus as a function of time. Substituting into Equation 5 at two different times and counting rates will permit the elimination of $\log A_0$ and the evaluation of k. A more accurate method would be to measure the activity A of the sample at several times and to make a graph of $\log A$ as a function of time. Since $\log A$ varies linearly with time, the slope of the graph of $\log A$ versus t should be constant and equal to $-k/2.3$.

In this experiment we will use the latter procedure to measure the half-life of a radioactive isotope. Since most naturally occurring radioactive isotopes have very long half-lives, and thus could not be studied by this method, we will use synthetic radioactive isotopes prepared in this laboratory. Many nuclei, when bombarded with slow neutrons, absorb the neutrons and so undergo nuclear reactions. The nuclei so formed are typically radioactive but do not decay by neutron emission. Rather, they emit electrons of high energy and are thereby converted to nuclei of one higher atomic number. Naturally occurring iodine is typical in its behavior in this regard:

On bombardment with slow neutrons: $^{127}_{53}\text{I} + ^{1}_{0}\text{n} \rightarrow ^{128}_{53}\text{I}$

Decay reaction: $^{128}_{53}\text{I} \rightarrow ^{128}_{54}\text{Xe} + ^{0}_{-1}\text{e}$

The electrons, which are called β particles in such reactions, can be readily detected in a counter and so used to measure the decay rate. The isotopes we shall be using have half-lives of the order of a few hours, so that they can be conveniently studied in the course of a laboratory period. The radiation emitted is of relatively low energy and of short duration, and is not particularly hazardous. You should, however, use due caution and not get any sample into your mouth or let it remain for any length of time on your skin.

EXPERIMENTAL PROCEDURE

Obtain a test tube containing an unknown radioactive sample from the stockroom.

Your instructor will demonstrate the use of the radioactivity counter in your laboratory. Do not make any adjustments of the counter settings unless you are specifically directed to do so.

Pour your sample into the planchet provided and smooth it out with the spatula so that it lies in a layer of uniform thickness. Place the planchet in the counter; turn the counter on and measure the number of counts recorded in a one-minute interval. Record the time at which you started the counter. Remove the planchet from the counter and place an empty planchet in the counter. Record the number of background counts obtained in a one-minute interval with the empty planchet.

Wait about 15 minutes and repeat the procedure, noting the number of counts per minute and the time you begin to count. If there is not too much congestion from other students wishing to use the counter, measure the background counting rate a second time.

Repeat the procedure at about 15-minute intervals until you have obtained six counting rates at six different times. During the course of the period you should also obtain about four measurements of the background radiation counting rate.

When you have finished the experiment, dispose of your sample as directed by your laboratory instructor.

Name ______________ Section ________________

DATA AND CALCULATIONS: Determination of the Half-life of a Radioactive Isotope

Unknown no. ____________

Count obtained in one minute	Time when counter was turned on	Total elapsed time	Corrected counting rate* = activity, A	$\log_{10}$ corrected counting rate = $\log_{10} A$
________	________	________	________	________
________	________	________	________	________
________	________	________	________	________
________	________	________	________	________
________	________	________	________	________
________	________	________	________	________

Background count ____________ ____________ ____________ ____________

Average background ____________ cpm obtained in one minute.

*Subtract the average background counting rate from the counts per minute obtained with the sample to obtain the corrected counting rate, or the activity, A, of the sample.

On the graph paper provided, make a graph of $\log_{10}A$ as a function of elapsed time.

Slope of line obtained in the graph $= \frac{\Delta \log A}{\Delta t} =$ ____________

Slope of the line $= -\frac{k}{2.303}$; $k =$ ____________ min^{-1}

By Equation 4, $t_{1/2} = \frac{0.693}{k} =$ ____________ $=$ ____________ min

Name ______________________________ Section ______________

DETERMINATION OF THE HALF-LIFE OF A RADIOACTIVE ISOTOPE (Data and Calculations)

 Name ______________ Section ____________________

ADVANCE STUDY ASSIGNMENT: Determination of the Half-life of a Radioactive Isotope

1. In experiments of this sort the activity ratio A/A_0 can be taken to be equal to the active nuclei ratio n/n_0. Why is this relation valid?

2. A certain sample of a compound containing a radioactive isotope produced 351 counts in one minute at the beginning of the experiment and a count of 90 in one minute when 68 minutes had passed. If the background count was 20 cpm, what is the decay constant k and the half-life of the radioactive species?

k = ______________ min^{-1}

$t_{1/2}$ = ______________ min

SECTION 15
Qualitative Analysis

Introduction to the Qualitative Analysis of Cations and Anions

The remaining experiments in this manual are devoted to that area of chemistry called qualitative analysis, in which one studies the methods by which one can determine the nature, but not the amount, of the species in a mixture. In these experiments you will usually be asked to analyze unknown solutions containing for the most part metallic cations and inorganic anions in aqueous solutions. The scheme of analysis we will use will allow for the identification of 22 cations and 15 anions.

Since the general problem of the analysis of a complex mixture of ions is by no means simple, the scheme of analysis is broken down into several parts; each part involves a fairly small group of ions which can be isolated from the general mixture, or at least studied as a separate set, on the basis of some property which is common to the ions in the group.

Analysis of Cations. The procedure for determining which cations are in a solution is somewhat more systematic than that used with anions and is dealt with first. In our scheme we separate the cations into four Groups. By means of selective precipitations, these Groups are removed one at a time and in a definite order from the general mixture. The cations in Group I are removed first, leaving the cations in Groups II, III, and IV in solution; from that solution the Group II cations are then precipitated, leaving Groups III and IV in solution, and so on.

The members of each Group, and the conditions under which that Group is separated, are as follows:

Group I	Ag^+, Hg_2^{2+}, Pb^{2+}	Precipitated as chlorides under strongly acidic conditions
Group II	Cu^{2+}, Cd^{2+}, Bi^{3+}, Sn^{2+} and Sn^{4+}, Hg^{2+}, Sb^{3+} and Sb^{5+}, (Pb^{2+})	Precipitated as sulfides under mildly acidic conditions
Group III	Al^{3+}, Zn^{2+}, Cr^{3+}, Fe^{2+} and Fe^{3+}, Ni^{2+}, Co^{2+}, Mn^{2+}	Precipitated as sulfides or hydroxides under slightly basic conditions
Group IV	Ba^{2+}, Ca^{2+}, Mg^{2+}, Na^+, K^+, NH_4^+	Remain in solution after precipitation of Group III cations

After separation, the cations within a Group are further resolved by means of a series of chemical reactions into sets of soluble and insoluble fractions, until the resolution is sufficient to allow identification of each cation by one or more tests specific to that ion. During the course of these separations all the different kinds of chemical reactions we have studied in this course will be used; in addition to precipitations, we will employ acid-base reactions, complex ion formation, oxidation-reduction, and combinations of these kinds of reactions to accomplish the analyses.

Analysis of Anions. In carrying out the qualitative analysis of anions we proceed in a manner somewhat similar to that outlined above. The anions fall into four Groups, each with a characteristic property common to the anions in the Group. Here, however, the anions in a Group are either separated from the general mixture before analysis or dealt with by "spot tests" designed to detect the ion directly in the general mixture. A sequence of Group precipitations such as is used in cation analysis is not easily accomplished with the anions, making anion analysis somewhat less systematic. It is also made more difficult by the fact that some anions tend under certain conditions to react with other anions and thus to be converted to other species.

The members of the anion Groups, along with their characteristic properties, are listed below:

Silver Group	Cl^-, Br^-, I^-, SCN^-	Precipitated by Ag^+ ion under strongly acidic conditions
Calcium-Barium Group	SO_4^{2-}, PO_4^{3-}, CrO_4^{2-}, $C_2O_4^{2-}$	Precipitated by Ca^{2+} ion or Ba^{2+} ion at proper pH
Soluble Group	NO_3^-, NO_2^-, ClO_3^-, $C_2H_3O_2^-$	Not easily precipitated
Volatile Acid Group	CO_3^{2-}, SO_3^{2-}, S^{2-}	Evolve gases on acidification

For the most part we will limit each qualitative analysis experiment to the study of the ions in one or, at most, two groups. At the beginning of each experiment there is a discussion of the properties of each of the ions in the Group, including the properties actually used in the analysis scheme as well as others. This is followed by a detailed procedure by which a solution containing the ions in the Group can be analyzed for the presence of those ions. The laboratory assignments for each experiment include carrying out the procedure with a known solution containing all of the ions in the Group and then using that procedure to analyze an unknown solution which may contain any of those ions. Following this you may be asked to devise your own scheme for the analysis of a sample of limited possible composition, containing only a few ions; for this problem you may use a simplified version of the standard procedure or a scheme based on other properties of the ions included in the discussion section.

In the experiments involving single groups of ions, the solutions used will not contain any interfering ions of opposite charge. The sources of cations in solution will be nitrates or chlorides, and the anion systems will be obtained from sodium or potassium salts. In general mixtures, where the cations and anions may react with each other and there is some likelihood of anion-anion reactions, the situation is considerably more complicated. In the last experiment we will consider mixtures of this sort and will ask you to do an analysis for both cations and anions. In that experiment we will work with solid mixtures and will describe methods for preparing solutions prior to analysis as well as for avoiding difficulties caused by unwanted ion-ion reactions.

In addition to giving you the nontrivial (and perhaps sometimes frustrating) experience of following a rather complicated set of directions for carrying out series of chemical reactions, studies in qualitative analysis offer you an opportunity for working with many different kinds of chemical substances and learning a good deal about their behavior under varying conditions. The procedures used illustrate very well how the principles of chemical equilibrium can be applied to make systems react in desired ways to furnish needed information. If you examine the procedures carefully, you will find that they are fairly easily understood in terms of the laws of chemistry and the properties of the ions being studied, and that, given time, you could have developed them yourself. Such examination should make it clearer to you what is accomplished in each stage in the procedure. If you know why you are asked to wash a precipitate a given way, or why a mixture must be heated or boiled, you are more likely to perform the operation properly.

LABORATORY PROCEDURES

Good laboratory technique in qualitative analysis is important if you are to get results like those described in the procedures. Sloppy, careless work will produce precipitates of the wrong color, or precipitates where you should get solutions, and in general will make your analytical life less pleasant and successful than it might be. Experience is certainly crucial to good technique, but a little advice before you begin these experiments might be useful in helping you get started properly.

Our qualitative analyses will be carried out on what is commonly called the semimicro level. The amounts of chemicals we use are neither large, of the order of grams, nor very small, of the order of micrograms. The sample solutions are typically about 0.1 *M*, and we work with volumes of about 1 ml, which means that there will be, on the average, about 10 mg of solute in the sample. The identification tests for the most part will be ineffective if you have less than 1 or 2 mg of solute present, so you must carry out the procedures carefully enough to avoid losing the major portion of any component somewhere during the analysis.

Separation of Solid Precipitates from Solutions. One of the reasons that we work at the semimicro level is that at that level one can very conveniently use small centrifuges to separate a precipitate from a solution. The common laboratory centrifuge will accept a small semimicro test tube holding about 8 ml; such tubes (13 mm × 100 mm) are large enough to hold the reaction mixtures which we will prepare and will be used almost exclusively in our work.

In a previous experiment you may have used centrifugation to remove solid PbI_2 from solution. In general, to centrifuge a sample, put the test tube containing the precipitate and solution into one of the locations in the centrifuge and another test tube containing a similar amount of water on the opposite side of the rotor. (You may find that such a tube is permanently taped in the centrifuge, in which case you should put your test tube in the opposite slot.) Turn on the centrifuge and let it run for about 30 seconds, during which time most precipitates will settle to a compact mass in the bottom of the tube. If your sample is still suspended, centrifuge it again; if this still does not work, you may find it helpful to heat the sample in the water bath for a few minutes, thereby promoting formation of larger crystals of solid, which tend to centrifuge out more easily.

Measuring Out Amounts of Solutions or Solids. A typical step in a procedure is to add 1 ml of a reagent, or 0.1 g of a solid, to a solution. Perhaps surprisingly, this is almost *never* done by using a graduated cylinder or a balance to measure out the amount of liquid or solid. The direction given means to add about 1 ml, say ±0.2 ml, or about 0.1 g ± 0.02 g. Measuring out an approximate volume of this sort is easy, and fast, if you know roughly the volume that 1 ml occupies in a semimicro test tube. This can be determined by putting about 5 ml of water in a small graduated cylinder and then pouring the water into the test tube, 1 ml at a time. After you have done this a few times you should be able to judge the increase in level that corresponds to 1 ml, and, indeed, to 0.5 ml. In general, use the medicine dropper in the reagent bottle to transfer solution directly to the test tube containing your sample. *Never* contaminate a reagent solution by dipping your own eye dropper or pipet into it. Add distilled water directly from your squeeze bottle, again estimating volume from the change in level of the liquid. If you wish, you can measure volume by counting drops from the medicine dropper. Most medicine droppers deliver about the same volume per drop, and you can check your own dropper to see how many drops equal 1 ml. Typical droppers deliver 10 to 15 drops per milliliter, with 12 drops being a good average, at least in our laboratories.

Dispensing a given approximate amount of solid can be accomplished in a way similar to that used with liquids. One usually adds a small amount of solid from the tip of a small spatula, and the problem is to determine the space that, say, 0.1 g of solid occupies. To find out, work with a sample of a typical solid, such as powdered limestone, $CaCO_3$, and a sensitive top.loading or triple beam balance. Put a small beaker on the balance and weigh it. Then add portions of the solid on the end of the spatula, weighing each, until you can add a sample that you are sure weighs 0.1 g ± 0.02 g. If you assume that an equal volume of any other solid will weigh about 0.1 g, you will not go too far wrong.

Precipitating a Solid. One of the most common reactions in qualitative analysis is the precipitation of substances from solution. To accomplish a precipitation, add the indicated amount of precipitating reagent to the sample solution and stir well with your glass stirring rod. Heat the solution in the water bath if so directed. Since some precipitates form slowly, they must be given time to form completely. It is hard to overstir, but students frequently do not mix reagents thoroughly enough. When the precipitation is believed to be complete, centrifuge out the solid, and before decanting the liquid, add a drop or two of the precipitating reagent, just to make sure that you added enough precipitant the first time. The directions usually specify enough reagent to furnish an excess, but it is good insurance to test, just the same.

Washing a Solid. The liquid decanted from the test tube after centrifuging out a solid does not in general contain any of the solid and may be used directly in a following step. The solid remaining in the tube, however, has residual liquid around it. Since this liquid contains ions that may interfere with further tests on the solid, they must be removed. This is accomplished by diluting the liquid with a wash liquid, often water, which does not interfere with the analysis, dissolve the solid, or precipitate any substances from solution.

To wash the solid, add the indicated amount of wash liquid to the test tube and mix well with your glass stirring rod, dispersing the solid well in the wash liquid. Simply pouring in the wash liquid and pouring it out again is not effective. After mixing thoroughly, centrifuge out the solid and decant the wash liquid, which usually may be discarded. The washing operation, in key separations, is best done twice, because an uncontaminated precipitate tends to give much better results than one mixed with even a little chemical trash.

Heating a Mixture. Many reactions are best carried out when the reagents are hot. We *never*, or almost never, heat a test tube containing a reaction mixture directly in a Bunsen flame. It is more convenient and much more considerate of your neighbor to heat the test tube in a water bath. A 150 ml beaker containing about 100 ml of water makes a very adequate water bath.

When you are following a procedure in which you need to heat a solution, keep the water bath hot or boiling by using a small flame to heat the beaker on a piece of asbestos-covered wire gauze. Then the bath is ready whenever required, and you do not have to wait 10 minutes for the water to heat. The test tube, or tubes, can be put directly into the bath, supported against the wall of the beaker. In a water bath you can bring the mixture under study to approximately 100°C without boiling it. If you heat the sample in an open flame, it inevitably bumps out of the tube and onto the laboratory bench, or onto you or someone else. Therefore, *do not* heat test tubes containing liquids over an open flame.

Evaporating a Liquid. In some cases it will be necessary to boil down a liquid to a small volume. This may be done to concentrate a species or to remove a volatile reagent, or perhaps because the reaction will proceed readily only in a boiling solution. When this operation is necessary, we perform the boiling in a small 30 ml beaker on a square of asbestos-covered wire gauze and use a small Bunsen flame judiciously applied to maintain controlled, gentle boiling. Since the volumes involved usually are of the order of 3 or 4 ml, overheating can easily occur.

If you are supposed to stop the evaporation at a volume of 1 ml or so, make sure that you do not heat to dryness, because you may decompose the sample or render it inert. Since concentrated solutions or slurries tend to bump, it is often helpful to encourage smooth boiling by scratching the bottom of the beaker with a stirring rod as the boiling proceeds. Good judgment in boiling down a sample is important, so use it.

Occasionally the liquid that is evaporated is highly acidic with HCl or HNO_3, and the boiling causes evolution of noticeable amounts of toxic gases into the laboratory. In some cases the amounts are small enough to be ignored. If you or anyone else notices that bothersome vapors are escaping from your boiling mixture, transfer your operation to the hood. In some laboratories each station has its own small hood; in such a case, carry out all your evaporations under your hood.

Transferring a Solid. Sometimes it is necessary to transfer a solid from the beaker in which it was prepared to a test tube for centrifuging, or from the test tube to the beaker. The amount of solid involved is never large, of the order of 50 mg at most. We always perform such transfers in the presence of a liquid, which serves as a carrier.

When you are ready to make the transfer, stir the solid well into the liquid, forming a slurry, and then, without delay, pour the slurry into the other container. The transfer is not quantitative, but if done properly, you can move 90 per cent of the sample to the other container. Forget about the rest. In general, we do not attempt to transfer wet solids with a spatula, because it is not easy, and all too often the spatula reacts with the liquid present, contaminating it.

Handling a Stirring Rod. You will find that a glass stirring rod is a very useful tool and that you need it in nearly every step in each procedure. The problem is that each time it is used, it gets wet with the solution being treated, and then it must be cleaned before it can be used again. This is a minor problem, but a bothersome one. The best solution we have found is to keep a 250 or 400 ml beaker full of distilled water handy as a storage place for stirring rods. After you have used a rod, swirl it around in the water in the beaker to clean it, and then leave it in the water. Solutes and solids accumulate, but they really amount to tiny traces when diluted in the water. Change the water occasionally to ensure that no significant contamination occurs. We have found this procedure for handling stirring rods to work very well and have had no spurious test results yet.

Adjusting the pH of a Solution. One of the most important variables controlling chemical reactions is the pH of the solution. Frequently it is necessary to make a basic solution acidic, or vice versa, in order to make a desired reaction take place. For instance, if you are directed to add 6 *M* HCl to an alkaline mixture until it is acidic, you should proceed in the following way. Knowing how the alkaline solution was prepared, make a quick mental calculation of about how much acid is needed—1 drop, 1 ml, or perhaps more. Then add the acid, drop by drop, until you think the pH is about right. Mix well with your stirring rod and then touch the end of the rod to a piece of blue litmus paper on a piece of paper towel or filter paper. If the color does not change, add another drop or two of acid, mix and test again. Frequently the system changes its character at the neutral point; a precipitate may dissolve or form, or the color may change. In any event, add enough acid so that, after mixing, the litmus paper turns red when touched with the stirring rod. Similarly, if you are told to make a solution basic with 6 *M* NH_3 or 6 *M* NaOH, add the reagent, drop by drop, until the solution, after being well mixed, turns red litmus blue. Adjustment of pH is not difficult, but it must be done properly if the desired reaction is to occur.

EXPERIMENT 32

Qualitative Analysis of the Group I Cations: Ag^+, Pb^{2+}, Hg_2^{2+}

SEPARATION OF THE GROUP I CATIONS

In the classical qualitative analysis scheme, the first ions which are determined are Ag^+, Pb^{2+}, and Hg_2^{2+}. Of all the common cations, only these form insoluble chlorides. These cations comprise Group I in the scheme and are separated from a general salt solution by precipitation of their chlorides under acidic conditions. The chloride precipitate is then analyzed for the possible presence of silver, lead, and mercury(I) on the basis of the characteristic properties of those cations.

PROPERTIES OF THE GROUP I CATIONS

Ag^+. Silver has only a few water soluble salts, of which the nitrate is certainly the most common. Most of the insoluble silver salts dissolve in cold 6 *M* HNO_3, the main exceptions being the silver halides, AgSCN, and Ag_2S. Silver ion forms many stable complexes; of these. the best known is probably the $Ag(NH_3)_2^+$ ion. This complex is sufficiently stable to be produced when AgCl or AgSCN is treated with 6 *M* NH_3; the reaction which occurs is useful for dissolving those solids. AgBr and AgI are less soluble than AgCl; AgBr will go into solution in 15 *M* NH_3 but AgI is so insoluble that it will not. The silver thiosulfate complex ion, $Ag(S_2O_3)_2^{3-}$, is extremely stable, and is important in photography, where it is formed in the "fixing" reaction in which AgBr is removed from the developed negative.

Pb^{2+}. Lead nitrate and acetate are the only well known soluble lead salts. Lead chloride is not nearly as insoluble in water as are the chlorides of silver and mercury(I), and becomes moderately soluble if the water is heated. $PbSO_4$ is one of the relatively few insoluble sulfates. Lead forms a stable hydroxide complex ion and a weak chloride complex. Although lead ordinarily has an oxidation number of +2, there are some Pb(IV) compounds, of which the most common is PbO_2 (brown); this compound is insoluble in most reagents, but will dissolve in 6 *M* HNO_3 to which some H_2O_2 has been added.

Hg_2^{2+}. Mercury(I) has only one soluble salt, the nitrate, and even with this compound, excess HNO_3 must be present to keep basic Hg(I) salts from precipitating. The Hg(I) ion, sometimes called mercurous ion, is relatively unstable; it will slowly oxidize to Hg(II) if exposed to air, and can be reduced to the metal by reducing cations (e.g., Sn^{2+}). In the presence of species that form Hg(II) complex ions or insoluble salts, mercurous ion often undergoes a disproportionation reaction to Hg (solid, black) and the Hg(II) compound. Mercury(I) chloride has a very characteristic reaction with ammonia:

$$Hg_2Cl_2(s) + 2\ NH_3(aq) \rightarrow Hg(s) + HgNH_2Cl(s) + NH_4^+(aq) + Cl^-(aq)$$

In Table 32.1 we have summarized some of the general solubility properties of the Group I cations. There is a good deal of information in the table, and you should learn to properly interpret and use the information it contains. For example, in the entry for Ag^+

TABLE 32.1 SOLUBILITY PROPERTIES OF THE GROUP I CATIONS

	Ag^+	Pb^{2+}	Hg_2^{2+}
Cl^-	C, A+ (white)	HW, C, A+ (white)	O+ (white)
OH^-	C, A (brown)	C, A (white)	D (black)
SO_4^{2-}	S−, C (white)	C (white)	S−, A (white)
CrO_4^{2-}	C, A (dk red)	C (yellow)	A (orange)
CO_3^{2-}, PO_4^{3-}	C, A (white)	C, A (white)	A (white)
S^{2-}	O (black)	O (black)	D (black)
Complexes	NH_3, $S_2O_3^{2-}$	OH^-	—

Key:

- S soluble in water, >0.1 mole/liter
- S− slightly soluble in water, ~0.01 mole/liter
- HW soluble in hot water
- A soluble in acid (6 *M* HCl or other non-precipitating, nonoxidizing acid)
- I insoluble in any common solvent
- A+ soluble in 12 *M* HCl
- B soluble in hot 6 *M* NaOH containing S^{2-} ion
- O soluble in hot 6 *M* HNO_3
- O+ soluble in hot aqua regia
- C soluble in solution containing a good complexing ligand
- D unstable, decomposes

and CrO_4^{2-} we have C, A (dk red). This means that if water solutions containing Ag^+ and CrO_4^{2-} ions are mixed, we obtain a precipitate of dark red Ag_2CrO_4; this substance is not soluble in water but would dissolve in an acidic solution such as 6 *M* HNO_3, which would not contain a precipitating anion, and in solutions containing ligands which form stable complexes with silver. The entry under Complexes tells us that those ligands normally encountered in qualitative analysis include NH_3 and $S_2O_3^{2-}$.

GENERAL SCHEME OF ANALYSIS

The procedure used for the qualitative analysis of the Group I cations makes simple, straightforward use of some of the properties of these ions. Following separation of the chloride precipitate, the solid is treated with hot water to dissolve any $PbCl_2$ that is present. The hot solution containing Pb^{2+} ion is then mixed with a solution of K_2CrO_4; if lead is present, a yellow precipitate of $PbCrO_4$ will be produced. The remaining chloride precipitate is treated with 6 *M* NH_3. If Hg(I) is present, a black precipitate containing Hg(s) will form. Any silver chloride present will dissolve as $Ag(NH_3)_2^+$; after separation from the solid, the solution of the silver complex ion is acidified, which destroys the complex and reprecipitates white AgCl. In the presence of large amounts of Hg_2^{2+}, silver ion may be reduced to metallic silver on addition of NH_3 to the chloride precipitate; under such conditions the black precipitate which is obtained in that step is dissolved in aqua regia, and the resulting solution is tested for silver.

PROCEDURE FOR ANALYSIS OF GROUP I CATIONS

WEAR YOUR SAFETY GLASSES WHILE PERFORMING THIS EXPERIMENT.

Unless told otherwise, you may assume that 10 ml of your sample contains the equivalent of about 1 ml of 0.1 *M* solutions of the nitrate salts of one or more of the Group I cations, plus possibly ions from Groups II, III, and IV. Roughly speaking, this amounts to about 10 mg of each cation present. This is a very sufficient amount for good qualitative tests, *as long as you do not lose any component cations* by improperly carrying out or interpreting any step.

Step 1. To 5 ml of your sample in a test tube, add 0.5 ml 6 *M* HCl. Stir well and centrifuge. Decant the liquid, which may contain ions from groups to be discussed later, into a test tube and save it, if necessary, for further analysis; to make sure precipitation of Group I cations was complete, add 1 drop of 6 *M* HCl to the liquid. Wash the precipitate with 2 ml water and 3 drops of 6 *M* HCl. Stir well. Centrifuge and discard the wash liquid. Wash the precipitate again with water and HCl; centrifuge and discard the wash.

Step 2. To the precipitate from Step 1, which contains the chlorides of the Group I cations, add about 4 ml water. Heat in the boiling water bath for at least three minutes, stirring constantly. Centrifuge quickly and decant the liquid, which may contain Pb^{2+}, into a test tube.

Step 3. *Confirmation of the presence of lead.* To the liquid from Step 2 add 2 drops of 6 *M* acetic acid and 3 or 4 drops of 1 *M* K_2CrO_4. The formation of a yellow precipitate of $PbCrO_4$ confirms the presence of lead. Centrifuging out the solid may help with the identification, because the liquid phase is orange.

Step 4. *Confirmation of the presence of mercury.* If lead is present, wash the precipitate from Step 2 with 6 ml water in the boiling water bath. Centrifuge and test the liquid for Pb^{2+}. Continue the washings until no positive reaction to the lead test is obtained. To the washed precipitate add 2 ml 6 *M* NH_3 and stir well. A black or dark gray precipitate establishes the presence of the mercury(I) ion. Centrifuge and decant the liquid, which may contain $Ag(NH_3)_2^+$, into a test tube.

Step 5. *Confirmation of the presence of silver.* To the liquid from Step 4 add 3 ml 6 *M* HNO_3. Check with litmus to see that the solution is acidic. A white precipitate of AgCl confirms the presence of silver.

Step 6. *Alternative confirmation of the presence of silver.* If the test for silver ion was inconclusive, and mercury was present, add 1 ml 12 *M* HCl and 0.5 ml 6 *M* HNO_3 to the precipitate from Step 4. Heat in the water bath until solution is essentially complete. Pour the liquid into a 30 ml beaker and boil it gently for a minute. Add 3 ml water. If a white precipitate forms, it is probably AgCl. Centrifuge and discard the liquid. To the precipitate, add 0.5 ml 6 *M* NH_3; with stirring, the precipitate should dissolve. Add 1 ml 6 *M* HNO_3; if silver is present, a precipitate of AgCl forms.

COMMENTS ON PROCEDURE FOR ANALYSIS OF GROUP I CATIONS

Step 1. In this step the cations of Group I are precipitated as their chlorides. Both silver and lead ions can form chloride complexes in solutions when the chloride ion concentrations are high. In our procedure, $[Cl^-]$ is about 1 *M*, which decreases the salt solubilities by the common ion effect, but is not great enough to cause appreciable amounts of the complex ions to form. If, of the Group I cations, only lead is present, it may not precipitate unless its concentration is ~ 0.1 *M* or greater.

Step 2. The $PbCl_2$ is sufficiently soluble in hot water to allow its separation from the other chlorides by simply heating the precipitate, with mixing, in water. The centrifuging should be done quickly to avoid reprecipitation of $PbCl_2$ on cooling.

Step 3. We acidify the liquid to minimize precipitation of other chromates from residual amounts of ions in other groups. The liquid is orange because of the conversion of CrO_4^{2-} to $Cr_2O_7^{2-}$ in the acid medium.

Step 4. If lead chloride is not completely removed, it is converted to a white, basic, insoluble salt on addition of NH_3. This could cause confusion, but should not interfere with later identifications. The AgCl dissolves readily in 6 *M* NH_3, with formation of the silver ammonia complex ion. If Hg_2Cl_2 is present, it reacts with NH_3, forming black Hg and white insoluble $HgNH_2Cl$. The mixture is black or dark gray if mercury(I) ion is present.

Step 5. The silver ammonia complex ion is destroyed by acid, and the released silver ion precipitates with the chloride ion in solution. The formation of white AgCl is definitive evidence for the presence of silver.

Step 6. If both mercury(I) ion and silver ion are present, the $Ag(NH_3)_2^+$ and mercury, both present in Step 4, tend to undergo an oxidation-reduction reaction:

$$2\ Ag(NH_3)_2^+(aq) + Hg(s) + Cl^-(aq) \rightarrow 2\ Ag(s) + HgNH_2Cl(s) + NH_4^+(aq) + 2\ NH_3(aq)$$

If sufficient mercury is present, nearly all the silver may be reduced and a very doubtful test for Ag^+ obtained in Step 5. If it appears that this is the case, carrying out Step 6 should be helpful. On being dissolved in aqua regia, the mercury exists as $HgCl_4^{2-}$ and the silver as $AgCl_2^-$. Adding water to the strongly acid solution reprecipitates white AgCl, which can then be separated from the $HgCl_4^{2-}$ by centrifuging. The solution of AgCl in NH_3 and reprecipitation on addition of HNO_3 is definitive confirmation of the presence of silver.

LABORATORY ASSIGNMENTS

Perform one or more of the following, as directed by your instructor:

1. Make up a sample containing about 1 ml of 0.1 *M* solutions of the nitrate salts of each of the cations in Group I. Go through the standard procedure for analysis of the Group I cations, comparing your observations with those that are given. Then obtain a Group I unknown from your instructor and analyze it to determine possible presence of Ag^+, Pb^{2+}, and Hg_2^{2+}. On a Group I flow chart, indicate your observations and conclusions about the unknown and submit the completed chart to your instructor.

2. If a sample may contain *only* cations from Group I, it is possible to analyze it by several procedures that are quite different from the one given in this book. Develop a scheme for analysis of such a sample, starting with the addition of 6 *M* NaOH in excess. Draw a complete flow chart for your procedure, indicating reagents to be added at each step and the formulas and colors of all species present during the course of the analysis. Test your procedure with a Group I known, and then use your method to analyze an unknown sample. In another color, indicate on your flow chart your observations on the unknown and your conclusions regarding its composition.

Note: In this and all succeeding laboratory assignments in this manual, the first assigned problem involves your acquiring some familiarity with the standard procedure for analysis. Succeeding problems require your developing and using your own schemes for analyzing particular unknown mixtures. In setting up your procedures, you may use steps from the standard schemes, but you should also examine the characteristic properties of the individual ions to see if some of them might be profitably used in your scheme. In all probability, the best method for analyzing any given limited mixture of ions will be partly based on the standard procedure and partly based on ion properties that were not made use of in the standard approach.

Outline of Procedure for Analysis of Group I Cations (Group I Flow Chart)

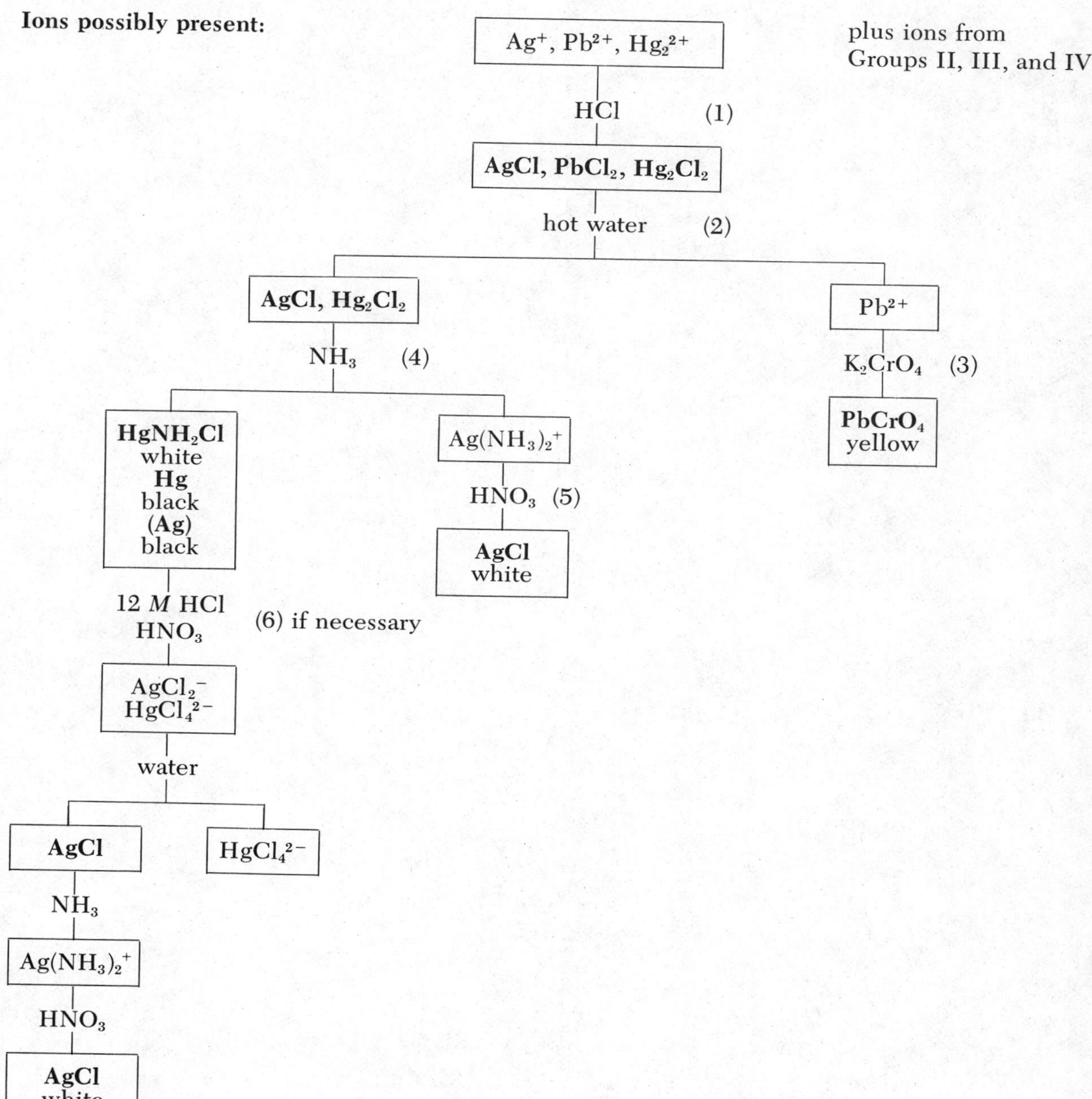

Name ______________________ Section ____________

OBSERVATIONS: Analysis of Group I Cations

Assignment 1 Flow Chart Showing Behavior of Unknown

Assignment 2 Flow Chart

EXP. 32 Name ______________________ Section ______________

ADVANCE STUDY ASSIGNMENT: Analysis of Group I Cations

1. Write balanced net ionic equations for the following reactions:
   a. The precipitation of the chloride of Hg_2^{2+}.

   b. The confirmatory test for Pb^{2+}.

   c. The dissolving of AgCl in aqueous ammonia.

2. You are given an unknown solution that contains only one of the Group I cations and no other metallic cations. Develop the simplest procedure you can think of to determine which cation is present. Draw a flow chart showing the procedure and the observations to be expected at each step with each of the possible cations.

3. A solution may contain Ag^+, Pb^{2+}, and Hg_2^{2+}. A white precipitate forms on addition of 6 *M* HCl. The precipitate is insoluble in hot water, and turns black on addition of ammonia. Which of the ions are present, which are absent, and which remain undetermined? State your reasoning.

Present ______________

Absent ______________

In doubt ______________

EXPERIMENT 33

Qualitative Analysis of the Group II Cations: Cu^{2+}, Bi^{3+}, Hg^{2+}, Cd^{2+}, (Pb^{2+}), Sn^{2+} and Sn^{4+}, Sb^{3+} and Sb^{5+}

SEPARATION OF THE GROUP II CATIONS

The second set of cations to be removed from a general mixture includes those ions which form insoluble sulfides in the presence of H_2S under highly acidic conditions. These ions make up Group II in the standard qualitative analysis scheme. They precipitate as sulfides at pH 0.5 and are separated from the remaining cations. Since seven different metals form cations which fall into Group II, the procedure for analysis of the ions in this Group is relatively complicated.

PROPERTIES OF THE GROUP II CATIONS

Cu^{2+}. Although copper can exist in the +1 oxidation state, copper(I), or cuprous, compounds are relatively rarely encountered. The solution chemistry of copper, for the most part, is that of the copper(II), cupric, Cu^{2+} ion. Most copper(II) salts exist as hydrates in the solid state and are either blue or green. Copper(II) complexes are very common. Copper(II) is fairly easily reduced to copper(I) or to the metal by the more active metals, such as iron or zinc, or by other strong reducing species, including the hydrosulfite, or dithionite, ion, $S_2O_4^{2-}$. Copper(II) has a characteristic oxidation-reduction reaction with iodide ion; brown I_2 and a white precipitate of CuI are produced:

$$2\ Cu^{2+}(aq) + 4\ I^-(aq) \rightarrow 2\ CuI(s) + I_2(aq)$$

Bi^{3+}. Bismuth ordinarily occurs in the +3 state, but in some strong oxidizing agents it exists as bismuth(V). Bismuth salts are nearly all colorless; they are insoluble in water, but moderately soluble in strong acids, particularly HCl. Bismuth does not tend to form many complex ions. It is reduced to the metal by strong reducing agents, including Sn(II) in basic solution:

$$2\ Bi(OH)_3(s) + 3\ Sn(OH)_4^{2-}(aq) \rightarrow 2\ Bi(s) + 3\ Sn(OH)_6^{2-}(aq)$$

If a solution of a bismuth salt in HCl is added to a large volume of water, the bismuth will precipitate as a white basic salt. In the absence of antimony salts, which behave similarly, this reaction serves as a definitive test for the presence of bismuth ion:

$$Bi^{3+}(aq) + Cl^-(aq) + H_2O \xrightarrow{Aq} BiOCl(s) + 2\ H^+(aq)$$

Cd^{2+}. Cadmium ordinarily exists in its compounds in the +2 state. Its salts are usually colorless, and many of them are soluble in water. Cadmium ion forms several complexes, including those with ammonia, halide ions, and cyanide ions. Cadmium is not readily reduced to the metal, and has about the same reduction potential as iron. Cadium sulfide, CdS, has a characteristic yellow color and is the most soluble of the

Group II sulfides. Addition of 6 *M* NaOH to a solution containing $Cd(NH_3)_4^{2+}$ will precipitate a white basic salt which is essentially insoluble in excess ammonia; $Cu(NH_3)_4^{2+}$ will not precipitate under these conditions.

Hg^{2+}. Mercury(II) compounds are much more common than those of Hg(I); the chloride, bromide, cyanide, and acetate are among the mercuric salts which are soluble in water. Mercury(II) salts in water are often only very slightly ionized. The Hg^{2+} ion forms several complexes, including HgS_2^{2-} and $HgCl_4^{2-}$. Mercury(II) sulfide, HgS, is black and is the least soluble of all known sulfides. Mercury(II) is readily reduced to either mercury(I) or to metallic mercury. The deposit of bright mercury on a piece of copper is a common test for the presence of mercury ions in solution. Tin(II) chloride, $SnCl_2$, in acid solution reduces Hg(II) compounds to white Hg_2Cl_2 and/or black metallic mercury.

Sn^{2+} and Sn^{4+}. Tin in its compounds exists in either the +2, stannous, or the +4, stannic, state. Tin(II), particularly in basic solution, is a good reducing agent. In either state tin forms many complex ions; in solution tin is usually in the form of a complex anion, such as $SnCl_6^{4-}$ or $Sn(OH)_4^{2-}$. Most tin compounds are colorless; they are essentially all insoluble in water, but will dissolve in either basic or acidic media. Tin(IV) can be reduced to tin(II) by active metals such as iron or aluminum in HCl solution. Tin metal will dissolve in 6 *M* HCl.

Sb^{3+} and Sb^{5+}. Antimony salts, like those of tin, are typically insoluble in water. The most common salt of antimony, $SbCl_3$, dissolves readily in moderately strong HCl, forming $SbCl_6^{3-}$, and in NaOH solution, where the antimony species present is the $Sb(OH)_4^-$ complex ion. Sb(III) compounds are much more common than those of Sb(V), the latter being good oxidizing agents. Antimony sulfides are soluble in hot NaOH solution containing S^{2-} ion and in 12 *M* HCl, as is tin(IV) sulfide. Antimony is reduced to the metal by good reducing agents, such as aluminum in acid solution.

TABLE 33.1 SOLUBILITY PROPERTIES OF THE GROUP II CATIONS

	Cu^{2+}	Bi^{3+}	Cd^{2+}
Cl^-	S	A (white)	S
OH^-	C, A (blue)	A (white)	C, A (white)
SO_4^{2-}	S	A (white)	S
CrO_4^{2-}	C, A (brown)	A (yellow)	C, A (white)
CO_3^{2-}, PO_4^{3-}	C, A (blue)	A (white)	C, A (white)
S^{2-}	O (black)	O (dk brown)	A, O (yellow)
Complexes	NH_3	Cl^-	NH_3
	Hg^{2+}	**Sn^{2+}, Sn^{4+}**	**Sb^{3+}**
Cl^-	S	C, A (white)	C, A (white)
OH^-	A (yellow)	C, A (white)	C, A (white)
SO_4^{2-}	S	C, A (white)	C, A (white)
CrO_4^{2-}	S^- (red)	S	C, A (yellow)
CO_3^{2-}, PO_4^{3-}	A (red)	C, A (white)	C, A (white)
S^{2-}	O^+, B (black)	A^+, C, B (tan)	A^+, C, B (red-orange)
Complexes	Cl^-, S^{2-}	OH^-	OH^-

Key:

S soluble in water, >0.1 mole/liter
S^- slightly soluble in water, ~0.01 mole/liter
HW soluble in hot water
A soluble in acid (6 *M* HCl or other nonprecipitating, nonoxidizing acid)
I insoluble in any common solvent
A^+ soluble in 12 *M* HCl
B soluble in hot 6 *M* NaOH containing S^{2-} ion
O soluble in hot 6 *M* HNO_3
O^+ soluble in hot aqua regia
C soluble in solution containing a good complexing ligand
D unstable, decomposes

In Table 33.1 we have listed some of the common solubility properties of the Group II cations.

GENERAL SCHEME OF ANALYSIS

In the standard scheme for analysis of the Group II cations, following separation of the sulfides, the solid is treated with strong NaOH solution and sulfide ion, which dissolve the sulfides of the tin subgroup (mercury, tin, and antimony) and allow their separation from those of the copper subgroup (CuS, CdS, and Bi_2S_3).

The sulfides in the copper subgroup are dissolved in hot 6 *M* HNO_3 and the solution treated with ammonia; in excess NH_3 both Cu^{2+} and Cd^{2+} form complexes, while Bi^{3+} precipitates as the hydroxide along with Pb^{2+} if it is present. Copper is identified by the color of its ammonia complex ion, and cadmium by precipitation of CdS after separation from copper ion. Bismuth is identified by precipitation of BiOCl or by reduction to the metal after separation from lead. Although lead is not likely to be present in appreciable amounts, its presence can be confirmed by precipitation, first as the chloride and then as the sulfate.

The members of the tin subgroup are reprecipitated as the sulfides, and HgS is separated out by treatment with concentrated HCl, in which it is insoluble. The mercuric sulfide is dissolved in aqua regia, and presence of Hg(II) is established by its reactions with copper metal and stannous chloride solution. The solution of tin and antimony is divided. In one half of the sample, tin is reduced to Sn(II), where it is identified by its characteristic reaction with $HgCl_2$ solution. Antimony is detected in the other part of the sample by precipitation as Sb_2OS_2.

As you can see from the previous discussion, the procedure for analysis of the Group II cations includes a large number of steps and many different kinds of reactions. Indeed, the Group II analysis involves what is probably the most complicated sequence of chemical reaction steps that you will encounter in undergraduate chemistry. Successful analyses of Group II cations require both care in carrying out the steps in the procedure and some knowledge of what is happening in each step. Students who become familiar with the procedure before coming to the laboratory and then use it properly will have little difficulty in achieving good results, but those who try to rely completely on following the "cookbook" will most likely get into trouble.

PROCEDURE FOR ANALYSIS OF GROUP II CATIONS

WEAR YOUR SAFETY GLASSES WHILE PERFORMING THIS EXPERIMENT.

Unless directed otherwise, you may assume that a 10 ml sample contains the equivalent of about 1 ml of 0.1 *M* solutions of the nitrate or chloride salts of one or more of the Group II cations. If you are working with a general unknown, your sample is the HCl solution decanted from the Group I precipitate and may contain ions from Groups II, III, and IV.

Step 1. Pour 5 ml of your Group II sample or your general unknown into a 30 ml beaker. Add 0.5 ml 3% H_2O_2, and carefully boil the solution down to a volume of about 2 ml.

Step 2. Swirl the liquid around in the beaker to dissolve any salts that may have crystallized, and then pour the solution into a test tube. Add 6 *M* NaOH a little at a time, until the pH becomes 0.5. (The way to accomplish this is discussed in the comments on procedure following this section.) When the pH has been properly established, add 1 ml 1 *M* thioacetamide and stir.

Heat the test tube in the boiling water bath for at least five minutes. If any Group II ions are present, a precipitate will form; its color will typically be initially light, gradually darkening and finally becoming black. Continue to heat the test tube for at least two minutes after the color has stopped changing. Cool the test tube under the water tap and let stand for a minute or so. Centrifuge out the precipitate and decant the solution into a test tube. Add 1 ml 1 *M* NH_4Cl and 1 ml water to precipitate and put it aside.

Check the pH of the decanted solution. If it is too low (too acid), add 0.5 *M* $NaC_2H_3O_2$, drop by drop with stirring, until the pH is again 0.5. A brown or yellow precipitate may form during this adjustment, indicating that not all of the Group II cations precipitated the first time. In any event, add 0.5 ml 1 *M* thioacetamide to the decanted solution at pH 0.5, and heat for three minutes in the boiling water bath. Cool the test tube under the water tap and let stand for a minute. Centrifuge out any precipitate, and decant the liquid, which should be saved only if it may contain ions from groups to be studied later. Add 1 ml 1 *M* NH_4Cl and 1 ml water to the precipitate, stir, and pour the slurry into the test tube containing the first portion of Group II precipitate. Stir well, centrifuge, and decant, discarding the liquid. Wash the precipitate once again with 3 ml water. Centrigue, and discard the wash liquid.

Step 3. To the precipitate from Step 2 add 1 ml water and 1 ml 1 *M* NaOh. Heat in the water bath, with stirring, for two minutes. Any SnS_2 or Sb_2S_3 should dissolve. The residue will typically be dark and may contain CuS, Bi_2S_3, PbS, CdS, and HgS. Centrifuge and decant the yellow liquid into a test tube (Label 3). Wash the precipitate twice with 2 ml water and 1 ml 1 *M* NaOH. Stir, centrifuge, and decant, discarding the wash each time.

Step 4. To the precipitate from Step 3, add 1 ml water and 1 ml 6 *M* HNO_3. Heat in the boiling water bath. Most of the reaction will occur within about a minute, as some of the sulfides dissolve and sulfur is formed. There may be a substantial amount of dark residue, which is mainly HgS and free sulfur. Continue heating until no further reaction appears to occur, at least two minutes after the initial changes. Centrifuge and decant the solution, which may contain Cu^{2+}, Bi^{3+}, Cd^{2+}, and Pb^{2+}, into a test tube. Wash the dark residue with 2 ml water, centrifuge, and discard the wash. Then add 1 ml water to the residue and put it aside (Label 4).

Step 5. To the solution from Step 4, add 6 *M* NH_3 until the solution is basic to litmus. Then add 0.5 ml more and stir. If copper is present, the solution will turn blue. A white precipitate in the solution is indicative of bismuth (or, possibly, lead). Centrifuge and decant the solution, which may contain $Cu(NH_3)_4^{2+}$ and $Cd(NH_3)_4^{2+}$, into a test tube. Wash the precipitate with 1 ml water and 0.5 ml 6 *M* NH_3. Stir, centrifuge, and discard the wash.

Step 6. To the precipitate from Step 5, add 0.5 ml 6 *M* HCl and 0.5 ml water. Stir to dissolve any $Bi(OH)_3$ that is present. A white insoluble residue may contain lead. Centrifuge and decant the solution into a test tube. Wash the residue with 1 ml water and 0.5 ml 6 *M* HCl. Centrifuge and discard the wash.

Step 7. *Confirmation of the presence of bismuth.* Add 2 or 3 drops of the decantate from Step 6 to 300 ml water in a beaker. A white cloudiness due to precipitation of BiOCl appears if the sample contains bismuth. To the rest of the decantate, add 6 *M* NaOH until it is definitely basic; a white precipitate is $Bi(OH)_3$. To the mixture add 2 drops 0.1 *M* $SnCl_2$ and stir; if bismuth is present, it will be reduced to black metallic bismuth.

Step 8. *Confirmation of the presence of lead.* To the white precipitate from Step 6 add 1 ml 0.5 *M* $NaC_2H_3O_2$, sodium acetate. Heat gently if necessary to dissolve any lead-containing salts. Add 1 ml water and 1 ml 6 *M* H_2SO_4. A white precipitate of $PbSO_4$ establishes the presence of lead.

Step 9. *Confirmation of the presence of copper.* If the solution from Step 5 is blue, copper must be present, since the color is characteristic of $Cu(NH_3)_4^{2+}$. To further confirm the presence of Cu(II), add 6 *M* acetic acid to half of the blue solution from Step 5 until the color fades and the solution becomes acidic.* Then add a drop or two of 0.2 *M* $K_4Fe(CN)_6$, which will produce a red-brown, or purplish, precipitate of $Cu_2Fe(CN)_6$ in the presence of copper.

Step 10. *Confirmation of the presence of cadmium.* Take the other half of the decantate from Step 5 and, if it is blue, add about 0.3 g solid $Na_2S_2O_4$, sodium hydrosulfite, to that liquid; it should be quickly decolorized, owing to reduction of Cu(II) to Cu(I). Put the test tube in the boiling water bath, where further reduction to copper metal will occur. After a minute, centrifuge out the black or reddish copper and decant the liquid into a test tube. Add 1 ml 1 *M* thioacetamide to the liquid, or to the original colorless decantate, and heat in the water bath; precipitation of yellow CdS confirms the presence of cadmium.

Step 11. To the precipitate from Step 4 add 1 ml 6 *M* HCl and 1 ml 6 *M* HNO_3. Put the test tube in the water bath. The dark precipitate, which is mainly HgS, should dissolve in a minute or two, leaving some insoluble sulfur residue. Pour the contents of the tube into a 30 ml beaker and boil gently for about a minute to drive out any remaining H_2S. Add 2 ml water to the solution and stir. Centrifuge, if necessary, to remove sulfur.

Step 12. *Confirmation of the presence of mercury.* Pour half of the liquid from Step 11 into a test tube. Immerse a piece of heavy copper wire in the liquid for a minute; a shiny deposit of liquid mercury on the wire will confirm the presence of mercury. To the other half of the liquid from Step 11, in a test tube add 1 or 2 drops 0.1 *M* $SnCl_2$; a white, somewhat glossy precipitate of Hg_2Cl_2 again proves the presence of mercury.

Step 13. To the decantate from Step 3 add 6 *M* HCl drop by drop until the mixture becomes acidic (pH ~0.5, green color on methyl violet). The precipitate which forms may contain the sulfides of Sb(III) and Sn(IV). Stir well for half a minute, centrifuge, and discard the liquid.

Step 14. To the precipitate from Step 13, add 2 ml 6 *M* HCl. Stir and transfer the mixture to a 30 ml beaker. Boil the liquid gently for one minute to drive out H_2S and to dissolve most of the sulfides. A black residue is mainly HgS. Add 1 ml 6 *M* HCl. Centrifuge out any solid residue and transfer the liquid to a test tube. Discard the solid.

Step 15. *Confirmation of the presence of tin.* To half of the solution from Step 14, in a test tube, add a 1 cm length of 24 gauge aluminum wire. Heat the test tube in the water bath to promote reaction of the Al and production of H_2. In this reducing medium any tin present will be converted to Sn^{2+} and any antimony to the metal, which will appear as black specks. Heat for two minutes after the wire has all reacted, centrifuge

*If you are working with a general unknown and precipitated Group II at too high a pH, zinc may be in the acidified liquid from Step 9. To test for zinc there, add 1 drop 0.1 *M* $Cu(NO_3)_2$, if copper is absent, and 1 ml zinc reagent. A dark precipitate, which may form slowly, is good evidence for the presence of zinc.

out any solid and decant the liquid into a test tube. To the liquid add a drop or two of 0.1 *M* $HgCl_2$. A white or gray cloudiness, produced as Hg_2Cl_2 slowly forms, establishes the presence of tin.

Step 16. *Confirmation of the presence of antimony.* To the other half of the solution from Step 14, add 6 *M* NH_3 until the solution is basic to litmus. Any precipitate which forms may be ignored; it will not interfere, but does indicate that either tin or antimony must be present. Add 6 *M* $HC_2H_3O_2$ until the mixture becomes acidic; add 0.5 ml more. Add a little (approximately 0.4 g) solid sodium thiosulfate, $Na_2S_2O_3$, and put the test tube in the boiling water bath for a few minutes. If the mixture contains antimony, a peach-colored precipitate of Sb_2OS_2 will form.

COMMENTS ON PROCEDURE FOR ANALYSIS OF GROUP II CATIONS

Step 1. Here the solution is concentrated, and all ions are brought to their higher states of oxidation. Tin(II) and antimony(III), if present, are oxidized to tin(IV) and antimony(V). This is important, particularly in the case of tin, because unless SnS_2 is the sulfide precipitated, tin will not behave as it should in Step 3.

Step 2. At this point all the Group II sulfides are precipitated with hydrogen sulfide. The reaction that occurs is in all cases analogous to that for copper:

$$Cu^{2+}(aq) + H_2S(aq) \rightarrow CuS(s) + 2\ H^+(aq)$$

Since the solubility products of the Group II sulfides are very low, they precipitate in the presence of even extremely low concentrations of S^{2-} ion. The precipitation is carried out at a pH of 0.5, where $[S^{2-}]$ is only about 1×10^{-21} *M*. The values of the solubility products of some common metallic sulfides are as follows:

Group II		Group III	
HgS	1×10^{-52}	CoS	1×10^{-21}
CuS	1×10^{-36}	NiS	1×10^{-22}
CdS	1×10^{-26}	ZnS	1×10^{-23}
PbS	1×10^{-27}	FeS	6×10^{-18}

Under the conditions of the precipitation, the metallic cations are all about 0.01 *M*; therefore, $[M^{2+}][S^{2-}] = (1 \times 10^{-2})(1 \times 10^{-21}) \approx 1 \times 10^{-23}$. This means that those sulfides in the left column, $K_{sp} < 10^{-23}$, will precipitate, whereas those in the right column, $K_{sp} \geq 10^{-23}$, will not. This difference in sulfide solubilities is the basis of the separation of the Group II cations (left column) from Group III cations (right column).

Clearly, if the separation is to be effective, the $[H^+]$ must be properly set before precipitation is carried out, since $[S^{2-}]$ is controlled by the pH of the solution. The pH adjustment is probably most easily accomplished with an acid-base indicator. We find that methyl violet is quite suitable. On a piece of filter paper, put about 10 drops of methyl violet indicator, making 10 spots about ¾ inch in diameter. Let these dry in the air. Make up a solution of HCl about 0.3 *M* in H^+ ion by diluting 10 ml of a 1 *M* HCl solution with 20 ml of water and stirring. Put a drop of this solution on a spot of indicator. The blue-green color is that of a solution of the desired pH. Add NaOH, drop by drop, to your cation solution, with stirring, until the color of the indicator when touched with a drop of solution from your stirring rod matches that of the standard spot. (Methyl violet is violet at a pH of 2 and yellow at a pH of 0). If you go past the desired pH (too blue a spot), add a drop or two of 6 *M* HCl.

The source of H_2S in our procedure is thioacetamide, CH_3CSNH_2. This organic compound hydrolyzes when heated in acidic or basic solutions, producing H_2S; in acidic systems the reaction is:

$$CH_3CSNH_2(aq) + 2\ H_2O + H^+(aq) \rightarrow CH_3COOH(aq) + NH_4^+(aq) + H_2S(aq)$$

Generating H_2S in small amounts by this reaction is advantageous, because the gas is both bad-smelling and highly toxic. Also, it is produced slowly, which tends to allow the formation of more compact sulfide precipitates.

As you proceed to adjust the pH you will probably find that a precipitate forms. This precipitate consists of basic salts or hydroxides of tin, bismuth, and antimony and will cause no trouble. You may find, however, that accurate pH adjustment is initially difficult, since some of the cations in Group II may interact with the indicator. This again is not serious, since the readjustment of pH following the first precipitation is considerably easier to carry out. It is important that you fix the final pH properly, since too acid a solution (too green indicator) will not allow precipitation of CdS (yellow), while in too basic a solution (too blue an indicator), sulfides from Group III, particular ZnS (white), will tend to come down. If you are working *only* with Group II, it is advisable to make your final pH, following the initial precipitation, a little high (a little too blue an indicator spot), since then you can be sure that any CdS present will be precipitated. If you must separate Group II from Group III, set the final pH very carefully, and also observe the color of any precipitate which forms when you add each drop of $NaC_2H_3O_2$ solution; a light-colored precipitate (ZnS), not yellow, implies too basic a solution, to which you should add a drop of 6 *M* HCl.

Step 3. In this step the sulfides of copper, bismuth, cadmium, and mercury are separated from those of tin and antimony. The former do not dissolve in basic solution, whereas the latter do, according to reactions analogous to that observed with tin:

$$SnS_2(s) + 6\ OH^-(aq) \rightleftarrows Sn(OH)_6^{2-}(aq) + 2\ S^{2-}(aq)$$

Since Sn(II) sulfide would not dissolve, we oxidize tin in Step 1. It is likely that tin and antimony also dissolve as sulfide complexes in this step, but this causes no difficulty. Most of the HgS remains in the sulfide residue.

Step 4. The sulfides of copper, bismuth, and cadmium dissolve readily in hot 6 *M* HNO_3, a typical reaction being:

$$Bi_2S_3(s) + 8\ H^+(aq) + 2\ NO_3^-(aq) \rightarrow 2\ Bi^{3+}(aq) + 3\ S(s) + 2\ NO(g) + 4\ H_2O$$

Any HgS present is not affected by the nitric acid and remains as a black residue.

Step 5. The blue copper ammonia complex ion will form at this point if the solution contains Cu^{2+} ion. A white precipitate simultaneously formed is highly indicative of bismuth, although if lead is present it will also come down. Cadmium and copper form stable ammonia complex ions, whereas bismuth and lead do not; typically:

$$Cd^{2+}(aq) + 4\ NH_3(aq) \rightleftarrows Cd(NH_3)_4^{2+}(aq)$$

$$Bi^{3+}(aq) + 3\ NH_3(aq) + 3\ H_2O \rightleftarrows Bi(OH)_3(s) + 3\ NH_4^+(aq)$$

The blue color of the solution in Step 5 or Step 9 is confirmatory for the presence of copper. If additional assurance is needed, the precipitation of $Cu_2Fe(CN)_6$ is easy and very sensitive to small amounts of Cu^{2+} ion.

Step 7. There are two very good confirmatory tests for bismuth. Simply pouring a drop or two of the acidic solution of Bi^{3+} into water produces a characteristic white cloudiness owing to formation of BiOCl. Alternatively, if you make the bismuth solution basic with NaOH and add a drop of $SnCl_2$ solution, an oxidation-reduction reaction occurs, in which black metallic bismuth is formed.

Step 8. In all probability you do not have appreciable amounts of lead appearing in Group II, because the chloride precipitation in Group I is quite effective. Any lead salt you do have will be soluble in acetic acid; addition of sulfuric acid will precipitate $PbSO_4$. Bismuth will not interfere with this test.

Step 10. Here copper is reduced with sodium hydrosulfite, $Na_2S_2O_4$, also called sodium dithionite; addition of the solid to the cold solution causes reduction of copper to the Cu(I) state, and on warming or standing, brown or black metallic copper is produced:

$$2\ Cu(NH_3)_4^{2+}(aq) + S_2O_4^{2-}(aq) + 2\ H_2O \rightarrow 2\ Cu^+(aq) + 2\ SO_3^{2-}(aq) + 4\ NH_4^+(aq) + 4\ NH_3(aq)$$

Any other cations forming dark sulfides are also reduced, so that only bright yellow CdS is produced when the final solution is treated with sulfide.*

Step 11. Mercuric sulfide is readily soluble in aqua regia. The solvent used is a rather mild aqua regia:

$$3\ HgS(s) + 12\ Cl^-(aq) + 2\ NO_3^-(aq) + 8\ H^+(aq) \rightarrow 3\ HgCl_4^{2-}(aq) + 2\ NO(g) + 4\ H_2O + 3\ S(s)$$

Any sulfur formed does not interfere with the tests for mercury.

Step 12. There are two good confirmatory tests for the mercuric ion. The simplest is to put a drop of the solution from Step 14 on a copper penny or to dip a piece of copper wire in the solution. If mercury is present, it quickly deposits as a shiny metal on the copper:

$$HgCl_2(aq) + Cu(s) \rightarrow Hg(l) + Cu^{2+}(aq) + 2\ Cl^-(aq)$$

Probably the most common test is to add a drop or two of $SnCl_2$ solution to the solution being examined; if mercury(II) is present, it is reduced to the mercurous state or to the black metal:

$$2\ HgCl_2(aq) + Sn^{2+}(aq) \rightarrow Hg_2Cl_2(s) + Sn^{4+}(aq) + 2\ Cl^-(aq)$$

Step 13. When the solution from Step 3 is acidified, the hydroxo complexes of tin and antimony are destroyed and the sulfides reprecipitate; reactions like the following one occur:

$$Sn(OH)_6^{2-}(aq) + 2\ S^{2-}(aq) + 6\ H^+(aq) \rightarrow SnS_2(s) + 6\ H_2O$$

Step 14. The sulfides of tin and antimony dissolve readily in 6 *M* HCl at 100°C, with the formation of chloro complex ions. Mercuric sulfide is not soluble in this medium, so a black residue may be observed.

Step 15. Tin is reduced to the +2 state by Al in the presence of acid. The reduction is probably accomplished more by the H_2 gas produced than by the aluminum metal. Sn(II) may be reduced by Al to the metal, but will redissolve in the strongly acidic solution. Any antimony present will be converted to the metal, as will any traces of bismuth. The confirmatory test is again the reaction of $HgCl_2$ with Sn(II).

*See the footnote to Step 11 in the procedure section of Experiment 34 for a further test for cadmium.

Step 16. Indications of the presence of antimony appear several times in the procedure. If tin is present, it will not precipitate on addition of the thiosulfate solution. The color of the Sb_2OS_2 is very similar to that of Sb_2S_3.

LABORATORY ASSIGNMENTS

Perform one or more of the following, as directed by your instructor:

1. Make up a sample containing about 1 ml of 0.1 *M* solutions of the nitrate or chloride salts of each of the cations in Group II. Your instructor will tell you whether you should include Pb^{2+} in the sample. Go through the standard procedure for analysis of the Group II cations, comparing your observations with those that are given. Then obtain a Group II unknown from your instructor and analyze it according to the procedure. On a Group II flow chart, indicate your observations and conclusions regarding the composition of the unknown. Submit the completed chart to your instructor.

2. You will be given an unknown that may contain no more than two cations, both chosen from Group II. You will be told which two cations may be present. Develop as simple a scheme as you can to analyze a solution which might contain one, or both, or none of those ions. Use your scheme to analyze the unknown. Report the results you obtain, along with the procedure you used, to your instructor. Your instructor will then assign you another pair of Group II cations to consider, and an unknown to analyze. Your grade will depend on correct analyses of the unknowns and the number of different analyses you are able to complete in the time allowed. Some possible pairs of cations that may be assigned are the following:

Cu^{2+}, Hg^{2+}	Bi^{3+}, Pb^{2+}	Cd^{2+}, Sb^{3+}
Cd^{2+}, Sn^{4+}	Bi^{3+}, Sb^{3+}	Pb^{2+}, Cu^{2+}

3. Use the analysis scheme from Problem 3 of the Advance Study Assignment to determine the Group II cation present in one or more unknown solutions.

Outline of Procedure for Analysis of Group II Cations

Ions possibly present:

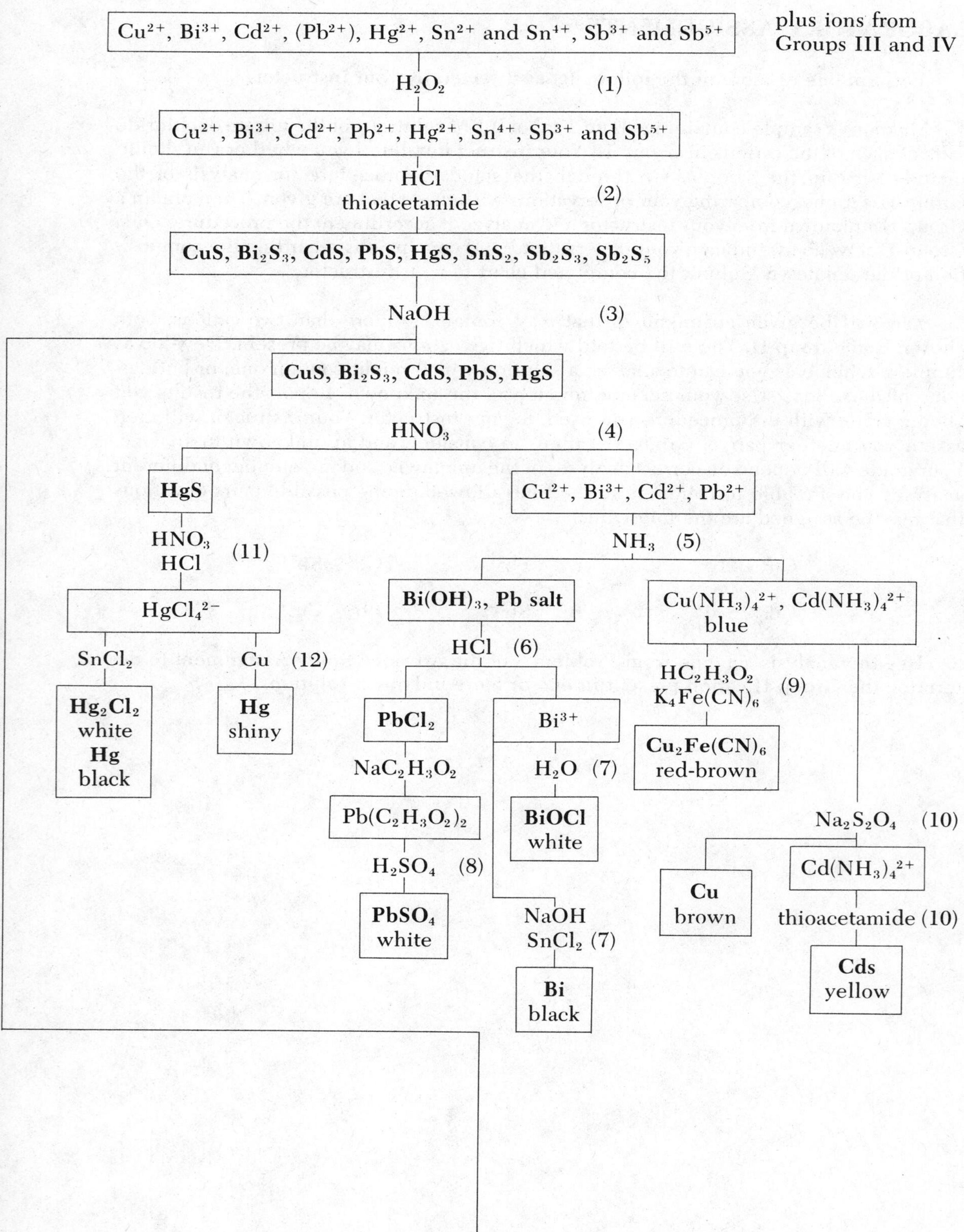

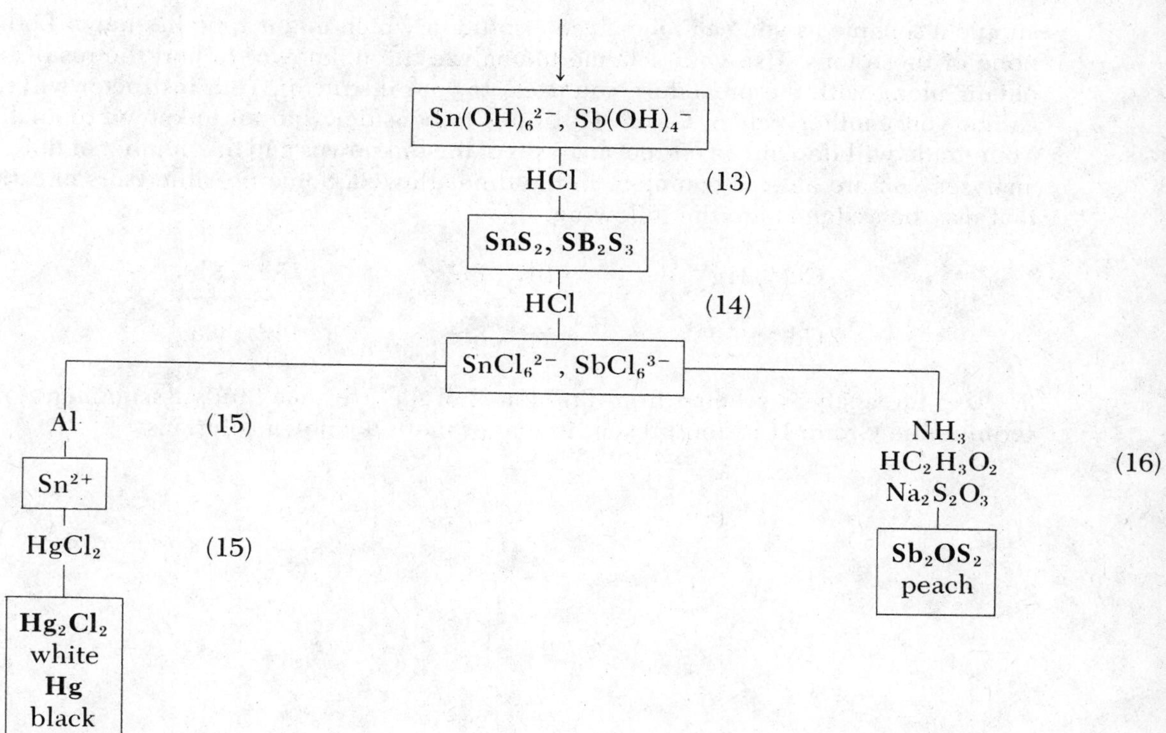
$Sn(OH)_6^{2-}$, $Sb(OH)_4^-$
HCl (13)
SnS_2, SB_2S_3
HCl (14)
$SnCl_6^{2-}$, $SbCl_6^{3-}$
Al (15)
Sn^{2+}
$HgCl_2$ (15)
Hg_2Cl_2
white
Hg
black
NH_3
$HC_2H_3O_2$ (16)
$Na_2S_2O_3$
Sb_2OS_2
peach

simple a scheme as you can to analyze a solution which might contain one, or both, or none of those ions. Use your scheme to analyze the unknown. Report the results you obtain, along with the procedure you used, to your instructor. Your instructor will then assign you another pair of Group II cations to consider, and an unknown to analyze. Your grade will depend on correct analyses of the unknowns and the number of different analyses you are able to complete in the time allowed. Some possible pairs of cations that may be assigned are the following:

Cu^{2+}, Hg^{2+} Bi^{3+}, Pb^{2+} Cd^{2+}, Sb^{3+}

Cd^{2+}, Sn^{4+} Bi^{3+}, Sb^{3+} Pb^{2+}, Cu^{2+}

3. Use the analysis scheme from Problem 3 of the Advance Study Assignment to determine the Group II cation present in one or more unknown solutions.

Name ______________________ Section ______________

OBSERVATIONS: Analysis of Group II Cations

Flow Chart Showing Behavior of Unknown

 Name ______________________ Section ______________

ADVANCE STUDY ASSIGNMENT: Analysis of Group II Cations

1. Write balanced net ionic equations for the following reactions:
   a. The confirmatory test for tin (step 15).

   b. A confirmatory test for bismuth (step 7).

   c. The reaction by which CuS is dissolved (step 4).

2. You are given solutions which contain one and only one of the cations in each of the following pairs. For each pair, indicate how you would proceed to determine which cation is present.
   a. Cu^{2+}, Bi^{3+}

   b. Cd^{2+}, Sn^{4+}

   c. Hg^{2+}, Cd^{2+}

   d. Cu^{2+}, Sb^{3+}

3. A solution may contain only one cation from Group II and no other metallic cations. Develop a simple scheme to identify the cation. On the back of this sheet, draw a flow chart showing the procedure and observations that establish which cation is present.

4. A solution may contain any of the cations in Group II. The initial sulfide precipitate is unaffected by NaOH. The residue resulting from treatment with NaOH partially dissolves in nitric acid; addition of NH_3 to the acid solution produces a colorless solution and no precipitate. On the basis of these observations, state which of the ions in Group II are present, absent, or still in doubt.

Present ______________

Absent ______________

In doubt ______________

EXPERIMENT 34

Qualitative Analysis of the Group III Cations: Ni^{2+}, Co^{2+}, Fe^{2+} and Fe^{3+}, Mn^{2+}, Cr^{3+}, Al^{3+}, Zn^{2+}

SEPARATION OF THE GROUP III CATIONS

In the discussion of the procedure for precipitating the Group II cations, we noted that the relatively low solubility of their sulfides as compared to those of the Group III cations allowed for the separation of Group II by sulfide precipitation under moderately acidic conditions. In slightly alkaline sulfide media the Group III cations will precipitate as either sulfides or hydroxides. This property allows one to separate these cations from those in Group IV, none of which precipitate in a buffered sulfide solution maintained at a pH of about 9.

PROPERTIES OF THE GROUP III CATIONS

Ni^{2+}. Nickel salts, like those of most of the other members of Group III, are typically colored. The hydrates are all green, the color of the $Ni(H_2O)_6^{2+}$ complex ion. Nickel forms several complex ions, many of which have characteristic colors; the blue $Ni(NH_3)_6^{2+}$ ion is perhaps the most common of these. Nickel sulfide, NiS, when first precipitated tends to be colloidal and difficult to settle by centrifuging; it is not very soluble in 6 *M* HCl, even though it cannot be precipitated from acidic solutions. Nickel forms a very characteristic rose-red precipitate with an organic reagent called dimethylglyoxime.

Co^{2+}. Cobalt(II) salts in water solution are characteristically pink, the color of the hydrated cobalt ion, $Co(H_2O)_6^{2+}$. Cobalt(II) forms several complex ions. When heated to boiling, the color of cobalt chloride solutions turns from pink to blue, as the hydrated cobalt ion is converted to species such as $CoCl_3(H_2O)_3^-$. Cobalt sulfide, like NiS, does not dissolve readily in 6 *M* HCl even when heated. Co(II) reacts with thiocyanate solutions to form a blue complex, $Co(SCN)_4^{2-}$, whose stability is much greater in ethanol than in water. Addition of KNO_2 to solutions of Co^{2+} produces a characteristic yellow precipitate of $K_3Co(NO_2)_6$:

$$Co^{2+}(aq) + 7NO_2^-(aq) + 3K^+(aq) + 2H^+(aq) \rightarrow K_3Co(NO_2)_6(s) + NO(g) + H_2O$$

Under strongly oxidizing conditions Co(II) can be converted to Co(III), which has a stability that is enhanced in a complex species like $Co(NH_3)_6^{3+}$, or an insoluble substance such as the yellow cobaltinitrite produced in the reaction above.

Mn^{2+}. Manganese exists in its common compounds in perhaps more different oxidation states than any other element, i.e., +2, +3, +4, +6, and +7. The only cation of manganese is Mn^{2+}, which is very pale pink in solution. The common Mn(IV) compound is MnO_2, a dark brown oxide that, like many higher oxides, will dissolve in acids only if a reducing agent like H_2O_2 is present:

$$MnO_2(s) + H_2O_2(aq) + 2\ H^+(aq) \rightarrow Mn^{2+}(aq) + O_2(g) + 2\ H_2O$$

Potassium permanganate, $KMnO_4$, a deep purple substance that is soluble in water and is a strong oxidizing agent in acid solution, contains manganese in its highest oxidation state, +7; the MnO_4^- ion is formed when sodium bismuthate, $NaBiO_3$, is added to Mn^{2+} under acidic conditions:

$$2\ Mn^{2+}(aq) + 5\ BiO_3^-(aq) + 14\ H^+(aq) \rightarrow 2\ MnO_4^-(aq) + 5\ Bi^{3+}(aq) + 7\ H_2O$$

The Mn^{2+} ion, unlike most of the Group III cations, does not form many complexes. The sulfide, MnS, is pink and readily soluble in dilute acids.

Fe^{2+} and Fe^{3+}. Iron in its compounds is ordinarily in the +2, ferrous, or the +3, ferric, state. The latter is more common, since most ferrous compounds oxidize in the air, particularly if water is present. Iron(II) compounds are usually found as hydrates and are light green. Iron(III) salts are also ordinarily obtained as hydrates and are often yellow or orange. Both Fe^{2+} and Fe^{3+} form many complexes, of which perhaps the most stable are those with cyanide, $Fe(CN)_6^{4-}$ and $Fe(CN)_6^{3-}$. The $FeSCN^{2+}$ ion has a very characteristic deep red color. Metallic iron is a good reducing agent, dissolving readily in 6 *M* HCl with evolution of hydrogen. Conversion of Fe(II) to Fe(III) or the reverse is easily accomplished by common oxidizing agents (air, H_2O_2 in acid) or by many reducing agents (H_2S, Sn^{2+}, I^-).

Al^{3+}. Aluminum in its compounds is found essentially only in the +3 state. Aluminum salts are typically colorless and soluble in water and in strong acids and bases, but not in ammonia. Aluminum metal is a strong reducing agent and dissolves easily in dilute strong acids and bases, with evolution of hydrogen. Aluminum is typically detected as the hydroxide, which is brought down in an NH_3 solution buffered with NH_4^+; a dye called aluminon, which adsorbs on $Al(OH)_3$ to form a so-called red lake, is often added to the solution of Al^{3+} before the hydroxide is precipitated.

Cr^{3+}. Chromium is ordinarily encountered in the laboratory in either the +3 or the +6 oxidation state. The common cation is Cr^{3+}, which forms several complexes, essentially all of which are colored; $Cr(H_2O)_6^{3+}$ is reddish-violet in solution. As with aluminum, the precipitate obtained in the Group III precipitation is the hydroxide, $Cr(OH)_3$, rather than the sulfide. Chromium(III) can be oxidized to Cr(VI) with several oxidizing agents (ClO_3^- in 16 *M* HNO_3, H_2O_2 in 6 *M* NaOH, ClO^- in 6 *M* NaOH) and it is in the latter state that it is usually identified. In neutral or basic solutions, Cr(VI) exists as the bright yellow chromate, CrO_4^{2-}, ion. If acid is added to this species, orange dichromate ion, $Cr_2O_7^{2-}$, is produced:

$$2\ CrO_4^{2-}(aq) + 2\ H^+(aq) \rightleftharpoons Cr_2O_7^{2-}(aq) + H_2O$$

If H_2O_2 is added to a solution containing $Cr_2O_7^{2-}$ ion, a transitory blue color, due to CrO_5, is observed.

Zn^{2+}. Zinc compounds are typically colorless and hydrated. Most of the salts are soluble in water, dilute acids, strong bases, and ammonia. Zinc ion forms many complexes, the stabilities of two of which explain the solubility of zinc(II) in excess hydroxide and ammonia. Zinc sulfide, ZnS, is white and soluble in dilute strong acids but not in NaOH solutions. Zinc metal is a good reducing agent, reacting with dilute acids to yield hydrogen. In its compounds zinc occurs ordinarily only in the +2 state. In the presence of potassium ferrocyanide, zinc ion forms a characteristic precipitate, $K_2Zn_3[Fe(CN)_6]_2$ (usually blue-green).

In Table 34.1 we have listed the common solubility properties of the Group III cations. In interpreting this and the other solubility tables, you should note that, unless a cation forms an ammonia complex ion, addition of ammonia to that species will typically precipitate its hydroxide or a basic oxide; this will happen with all cations whose hydroxides are insoluble in water and is caused by the fact that NH_3 in solution behaves as a weak base.

TABLE 34.1 SOLUBILITY PROPERTIES OF THE GROUP III CATIONS

	Ni^{2+}	Co^{2+}	Fe^{2+}	Fe^{3+}
Cl^-	S	S	S	S
OH^-	A (green)	A (tan)	A (green)	A (red-brown)
SO_4^{2-}	S	S	S	S
CrO_4^{2-}	S	C, A (brown)	D (brown)	A (tan)
CO_3^{2-}, PO_4^{3-}	C, A (green)	C, A (violet)	A (green)	A (tan)
S^{2-}	A^+, O^+ (black)	A^+, O^+ (black)	A (black)	D (black)
Complexes	NH_3	NH_3*	—	—

	Mn^{2+}	Cr^{3+}	Al^{3+}	Zn^{2+}
Cl^-	S	S	S	S
OH^-	A (white)	C, A (green)	C, A (white)	C, A (white)
SO_4^{2-}	S	S	S	S
CrO_4^{2-}	S	A (tan)	C, A (orange)	C, A (yellow)
CO_3^{2-}, PO_4^{3-}	A (white)	A (green)	C, A (white)	C, A (white)
S^{2-}	A (pink)	D (green)	D (white)	A (white)
Complexes	—	OH^-*	OH^-	NH_3, OH^-

*Although cobalt forms ammonia complexes, some of them are insoluble, so that tests for solubility should be made for mixtures of interest. Chromium hydroxide coprecipitated with other hydroxides may be insoluble in 6 *M* NaOH.

Key:

- S soluble in water, >0.1 mole/liter
- S^- slightly soluble in water, ~0.01 mole/liter
- HW soluble in hot water
- A soluble in acid (6 *M* HCl or other non-precipitating, nonoxidizing acid)
- I insoluble in any common solvent
- A^+ soluble in 12 *M* HCl
- B soluble in hot 6 *M* NaOH containing S^{2-} ion
- O soluble in hot 6 *M* HNO_3
- O^+ soluble in hot aqua regia
- C soluble in solution containing a good complexing ligand
- D unstable, decomposes

GENERAL SCHEME OF ANALYSIS

The qualitative analysis scheme for the Group III cations proceeds rather more easily than that for Group II. Following separation of the Group III precipitate from the solution containing the Group IV cations, we treat the precipitate with 6 *M* HCl, which puts all the cations except for Ni^{2+} and Co^{2+} into solution. The precipitate of NiS and CoS is dissolved in aqua regia, and the two cations are identified by their reactions with specific reagents. The hydrochloric acid solution of the other cations is made strongly basic and treated with sodium hypochlorite, which oxidizes Cr(III) to Cr(VI), Fe(II) to Fe(III), and Mn(II) to Mn(IV) or Mn(VII). Following treatment with NH_3, the solid phase contains $Fe(OH)_3$, MnO_2, and some $Ni(OH)_2$, and the solution phase contains CrO_4^{2-}, $Zn(OH)_4^{2-}$, and $Al(OH)_4^-$. The iron and nickel hydroxides are dissolved in H_2SO_4, leaving solid MnO_2, which is then dissolved and tested for the presence of manganese. The Fe^{3+} and Ni^{2+} ions are separated by treatment with ammonia, and identified with specific reagents.

The solution of CrO_4^{2-}, $Zn(OH)_4^{2-}$, and $Al(OH)_4^-$ is acidified and then made basic with NH_3, which precipitates aluminum as the hydroxide, allowing its removal and identification. Chromate is precipitated as $BaCrO_4$, and zinc ion is detected with a reagent specific to it.

The tests for identification of the ions in Group III have the advantage that they are relatively free of interferences. In each case, reagents are used that form very characteristic colored precipitates or solutions with the given cations. Some of the identifying species and their properties are as follows:

Ni^{2+}: Nickel dimethylglyoxime, a rose-red precipitate

Co^{2+}: $Co(SCN)_4^{2-}$, a blue complex ion
Fe^{3+}: $FeSCN^{2+}$, a deep red complex ion
Mn^{2+}; MnO_4^-, a deep purple anion
Cr^{3+}: CrO_5, a deep blue unstable peroxide
Al^{3+}: $Al(OH)_3$ with aluminon, a red lake
Zn^{2+}: $K_2Zn_3[Fe(CN)_6]_2$, a light green precipitate

PROCEDURE FOR ANALYSIS OF GROUP III CATIONS

WEAR YOUR SAFETY GLASSES WHILE PERFORMING THIS EXPERIMENT.

Step 1. Unless directed otherwise, you may assume that 10 ml of your sample contains the equivalent of about 1 ml of 0.1 *M* solutions of the nitrate or chloride salts of one or more of the Group III cations. If you are working with a general unknown, your sample is the solution decanted after separation of the Group II sulfides. Pour 5 ml of your sample, or your general unknown, into a 30 ml beaker and boil the solution gently until the volume is reduced to about 2 ml. Add 1 ml 1 *M* NH_4Cl and swirl the beaker to dissolve any crystallized salts.

Pour the solution into a test tube and then, drop by drop, with stirring, add 6 *M* NH_3 until the solution is basic to litmus. Add another 0.5 ml 6 *M* NH_3. Then add 1 ml *1 M* thioacetamide, stir well, and put the test tube in the boiling water bath for at least five minutes, and at least two minutes after the color of the precipitate stops changing. Stir the mixture occasionally as precipitation proceeds.

Centrifuge out the precipitate and decant the liquid into a test tube. Add a few drops of 1 *M* thioacetamide to the liquid and put the test tube into the boiling water bath for a few minutes more to check for complete precipitation of Group III cations. Save the liquid, if necessary, for analysis of Group IV cations. Wash the precipitate twice with 1 ml 1 *M* NH_4Cl, 2 ml water, and a few drops of 6 *M* NH_3, stirring well and centrifuging between washes. Discard the wash liquid.

Step 2. To the precipitate from Step 1, which should contain the Group III sulfides or hydroxides, add 1 ml 6 *M* HCl and 1 ml water. Mix thoroughly, and pour the slurry into a 30 ml beaker. Boil the liquid gently for about a minute. A black residue is mainly CoS and NiS. Add 1 ml water, stir, and pour the slurry into a test tube. Centrifuge and decant the liquid, which may contain Al^{3+}, Fe^{2+}, Zn^{2+}, Cr^{3+}, and Mn^{2+}, as well as Ni^{2+}, into a test tube (Label 2). Wash the solid twice with 1 ml 6 *M* HCl and 1 ml water. Centrifuge and discard the wash liquid.

Step 3. To the precipitate from Step 2 add 1 ml 6 *M* HCl and 1 ml 6 *M* HNO_3. Stir, and put the test tube in the boiling water bath for about a minute. The precipitate should dissolve in a few moments, leaving almost no residue. Pour the solution into a 30 ml beaker and boil gently for one minute; add 2 ml water and pour the liquid back into a test tube.

Step 4. *Confirmation of the presence of cobalt.* Pour one third of the solution from Step 3 into a test tube and slowly add about 1 ml of a saturated solution of NH_4SCN in ethyl alcohol, C_2H_5OH. If Co^{2+} is present, a blue solution of $Co(SCN)_4^{2-}$ forms. To the rest of the solution add 6 *M* NaOH, drop by drop, until a precipitate remains after stirring. Then add 0.5 ml 6 *M* acetic acid to dissolve the precipitate. To half of this solution add 0.4 g solid KNO_2. Add 1 ml water and stir. A yellow precipitate of $K_3Co(NO_2)_6$, which may form over a period of ten minutes, also confirms the presence of cobalt.

Step 5. *Confirmation of the presence of nickel.* To the other half of the solution from Step 4, add 0.5 ml of dimethylglyoxime reagent. A rose-red precipitate proves the presence of nickel.

Step 6. To the liquid from Step 2, add 6 *M* NaOH, drop by drop, until the solution is basic, and then add 0.5 ml more. Pour the slurry into a 30 ml beaker and boil gently for two minutes, stirring to minimize bumping. Remove heat, and add 1 ml 1 *M* NaClO, sodium hypochlorite; swirl the beaker for 30 seconds. Boil the liquid for one minute. Manganese is likely if the foam looks purple. Add 0.5 ml 6 *M* NH_3 and boil for another minute. Transfer the mixture to a test tube and centrifuge out the solid. Decant the liquid, which may contain $Al(OH)_4^-$, $Zn(OH)_4^{2-}$, and CrO_4^{2-}, into a test tube (Label 6). Wash the solid twice with 2 ml water and 0.5 ml 6 *M* NaOH; centrifuge each time, discarding the wash.

Step 7. To the precipitate from Step 6, which may contain $Fe(OH)_3$, MnO_2, and $Ni(OH)_2$, add 1 ml water and 1 ml 6 *M* H_2SO_4. Stir and heat the tube for a few minutes in the water bath; centrifuge out any undissolved solid, which should contain essentially only MnO_2. Decant the liquid, which may contain Fe^{3+} and Ni^{2+}, into a test tube (Label 7). Wash the precipitate with 2 ml water and 1 ml 6 *M* H_2SO_4; centrifuge and discard the wash.

Step 8. To the precipitate from Step 7 add 1 ml water and 1 ml 6 *M* H_2SO_4; stir and then add 1 ml of 3 per cent H_2O_2. Put the test tube in the boiling water bath. The precipitate should dissolve readily on stirring, with possibly a small amount of residue. When it is essentially dissolved, pour the solution into a 30 ml beaker and boil gently for two minutes.

Step 9. *Confirmation of the presence of manganese.* Pour 1 ml of the liquid from Step 8 into a test tube and add 1 ml 6 *M* HNO_3. Add about 0.4 g of solid sodium bismuthate, $NaBiO_3$, with your spatula, and stir well. There should be a little solid bismuthate in excess. Let the mixture stand for a minute and then centrifuge it. If the solution phase is purple, the color is due to MnO_4^- ion and proves the presence of manganese.

Step 10. *Confirmation of the presence of iron.* To one third of the liquid from Step 7, add 2 ml water and 1 or 2 drops of 1 *M* KSCN. Formation of a deep red solution of the $FeSCN^{2+}$ complex ion is a definitive test for the presence of iron. To another third add 1 or 2 drops of 0.2 *M* $K_4Fe(CN)_6$. A dark blue solution or precipitate of $KFe[Fe(CN)_6]$ offers a comforting reassurance that iron is there.

Step 11. *Alternative confirmation of the presence of nickel.* To the remaining liquid from Step 7 add 6 *M* NH_3, drop by drop, until the solution is basic; add 4 or 5 drops more. Centrifuge out any brown precipitate of $Fe(OH)_3$ and decant the liquid into a test tube.* Add 0.5 ml of dimethylglyoxime to the liquid. The formation of a rose-red precipitate proves the presence of nickel.

Step 12. Returning to the solution from Step 6, add 6 *M* acetic acid slowly until the solution is definitely acidic after mixing. Transfer the solution to a 30 ml beaker and boil it down to a volume of about 3 ml. Pour the solution into a test tube. Add 6 *M* NH_3, drop by drop, until the solution is basic to litmus, and then add 5 drops of NH_3 in excess. Stir the mixture for a minute or so to bring the system to equilibrium. If aluminum is present, a light, translucent, gelatinous precipitate of $Al(OH)_3$ should be floating in the clear (possibly yellow) solution. Centrifuge out the solid, decanting the solution, which may contain CrO_4^{2-} and $Zn(NH_3)_4^{2+}$, into a test tube.

Step 13. *Confirmation of the presence of aluminum.* Wash the precipitate from Step 12 with 3 ml water once or twice, while warming it in the boiling water bath and stirring well. Centrifuge, and discard the wash. Dissolve the precipitate in 0.5 ml 6 *M*

*If you are working with a general unknown and, owing to too low a pH, failed to precipitate cadmium in Group II, it may be in the solution in Step 11. To test for cadmium in this step, acidify the decanted liquid with acetic acid after removing $Fe(OH)_3$. Add 1 ml 1 *M* thioacetamide and heat in the water bath. If cadmium is present, yellow CdS will precipitate.

HNO_3, discarding any insoluble residue. Add 1 ml water and 2 drops of aluminon reagent and stir thoroughly. At this point the solution is light orange because of the aluminon. Add 6 M NH_3, drop by drop, stirring well, until the solution becomes basic to litmus. If Al^{3+} is present, the precipitate of $Al(OH)_3$ re-forms and adsorbs the aluminon from the solution, producing a red precipitate of $Al(OH)_3$, called a lake. Centrifuge to concentrate the precipitate; discard the liquid. To the precipitate add 1 ml 1 M $(NH_4)_2CO_3$ and 3 drops 6 M NH_3. Stir for one minute and centrifuge. If the precipitate is still definitely red, aluminum is present.

Step 14. If the solution from Step 12 is yellow, chromium is probably present; if it is colorless, chromium is absent. If you suspect that chromium is there, pour the solution into a 30 ml beaker, bring the solution to a boil, remove the source of heat, and add 0.5 ml 1 M $BaCl_2$. In the presence of chromium, you obtain a very finely divided yellow precipitate of $BaCrO_4$, which may be mixed with a white precipitate of $BaSO_4$. Pour the slurry into a test tube and put the test tube in the boiling water bath for a few minutes; then centrifuge out the solid and decant the solution into a test tube. Wash the precipitate with 2 ml water; centrifuge and discard the wash.

Step 15. *Confirmation of the presence of chromium.* To the precipitate from Step 14, add 0.5 ml 6 M HNO_3 and stir to dissolve the $BaCrO_4$. Add 1 ml water, stir the solution, cool it under the water tap, and then add 2 drops of 3 per cent H_2O_2. A blue solution, which may fade quite rapidly, is confirmatory evidence for the presence of chromium.

Step 16. *Confirmation of the presence of zinc.* If you tested for the presence of chromium, use the solution from Step 14. If you were sure chromium was absent, use the solution from Step 12. Make the solution slightly acidic to litmus with 6 M HCl added drop by drop. Add 3 drops in excess and then add about 3 drops of 0.2 M $K_4Fe(CN)_6$ and stir. If zinc is present, you will obtain a light green precipitate of $K_2Zn_3[Fe(CN)_6]_2$. Centrifuge to make the precipitate more compact for examination. Decant the liquid, which may be discarded. To the precipitate add 5 drops 6 M NaOH; the solid should dissolve readily with stirring, and possibly some heating in the water bath. If there is an insoluble residue, centrifuge it out and decant the liquid into a test tube. To the liquid add 0.5 ml water and then 6 M HCl, drop by drop until acidic to litmus (about 6 drops). Re-formation of the green precipitate confirms the presence of zinc.

COMMENTS ON PROCEDURE FOR ANALYSIS OF GROUP III CATIONS

Step 1. As noted previously, the Group II sulfides are extremely insoluble and precipitate with H_2S in acid solution. The sulfides of the cations in Group III are more soluble than those in Group II and can be precipitated by sulfide ion in a slightly basic solution. An ammonia–ammonium chloride buffer is typically used for controlling pH; since in the precipitating medium the concentrations of hydroxide and sulfide ions are low, about 10^{-5} M and 10^{-6} M, respectively, hydroxide and sulfide complexes do not form, and Group IV cations, if present, do not precipitate. Because of the extreme insolubility of $Al(OH)_3$ and $Cr(OH)_3$, these compounds, rather than their more soluble sulfides, are precipitated.

In the procedure used, the pH is fixed before thioacetamide is added, and some hydroxides may be precipitated, i.e., $Fe(OH)_3$ (rust red), $Fe(OH)_2$ (green), $Cr(OH)_3$ (gray-green), and $Al(OH)_3$ (white). On formation of the sulfides, the color changes. The sulfides have the following colors: FeS (black), CoS (black), MnS (pink), NiS (black), and ZnS (white). Because the sulfide ion reduces iron from the +3 state, FeS, rather than $Fe(OH)_3$ or Fe_2S_3, should be the iron precipitate.

On centrifuging out the precipitate, you may find that the remaining liquid is dark, with some fine particles dispersed in it. The NiS does not settle out as completely as a well behaving precipitate should and is responsible for the darkness in the solution. Most of the NiS does come down, though; no real problem is created, just perhaps a little question in one's mind.

Step 2. The relative insolubilities of CoS and NiS make it possible to separate these sulfides from the others by treatment with 6 *M* HCl. Almost no cobalt(II) dissolves, but some nickel(II) does, and one therefore probably obtains a test for nickel both from the precipitate and from the solution.

Step 3. If cobalt is present, when you add the water to the hot solution, the color will usually change from blue-green to a very light pink.

Step 4. The use of an alcohol solution of NH_4SCN enhances the stability of the cobalt thiocyanate complex ion and makes the test quite sensitive. If you add the thiocyanate slowly, the lower water layer will typically be red, due to traces of iron, and the upper alcohol layer will be blue. The formation of yellow potassium hexanitrocobaltate(III), $K_3[Co(NO_2)_6]\cdot 3H_2O$, is a less sensitive test for cobalt, but it is also satisfactory. In neither test does nickel interfere.

Step 5. The classic dimethylglyoxime test for nickel is hard to beat. Cobalt does form a colored complex ion with dimethylglyoxime, which must not be confused with a precipitate. However, once you have seen the nickel precipitate made by adding dimethylglyoxime to a dilute nickel solution, you will remember how it looks. Dimethylglyoxime has the formula:

$$\begin{array}{l} CH_3{-}C{=}N{-}OH \\ \quad\quad\;\; | \\ CH_3{-}C{=}N{-}OH \end{array}$$

and two of these molecules attach to each Ni^{2+} ion in the complex.

Step 6. In this step sodium hypochlorite, NaClO, a very strong oxidizing agent and the main component of household bleach, is used to convert Cr(III) to CrO_4^{2-}. Some of the manganese present may be oxidized to permanganate ion, MnO_4^-, which is deep purple in color. Following the oxidation, NH_3 is added to remove excess hypochlorite and to reduce manganese to Mn(IV), where it precipitates as MnO_2. Some of the key reactions are:

$$2\ Cr^{3+}(aq) + 3\ ClO^-(aq) + 10\ OH^-(aq) \rightarrow 2\ CrO_4^{2-}(aq) + 3\ Cl^-(aq) + 5\ H_2O$$

$$3\ ClO^-(aq) + 2\ NH_3(aq) \rightarrow 3\ Cl^-(aq) + N_2(g) + 3\ H_2O$$

$$2\ MnO_4^-(aq) + 2\ NH_3(aq) \rightarrow 2\ MnO_2(s) + N_2(g) + 2\ OH^-(aq) + 2\ H_2O$$

Never acidify hypochlorite solutions, since chlorine or explosive vapors may be produced. Excess ClO^- ion can be destroyed by adding 6 *M* NH_3 in excess to the basic solution and boiling.

Step. 7. Of the three solids possibly present, only the MnO_2 is so weakly basic that it resists solution in acid; some of the manganese does dissolve, but the bulk remains as a brown solid. If the decanted liquid is dark colored, heat it in the water bath for a few minutes. Centrifuge again to remove the MnO_2 that precipitates, and use the decanted, (usually) light tan liquid in Step 10.

Step 8. In acid solution H_2O_2 reduces many higher oxides, including MnO_2, forming more basic oxides; in this case, MnO, or $Mn(OH)_2$, is produced and dissolves very easily in acid.

Step 9. This is the classic test for the presence of manganese. The only interference is by chlorides and other species that can be oxidized, but in excess bismuthate even these finally are all oxidized and the deep purple MnO_4^- ion forms.

Step 10. The test for Fe^{3+} is another one that is hard to miss. Nitric acid also gives a red coloration, which is the reason H_2SO_4 is used in dissolving $Fe(OH)_3$. The test with $K_4Fe(CN)_6$ is extremely sensitive, and should be dark blue.

Step 11. We have always obtained a confirmatory reaction for nickel at this point when nickel was present. It has tended to be somewhat weaker than that in Step 5, however.

Steps 12 and 13. Of all the cations in the analysis scheme, aluminum is most likely to appear to be present when it is actually not there. The false positive test arises mainly from residual Cr^{3+}, which will behave much like Al^{3+}. The aluminum lake is unique in that it will remain reddish in the presence of 1 *M* $(NH_4)_2CO_3$, whereas lakes due to other cations will become either white or light tan in color.

Steps 14 and 15. Sometimes, although the solution in Step 14 is yellow, the precipitate obtained on addition of barium ion is not very soluble in 6 *M* HNO_3 in Step 15, to the extent that no chromium test is obtained. This insolubility may be due to coprecipitation of sulfate with the chromate or to other chromium oxyanions which do not behave quite like CrO_4^{2-}. In any event, if the barium salt does not dissolve readily in 6 *M* HNO_3, transfer the slurry to a 30 ml beaker, add 1 ml 6 *M* HNO_3 more, and boil gently for two minutes, stirring frequently to minimize spattering. Centrifuge out any undissolved solid and use the liquid for the chromium test. The blue species formed when H_2O_2 is added to the acidified chromate solution is thought to be CrO_5, an unstable peroxide:

$$Cr_2O_7^{2-}(aq) + 4\ H_2O_2(aq) + 2\ H^+(aq) \rightarrow 2\ CrO_5(aq) + 5\ H_2O$$

Step 16. Potassium zinc hexacyanoferrate(II), $K_2Zn_3[Fe(CN)_6]_2$, is nearly white when pure. In this test it is usually light green or blue-green because of contamination with a trace of iron. Under the acidic conditions that prevail, other cations likely to be present do not interfere.

LABORATORY ASSIGNMENTS

Perform one or more of the following, as directed by your instructor:

1. Make up a sample containing about 1 ml of 0.1 *M* solutions of the nitrate or chloride salts of each of the cations in Group III. Go through the standard procedure for analysis of the Group III cations, comparing your observations with those that are noted. Then obtain a Group III unknown from your instructor and analyze it according to the procedure. On a Group III flow chart, indicate your observations and conclusions regarding the composition of the unknown. Submit the completed chart to your instructor.

2. You will be assigned in advance an unknown that may contain only those Group III cations in one of the following sets. Before coming to laboratory, develop a procedure by which you can analyze for the ions in your set. Do not include any unnecessary steps; try to make the procedure as simple as possible. Draw a complete flow chart for your scheme, indicating the reagents to be used in each step and the observations that will confirm the presence of each cation. Test your procedure with a sample containing all

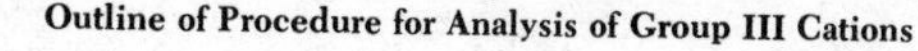

Outline of Procedure for Analysis of Group III Cations

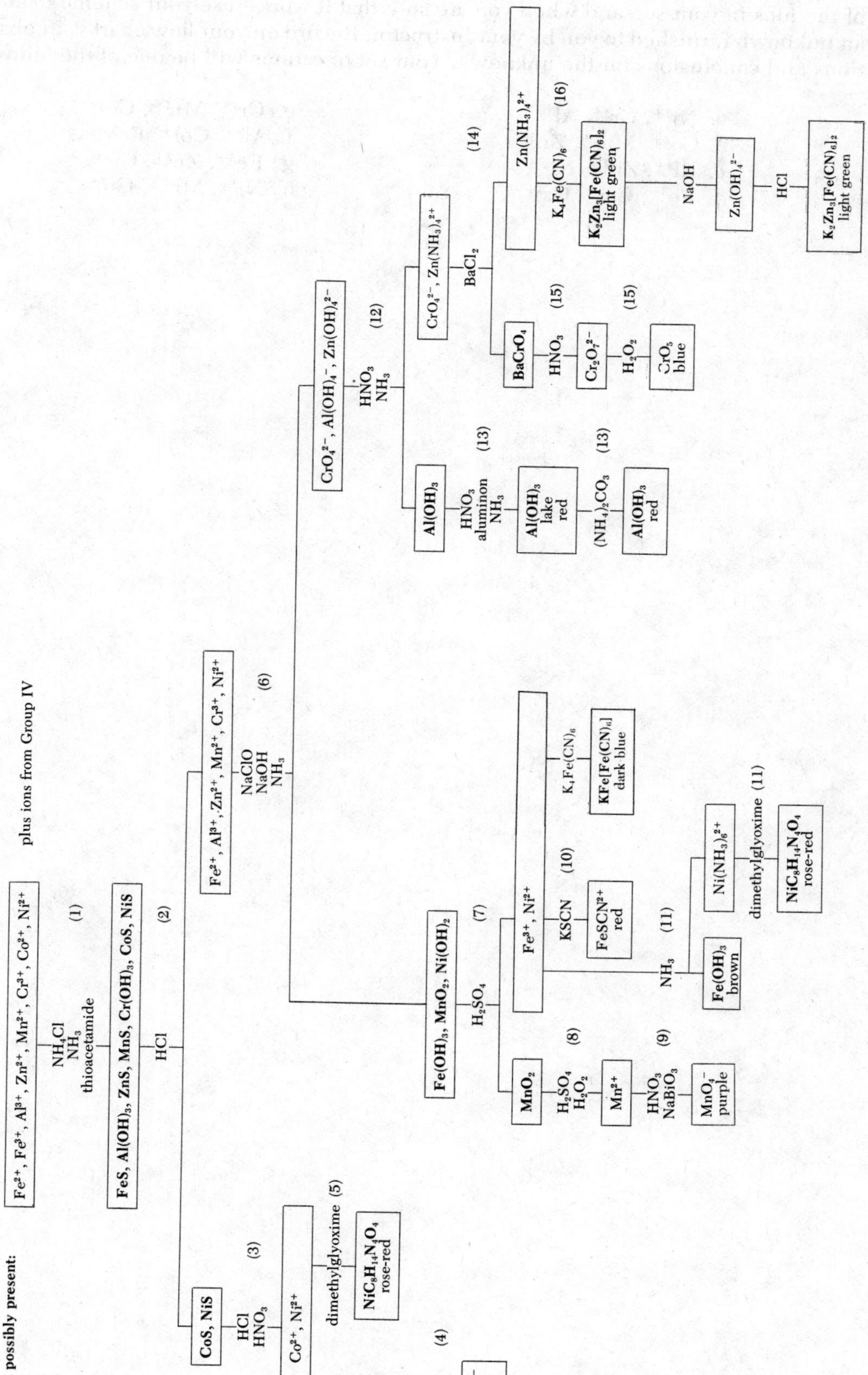

Ions possibly present: Fe^{2+}, Fe^{3+}, Al^{3+}, Zn^{2+}, Mn^{2+}, Cr^{3+}, Co^{2+}, Ni^{2+} plus ions from Group IV

- NH_4Cl, NH_3, thioacetamide (1) → **FeS, $Al(OH)_3$, ZnS, MnS, $Cr(OH)_3$, CoS, NiS**
  - HCl (2)
    - **CoS, NiS**
      - HCl, HNO_3 (3) → Co^{2+}, Ni^{2+}
        - NH_4SCN (4) → $Co(SCN)_4^{2-}$ blue
        - dimethylglyoxime (5) → **$NiC_8H_{14}N_4O_4$** rose-red
    - Fe^{2+}, Al^{3+}, Zn^{2+}, Mn^{2+}, Cr^{3+}, Ni^{2+}
      - NaClO, NaOH, NH_3 (6)
        - **$Fe(OH)_3$, MnO_2, $Ni(OH)_2$**
          - H_2SO_4 (7)
            - **MnO_2**
              - H_2SO_4, H_2O_2 (8) → Mn^{2+}
                - HNO_3, $NaBiO_3$ (9) → MnO_4^- purple
            - Fe^{3+}, Ni^{2+}
              - KSCN (10) → $FeSCN^{2+}$ red
              - $K_4Fe(CN)_6$ → **$KFe[Fe(CN)_6]$** dark blue
              - NH_3 (11)
                - **$Fe(OH)_3$** brown
                - $Ni(NH_3)_6^{2+}$
                  - dimethylglyoxime (11) → **$NiC_8H_{14}N_4O_4$** rose-red
        - CrO_4^{2-}, $Al(OH)_4^-$, $Zn(OH)_4^{2-}$
          - HNO_3, NH_3 (12)
            - **$Al(OH)_3$**
              - HNO_3, aluminon, NH_3 (13) → **$Al(OH)_3$** lake red
                - $(NH_4)_2CO_3$ (13) → **$Al(OH)_3$** red
            - CrO_4^{2-}, $Zn(NH_3)_4^{2+}$
              - $BaCl_2$ (14)
                - **$BaCrO_4$**
                  - HNO_3 (15) → $Cr_2O_7^{2-}$
                    - H_2O_2 (15) → CrO_5 blue
                - $Zn(NH_3)_4^{2+}$
                  - $K_4Fe(CN)_6$ (16) → **$K_2Zn_3[Fe(CN)_6]_2$** light green
                    - NaOH → $Zn(OH)_4^{2-}$
                      - HCl → **$K_2Zn_3[Fe(CN)_6]_2$** light green

of the ions in your set, and when you are sure that it works, use your scheme to analyze an unknown furnished to you by your instructor. Record on your flow chart your observations and conclusions for the unknown. Your set of cations will be one of the following:

a. Ni^{2+}, Cr^{3+}, Al^{3+}
b. Co^{2+}, Mn^{2+}, Zn^{2+}
c. Al^{3+}, Zn^{2+}, Ni^{2+}
d. Fe^{3+}, Co^{2+}, Cr^{3+}
e. Cr^{3+}, Mn^{2+}, Co^{2+}
f. Al^{3+}, Co^{2+}, Fe^{3+}
g. Fe^{3+}, Zn^{2+}, Cr^{3+}
h. Ni^{2+}, Mn^{2+}, Cr^{3+}

Name ______________________ Section ______________

OBSERVATIONS: Analysis of Group III Cations

Flow Chart Showing Behavior of Unknown

 Name ________________ Section ________________

ADVANCE STUDY ASSIGNMENT: Analysis of Group III Cations

1. Write balanced net ionic equations for the following reactions:
   a. The confirmatory test for chromium (step 15).

   b. The reaction by which NiS is dissolved (step 3).

   c. The reaction by which MnS is dissolved (step 2).

   d. The reaction by which Mn^{2+} is converted to MnO_4^- by ClO^- in NaOH solution.

2. You are given solutions which contain one of the cations in each of the following sets. For each set, indicate how you would proceed to determine which cation is present.
   a. Al^{3+} Fe^{3+} Mn^{2+}

   b. Mn^{2+} Co^{2+} Al^{3+}

   c. Cd^{2+} Zn^{2+} Ni^{2+}

   d. Pb^{2+} Cr^{3+} Cu^{2+}

3. A solution may contain any of the cations in Group III. Addition of NH_3 and NH_4Cl to the solution gives a reddish precipitate which turns black when H_2S is added. The final precipitate is completely soluble in HCl. Treatment of the HCl solution with NaOCl and NaOH produces a colorless solution and a precipitate that is completely soluble in H_2SO_4. Given this information, state which ions must be present, are absent, or are still in doubt.

Present ________________

Absent ________________

In doubt ________________

EXPERIMENT 35

Qualitative Analysis of the Group IV Cations: Ba^{2+}, Ca^{2+}, Mg^{2+}, Na^{+}, K^{+}, NH_4^{+}

SEPARATION OF SOME OF THE GROUP IV CATIONS

The ions remaining in solution after the separation of the Group III cations are those of the alkaline earths, the alkali metals, and the ammonium ion. Barium and calcium are separated from the rest of the ions by precipitation of their carbonates under slightly basic conditions. Sodium, potassium, ammonium, and, for the most part, magnesium ions do not precipitate under such conditions. The cations in Group IV have rather less distinctive chemical properties than do the other cations we have studied, so their detection depends in some cases more on physical than on chemical behavior.

PROPERTIES OF THE GROUP IV CATIONS

Ba^{2+}. Most of the common barium salts are soluble in water or dilute strong acids and are colorless in solution. The main exception is the sulfate, $BaSO_4$, a finely divided white powder which is essentially insoluble in all common reagents. Barium chromate, $BaCrO_4$, is insoluble in acetic acid but will dissolve in solutions of strong acids. The oxalate and phosphate are soluble in acidic systems at a pH of 3 or less. Barium hydroxide is a strong base and is moderately soluble in water (~0.2 moles/liter). Barium exists in its compounds essentially only in the +2 state and is not reducible to the metal in aqueous systems.

Ca^{2+}. Calcium salts are typically soluble in water or dilute acids. Like barium, calcium does not form many common complex ions. Although the hydroxide is less soluble than $Ba(OH)_2$, it will not precipitate in ammonia. Calcium oxalate, CaC_2O_4, is white and not appreciably soluble in acetic acid, but it will dissolve in dilute strong acid solutions. Calcium in its compounds occurs in the +2 state, and the ion is very difficult to reduce to the metal.

Mg^{2+}. Magnesium salts are all soluble in water or dilute acids. Compounds of magnesium are essentially all white and frequently crystallize as hydrates. Magnesium has the least soluble hydroxide of all the alkaline earths; in the presence of magnesium reagent (4-(*p*-nitrophenylazo)resorcinol) the hydroxide forms a blue lake. Magnesium oxalate is moderately soluble at pH 5 or below. In an ammonia-ammonium chloride buffer, magnesium ion will form a characteristic white precipitate on addition of Na_2HPO_4 solution:

$$Mg^{2+}(aq) + NH_3(aq) + HPO_4^{2-}(aq) \rightleftharpoons NH_4MgPO_4(s)$$

NH_4^+. Although ammonium ion is not a metallic cation, it forms salts with properties similar to those of alkali metals and is usually included in schemes of qualitative analysis. Ammonium salts are white and soluble in water; if the anion is that of a strong acid, the ammonium salt solution will be slightly acidic. Addition of strong bases to solutions containing ammonium ion causes formation and evolution of NH_3:

$$NH_4^+(aq) + OH^-(aq) \rightleftharpoons NH_3(g) + H_2O$$

The gas can be detected by its odor or by its ability to turn red litmus paper blue. Ammonium salts are much more volatile and unstable when heated than are those of the other cations. The products obtained on heating are often NH_3 and an acid, but N_2 or N_2O may also be produced, depending on the salt.

Na^+. Sodium salts are typically water soluble and white. The Na^+ ion in water solution is essentially inert. The hydroxide is very soluble and is the common laboratory source of OH^- ion. Sodium does not form any common complex ions; its salts are frequently obtained as hydrates. It is difficult to detect sodium by precipitation of an insoluble salt; one of the least soluble compounds of sodium is the zinc uranyl acetate, $NaZn(UO_2)_3(C_2H_3O_2)_9$, a yellow substance that can be precipitated from moderately concentrated solutions of Na^+. The most common test for sodium in qualitative analysis is the flame test. In a Bunsen flame, sodium salts give off a very strong characteristic yellow light. Since even traces of Na^+ produce the flame, care is necessary in interpreting the test.

K^+. The salts of potassium are similar to those of sodium in their general properties. Potassium hydroxide is very soluble and is a strong base. There are no highly insoluble, easily prepared compounds of potassium; among the least soluble potassium salts is the hexachloroplatinate(IV), K_2PtCl_6. Ordinarily, potassium is detected in qualitative analysis by its characteristic violet flame test, which is much less sensitive than that for sodium.

In Table 35.1 we have listed some of the common solubility properties of the Group IV cations. As a group these cations have by far the most soluble salts; nearly all of their salts will dissolve in very dilute acids.

GENERAL SCHEME OF ANALYSIS

Following separation of the Group IV precipitate, containing $BaCO_3$, $CaCO_3$, and possibly some $MgCO_3$, from the soluble cations, Na^+, K^+, and NH_4^+, the precipitate is dissolved in acetic acid. Addition to the resulting solution of chromate, oxalate, and phosphate ions in a succession of steps causes precipitation of $BaCrO_4$, CaC_2O_4, and $MgNH_4PO_4$ and thereby allows separation of the alkaline earth cations. Specific tests

TABLE 35.1 SOLUBILITY PROPERTIES OF THE GROUP IV CATIONS

	Ba^{2+}	Ca^{2+}	Mg^{2+}	Na^+, K^+, NH_4^+
Cl^-	S	S	S	S
OH^-	S	S⁻	A (white)	S
SO_4^{2-}	I (white)	S⁻	S	S
CrO_4^{2-}	A (yellow)	S	S	S
CO_3^{2-}, PO_4^{3-}	A (white)	A (white)	A (white)	S
S^{2-}	S	S	S	S
Complexes	–	–	–	–

Key:

S soluble in water, >0.1 mole/liter
S^- slightly soluble in water, ~0.01 mole/liter
HW soluble in hot water
A soluble in acid (6 *M* HCl or other non-precipitating, nonoxidizing acid)
I insoluble in any common solvent
A^+ soluble in 12 *M* HCl
B soluble in hot 6 *M* NaOH containing S^{2-} ion
O soluble in hot 6 *M* HNO_3
O^+ soluble in hot aqua regia
C soluble in solution containing a good complexing ligand
D unstable, decomposes

for each cation establish their presence in the solution. Sodium and ammonium ions are tested for in an untreated sample; sodium is identified by its characteristic flame, and ammonium ion by the evolution of NH_3 upon treatment with base. Potassium ion is also detected by a flame test, made either on the original solution or on the liquid decanted from the Group IV precipitate.

PROCEDURE FOR ANALYSIS OF GROUP IV CATIONS

WEAR YOUR SAFETY GLASSES WHILE PERFORMING THIS EXPERIMENT.

Step 1. If you are working with only the Group IV cations, you may assume, unless told otherwise, that 10 ml of sample contains the equivalent of 1 ml of 0.1 *M* solutions of the nitrate or chloride salts of one or more of those cations. Pour 5 ml of your Group IV sample into a 30 ml beaker and boil the solution down to a volume of 2 ml. Then add 0.5 ml 6 *M* HCl, swirl to dissolve any crystals on the walls of the beaker, and transfer the solution to a test tube.

If you are analyzing a general unknown, prepare for Group IV analysis by transferring the solution remaining after removal of the Group III cations to a 30 ml beaker and boiling it down to a volume of 2 ml. Transfer the liquid to a test tube and centrifuge out any solid matter, which you may discard. Put the liquid back into the beaker, add 1 ml 6 *M* HCl, and proceed to boil the material essentially to dryness. Transfer the beaker to a hood, and carefully heat the dry solid to drive off all the ammonium salts that were added in previous steps. Stop heating the solid when the visible smoke from these salts is no longer being evolved. Let the beaker cool, and then add 0.5 ml 6 *M* HCl and 2 ml water. Warm the solution gently to dissolve the remaining salts; discard any insoluble material after centrifuging it out. Pour the solution into a test tube.

Step 2. To your Group IV sample prepared in Step 1, add 6 *M* NH_3 until the solution becomes basic; add 0.5 ml more: Then add 1 ml 1 *M* $(NH_4)_2CO_3$ and stir. Put the test tube in the hot, *but not boiling*, water bath, and without any heating, leave the tube in the bath for two minutes, stirring occasionally. Centrifuge and decant the liquid, which may contain K^+ and Mg^{2+}, into a test tube (Label 2). Wash the precipitate, which may contain $BaCO_3$, $CaCO_3$, and possibly some $Mg(OH)_2$ or $MgCO_3$, with 2 ml water. Centrifuge out the precipitate, and discard the wash.

Step 3. *Confirmation of the presence of barium.* Add 0.5 ml 6 *M* acetic acid to the precipitate from Step 2 and stir to dissolve the solid. Add 1 ml water and 2 drops 6 *M* NH_3 and mix; then add 0.5 ml 1 *M* K_2CrO_4. A yellow precipitate indicates the presence of barium. Stir for a minute and centrifuge out the solid. Decant the liquid, which may contain Ca^{2+} and Mg^{2+}, into a test tube. Wash the solid with 3 ml water; centrifuge, and discard the wash. Dissolve the solid in 0.5 ml 6 *M* HCl; add 1 ml water. Then add 0.5 ml 6 *M* H_2SO_4, and stir the solution for 30 seconds. A white precipitate of $BaSO_4$ establishes the presence of barium. Centrifuge to separate the white solid from the orange solution, which may be discarded.

Step 4. *Confirmation of the presence of calcium.* Add 6 *M* NH_3 to the decanted orange liquid from Step 3 until it becomes basic; at this point the solution becomes yellow. Add 0.5 ml 1 *M* $K_2C_2O_4$, stir and let the solution stand for a minute. A white precipitate of $CaC_2O_4 \cdot H_2O$ is confirmation for the presence of calcium. Centrifuge out the white solid, and pour the liquid, which may contain Mg^{2+}, into a test tube. Wash the solid with 3 ml of water; centrifuge, and discard the wash.

Dissolve the solid in 2 drops of 6 *M* HCl. Perform a flame test several times on the resulting solution. A fleeting orange-red sparkly flame is due to calcium. This color appears before the yellow sodium flame, and it is best observed if you have a small drop of the solution on the test loop; the color lasts only a fraction of a second. Compare your observations here with those obtained with a 0.1 *M* $Ca(NO_3)_2$ solution.

Step 5. *Confirmation of the presence of magnesium.* To the solution from Step 4, add 0.5 ml 1 *M* Na_2HPO_4. Stir the solution, warm it gently in the water bath, and let it stand for a minute. A white precipitate is highly indicative of the presence of magnesium. Centrifuge out the solid, and discard the liquid. Wash the solid with 3 ml of water; centrifuge, and discard the wash. Dissolve the solid in a few drops of 6 *M* HCl. Add 1 ml water and then 2 or 3 drops of magnesium reagent, 4-(*p*-nitrophenylazo)resorcinol. Stir the solution, and then, drop by drop, add 6 *M* NaOH until the solution is basic. If magnesium is present, a medium blue precipitate of $Mg(OH)_2$ with adsorbed magnesium reagent forms. Centrifuge out the precipitate from the almost colorless solution for better observation of the solid.

Step 6. *Alternative confirmation of the presence of magnesium.* Repeat Step 5 on one half of the solution obtained in Step 2. If magnesium is present in your sample, you will probably detect it in both Step 5 and Step 6; we have found that the amount of blue precipitate is usually greater in Step 6.

Step 7. *Confirmation of the presence of sodium and potassium.* Perform a flame test on 1 ml of the *original* sample, using a portion that has not been treated in any way. A strong yellow flame, which persists for several seconds, is confirmatory evidence for the presence of sodium. Since the test is *very* sensitive to traces of sodium, compare the intensity and duration of the flame you obtain with that from a sample of distilled water and that from 0.1 *M* NaCl solution.

We also perform a flame test on the original sample to detect potassium. The potassium flame is violet and usually lasts for only a moment, perhaps ½ second. The test is much less sensitive than that for sodium, and is best observed with crystals obtained by evaporating 1 ml of sample to near dryness. Look for the potassium flame through one or two thicknesses of blue cobalt glass, which absorbs any sodium emission. The flame from potassium looks reddish-violet through the glass. Compare the flame you observe with that from saturated KCl solution.

Since potassium is much less likely to be a contaminant in your reagents than is sodium, it is also possible to perform a meaningful test for potassium on the other half of the solution from Step 2. Boil that solution down to a volume of only a few drops, and carry out the test for potassium on those drops. Because this solution may be quite concentrated in K^+, the test for potassium should be easy to see. In addition, other cations that might interfere with the potassium test in the original sample are not present in the solution remaining after the Group IV precipitation.

Step 8. *Confirmation of the presence of NH_4^+ ion.* Pour the 1 ml of *original* sample used in the flame test for Na^+, or 1 ml of a fresh sample, into a 30 ml beaker. Moisten a piece of red litmus paper and put it on the bottom of a small watch glass. Add 1 ml 6 *M* NaOH to the sample in the beaker and swirl to stir. Cover the beaker with the watch glass, and then gently heat the solution to the boiling point; do not boil it, and be careful that no liquid solution comes in contact with the litmus paper. If ammonium ion is present, the litmus paper gradually turns blue as it is exposed to the evolved vapors of NH_3. Remove the watch glass and try to smell the ammonia. If only a small amount of ammonium ion is present, the odor test will probably not detect it, whereas the litmus test will.

COMMENTS ON PROCEDURE FOR ANALYSIS OF GROUP IV CATIONS

Step 1. If you have been working with a general unknown, by the time you get to Group IV analysis you have added a substantial number of reagents to the original sample. In particular, ammonium salts have been added; they dilute the Group IV cations and make their precipitation and detection more difficult. Since all ammonium salts are relatively volatile, they are removed from the Group IV metallic cations by simple heating. While subliming the ammonium salts, do not overheat the solid, but keep the temperature at the point at which the salts sublime relatively slowly and smoothly. The nonvolatile salts remaining are easier to dissolve if they have not been heated above the minimal temperature necessary for sublimation.

If you have sufficient general unknown, it is probably best to prepare your sample of Group IV cations by precipitating in one step Groups I, II, and III from a new sample, using Step 1 in the Group III Procedure. This will minimize dilution effects.

Step 2. In this step the carbonates of barium, calcium, and possibly the hydroxide or carbonate of magnesium precipitate. The warming of the mixture promotes formation of well defined precipitates. In the ammonia–ammonium chloride buffer used, magnesium hydroxide or carbonate should not precipitate, but Mg^{2+} does tend to coprecipitate with the other alkaline earths.

Step 3. Neither calcium nor magnesium chromate precipitates under the slightly acidic conditions that prevail here. However, $BaCrO_4$ is essentially quantitatively removed. Its solubility in HCl and reprecipitation of the Ba^{2+} as barium sulfate is definitive evidence for the presence of barium. Lead would not interfere with this test.

Step 4. Neither magnesium oxalate nor barium oxalate from the residual barium present precipitates at this point. A precipitate on addition of oxalate is really definitive evidence for the presence of calcium. Nevertheless, the flame test gives an added degree of confidence that is very reassuring. The calcium flame test lasts only a moment and typically consists of a few red-orange flashes plus a small amount of flame.

In performing a flame test, we use a piece of platinum or chromel wire sealed into the end of a piece of soft glass tubing. Before carrying out the test, make a small loop on the end of the wire and then clean the wire by heating it in a nonluminous Bunsen flame until the flame is colorless; usually the wire will give off a yellow flame initially, but this will gradually disappear as the trace of sodium which causes the color vaporizes. Flame tests are best carried out on concentrated solutions or small crystals. To carry out the test, dip the wire into the solution and then put the wire in the Bunsen flame. To pick up a small amount of solid, heat the wire and touch it to the crystals, which will usually adhere sufficiently to be put into the flame.

Steps 5 and 6. The blue lake test for magnesium is excellent. There is interference if cobalt or nickel is present, but that is highly unlikely. You will see the blue $Mg(OH)_2$ precipitate gradually forming as you add the NaOH. Considering that this is the last cation to be precipitated in this scheme, the test is remarkably sensitive.

Step 7. It is very difficult to carry out convincing precipitations of the salts of sodium, potassium, and ammonium ions. The flame tests for sodium and potassium are quite adequate, but they must be done with care. Be sure that your wire is as clean as you can make it before attempting any flame tests. Because your sample will probably show positive results of a sodium test even if almost no sodium is present, be sure to compare your sample with a standard NaCl solution and with distilled water. The potassium test is more easily observed in a partially darkened room.

Step 8. If only a small amount of ammonium salt is present, you probably cannot smell the NH_3 that is evolved. Spattering from the alkaline sample of course will turn the litmus paper blue, but that will not give the smooth, gradual change in color that you get from the NH_3 vapors. Obviously, this test must be done on a sample that has not had either ammonia or ammonium salts added to it.

LABORATORY ASSIGNMENTS

Perform one or more of the following, as directed by your instructor:

1. Make up a sample containing about 1 ml of 0.1 *M* solutions of the nitrate or chloride salts of each of the Group IV cations. Go through the standard procedure for analysis of Group IV, comparing your observations with those that are described. Obtain a Group IV unknown from your instructor and analyze it according to the procedure. On a Group IV flow chart, indicate your observations and conclusions regarding the composition of the unknown. Submit the completed chart to your instructor.

2. A week in advance, your instructor will assign you a set of seven cations, chosen from the 22 ions in Groups I through IV. Before coming to the laboratory, develop a procedure that you can use to analyze for the ions in your set. Do not include any unnecessary steps, and make the procedure as simple as possible. Draw a complete flow chart for your scheme, indicating the reagents to be used in each step and the observations that will confirm the presence of each cation. Test your procedure with a sample containing all of the seven ions in your set. When you are sure that your methods work, obtain an unknown for your set of ions from your instructor. Record your observations and conclusions on your flow chart. Your grade will depend on the analytical results you obtain and on the validity of the procedure you develop.

Outline of Procedure for Analysis of Group IV Cations

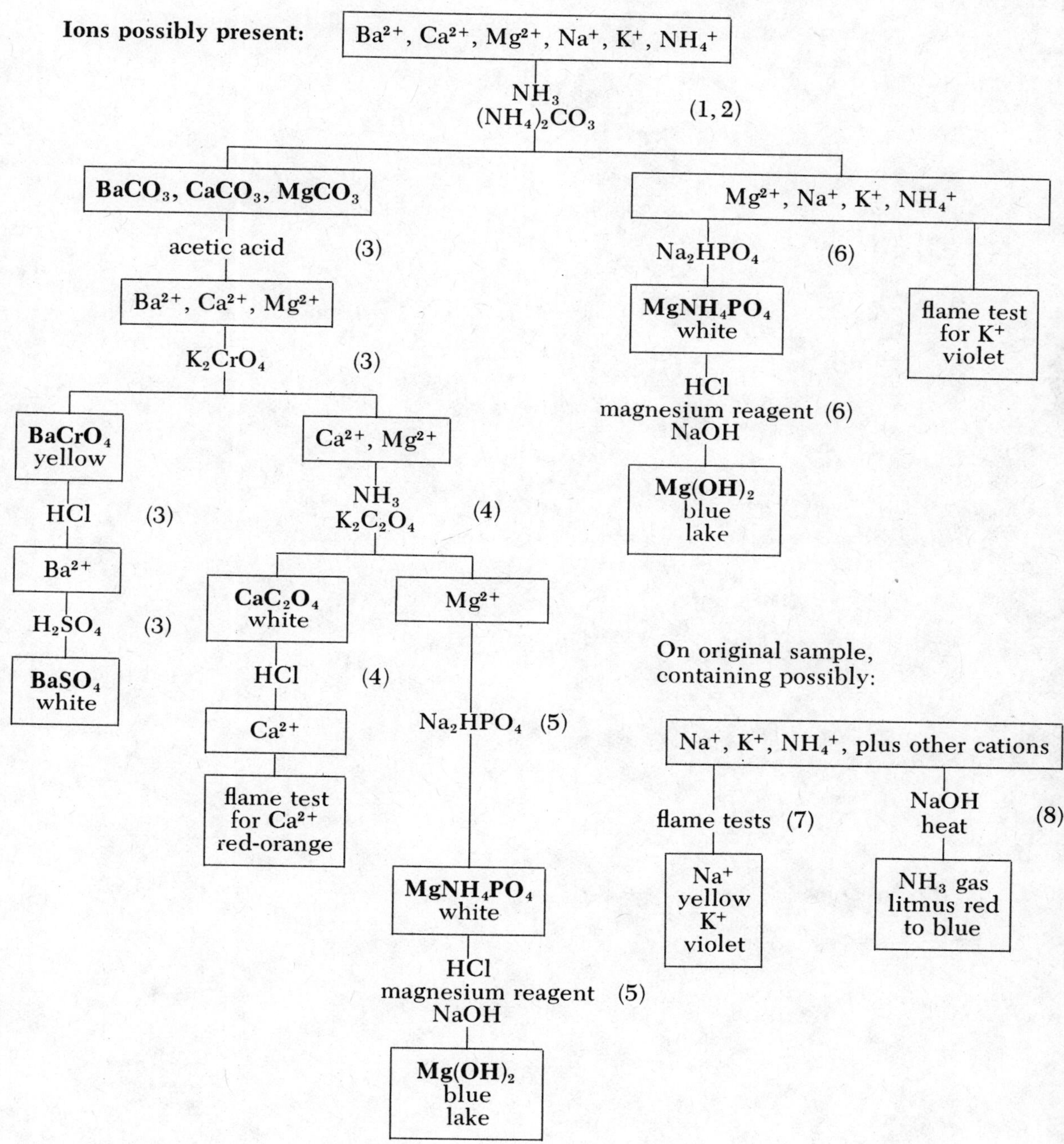

Name ______________________ Section ______________

OBSERVATIONS: Analysis of the Group IV Cations

Flow Chart Showing Behavior of Unknown

 Name ______________________ Section ______________

ADVANCE STUDY ASSIGNMENT: Analysis of the Group IV Cations

1. Write balanced net ionic equations for the following reactions:
   a. The precipitation of Ca^{2+} in Step 2 in the Group IV Procedure.

   b. The final precipitation of Ba^{2+}.

   c. The confirmatory test for Mg^{2+} ion.

2. For each of the following pairs of ions, name a reagent which, when added in excess to a 0.1 *M* solution containing both ions, will precipitate the first and leave the second in solution.

a. Mg^{2+}, Ba^{2+} ______________	d. Mg^{2+}, Pb^{2+} ______________
b. Ba^{2+}, Mg^{2+} ______________	e. Ag^{+}, Ni^{2+} ______________
c. Al^{3+}, Ca^{2+} ______________	f. Cd^{2+}, Zn^{2+} ______________

3. Explain why $Ca(OH)_2$ does not precipitate when 6 *M* NH_3 is added to a solution of Ca^{2+}, although $Bi(OH)_3$ is formed when NH_3 is added to a solution containing Bi^{3+}.

4. An unknown contains four cations, chosen from Groups I through III. The unknown is initially colorless; on addition of 6 *M* NaOH, a white precipitate is obtained, which dissolves completely in excess reagent. If 6 *M* NH_3 is added to the original sample, a white precipitate is again obtained, but it is essentially insoluble in excess NH_3. On the basis of this information, can you name the ions in the unknown?

EXPERIMENT 36

Qualitative Analysis of Anions, I The Silver Group: Cl^-, Br^-, I^-, SCN^- The Calcium-Barium-Iron Group: SO_4^{2-}, CrO_4^{2-}, PO_4^{3-}, $C_2O_4^{2-}$

SEPARATION OF THE ANIONS IN THE SILVER GROUP AND THE CALCIUM-BARIUM-IRON GROUP

In anion analysis the use of groups is more limited than is the case with the cations. In this scheme we separate two groups of anions from the general mixture. Each group separation is usually made from an original sample, rather than sequentially as in cation analysis; this is both convenient and advantageous, since contamination by added reagents is minimized. The Silver Group includes those anions which form insoluble salts with Ag^+ ion in strongly acidic solution. The Calcium-Barium-Iron Group anions form insoluble salts with Ca^{2+}, Ba^{2+}, or Fe^{3+} under slightly acidic conditions. Following separation of the group precipitates, they are dissolved and analyzed on the basis of characteristic properties of the individual anions.

PROPERTIES OF THE ANIONS IN THE SILVER GROUP

Cl^-. Chlorides are among the most common commercially available salts, and, being typically soluble, they are often used as sources of metallic cations in solution. Only the chlorides of the Group I cations plus the oxychlorides of antimony and bismuth are insoluble in water. Chloride complexes are quite common and are frequently formed when otherwise insoluble species, such as Sb_2S_3 or AgCl, are dissolved in 12 *M* HCl, the best source of concentrated chloride ion. Chloride ion is not very reactive chemically and is ordinarily detected by formation of AgCl; that salt is insoluble in acids but soluble in ammonia:

$$AgCl(s) + 2\ NH_3(aq) \rightleftharpoons Ag(NH_3)_2^+(aq) + Cl^-(aq)$$

Chloride ion is not easily oxidized to chlorine, Cl_2, but the reaction may occur with strong oxidizing agents like $KMnO_4$ or MnO_2 in very acidic solution:

$$2\ Cl^-(aq) + MnO_2(s) + 4\ H^+(aq) \rightarrow Cl_2(g) + Mn^{2+}(aq) + 2\ H_2O$$

Br^-. Bromide salts resemble the chlorides in most of their general properties. Those metals that have insoluble chlorides have insoluble bromides; as a class, however, the bromides are less soluble than chlorides. AgBr (light tan) is essentially insoluble in 6 *M* NH_3. Hydrobromic acid, which is a solution of HBr gas in water, is, like HCl, a strong acid. Bromides are more easily oxidized than chlorides, and yield bromine on addition of such oxidizing agents as Cl_2, 15 *M* HNO_3, and $KMnO_4$ in the presence of strong acids. Ordinarily, bromine, Br_2, is detected by its orange color in CCl_3CH_3, TCE, in which it is much more soluble than in water.

I^-. Iodides are similar in many ways to the other halide salts, with the exception that they are much more easily oxidized, especially in solution. Iodides are oxidized to I_2 by such reagents as $K_2Cr_2O_7$, KNO_2, H_2O_2, and Cu^{2+} in mildly acidic solutions; stronger oxidizing agents tend to further oxidize I_2 to IO_3^-, which is colorless. The reaction with Cu^{2+} ion is unique for the halides:

$$2\ Cu^{2+}(aq) + 4\ I^-(aq) \rightarrow I_2(aq) + 2\ CuI(s)$$

Silver iodide is a yellow solid, and is so insoluble as to be essentially unaffected by 15 M NH_3. Like the other silver halides, AgI can be reduced readily with zinc in acid solution. Iodide ion often is detected by oxidation to I_2, which has a characteristic purple color in CCl_3CH_3.

SCN^-. The thiocyanates resemble the halides in many of their properties, including the insolubility of the silver salt. Like AgCl, AgSCN is soluble in 6 M NH_3. One of the characteristic properties of the SCN^- ion is the deep red color of the $FeSCN^{2+}$ complex ion formed when Fe^{3+} ion is added to solutions of thiocyanates. The thiocyanate ion is easily oxidized, yielding several possible products including sulfate ion, by such species as hot 6 M HNO_3, and $K_2Cr_2O_7$, KNO_2, or H_2O_2 in acid solution. Thiocyanate can also be reduced to H_2S and other species by zinc in dilute H_2SO_4; it is unaffected by zinc in acetic acid.

PROPERTIES OF THE ANIONS IN THE CALCIUM-BARIUM-IRON GROUP

SO_4^{2-}. Sulfate salts are typically soluble in water and are frequently available in chemical stockrooms. Among the common sulfates, only $PbSO_4$ and $BaSO_4$ are insoluble, and, as might be expected, these two salts are often used in sulfate analysis. $PbSO_4$ can be dissolved in strong NaOH solution or in hot concentrated ammonium acetate, in both cases owing to formation of very stable lead complex ions. Barium sulfate is one of the few common salts which is insoluble in all common solvents. Sulfuric acid, H_2SO_4, from which sulfates can be considered to be derived, is made by dissolving SO_3 in water. Once dissolved, the oxide is not volatile; to drive SO_3 from sulfuric acid one must first boil off most of the water; then, at temperatures above 300°C, SO_3 begins to evolve as a choking gas. Sulfuric acid is one of the strong acids; in the concentrated solution, 18 M H_2SO_4, the acid is also a powerful dehydrating agent and a moderately strong oxidizing agent.

PO_4^{3-}. Phosphate salts are derived from phosphoric acid, H_3PO_4. This weak acid ionizes in three steps, with the successive hydrogen ions being increasingly difficult to remove. The parent acid can be made by dissolving solid P_4O_{10} in water. Most phosphates are insoluble in water but will dissolve in dilute acids. $FePO_4$ is one of the few phosphates that can be precipitated in 1 M $HC_2H_3O_2$ solution. The various phosphate ions are not susceptible to either reduction or oxidation. In hot nitric acid solution, phosphates form a characteristic yellow precipitate of ammonium phosphomolybdate on addition of ammonium molybdate:

$$H_2PO_4^-(aq) + 12\ MoO_4^{2-}(aq) + 3\ NH_4^+(aq) + 22\ H^+(aq) \rightarrow (NH_4)_3PO_4 \cdot 12\ MoO_3(s) + 12\ H_2O$$

CrO_4^{2-}. Chromate salts are all colored, and are usually yellow or red. Most of these salts are insoluble in water but are soluble in solutions of strong acids. $BaCrO_4$ is precipitated in the Group IV analysis scheme from acetic acid solution, but will dissolve in 6 M HCl. Lead chromate, $PbCrO_4$, is bright yellow and so insoluble that it will not dissolve in dilute strong acids; it will, however, go into solution in 6 *M* NaOH. In acids, the CrO_4^{2-} ion dimerizes to form orange $Cr_2O_7^{2-}$ ion. Dichromate ion is a good oxidizing agent in strong acid solution, oxidizing such species as SCN^-, I^-, and SO_3^{2-} quite readily, being itself reduced to Cr^{3+}. An unstable blue peroxide, CrO_5, is formed when H_2O_2 is added to strongly acidic dichromate solutions:

$$Cr_2O_7^{2-}(aq) + 4\ H_2O_2(aq) + 2\ H^+(aq) \rightarrow 2\ CrO_5(aq) + 5\ H_2O$$

$C_2O_4^{2-}$. Most of the oxalates are insoluble in water, the exceptions being those of the alkali metals, magnesium, and chromium. The most insoluble oxalate is $CaC_2O_4 \cdot H_2O$, which can be precipitated from acetic acid solution. All of the oxalates will dissolve in 6 *M* HCl with formation of the weak acid, $H_2C_2O_4$. The oxalate ion is a good complexing agent, forming stable complexes with Sn^{4+}, Fe^{3+}, and Cu^{2+}. The oxalate ion can be slowly oxidized and converted to CO_2 by hot strong oxidizing agents, such as $KMnO_4$ in hot 6 *M* H_2SO_4:

$$5\ H_2C_2O_4(aq) + 2\ MnO_4^-(aq) + 6\ H^+(aq) \rightarrow 10\ CO_2(g) + 2\ Mn^{2+}(aq) + 8\ H_2O$$

GENERAL SCHEME OF ANALYSIS

Following separation of the silver salts of the halides and SCN^- ion, they are treated with zinc in weakly acid solution, freeing the anions and reducing the silver ion to the metal. Thiocyanate is identified by formation of the red $FeSCN^{2+}$ complex ion and by oxidation to SO_4^{2-} ion, which is precipitated as $BaSO_4$. Iodide and bromide are oxidized to the elements sequentially by increasingly stronger oxidizing agents, and their presence is established by their characteristic colors in TCE solution. Chloride is precipitated as AgCl after all of the other anions in the group have been oxidized.

In the analysis of the Calcium-Barium-Iron Group, calcium oxalate is precipitated first. Oxalate is identified by reaction with permanganate. Barium ion is then added to precipitate sulfate and chromate ions. The presence of sulfate is established by the insolubility of $BaSO_4$, and that of chromate by its reaction with peroxide. Finally, phosphate is precipitated by adding Fe^{3+}, and identified, after being redissolved, by formation of its characteristic precipitate with molybdate.

PROCEDURE FOR ANALYSIS OF THE ANIONS IN THE SILVER GROUP

WEAR YOUR SAFETY GLASSES WHILE PERFORMING THIS EXPERIMENT.

Unless directed otherwise, you may assume that 10 ml of sample contains about 1 ml of 0.1 *M* solutions of the sodium salts of the anions in the Silver Group, plus possibly other anions of nonvolatile acids.

Step 1. To 5 ml of your sample add 6 *M* NH_3 or 6 *M* HNO_3 until the solution is just basic to litmus. Then add 0.5 ml 6 *M* HNO_3. Add 1 ml 0.5 *M* $AgNO_3$ and stir. Centrifuge out the solid, which may contain AgCl, AgBr, AgI, and AgSCN, and check for completeness of precipitation by adding another drop or two of $AgNO_3$. When all the precipitate has been brought down, centrifuge, and decant the liquid, which may be discarded. Wash the solid twice with 3 ml water, discarding the wash.

Step 2. To the precipitate add 2 ml 6 *M* $HC_2H_3O_2$ and about 0.3 g granular zinc (the volume of the zinc is roughly equal to that of the precipitate). Stir and put the test tube in the boiling water bath for 10 minutes, stirring occasionally as the reduction of the silver salts proceeds. Cool the test tube under the cold water tap until the evolution of hydrogen ceases; add 1 ml water, and then centrifuge the mixture, decanting the solution, which may contain Cl^-, Br^-, I^-, and SCN^- ions, into a test tube. Discard the solid residue.

Step 3. *Confirmation of the presence of thiocyanate.* Pour one-third of the liquid from Step 2 into a test tube and add, without stirring, 2 drops of 0.1 *M* $Fe(NO_3)_3$. If thiocyanate is present, the area where the drops hit the solution will turn a deep rust color owing to formation of $FeSCN^{2+}$. Since both iodides and acetates will darken slightly on addition of Fe^{3+} ion, confirm the presence of SCN^- by adding 0.5 ml 1 *M* $BaCl_2$, 0.5 ml 6 *M* HCl, and 1 ml 3% H_2O_2 to oxidize thiocyanate to SO_4^{2-}. Stir and put the test tube in the water bath for a minute. If thiocyanate is in the sample, a white cloudiness that is due to formation of $BaSO_4$ will slowly appear in the yellow liquid. Centrifuge out the solid to establish its color and amount.

Step 4. *Confirmation of the presence of iodide.* To the rest of the solution from Step 2 add 0.5 ml 1,1,1-trichloroethane, CCl_3CH_3 (TCE), and 1 ml 1 *M* KNO_2. Stopper the test tube and shake well. If iodide is present it will be oxidized to I_2 and extracted into the lower TCE layer, where it will have a characteristic purple color.

Step 5. Shake the test tube until the upper water layer is essentially colorless. Let the layers settle, and with a medicine dropper transfer the upper (water) layer to another test tube. To this, add 0.5 ml 6 *M* HNO_3 and, slowly to avoid excessive foaming, add solid sulfamic acid to remove the excess nitrite. Continue adding solid, with stirring, until there is no more evolution of gas.

Step 6. *Confirmation of the presence of bromide.* To the solution from Step 5 add 0.5 ml TCE and 0.02 *M* $KMnO_4$, a few drops at a time, until the pink color remains for about 15 seconds of stirring. Stopper the test tube and shake. If bromide ion is present, it will be converted to Br_2 by the permanganate and extracted into the TCE layer, where it will have an orange color.

Step 7. Add 5 drops 0.02 *M* $KMnO_4$, stopper the tube, and shake for 15 seconds to complete oxidation of the bromide ion and extract as much Br_2 as possible into the TCE. Let the layers settle, and, using a medicine dropper, transfer the water layer to a 30 ml beaker. Boil the liquid down to a volume of 2 ml, adding 0.02 *M* $KMnO_4$ dropwise as the boiling proceeds until the liquid takes on a tan cloudiness. Add a few drops of 3% H_2O_2 to dissolve the MnO_2 which has formed, and transfer the solution to a test tube.

Step 8. *Confirmation of the presence of chloride.* To the solution from Step 7 add 0.5 ml 0.1 *M* $AgNO_3$. If chloride ion is present, you will observe a white cloudiness which turns to a curdy precipitate of AgCl. To confirm the identification, centrifuge out the solid and decant and discard the liquid. Wash the solid with 3 ml water, centrifuging and discarding the wash. Add 0.5 ml 6 *M* NH_3 to the solid and stir; if it is AgCl, the solid will dissolve in a few moments. Then add 1 ml 6 *M* HNO_3, which will cause the AgCl to reprecipitate and prove the presence of chloride.

PROCEDURE FOR THE ANALYSIS OF THE ANIONS IN THE CALCIUM-BARIUM-IRON GROUP

WEAR YOUR SAFETY GLASSES WHILE PERFORMING THIS EXPERIMENT.

It may be assumed that 5 ml of sample contains about 1 ml of 0.1 *M* solutions of the sodium salts of the anions in the Calcium-Barium-Iron Group plus possibly anions of the nonvolatile acids.

Step 1. To 5 ml of your sample add 6 *M* NaOH or 6 *M* HCl until the solution is just basic to litmus. Then add 1 ml 6 *M* acetic acid and mix thoroughly.

Step 2. *Confirmation of the presence of oxalate.* To the solution from Step 1 add 1 ml 1 *M* $CaCl_2$. Stir for 15 seconds and then put the test tube in the hot water bath for a few minutes. If a white precipitate forms (usually slowly), it is likely to be $CaC_2O_4 \cdot H_2O$ and therefore indicative of the presence of oxalate. Centrifuge out the solid and decant the liquid into a test tube. Wash the solid twice with 2 ml water, stirring well and warming each time for a minute in the water bath before centrifuging. Discard the wash liquids. To the solid add 2 ml 3 *M* H_2SO_4. Put the test tube in the water bath, stirring to help dissolve the solid. To the hot liquid add 0.02 *M* $KMnO_4$, a drop at a time, stirring after each drop. If oxalate is present, it will quickly bleach several drops of the purple solution.

Step 3. *Confirmation of the presence of sulfate.* To half of the liquid from Step 2 add 1 ml 1 *M* $BaCl_2$. Stir well and centrifuge out any solid which forms, discarding the liquid. Wash the solid, which may be yellow or white and may contain $BaCrO_4$ and $BaSO_4$, with 3 ml water; centrifuge and discard the wash. To the solid add 1 ml 6 *M* HNO_3 and 1 ml water. Stir and put the test tube in the water bath for about a minute. Any white solid remaining undissolved must be $BaSO_4$ and establishes the presence of sulfate in the sample. Centrifuge out the solid to ascertain its color and amount, and pour the liquid into a test tube.

Step 4. *Confirmation of the presence of chromate.* If the liquid from Step 3 is orange or yellow, chromate is very likely to be present. Cool the test tube under the cold water tap, and then add 1 ml 3% H_2O_2 to the liquid. A blue coloration, which may fade rapidly, is proof of the presence of chromate.

Step 5. *Confirmation of the presence of phosphate.* To the other half of the liquid from Step 2 add 1 ml 0.1 *M* $Fe(NO_3)_3$. Formation of a light tan precipitate is highly indicative of the presence of phosphate. Put the test tube in the water bath for a minute to promote coagulation of the solid and then centrifuge, discarding the liquid. Wash the solid with 3 ml water, and heat in the water bath for a minute. Centrifuge and discard the wash. To the solid add 1 ml 6 *M* HNO_3; the solid should readily dissolve with stirring. To the solution add 1 ml 0.5 *M* ammonium molybdate and place the test tube in the water bath. If the sample contains phosphate, a fine yellow precipitate of ammonium phosphomolybdate, which may form quite slowly, will be obtained.

COMMENTS ON THE PROCEDURE FOR ANALYSIS OF THE ANIONS IN THE SILVER GROUP

Step 1. The only silver salts which are insoluble in strongly acidic solutions are the silver halides and AgSCN. This precipitation allows a clean and quantitative separation of Cl^-, Br^-, I^-, and SCN^- ions from the other noninterfering anions. (If sulfide ion were present, it would precipitate here as Ag_2S; in the general procedure S^{2-} ion is removed with the other anions of volatile acids before this group separation is made.)

Step 2. Here zinc metal, or hydrogen gas, reduces the silver salts, producing black metallic silver and liberating the anions to the solution, which also ends up containing appreciable amounts of zinc acetate:

$$Zn(s) + 2\ HC_2H_3O_2(aq) \rightarrow Zn^{2+}(aq) + 2\ C_2H_3O_2^-(aq) + H_2(g)$$

$$2\ AgCl(s) + H_2(g) + 2\ C_2H_3O_2^-(aq) \rightarrow 2\ Ag(s) + 2\ Cl^-(aq) + 2\ HC_2H_3O_2(aq)$$

Step 3. Thiocyanate ion forms a very characteristic deep red complex ion with Fe^{3+}. Unfortunately, both I^- and acetate ions also interact with Fe^{3+} to form much less intensely colored orange species, which conceivably can confuse the thiocyanate test. The confirmation of the presence of SCN^- by its oxidation to sulfate and precipitation as $BaSO_4$ is definitive. Traces of sulfate may cause precipitation of $BaSO_4$ before addition of the peroxide; if this occurs, the precipitate should be centrifuged out and discarded before the solution is treated with peroxide and heated.

Step 4. Nitrite ion oxidizes I^- to I_2 very readily in weak acid solution. The purple color of I_2 in CCl_4 is an excellent test for presence of iodide ion:

$$2\ NO_2^-(aq) + 2\ I^-(aq) + 4\ H^+(aq) \rightarrow I_2(aq) + 2\ NO(g) + 2\ H_2O$$

Step 5. Sulfamic acid, NH_2SO_3H, reacts readily with nitrites to produce N_2 gas; we use the reaction here to destroy excess NO_2^-, which would interfere in a later step:

$$NH_2SO_3H(aq) + HNO_2(aq) \rightarrow N_2(g) + HSO_4^-(aq) + H^+(aq) + H_2O$$

Step 6. Permanganate ion under strongly acidic conditions will oxidize bromide ion to bromine, which has an orange color:

$$10\ Br^-(aq) + 2\ MnO_4^-(aq) + 16\ H^+(aq) \rightarrow 5\ Br_2(aq) + 2\ Mn^{2+}(aq) + 8\ H_2O$$

Chloride ion is not appreciably oxidized under the conditions prevailing here.

Step 7. Bromide ion must be completely removed from the solution if the test for chloride ion is to be reliable. In this step residual bromide ion is oxidized to bromine and driven out of the boiling solution.

Step 8. This is the old test for Ag^+, now applied to Cl^-, where it is equally effective.

COMMENTS ON THE PROCEDURE FOR ANALYSIS OF THE ANIONS IN THE CALCIUM-BARIUM-IRON GROUP

Step 2. Under the slightly acidic conditions in the solution, oxalate precipitates essentially quantitatively. Some sulfate ion will tend to come down if its concentration is high.

In the reaction which occurs, MnO_4^- ion oxidizes $C_2O_4^{2-}$ to CO_2 gas and is itself converted to colorless Mn^{2+}. Permanganate ion will decompose slowly in any hot solution, so you should compare the behavior of the test solution with that of 2 ml of hot 6 M H_2SO_4.

Step 3. $BaCrO_4$ and $BaSO_4$ are precipitated here if chromate and sulfate ions are present, but no other barium salts should come down.

There is only one barium salt that is insoluble under the conditions in the HNO_3 solution, and that salt is $BaSO_4$. Traces of sulfate will produce cloudiness, so you may want to compare the amount of precipitate with that obtained from one drop of 0.1 *M* Na_2SO_4, which contains about 1 mg SO_4^{2-}.

Step 4. The yellow color of CrO_4^{2-} plus the blue flash of CrO_5 make it hard to miss chromate ion in any solution in which it is present.

Step 5. The precipitate with molybdate will be yellow if phosphate is present. Interfering anions sometimes produce white precipitates.

LABORATORY ASSIGNMENTS

Perform one or more of the following, as directed by your instructor:

1. Make up a solution containing about 1 ml of 0.1 *M* solutions of the sodium salts of the anions in the Silver Group. Go through the standard procedure for analysis of the Group, comparing your results with those that are described. Then prepare a solution of the anions in the Calcium-Barium-Iron Group and analyze it by the standard procedure. Obtain an unknown which may contain anions from both of these Groups and determine its composition. Draw a flow chart for both Groups, showing your observations on the unknown. Note that, although the ions within a Group do not react chemically, ions in different Groups may react; in particular here, iodides and thiocyanates are unstable in the presence of chromates in acidic solutions. Consult Appendix III for information regarding behavior of these ions. In dealing with unknowns which exhibit such reactions, you may wish to carry out some experiments with knowns in order to observe directly the changes which occur.

2. Your instructor will assign you a set of four anions, chosen from the Silver and the Calcium-Barium-Iron Groups. Set up a procedure for analysis of a sample which may contain only those ions. Draw a complete flow chart for your scheme, indicating all reagents to be used and the observations that will confirm the presence of each anion. Test your procedure with a sample containing all four ions, and when you are sure your approach will work, obtain an unknown for that set of ions from your instructor. Record your observations and conclusions about the unknown on your flow chart and submit it to your instructor.

Outline of Procedure for Analysis of the Anions in the Silver Group

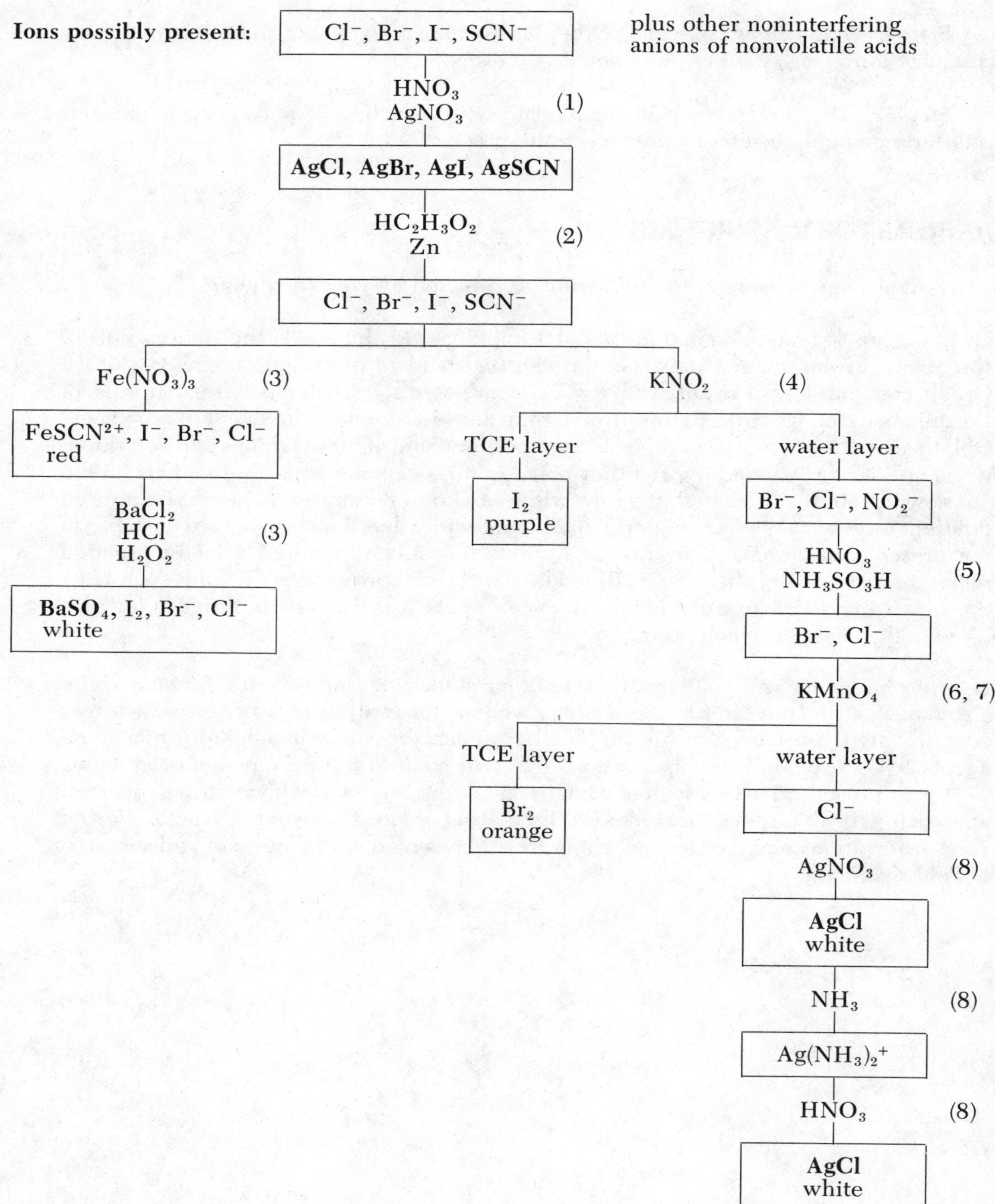

Outline of Procedure for Analysis of Anions in the Calcium-Barium-Iron Group

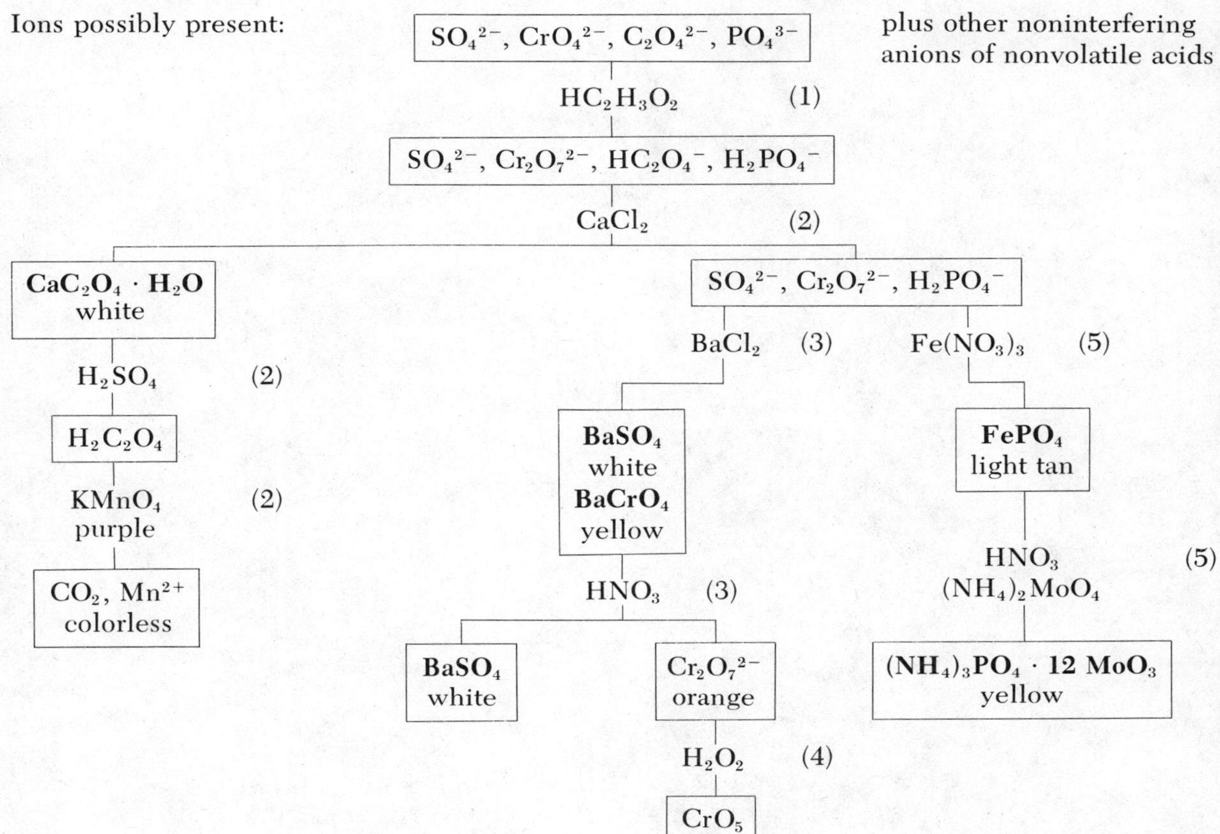

Name ______________________________ Section ________________

OBSERVATIONS: **Analysis of Anions in the Silver and Calcium-Barium-Iron Groups**

Flow Chart Showing Behavior of Unknown

EXP. 36 Name ______________________ Section ______________

ADVANCE STUDY ASSIGNMENT: Analysis of the Anions in the Silver Group and in the Calcium-Barium-Iron Group

1. Write balanced net ionic equations for the following reactions:
   a. The confirmatory test for bromide ion.

   b. The confirmatory test for oxalate ion.

   c. The confirmatory test for phosphate ion.

2. You are given solutions of the sodium salt of one of the anions in each of the following pairs. For each pair, indicate how you would proceed to determine which anion is present.
   a. I^-, Cl^-

   b. SCN^-, Br^-

   c. CrO_4^{2-}, SO_4^{2-}

   d. I^-, PO_4^{3-}

3. A solution may contain only one anion from the Silver Group and no other anions. On the back of this sheet, develop a simple scheme to identify the anion. Draw a flow chart showing your procedure and the observations that establish which anion is present.

4. A yellow solution may contain any anions in the Calcium-Barium-Iron and the Silver Groups. There is no oxidation-reduction reaction on acidification with HNO_3. Addition of $AgNO_3$ to the acidified solution yields a yellowish precipitate that is essentially insoluble in 6 *M* NH_3. There is no reaction observed when $BaCl_2$ is added to the same acidified solution. Addition of $CaCl_2$ to the original sample produces a white precipitate and a yellow solution. The precipitate is completely soluble in acetic acid. On the basis of this information, which anions are present, absent, and still in doubt?

Present ______________

Absent ______________

In doubt ______________

Qualitative Analysis of Anions, II The Soluble Group: NO_3^-, NO_2^-, ClO_3^-, $C_2H_3O_2^-$ The Volatile Acid Group: CO_3^{2-}, SO_3^{2-}, S^{2-}

Although group separations such as were used in the previous experiment are possible for some of the common anions, for several others such separations are not feasible. For those ions, spot tests are usually carried out on an original sample, in the presence of other anions. In some cases such spot tests are conclusive, but in others there are interferences with the tests if certain other ions are also in the solution. Usually it is possible to remove such interferences prior to carrying out the spot tests, but it certainly is true that in anion analysis it is much more often necessary to devise special procedures for dealing with particular samples than it is in cation analysis.

PROPERTIES OF THE ANIONS IN THE SOLUBLE GROUP

NO_3^-. Since essentially all nitrate salts are soluble in water, they are very commonly used to furnish required cations in laboratory stock solutions. In general, nitrates are quite resistant to reaction in neutral solution, but at high concentrations in highly acidic systems they become good oxidizing agents. Hot 6 *M* HNO_3 is a strong oxidizing agent, capable of oxidizing such species as I^-, SO_3^{2-}, and CuS. Nitrates can be reduced in 6 *M* NaOH solution to NH_3 by aluminum or zinc metal. The classic test for nitrates is the "brown ring" test, resulting from the reaction of a concentrated $FeSO_4$ solution with nitrates in strong sulfuric acid; in this test the nitrate ion is reduced to NO and combines with excess Fe(II) to form an unstable brown complex ion, $Fe(NO)^{2+}$:

$$3\ Fe^{2+}(aq) + NO_3^-(aq) + 4\ H^+(aq) \rightarrow 3\ Fe^{3+}(aq) + NO(aq) + 2\ H_2O$$
$$Fe^{2+}(aq) + NO(aq) \rightarrow Fe(NO)^{2+}(aq)$$

Unfortunately, nitrites, chromates, iodides, and bromides interfere with this test.

NO_2^-. Nearly all nitrite salts are soluble in water. The alkali nitrites, the common laboratory source of the NO_2^- ion, are made by strongly heating the corresponding nitrates. Nitrites can serve as both reducing and oxidizing agents, depending on conditions, and also are fairly good complexing agents. They are unstable in solution, decomposing slowly to nitrates. Since they interfere with many tests for other ions, once they have been detected it is best that they be removed from solution. This can be accomplished by treatment with excess sulfamic acid, NH_2SO_3H, in acidic solution:

$$NO_2^-(aq) + NH_2SO_3H(aq) \rightarrow N_2(g) + SO_4^{2-}(aq) + H^+(aq) + H_2O$$

The reaction is specific to nitrites and produces little, if any, nitrate. Among the oxidizing species we are studying, only nitrite will oxidize I^- ion in cold acetic acid solution. In dilute solutions of strong acids, nitrite ion will oxidize Fe^{2+} to Fe^{3+}; excess Fe^{2+} reacts with the NO produced, forming a brown solution of $Fe(NO)^{2+}$.

ClO_3^-. Chlorate salts are generally soluble in water, but are not commonly encountered in the laboratory, probably because they are more expensive than the nitrates. Chlorates in acidic solution are moderately good oxidizing agents, and will react, sometimes rather slowly unless heated, with such species as NO_2^-, SO_3^{2-}, and I^-. Hot 6 *M* HCl is oxidized by chlorates, producing a yellow solution:

$$2\ ClO_3^-(aq) + 2\ Cl^-(aq) + 4\ H^+(aq) \rightarrow 2\ ClO_2(g) + Cl_2(g) + 2\ H_2O$$

$C_2H_3O_2^-$. Acetates are characteristically soluble in water and are the most common salts of the organic acids. The parent acid, $HC_2H_3O_2$, is moderately volatile and has the odor of vinegar; the odor can be detected above moderately concentrated warm acetate solutions on treatment with 6 *M* H_2SO_4. In complex mixtures acetates are best detected by their very characteristic reaction with lanthanum nitrate in the presence of I_3^- ion; iodine adsorbed on the basic lanthanum acetate precipitate gives it a deep blue color. Sulfates and phosphates interfere with this test.

PROPERTIES OF THE ANIONS OF THE VOLATILE ACIDS

CO_3^{2-}. The acid associated with the carbonate ion is carbonic acid, made by dissolving CO_2 gas in water. This acid is quite weak and must dissociate twice to yield the carbonate ion. Carbonic acid cannot be prepared in pure form, and there is some question whether H_2CO_3 molecules exist in solution. Ordinarily, if we were told that a solution was 0.02 *M* H_2CO_3, we would say that the solution contains 0.02 moles CO_2 per liter. When a carbonate solution is treated with acid, carbonic acid tends to form, and if the solubility of CO_2 is exceeded, CO_2 gas will effervesce from the system:

$$CO_3^{2-}(aq) + 2\ H^+(aq) \rightleftarrows (H_2CO_3)(aq) \rightleftarrows CO_2(g) + H_2O$$

Most carbonates are insoluble in water, but dissolve in acids by a reaction similar to the one above, and give off CO_2 in the process. It is possible to prepare hydrogen carbonates, with $NaHCO_3$ being the one most commonly encountered. That salt is also called sodium bicarbonate, or baking soda.

The usual test for carbonates is effervescence on treatment with acid; this will occur with solids and moderately concentrated solutions. The CO_2 driven off is passed into a solution of $Ba(OH)_2$, and causes precipitation of white $BaCO_3$. Sulfites and nitrites may interfere, but can usually be removed before the test is made.

SO_3^{2-}. Sulfites can be considered to be derived from sulfurous acid, made by dissolving SO_2 in water. Like carbonic acid, sulfurous acid cannot be isolated in pure form. The acid is weak, but considerably stronger than carbonic acid. Acidified sulfites, whether solid or in solution, evolve SO_2 gas, which can be fairly easily detected by its sharp odor of burning sulfur. Since the gas is not very soluble in water, it is readily driven from a boiling solution. Many sulfites are insoluble in water but soluble in acids; hydrogen sulfites can be prepared and are more soluble than the corresponding sulfites.

The detection of sulfites can be accomplished by the odor test, but in dilute solution it is usually done by oxidation of the sulfite to sulfate (by such reagents as H_2O_2, CrO_4^{2-}, or NO_2^- in acidic solution) and subsequent precipitation as $BaSO_4$. Since sulfites are oxidized by moist air, sulfite solutions will also usually give a positive test for sulfate ion.

S^{2-}. Sulfide ion in solution is most easily detected by the odor of its parent acid, H_2S, which smells like rotten eggs. The acid is very weak, so it exists in appreciable concentrations even in highly alkaline solutions:

$$S^{2-}(aq) + 2\ H_2O \rightleftharpoons H_2S(g) + 2\ OH^-(aq)$$

Sulfides are typically insoluble; some, like ZnS, will dissolve in 6 *M* HCl, but others, such as CuS, require oxidation in 6 *M* HNO_3. H_2S gas could be detected by smell over ZnS when treated with acid, but with CuS the sulfur would end up as either the element or sulfate ion, and there would be very little if any odor of H_2S.

Hydrogen sulfide can be spotted by its unforgettable odor. An alternate test is to pass the gas over a piece of filter paper that has been moistened with lead nitrate solution; formation of shiny black or brown PbS is confirmatory evidence for the presence of sulfide.

PROCEDURE FOR THE ANALYSIS OF ANIONS IN THE SOLUBLE AND VOLATILE ACID GROUPS

WEAR YOUR SAFETY GLASSES WHILE PERFORMING THIS EXPERIMENT.

Unless told otherwise, you may assume that 5 ml of sample contains 1 ml of 0.1 *M* solutions of the sodium salts of the anions in the Soluble and Volatile Acid Groups plus possibly other nonreacting anions. The tests for the anions in these Groups are all "spot" tests, made on the original sample. Where interferences may occur, the interfering anions are removed before the test is made. The tests are carried out first for those anions for which there are the smallest number of interferences.

Step 1. *Test for the presence of nitrite.* To 1 ml of sample solution add 0.5 ml 6 *M* H_2SO_4. In a separate test tube, dissolve 0.1 g $FeSO_4 \cdot 7H_2O$ in 1 ml water. Mix the two solutions. If nitrite is present, you will obtain a dark, greenish brown solution of $Fe(NO)^{2+}$.

Step 2. *Test for the presence of chlorate.* To 1 ml of sample solution add 0.5 ml 6 *M* HNO_3 and 2 drops 0.1 *M* $AgNO_3$. If a precipitate forms, add 2 ml 0.1 *M* $AgNO_3$, stir, and centrifuge; add a drop of $AgNO_3$ to the liquid to ascertain that all Silver Group anions have precipitated, and that Ag^+ is in excess. To the decanted liquid add 1 ml 1 *M* KNO_2. If chlorate is present, it is reduced by nitrite, and the chloride ion produced reacts with excess Ag^+ to form white AgCl.

Step 3. *Test for the presence of sulfide.* Smell the sample. If it contains sulfide you should be able to detect the very characteristic and unpleasant odor of H_2S. To further confirm the presence of this ion, pour 1 ml of sample into a 30 ml beaker. On a strip of filter paper, 1/4" × 2", put a drop or two of 0.2 *M* $Pb(NO_3)_2$; place the filter paper on the bottom of a small watch glass. Add 1 ml 6 *M* H_2SO_4 to the sample and cover the beaker with the watch glass. Heat the liquid gently. If sulfide is present, the paper will turn shiny black or brown as PbS is formed by reaction of Pb^{2+} with the H_2S evolved.

Step 4. *Test for the presence of sulfite.* To 1 ml of sample add 1 ml 6 *M* HCl and stir. You may be able to detect the sharp odor of SO_2 above the solution. Add 1 ml 1 *M* $BaCl_2$ to the acidified solution and, after stirring, centrifuge out any precipitate of $BaSO_4$. Decant the clear liquid into a test tube and add 1 ml 3% H_2O_2. If sulfite is present, its oxidation to sulfate causes a new precipitate of $BaSO_4$ to form quickly. See comments for interferences.

Step 5. *Test for the presence of acetate.* To 1 ml of sample add 6 *M* NH_3 or 6 *M*

HNO_3 until the liquid is just basic to litmus. Add 1 drop 1 *M* $BaCl_2$. If a precipitate forms, add 1 ml more of the $BaCl_2$ to bring down the anions in the Calcium-Barium-Iron Group. Stir, centrifuge, and decant the clear liquid into a test tube. Add a drop of $BaCl_2$ to make sure that the precipitation was complete. To 1 ml of the liquid add 0.1 *M* KI_3, drop by drop, until the solution takes on a fairly strong rust color. Add 0.5 ml 0.1 *M* $La(NO_3)_3$ and 3 drops 6 *M* NH_3. Stir and put the test tube in the water bath. In the presence of acetate the orange gelatinous liquid will gradually darken over a period of several minutes, finally acquiring a dark blue or black color.

Step 6. *Test for the presence of carbonate.* To 1 ml of sample add 0.5 ml 6 *M* HCl and stir. Check for the presence of small bubbles effervescing from solution, which is indicative of the presence of carbonate, particularly if the solution is moderately concentrated. Put a stopper *loosely* on the tube and put it in the water bath for a minute. While the tube is warming, draw a little clear, saturated $Ba(OH)_2$ solution into a medicine dropper. Take the test tube out of the water bath, remove the stopper, and put the medicine dropper into the tube so that the tip of the dropper is about 1/4" above the liquid surface. Squeeze a drop of $Ba(OH)_2$ so that it hangs from the dropper. If carbonate is present, the CO_2 gas evolved from the solution will react with the hydroxide, forming a characteristic "skin" of $BaCO_3$ over the surface of the drop. See comments for interferences.

Step 7. *Test for the presence of nitrate.* To 1 ml of sample, *carefully* add 2 ml 18 *M* H_2SO_4; because this is concentrated acid, add it slowly, mixing all the while. Cool the hot test tube under the water tap. In another test tube dissolve about 0.1 g $FeSO_4 \cdot 7H_2O$ in 1 ml water. Holding the tube containing the H_2SO_4 at an angle of about 45 degrees, let 5 drops of the $FeSO_4$ solution from a medicine dropper run down the side of the tube and form a layer over the acid. Let the tube stand for a few minutes, and look for a brown ring which will form at the junction of the two layers if nitrate is present. See comments for interferences.

COMMENTS ON THE PROCEDURE FOR ANALYSIS OF THE ANIONS IN THE SOLUBLE AND VOLATILE ACID GROUPS

Step 1. Nitrite will react with I^-, SCN^-, SO_3^{2-}, S^{2-}, CrO_4^{2-}, and ClO_3^- in weakly acidic solutions, so that if any of these ions are present, it is likely that nitrite is not. In this test, some of these ions produce colored solutions, but the $Fe(NO)^{2+}$ complex is very dark and quite distinctive, so that there should be no problem with interferences. Given a positive nitrite test, the ions with which it reacts are probably not present. Since they interfere with several tests, nitrites should generally be removed by adding excess sulfamic acid to the acidified sample; nitrite leaves as nitrogen gas, and sulfate ion is introduced into the system.

Step 2. Chlorate ion reacts slowly with oxidizable species under acidic conditions. Species which react with nitrite may interfere by removing it, so nitrite should be in excess; products of such reactions will not precipitate with Ag^+. Silver ion must of course also be in excess if AgCl is to form.

Step 3. Sulfide ion is really hard to miss, once you know what H_2S smells like.

Step 4. The test depends on the oxidation of SO_3^{2-} ion to SO_4^{2-} and its precipitation as $BaSO_4$. Both sulfide and thiocyanate can interfere with this test, since their oxidation products may also be sulfates. The oxidation of sulfide is slow, whereas that of SO_3^{2-} and SCN^- is quite rapid. If you can smell SO_2 above the acidified solution, that is a good test. Sulfite, if present, will always contain sulfate but thiocyanate will not.

Beware of tests for sulfite by $BaSO_4$ precipitation in the presence of SCN^- in solutions which do not contain sulfate ion or evolve SO_2 on acidification.

Step 5. The odor of acetate is not very strong, so that it will be hard to detect over dilute solutions. The basic lanthanum acetate precipitate adsorbs I_2 much as starch does, resulting in a medium to very dark blue color for the solid, depending on the acetate concentration. If heavy metal cations are present they will precipitate when the sample is made basic. Centrifuge out the solid before adding $BaCl_2$. The addition of $BaCl_2$ in excess removes the interfering anions.

Step 6. The skin of $BaCO_3$ which forms on the dropper is quite characteristic, and allows detection of carbonate at concentrations of 0.01 *M* and above. There will be noticeable effervescence from solutions which are 0.1 *M* in CO_3^{2-} and above. Sulfites and nitrites may interfere with this test; the former give off SO_2 which will form $BaSO_3$ on the drop of $Ba(OH)_2$, and the latter tend to effervesce. If either ion is present, add 0.5 ml 3% H_2O_2 to the neutral solution before you acidify it; put the test tube in the hot water bath for a few minutes to allow the reaction to be completed. Cool the tube, add the acid, and proceed as before. The test for carbonate is difficult in the presence of sulfite, since any SO_2 that is liberated may interfere. Repeat the test if it is not conclusive, giving the H_2O_2 at least 3 minutes to complete the oxidation.

Step 7. The ring is caused by formation of brown $Fe(NO)^{2+}$ ion. Oxidizable or reducible anions, like I^-, Br^-, NO_2^-, and CrO_4^{2-} may interfere with the test. Iodides and bromides produce dark colored solutions, nitrites produce the same ring as nitrates only more so, and chromates form a green ring. Remove iodide and bromide by adding Ag_2SO_4 in 1 *M* H_2SO_4 in excess. Chromates will precipitate on addition of 1 *M* $BaCl_2$ in excess to the neutral solution. Nitrites decompose without formation of nitrate on addition of excess sulfamic acid to the slightly acidic sample. After removal of the many interferences, the test should be dependable. However, it would be wise, when interferences are present, to compare your test with that obtained with 0.01 *M* KNO_3.

LABORATORY ASSIGNMENTS

Perform one or more of the following, as directed by your instructor:

1. Carry out the standard tests for the identification of the anions in the Soluble and Volatile Acid Groups. For each test use a solution of the 0.1 *M* sodium salt of the anion. Repeat each test with a solution made by mixing two drops of the 0.1 *M* salt solution with 1 ml water. Using the standard tests, analyze an unknown which contains anions from the Soluble and Volatile Acid Groups. Since there are many possible anion-anion reactions and anion interferences for these tests, examine the Table of Anion-Anion Reactions in Appendix III and the interferences mentioned in the Comments on Procedure for this experiment before making your report on the composition of the unknown.

2. You will be given an unknown which contains the sodium salts of five of the anions studied in this and the previous experiment. The anions are selected so that there will be no anion-anion reactions occurring when the unknown is acidified with a strong acid. There may, however, be anion interferences with given tests. Before carrying out the tests for anions in the Calcium-Barium Group, acidify the sample with 6 *M* HCl and boil gently for two minutes to remove anions of the volatile acids. If sulfide is present, acidify the sample with 6 *M* H_2SO_4 and boil for two minutes before testing for anions in the Silver Group. Analyze the unknown for its composition, and check to see that it is consistent with the condition that it contains no reacting anions and that all interferences have been considered. In your report describe the behavior of the sample in each test as well as the anions it contains.

Name ______________________ Section ______________

OBSERVATIONS: Analysis of Anions in the Soluble and Volatile Acid Groups

Test	Stock Solution 0.1 *M* and 0.01 *M*	Unknown
Nitrite		
Chlorate		
Sulfide		
Sulfite		
Acetate		
Carbonate		
Nitrate		

 Name ______________ Section ______________

ADVANCE STUDY ASSIGNMENT: Analysis of Anions in the Soluble and the Volatile Acid Groups

1. Write balanced net ionic equations for the following reactions:
   a. The confirmatory test for sulfite ion.

   b. The removal of interferences with the carbonate test.

2. You are given solutions which contain the sodium salt of one of the anions in each of the following pairs. For each pair, indicate how you would proceed to determine which ion is present.
   a. SO_3^{2-}, SO_4^{2-}

   b. ClO_3^-, CO_3^{2-}

   c. NO_3^-, CrO_4^{2-}

3. A neutral solution contains only one anion, at a concentration of 0.3 *M*, chosen from the set of 15 we have studied. You are allowed to use up to five reagents to determine which ion it is. Draw up a complete flow chart on the back of this sheet, showing how you would proceed in performing the analysis.

Analysis of Solids and General Mixtures

So far in our work we have dealt with solutions of the ions under consideration, assuming in general that the cations were in the presence of nitrate or chloride ions and that the anions were obtained from solutions of their sodium or potassium salts. It is by no means necessary to limit qualitative analyses to such systems, although they are very useful when one is becoming familiar with the analytical procedures. At this point we are ready to look into methods by which somewhat more realistic problems, involving solutions containing several cations and anions, or solids consisting of mixtures of metals, salts, and oxides, might be handled. You will find, as you might expect, that the analysis of such mixtures makes use of the procedures you have already studied, but that ordinarily some preliminary steps are required or helpful before the standard procedures are applied.

If the sample is a solid, it will be necessary to put it into solution, at least in part, before attempting its analysis. In some cases the problem of finding suitable solvents is by no means trivial, so that it is certainly true that analyzing an unknown solution is in general easier than analyzing an unknown solid. In the following discussion we will assume that the sample is a solid which may contain metals, salts, and oxides. Adaptation of the approach to allow treatment of solutions is relatively easy and will be included, where appropriate, in the procedure we describe.

PROCEDURE FOR ANALYSIS { WEAR YOUR SAFETY GLASSES WHILE PERFORMING THIS EXPERIMENT.

This procedure requires that you have available at least a gram of solid sample. The sample should be finely divided, preferably powdered, since powders tend to dissolve more readily than large crystals. If the sample does not appear to be affected reasonably promptly by the reagents in Step 1, it may be helpful to grind it in a mortar, *testing first* with a tiny portion to make sure that it will not explode.

Step 1. *Solubility characteristics and detection of anions in the Volatile Acid Group.* Determine the solubility of the sample in the reagents listed, using about 50 mg of solid (enough to cover a 1/16 inch circle on the end of a small spatula) and about 0.5 ml of reagent in a test tube; test with the following reagents:

1. water
2. 6 *M* H_2SO_4
3. 6 *M* HCl
4. 6 *M* HNO_3
5. 6 *M* NH_3
6. 6 *M* NaOH

With each reagent, stir the solid with your stirring rod for a minute or two, observing any changes in color of the solid or the solution; if a gas is evolved, note its color and odor. If the reaction with the solvent is slow at room temperature, put the test tube in the boiling water bath for up to five minutes, stirring occasionally.

The behavior of the solid in the various solvents may offer some clues as to its composition. In Appendix II and in the tables in the cation analysis experiments we have listed the solubility characteristics of most of the salts and hydroxides of the cations we have investigated; with respect to solubility properties, oxides often behave in much the same way as hydroxides, although oxides often take a relatively long time to react. The colors of the cations in solution are given in Appendix II, and the colors of solids are in the tables previously mentioned. Even if your solid is a mixture, it may be very helpful to compare its behavior with that of the substances in Appendix II, noting particularly its partial or complete solubility in 6 *M* HCl, hot 6 *M* HNO_3, 6 *M* NH_3, and 6*M* NaOH as well as its solubility in water.

Several anions, including those in the Volatile Acid Group, are easily, and perhaps best, identified in this Step. If you observe effervescence or detect any odor in the test with sulfuric acid, repeat the test with a larger sample, about 0.15 g of solid and 1 ml of 6 *M* H_2SO_4. You should be able to establish the presence of sulfides and sulfites by the odor of H_2S and SO_2, respectively, that those substances will give off. Carbonates will evolve CO_2, which is odorless, and active metals such as zinc, magnesium, and iron, will cause formation of hydrogen, also odorless. If you suspect hydrogen gas is being produced, trap in an inverted test tube the gas given off by a small sample, and try to ignite it in a Bunsen flame; if it is H_2, it will explode with a characteristic "pop." If they are present, nitrites will evolve brown NO_2 gas (choking) and the solution formed may be blue (this same gas will be produced by reaction of the less active metals, such as copper, mercury, lead, silver, cadmium, and cobalt when treated with hot 6 *M* HNO_3). With 6 *M* H_2SO_4, chlorates will give off a greenish yellow gas, ClO_2, which smells like chlorine, and acetates will evolve acetic acid, with its characteristic odor of vinegar. Although in many cases the test obtained here for an anion is quite reliable, it would be wise to proceed to perform the standard confirmatory test or tests for the ion at this point.

If you are working with a solution instead of a solid, the tests with the six reagents may be helpful in giving clues to the presence of particular cations; barium or lead are likely if a precipitate forms on addition of H_2SO_4, a Group I cation is present if 6 *M* HCl produces a precipitate, and the colors of precipitates and solutions formed on addition of 6 *M* NH_3 and 6 *M* NaOH may be very indicative. Neutralizing the solution and boiling it down to a small volume before treatment with 6 *M* H_2SO_4 will tend to enhance the reactions of the anions of the volatile acids and facilitate their detection.

Step 2. *Preparation of solutions to be used for anion analysis.* Treat about 0.2 g of the solid sample with 0.5 ml H_2SO_4 and 5 ml water. Dissolve as much of the solid as possible, stirring well for a few minutes without heating. Centrifuge out and discard any undissolved solid. The solution may be used in the procedures for the analysis of anions in the Silver Group and the Soluble Group, except for acetate ion. If sulfide is present, boil the solution gently for two minutes in a 30 ml beaker before adding $AgNO_3$ in the Silver Group procedure.

If cations appear to be interfering with any test in the Soluble Group, add 1 ml 2 *M* Na_2CO_3 to 1 ml of the test solution, stir thoroughly, centrifuge out the solid precipitate, which may be discarded, and decant the solution into a test tube. To the solution add 6 *M* H_2SO_4, drop by drop, until it is acidic to litmus, and then proceed with the test.

Step 3. Place about 0.2 g of the solid sample in a 30 ml beaker and add 2 ml 6 *M* HCl and 4 ml water. Stir and boil gently for two minutes to dissolve as much of the solid as possible and to drive out any volatile acids. Transfer the mixture to a test tube and centrifuge out and discard any undissolved solid. The solution may be used to test for the presence of acetate ion and the anions in the Calcium-Barium-Iron Group.

It is quite possible that you will encounter interferences by cations during the Calcium-Barium-Iron Group analyses. If this occurs, it may be helpful to attempt spot tests for the anions in that Group. These tests are similar to those in the Group procedure, but avoid some of the difficulties that may develop in the initial precipitation step. In each case use the HCl solution prepared in this Step in the following spot tests:

Test for the presence of sulfate. To 1 ml of solution add 1 ml 6 *M* HCl and then add a few drops of 1 *M* $BaCl_2$ and stir. If sulfate ion is present, a white, finely divided precipitate of $BaSO_4$ will form. Traces of sulfate will produce a cloudiness, but there are essentially no interferences.

Test for the presence of oxalate. Add 6 *M* NaOH to 1 ml of solution until just basic to litmus. Then add 0.5 ml 6 *M* acetic acid and 1 ml 1 *M* $CaCl_2$. Stir and let stand for up to 10 minutes. Formation of a white precipitate is highly indicative of the presence of oxalate. Centrifuge out any precipitate and decant the solution, which may be discarded. Wash the solid thoroughly twice with 4 ml water plus 0.5 ml 6 *M* acetic acid, centrifuging and discarding the wash each time. To the solid add 1 ml 6 *M* H_2SO_4 and put the test tube in the boiling water bath for a minute or so, stirring occasionally to facilitate solution of the solid. To the *hot* solution add, drop by drop, 0.02 *M* $KMnO_4$. If oxalate is present it will quickly bleach several drops of the purple solution.

Test for the presence of chromate. If it is to contain chromate, the solution must be yellow or orange. To 1 ml of solution add 1 ml 6 *M* HNO_3. Cool under the water tap and add 1 ml 3% H_2O_2. The rapidly fading blue color of CrO_5 is proof of the presence of chromate.

Test for the presence of phosphate. To 1 ml sample solution add 1 ml 6 *M* HNO_3. Then add 1 ml 0.5 *M* $(NH_4)_2MoO_4$ and stir. Warm the test tube in the boiling water bath for a minute or two, and then let it stand in the air for up to 10 minutes. In the presence of phosphate a *yellow* precipitate of ammonium phosphomolybdate will form.

Under some circumstances, some of the above spot tests are also subject to interferences by cations or anions. If these occur, postpone analysis for the affected anions until the solution for cation analysis has been prepared.

Step 4. *Preparation of the solution to be used for cation analysis.* Since most inorganic substances dissolve, at least in principle, in one or more of the six solvents used in Step 1, it is very likely that you found some of those solvents reasonably effective. If your solid is soluble in water, you can usually use the water solution for analysis of all of the cations. If it is soluble in one of the acid reagents, that is probably the best one to use for the cation analysis. If the solid is not completely soluble in any of the reagents, even when hot, select the acidic solvent that seems most effective. If there is no apparent difference between the solvent effects of the acids, use 6 *M* HCl.

To a sample of solid weighing about 0.25 g, in a 30 ml beaker, add 2 ml of the solvent that seems most appropriate. If that solvent is water, add 2 ml 6 *M* HNO_3 in addition to the water. Add 3 ml more of water and bring the liquid to a boil, boiling gently until the volume of liquid decreases to about 2 ml. Then add 4 ml water and swirl to dissolve any crystals that may have formed. Transfer the liquid, plus any undissolved or precipitated solid, to a test tube and centrifuge out any solid. Decant the solution into a test tube; this is the solution to be used for cation analysis. Wash any undissolved solid twice with 3 ml portions of water. Decant and discard the wash, saving the solid for later analysis.

Step 5. In the absence of phosphate and oxalate ions, you may use the solution prepared in Step 4 for analysis of the cations in Groups I to IV. If either of these anions is present, it must be removed from the cations or else most or all of the Ba^{2+}, Ca^{2+}, and Mg^{2+} will precipitate with Group III in the general analysis. To accomplish this separation, put the cation solution from Step 4 in a 30 ml beaker and add 2 *M* Na_2CO_3 until the mixture is basic to litmus; then add 0.5 ml more. Bring the mixture to a boil, and boil gently for two minutes, stirring to minimize bumping. This procedure should precipitate all of the cations present, except Na^+, K^+, and NH_4^+, as carbonates, leaving most of the anions in solution. By repeated centrifuging operations, collect all of the solid carbonate precipitate in one test tube; decant the liquid into another test tube and save it for possible anion analysis. Wash the precipitate thoroughly twice with 3 ml portions of water, centrifuging each time and discarding the wash. Dissolve the solid in 2 ml 6 *M* HCl and 4 ml water; heat the test tube in the water bath for a few minutes to drive out the CO_2 that is liberated. The resulting solution should be free of phosphate and oxalate ions (as well as the other anions initially present in the sample) and can be used for analysis of the cations present in the solid. The decanted liquid which you saved in this step should contain most of the anions in the original solid, plus only Na^+ ion and excess carbonate. If any of your previous anion analyses were not conclusive, carry out the treatment with carbonate as described, acidify the decanted liquid with an appropriate acid (a lot of CO_2 will bubble off), boil it down to a volume of about 5 ml, and use the resulting solution to make the necessary spot or Group anion analyses.

Step 6. *Identification of insoluble residues.* In Step 4 there may have been a residue that did not dissolve in the reagent that you used. This residue is likely to contain one or more of the following substances:

a. An insoluble sulfate:	$BaSO_4$, $PbSO_4$, or possibly $CaSO_4$
b. A silver salt:	AgCl, AgBr, AgI, AgSCN
c. A lead salt:	$PbSO_4$, $PbCl_2$, $PbCrO_4$
d. A mercury salt:	Hg_2Cl_2, HgS
e. An oxide:	SnO_2, PbO_2, MnO_2, Al_2O_3

Assuming for the moment that only one substance is present, since that is certainly a likely situation, it is profitable to seek a solvent for that substance. The following reagents may be effective solvents, and have the indicated properties:

1 *M* $Na_2S_2O_3$:	dissolves silver salts
6 *M* NaOH:	dissolves lead salts, but not PbO_2
6 *M* H_2SO_4 plus 3% H_2O_2:	dissolves MnO_2 and PbO_2
6 *M* NH_3:	dissolves AgCl and AgSCN
hot aqua regia; 12 *M* HCl plus 6 *M* HNO_3:	dissolves all of the solids except $BaSO_4$, $PbSO_4$ and possibly SnO_2 and Al_2O_3
2 *M* Na_2CO_3:	transposes sulfates and other insoluble salts to carbonates

In making tests, use about 0.5 ml of the reagent. If a reagent is ineffective, even when heated for five minutes in the water bath, centrifuge out the solid, decant the solvent, and wash the solid with 3 ml water. Centrifuge, discard the wash, and proceed with another potential solvent. In transposing solids, boil the solid with 3 ml 2 *M* Na_2CO_3 for five minutes or so. The solid carbonate that is formed may be dissolved in 6 *M* HNO_3 and the cation identified. The anion can be tested for in the solution after acidification, if this is necessary. *Do not assume* that solubility in a given solvent is a definite test for a given solid, since the list of solids we consider here is by no means complete.

COMMENTS ON THE PROCEDURE FOR ANALYSIS

Although we listed the steps in numerical order, analysis of solids in general is not necessarily accomplished in the sequence of steps we have given. Your problem is to determine the composition of the unknown, and you may find that it is most convenient for you first to find the cations in the sample, rather than the anions, or that some of each are identified before all of either the cations or anions are known. There is no one best procedure to use for analyzing a general mixture of ions, and you should use your chemical reasoning as best you can, adapting the suggested procedure to your special case.

Step 1. The results obtained from careful interpretation of the solubility behavior of the sample are often well worth the effort required. Changes in color of the solid or solution indicate that a reaction has occurred and may reveal which kinds of ions are involved. Partial or complete solubility in NH_3 or NaOH shows that complexes are being formed. The solvents we use relate directly to several of the categories listed in the tables in the section on cation analysis and in Appendix II.

For the most part the anions in the Volatile Acid Group should be identified in this

Step. If necessary, you can look for those anions in the solution in Steps 2 or 3, but any evolved gases will be most obvious on initial treatment with acid.

Step 2. There should be very little interference by cations with the procedure for analysis of the anions in the Silver Group. The tests for anions in the Soluble Group are, however, subject to many interferences; those interferences due to cations are easily removed by the treatment with Na_2CO_3, which will precipitate nearly all of the cations as carbonates. There will, of course, be considerable evolution of CO_2 when the solution is acidified with sulfuric acid, so don't just pour the acid in and expect the solution to stay in the test tube. Acetates are not tested for here, since sulfate ions from the H_2SO_4 will interfere with the acetate test.

Step 3. Since many cations will precipitate in the presence of oxalate and phosphate ions under basic or even slightly acidic conditions, the procedure for analysis of the Calcium-Barium-Iron Group may offer difficulty unless the cations are separated as in Step 5. The spot tests on the HCl solution may be very useful, however, and should be attempted if you have trouble with the Group procedure. Be very careful in interpreting the results of the spot tests. In the oxalate test, you must wash the calcium oxalate well to remove all traces of reducing anions. The chromate test is very good, but remember that the chromate ion may, under strongly acidic conditions, react with several anions; if this occurs, the Cr^{3+} ion is usually formed, and this will cause the solution to turn gray-blue or green. The precipitate in the phosphate test must be yellow and must persist. Given ambiguities in any of the spot tests, it is highly advisable to complete the anion analyses using the *solution* obtained in the carbonate treatment in Step 5.

Step 4. In many cases you will find that more than one of the solvents used in Step 1 will completely dissolve your solid sample. If, by some chance, it is soluble in either 6 *M* NH_3 or 6 *M* NaOH, this will greatly limit the cations that may be present in the sample. Do not, however, use a basic solvent in preparing the solution for cation analysis, since the procedure is based on acidic conditions prevailing during the analysis of Groups I and II. If no solvent will completely dissolve the sample, this is not serious, since identification of a residue is often fairly easily accomplished.

Step 5. Some of the anions we have studied, in addition to oxalate and phosphate, may produce anomalous results during analysis of the cations. (If chromate is present it will be reduced to Cr^{3+} by the Group II procedure, and you will get a test for chromium in Group III.) If your results in the cation tests are not satisfactory, it is advisable to carry out the separation of the cations by the carbonate precipitation in this Step. The precipitate obtained should be reasonably free of anions other than carbonate, but, since there are many salts that are insoluble under alkaline conditions, the anions in such salts will be found in the solution phase only if the conversion to the carbonate actually occurs. It should, but it may not. In principle, the treatment with carbonate should nicely separate the cations in the original sample from the anions, but dilution effects plus the difficulty that sometimes develops with the conversion to the carbonates make the approach less effective in general than one might believe. For some samples, however, the treatment will work very well and so should be considered if the analyses without the separation of the ions are not convincing. If the carbonate precipitate does not dissolve completely in HCl, the residue will be a Group I precipitate.

Step 6. There are really relatively few substances that will not dissolve in at least one of the solvents used in Step 1. Remember, though, that sulfides may well require hot 6 *M* HNO_3, and that oxides, if they have been prepared at high temperatures, may be slow to dissolve, even in hot acid. There are also some basic salts, containing both hydroxide ion and another anion, that are much less soluble than one would expect. The substances we have listed are the ones most commonly encountered, but it is possible that you will encounter one that is not included.

Once you have found a solvent for the solid, the specific tests for the cations are straightforward. Silver sulfide (black) will precipitate when the thiosulfate solution is acidified and heated; the anion in the salt can be determined by reduction of the insoluble silver salt with zinc and continuing with the Silver Group procedure. Lead will be brought down as a black sulfide if the hydroxide solution is treated with thioacetamide and heated. Mercury(II) can be identified by the standard procedure. Barium carbonate formed by conversion of the sulfate can be isolated and dissolved in HCl, and the sulfate is then reprecipitated by addition of H_2SO_4.

LABORATORY ASSIGNMENTS

Perform one or more of the following, as directed by your instructor:

1. You will be given a salt which contains one cation and one anion. Identify the salt. In your report, indicate the experiments you performed during the analysis that established the cation and the anion that are present.

2. You will be given a solution that contains two cations and two anions in addition to possibly H^+, Na^+, and NO_3^- ions. Determine the ions in the solution. Describe in your report the procedure you used and the results you obtained.

3. You will be given a solid mixture that may include salts, oxides, and hydroxides. The solid will contain three cations and three anions, in addition to possibly Na^+, OH^-, O^{2-}, and NO_3^- ions. Determine the ions present in the solid. In your report, describe completely the procedure you used, including those observations that confirmed the identification of each ion.

Name ______________________ Section ______________

OBSERVATIONS AND REPORT SHEET: Analysis of Solids and General Mixtures

Procedure used:

The following ions were found to be present:

________ ________ ________ ________ ________ ________

 Name ______________________ Section ______________

ADVANCE STUDY ASSIGNMENT: Analysis of Solids and General Mixtures

1. A sample contains the following salts: $CuCl_2$, $ZnCrO_4$, and $Ba(NO_3)_2$. Using the tables in the cation sections and Appendix II, determine which ions would go into solution when treated with each of the solvents in Step 1. Which solvent would you use for preparing the solution for cation analysis?

2. A sample may contain the following salts: $AgNO_3$, $CdBr_2$, and $Ni(C_2H_3O_2)_2$. Draw the simplest flow chart you can, showing how you would go about determining which salts are actually present. You may, of course, use a new sample of solid whenever that is necessary, but be sure that your overall procedure will accomplish the analysis.

3. A solid may contain Al, CaC_2O_4, $PbSO_4$, and $FeCl_3$. The mixture is colored, partially soluble in water, and completely soluble in 6 *M* HCl. On the basis of this information, what can you say about the composition of the mixture? What additional tests would you carry out to complete the analysis?

APPENDIX I

VAPOR PRESSURE OF WATER

Temperature °C	Pressure mm Hg	Temperature °C	Pressure mm Hg
0	4.6	26	25.2
1	4.9	27	26.7
2	5.3	28	28.3
3	5.7	29	30.0
4	6.1	30	31.8
5	6.5	31	33.7
6	7.0	32	35.7
7	7.5	33	37.7
8	8.0	34	39.9
9	8.6	35	42.2
10	9.2	40	55.3
11	9.8	45	71.9
12	10.5	50	92.5
13	11.2	55	118.0
14	12.0	60	149.4
15	12.8	65	187.5
16	13.6	70	233.7
17	14.5	75	289.1
18	15.5	80	355.1
19	16.5	85	433.6
20	17.5	90	525.8
21	18.7	95	633.9
22	19.8	97	682.1
23	21.1	99	733.2
24	22.4	100	760.0
25	23.8	101	787.6

APPENDIX II

SUMMARY OF SOLUBILITY PROPERTIES OF IONS AND SOLIDS

	Cl^-	SO_4^{2-}	CO_3^{2-} PO_4^{3-}	CrO_4^{2-}	OH^- O^{2-}	S^{2-}	Complexes
Na^+, K^+, NH_4^+	S	S	S	S	S	S	–
Ba^{2+}	S	I	A	A	S⁻	S	–
Ca^{2+}	S	S⁻	A	S	S⁻	S	–
Mg^{2+}	S	S	A	S	A	S	–
Fe^{3+} (yellow)	S	S	A	A	A	A	–
Cr^{3+} (blue-gray)	S	S	A	A	C, A	D, A	(OH^-)
Al^{3+}	S	S	C, A	C, A	C, A	D, C, A	OH^-
Ni^{2+} (green)	S	S	C, A	S	C, A	A⁺, O⁺	NH_3
Co^{2+} (pink)	S	S	C, A	C, A	A	A⁺, O⁺	(NH_3)
Zn^{2+}	S	S	C, A	C, A	C, A	A	OH^-, NH_3
Mn^{2+} (pale pink)	S	S	A	S	A	A	–
Cu^{2+} (blue)	S	S	C, A	C, A	C, A	O	NH_3
Cd^{2+}	S	S	C, A	C, A	C, A	A, O	NH_3
Bi^{3+}	A	A	A	A	A	O	Cl^-
Hg^{2+}	S	S	A	S⁻	A	O⁺, B	Cl^-, S^{2-}
Sn^{2+}, Sn^{4+}	C, A	C, A	C, A	S	C, A	C, A⁺, B	OH^-
Sb^{3+}	C, A	C, A	C, A	C, A	C, A	C, A⁺, B	OH^-
Ag^+	C, A⁺	S⁻	C, A	C, A	C, A	O	NH_3, $S_2O_3^{2-}$
Pb^{2+}	HW, C, A⁺	C	C, A	C	C, A	O	OH^-
Hg_2^{2+}	O⁺	S⁻	A	A	A	O⁺	–

Key:

S soluble in water, >0.1 mole/liter
S⁻ slightly soluble in water, ~0.01 mole/liter
HW soluble in hot water
A soluble in acid (6 *M* HCl or other non-precipitating, nonoxidizing acid)
I insoluble in any common solvent
A⁺ soluble in 12 *M* HCl
B soluble in hot 6 *M* NaOH containing S^{2-} ion
O soluble in hot 6 *M* HNO_3
O⁺ soluble in hot aqua regia
C soluble in solution containing a good complexing ligand
D unstable, decomposes

(For an example of the interpretation of this table, see Table 32.1 and the discussion preceding it.)

APPENDIX III

SOME ANION-ANION REACTIONS

Most anions are stable in solutions containing other anions, but those that are oxidizing agents may react with those that behave as reducing agents. The rate of reaction between such ions usually depends markedly on both the acidity of the solution and the temperature. The conditions for reaction between some common ions in solution are summarized in the table below:

		Oxidizing Agents			
		NO_2^-	CrO_4^{2-}	ClO_3^-	NO_3^-
Reducing Agents	I^-	A (cold)	A (cold)	A (cold)	A (hot)
	Br^-	A (hot)	NR	A (hot)	NR
	S^{2-}	N (cold)	B (hot)	A (cold)	A (cold)
	SO_3^{2-}	N (hot)	A (cold)	A (cold)	A (cold)
	SCN^-	A (cold)	A (cold)	A (hot)	NR
	NO_2^-	–	A (cold)	A (cold)	NR

Key: A (cold), reaction occurs in cold 1 *M* HCl
A (hot), reaction occurs in hot 1 *M* HCl
N (cold), reaction occurs in cold solution at pH 7
N (hot), reaction occurs in hot solution at pH 7
B (cold), reaction occurs in cold 1 *M* NaOH
B (hot), reaction occurs in hot 1 *M* NaOH
NR, no reaction under any of the above conditions

Example: For NO_2^- and SO_3^{2-} the entry is N (hot). This means that if 0.1 *M* solutions of NO_2^- and SO_3^{2-} are mixed at pH 7 and heated in a boiling water bath, an appreciable amount of SO_3^{2-} will be oxidized to SO_4^{2-} in about a minute. Since increased acidity greatly increases the rate of reactions of this sort, the reaction will also occur in cold, or hot, 1 *M* HCl, but not in cold or hot 1 *M* NaOH. Since lowering temperature decreases rate, the reaction will not occur to a significant extent in cold solution at pH 7, within a period of a few hours. At higher concentrations the reaction is more rapid. (In particular, 6 *M* HNO_3 is a much stronger oxidizing agent than 0.1 *M* NO_3^- ion in 1 *M* HCl.)

APPENDIX IV

TABLE OF ATOMIC WEIGHTS

(Based on Carbon-12)

	Symbol	Atomic No.	Atomic Weight		Symbol	Atomic No.	Atomic Weight
Actinium	Ac	89	[227]*	Mercury	Hg	80	200.59
Aluminum	Al	13	26.9815	Molybdenum	Mo	42	95.94
Americium	Am	95	[243]	Neodymium	Nd	60	144.24
Antimony	Sb	51	121.75	Neon	Ne	10	20.183
Argon	Ar	18	39.948	Neptunium	Np	93	[237]
Arsenic	As	33	74.9216	Nickel	Ni	28	58.71
Astatine	At	85	[210]	Niobium	Nb	41	92.906
Barium	Ba	56	137.34	Nitrogen	N	7	14.0067
Berkelium	Bk	97	[247]	Nobelium	No	102	[256]
Beryllium	Be	4	9.0122	Osmium	Os	76	190.2
Bismuth	Bi	83	208.980	Oxygen	O	8	15.9994
Boron	B	5	10.811	Palladium	Pd	46	106.4
Bromine	Br	35	79.904	Phosphorus	P	15	30.9738
Cadmium	Cd	48	112.40	Platinum	Pt	78	195.09
Calcium	Ca	20	40.08	Plutonium	Pu	94	[242]
Californium	Cf	98	[249]	Polonium	Po	84	[210]
Carbon	C	6	12.01115	Potassium	K	19	39.102
Cerium	Ce	58	140.12	Praseodymium	Pr	59	140.907
Cesium	Cs	55	132.905	Promethium	Pm	61	[145]
Chlorine	Cl	17	35.453	Protactinium	Pa	91	[231]
Chromium	Cr	24	51.996	Radium	Ra	88	[226]
Cobalt	Co	27	58.9332	Radon	Rn	86	[222]
Copper	Cu	29	63.546	Rhenium	Re	75	186.2
Curium	Cm	96	[247]	Rhodium	Rh	45	102.905
Dysprosium	Dy	66	162.50	Rubidium	Rb	37	85.47
Einsteinium	Es	99	[254]	Ruthenium	Ru	44	101.07
Erbium	Er	68	167.26	Samarium	Sm	62	150.35
Europium	Eu	63	151.96	Scandium	Sc	21	44.956
Fermium	Fm	100	[253]	Selenium	Se	34	78.96
Fluorine	F	9	18.9984	Silicon	Si	14	28.086
Francium	Fr	87	[223]	Silver	Ag	47	107.868
Gadolinium	Gd	64	157.25	Sodium	Na	11	22.9898
Gallium	Ga	31	69.72	Strontium	Sr	38	87.62
Germanium	Ge	32	72.59	Sulfur	S	16	32.064
Gold	Au	79	196.967	Tantalum	Ta	73	180.948
Hafnium	Hf	72	178.49	Technetium	Tc	43	[99]
Helium	He	2	4.0026	Tellurium	Te	52	127.60
Holmium	Ho	67	164.930	Terbium	Tb	65	158.924
Hydrogen	H	1	1.00797	Thallium	Tl	81	204.37
Indium	In	49	114.82	Thorium	Th	90	232.038
Iodine	I	53	126.9044	Thulium	Tm	69	168.934
Iridium	Ir	77	192.2	Tin	Sn	50	118.69
Iron	Fe	26	55.847	Titanium	Ti	22	47.90
Krypton	Kr	36	83.80	Tungsten	W	74	183.85
Lanthanum	La	57	138.91	Uranium	U	92	238.03
Lawrencium	Lw	103	[257]	Vanadium	V	23	50.942
Lead	Pb	82	207.19	Xenon	Xe	54	131.30
Lithium	Li	3	6.939	Ytterbium	Yb	70	173.04
Lutetium	Lu	71	174.97	Yttrium	Y	39	88.905
Magnesium	Mg	12	24.312	Zinc	Zn	30	65.37
Manganese	Mn	25	54.9380	Zirconium	Zr	40	91.22
Mendelevium	Md	101	[256]				

*A value given in brackets denotes the mass number of the longest-lived or best-known isotope.

APPENDIX V

TABLE OF LOGARITHMS

	0	1	2	3	4	5	6	7	8	9
1.0	.0000	.0043	.0086	.0128	.0170	.0212	.0253	.0294	.0334	.0374
1.1	.0414	.0453	.0492	.0531	.0569	.0607	.0645	.0682	.0719	.0755
1.2	.0792	.0828	.0864	.0899	.0934	.0969	.1004	.1038	.1072	.1106
1.3	.1139	.1173	.1206	.1239	.1271	.1303	.1335	.1367	.1399	.1430
1.4	.1461	.1492	.1523	.1553	.1584	.1614	.1644	.1673	.1703	.1732
1.5	.1761	.1790	.1818	.1847	.1875	.1903	.1931	.1959	.1987	.2014
1.6	.2041	.2068	.2095	.2122	.2148	.2175	.2201	.2227	.2253	.2279
1.7	.2304	.2330	.2355	.2380	.2405	.2430	.2455	.2480	.2504	.2529
1.8	.2553	.2577	.2601	.2625	.2648	.2672	.2695	.2718	.2742	.2765
1.9	.2788	.2810	.2833	.2856	.2878	.2900	.2923	.2945	.2967	.2989
2.0	.3010	.3032	.3054	.3075	.3096	.3118	.3139	.3160	.3181	.3201
2.1	.3222	.3243	.3263	.3284	.3304	.3324	.3345	.3365	.3385	.3404
2.2	.3424	.3444	.3464	.3483	.3502	.3522	.3541	.3560	.3579	.3598
2.3	.3617	.3636	.3655	.3674	.3692	.3711	.3729	.3747	.3766	.3784
2.4	.3802	.3820	.3838	.3856	.3874	.3892	.3909	.3927	.3945	.3962
2.5	.3979	.3997	.4014	.4031	.4048	.4065	.4082	.4099	.4116	.4133
2.6	.4150	.4166	.4183	.4200	.4216	.4232	.4249	.4265	.4281	.4298
2.7	.4314	.4330	.4346	.4362	.4378	.4393	.4409	.4425	.4440	.4456
2.8	.4472	.4487	.4502	.4518	.4533	.4548	.4564	.4579	.4594	.4609
2.9	.4624	.4639	.4654	.4669	.4683	.4698	.4713	.4728	.4742	.4757
3.0	.4771	.4786	.4800	.4814	.4829	.4843	.4857	.4871	.4886	.4900
3.1	.4914	.4928	.4942	.4955	.4969	.4983	.4997	.5011	.5024	.5038
3.2	.5051	.5065	.5079	.5092	.5105	.5119	.5132	.5145	.5159	.5172
3.3	.5185	.5198	.5211	.5224	.5237	.5250	.5263	.5276	.5289	.5302
3.4	.5315	.5328	.5340	.5353	.5366	.5378	.5391	.5403	.5416	.5428
3.5	.5441	.5453	.5465	.5478	.5490	.5502	.5514	.5527	.5539	.5551
3.6	.5563	.5575	.5587	.5599	.5611	.5623	.5635	.5647	.5658	.5670
3.7	.5682	.5694	.5705	.5717	.5729	.5740	.5752	.5763	.5775	.5786
3.8	.5798	.5809	.5821	.5832	.5843	.5855	.5866	.5877	.5888	.5899
3.9	.5911	.5922	.5933	.5944	.5955	.5966	.5977	.5988	.5999	.6010
4.0	.6021	.6031	.6042	.6053	.6064	.6075	.6085	.6096	.6107	.6117
4.1	.6128	.6138	.6149	.6160	.6170	.6180	.6191	.6201	.6212	.6222
4.2	.6232	.6243	.6253	.6263	.6274	.6284	.6294	.6304	.6314	.6325
4.3	.6335	.6345	.6355	.6365	.6375	.6385	.6395	.6405	.6415	.6425
4.4	.6435	.6444	.6454	.6464	.6474	.6484	.6493	.6503	.6513	.6522
4.5	.6532	.6542	.6551	.6561	.6571	.6580	.6590	.6599	.6609	.6618
4.6	.6628	.6637	.6646	.6656	.6665	.6675	.6684	.6693	.6702	.6712
4.7	.6721	.6730	.6739	.6749	.6758	.6767	.6776	.6785	.6794	.6803
4.8	.6812	.6821	.6830	.6839	.6848	.6857	.6866	.6875	.6884	.6893
4.9	.6902	.6911	.6920	.6928	.6937	.6946	.6955	.6964	.6972	.6981
5.0	.6990	.6998	.7007	.7016	.7024	.7033	.7042	.7050	.7059	.7067
5.1	.7076	.7084	.7093	.7101	.7110	.7118	.7126	.7135	.7143	.7152
5.2	.7160	.7168	.7177	.7185	.7193	.7202	.7210	.7218	.7226	.7235
5.3	.7243	.7251	.7259	.7267	.7275	.7284	.7292	.7300	.7308	.7316
5.4	.7324	.7332	.7340	.7348	.7356	.7364	.7372	.7380	.7388	.7396
5.5	.7404	.7412	.7419	.7427	.7435	.7443	.7451	.7459	.7466	.7474
5.6	.7482	.7490	.7497	.7505	.7513	.7520	.7528	.7536	.7543	.7551
5.7	.7559	.7566	.7574	.7582	.7589	.7597	.7604	.7612	.7619	.7627
5.8	.7634	.7642	.7649	.7657	.7664	.7672	.7679	.7686	.7694	.7701
5.9	.7709	.7716	.7723	.7731	.7738	.7745	.7752	.7760	.7767	.7774

TABLE OF LOGARITHMS—CONTINUED

	0	1	2	3	4	5	6	7	8	9
6.0	.7782	.7789	.7796	.7803	.7810	.7818	.7825	.7832	.7839	.7846
6.1	.7853	.7860	.7868	.7875	.7882	.7889	.7896	.7903	.7910	.7917
6.2	.7924	.7931	.7938	.7945	.7952	.7959	.7966	.7973	.7980	.7987
6.3	.7993	.8000	.8007	.8014	.8021	.8028	.8035	.8041	.8048	.8055
6.4	.8062	.8069	.8075	.8082	.8089	.8096	.8102	.8109	.8116	.8122
6.5	.8129	.8136	.8142	.8149	.8156	.8162	.8169	.8176	.8182	.8189
6.6	.8195	.8202	.8209	.8215	.8222	.8228	.8235	.8241	.8248	.8254
6.7	.8261	.8267	.8274	.8280	.8287	.8293	.8299	.8306	.8312	.8319
6.8	.8325	.8331	.8338	.8344	.8351	.8357	.8363	.8370	.8376	.8382
6.9	.8388	.8395	.8401	.8407	.8414	.8420	.8426	.8432	.8439	.8445
7.0	.8451	.8457	.8463	.8470	.8476	.8482	.8488	.8494	.8500	.8506
7.1	.8513	.8519	.8525	.8531	.8537	.8543	.8549	.8555	.8561	.8567
7.2	.8573	.8579	.8585	.8591	.8597	.8603	.8609	.8615	.8621	.8627
7.3	.8633	.8639	.8645	.8651	.8657	.8663	.8669	.8675	.8681	.8686
7.4	.8692	.8698	.8704	.8710	.8716	.8722	.8727	.8733	.8739	.8745
7.5	.8751	.8756	.8762	.8768	.8774	.8779	.8785	.8791	.8797	.8802
7.6	.8808	.8814	.8820	.8825	.8831	.8837	.8842	.8848	.8854	.8859
7.7	.8865	.8871	.8876	.8882	.8887	.8893	.8899	.8904	.8910	.8915
7.8	.8921	.8927	.8932	.8938	.8943	.8949	.8954	.8960	.8965	.8971
7.9	.8976	.8982	.8987	.8993	.8998	.9004	.9009	.9015	.9020	.9026
8.0	.9031	.9036	.9042	.9047	.9053	.9058	.9063	.9069	.9074	.9079
8.1	.9085	.9090	.9096	.9101	.9106	.9112	.9117	.9122	.9128	.9133
8.2	.9138	.9143	.9149	.9154	.9159	.9165	.9170	.9175	.9180	.9186
8.3	.9191	.9196	.9201	.9206	.9212	.9217	.9222	.9227	.9232	.9238
8.4	.9243	.9248	.9253	.9258	.9263	.9269	.9274	.9279	.9284	.9289
8.5	.9294	.9299	.9304	.9309	.9315	.9320	.9325	.9330	.9335	.9340
8.6	.9345	.9350	.9355	.9360	.9365	.9370	.9375	.9380	.9385	.9390
8.7	.9395	.9400	.9405	.9410	.9415	.9420	.9425	.9430	.9435	.9440
8.8	.9445	.9450	.9455	.9460	.9465	.9469	.9474	.9479	.9484	.9489
8.9	.9494	.9499	.9504	.9509	.9513	.9518	.9523	.9528	.9533	.9538
9.0	.9542	.9547	.9552	.9557	.9562	.9566	.9571	.9576	.9581	.9586
9.1	.9590	.9595	.9600	.9605	.9609	.9614	.9619	.9624	.9628	.9633
9.2	.9638	.9643	.9647	.9652	.9657	.9661	.9666	.9671	.9675	.9680
9.3	.9685	.9689	.9694	.9699	.9703	.9708	.9713	.9717	.9722	.9727
9.4	.9731	.9736	.9741	.9745	.9750	.9754	.9759	.9763	.9768	.9773
9.5	.9777	.9782	.9786	.9791	.9795	.9800	.9805	.9809	.9814	.9818
9.6	.9823	.9827	.9832	.9836	.9841	.9845	.9850	.9854	.9859	.9863
9.7	.9868	.9872	.9877	.9881	.9886	.9890	.9894	.9899	.9903	.9908
9.8	.9912	.9917	.9921	.9926	.9930	.9934	.9939	.9943	.9948	.9952
9.9	.9956	.9961	.9965	.9969	.9974	.9978	.9983	.9987	.9991	.9996

APPENDIX VI

SUGGESTED LOCKER EQUIPMENT

2 beakers, 30 or 50 ml
2 beakers, 100 ml
2 beakers, 250 ml
2 beakers, 400 ml
1 beaker, 600 cc
2 Erlenmeyer flasks, 25 or 50 ml
2 Erlenmeyer flasks, 125 ml
2 Erlenmeyer flasks, 250 ml
1 grad. cylinder, 10 ml
1 grad. cylinder, 25 or 50 ml
1 funnel, long or short stem
1 thermometer (150°C)
2 watch glasses, 3 or 4 in
1 crucible and cover, size #0
1 evaporating dish, small
2 medicine droppers
2 test tubes, 18 × 150 mm
8 test tubes, 13 × 100 mm
4 test tubes, 10 × 75 mm
1 test tube brush
1 file
1 spatula
1 test tube holder, wire
1 test tube rack
1 tongs
1 sponge
1 towel
1 plastic wash bottle
1 casserole, small